The Complete Guitar Player
Essential Acoustic Songs

T0079463

Published by:
Hal Leonard

Exclusive Distributors:
Hal Leonard,
7777 West Bluemound Road,
Milwaukee, WI 53213
Email: info@halleonard.com

Hal Leonard Europe Limited,
42 Wigmore Street Marylebone,
London, WIU 2 RY
Email: info@halleonardeurope.com

Hal Leonard Australia Pty. Ltd.
4 Lentara Court Cheltenham,
Victoria 9132, Australia
Email: info@halleonard.com.au

Order No. AM1009998
ISBN: 978-1-78558-305-6
This book © Copyright 2016 Hal Leonard

For all works contained herein:
Unauthorized copying, arranging, adapting, recording, Internet posting,
public performance, or other distribution of the music in this publication is
an infringement of copyright. Infringers are liable under the law.

Edited by James Welland.
Music processed by shedwork.com
Printed in the EU.

www.halleonard.com

The Complete Guitar Player
Essential Acoustic Songs

HAL•LEONARD®

Alone Again Or

Words & Music by Bryan MacLean

© Copyright 1968 Three Wise Boys Music LLC/Breadcrust Music.
Chester Music Limited trading as Campbell Connelly & Co.
All Rights Reserved. International Copyright Secured.

Practice the intro tab slowly at fi st, building up speed as you learn it. Otherwise, trying strumming in simple, constant eighth-notes for a similar effect

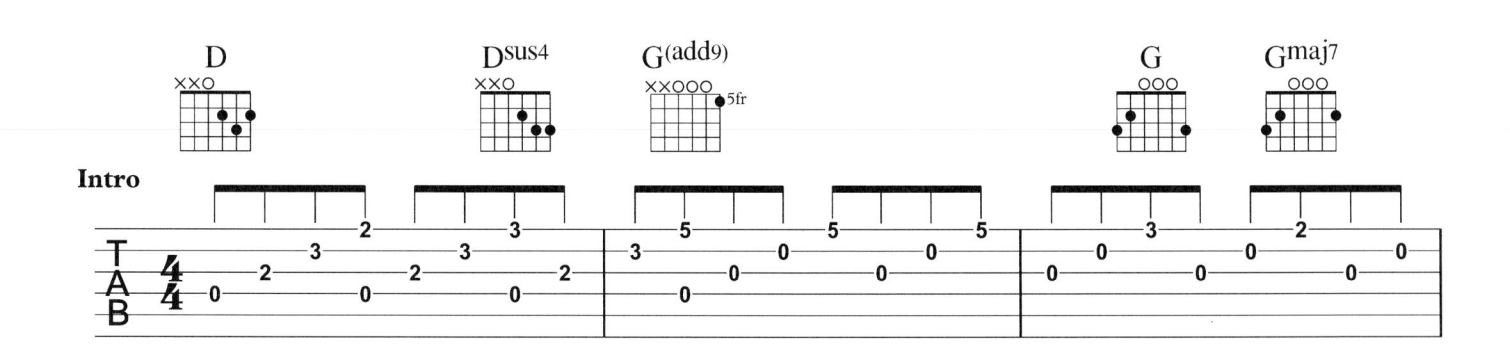

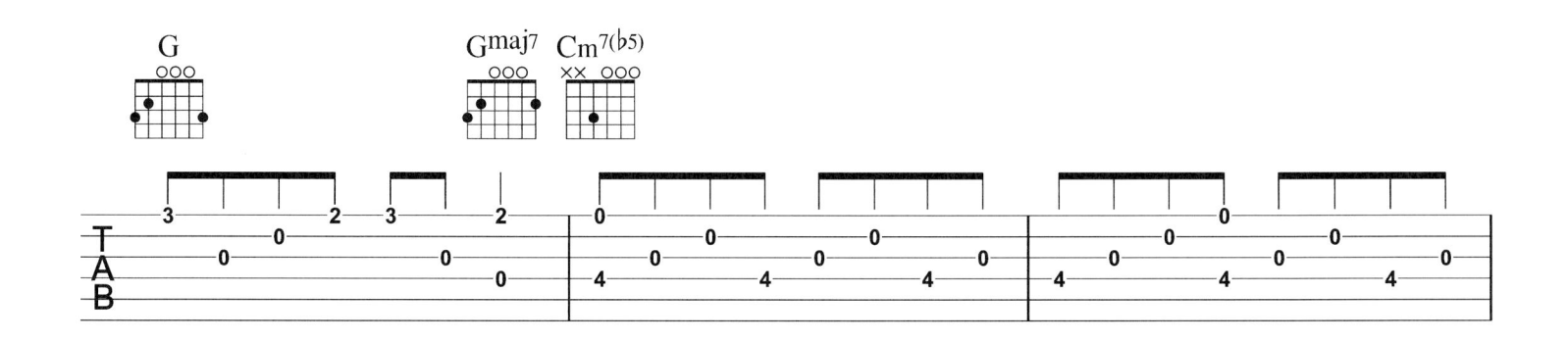

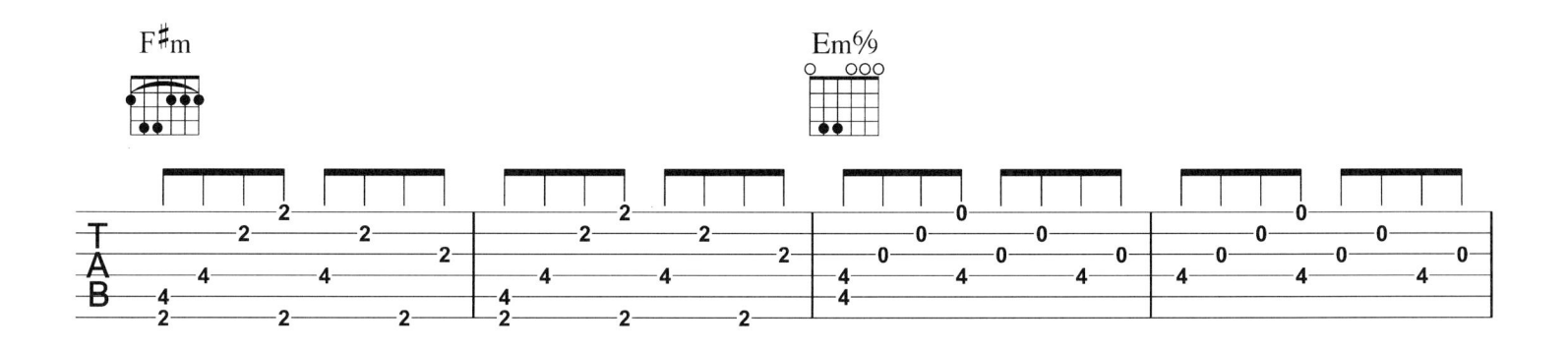

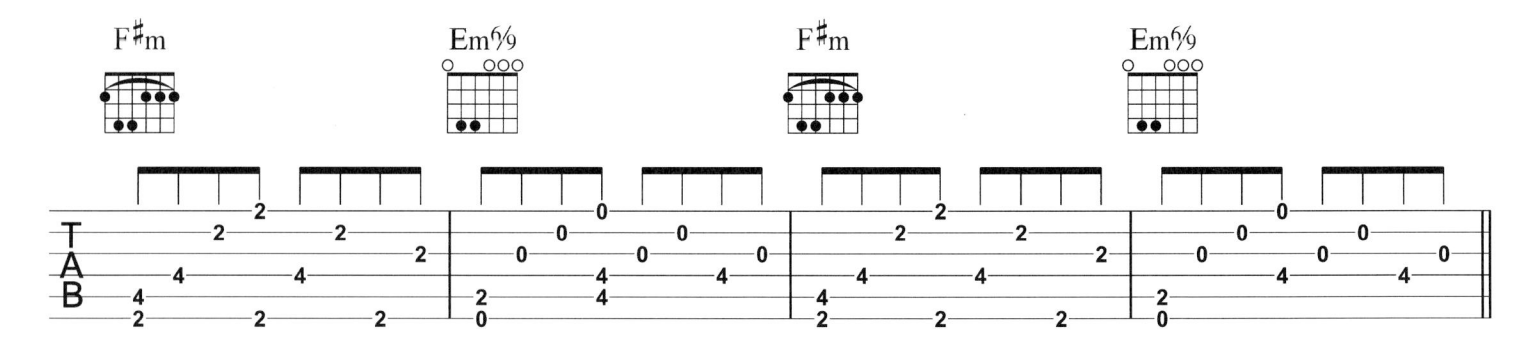

Verse

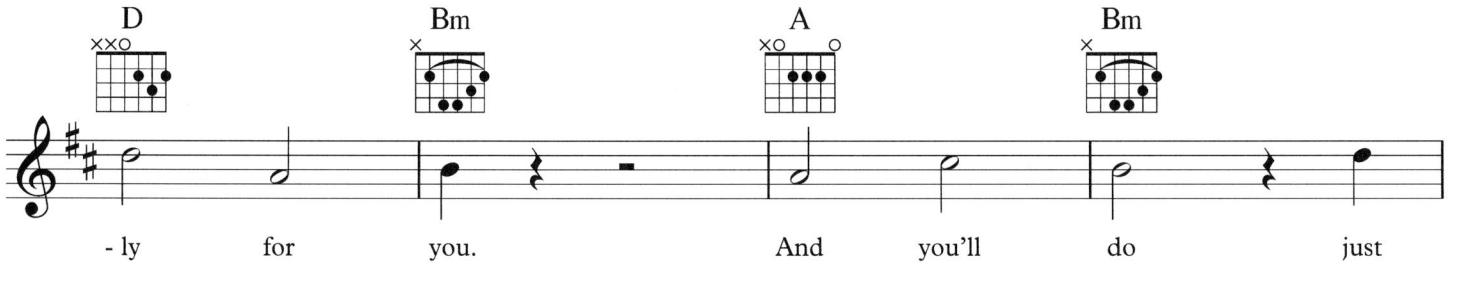

1. Yeah,_____ said it's__ all right_____ I won't for - get__

Instrumental on 𝄋 until ✳

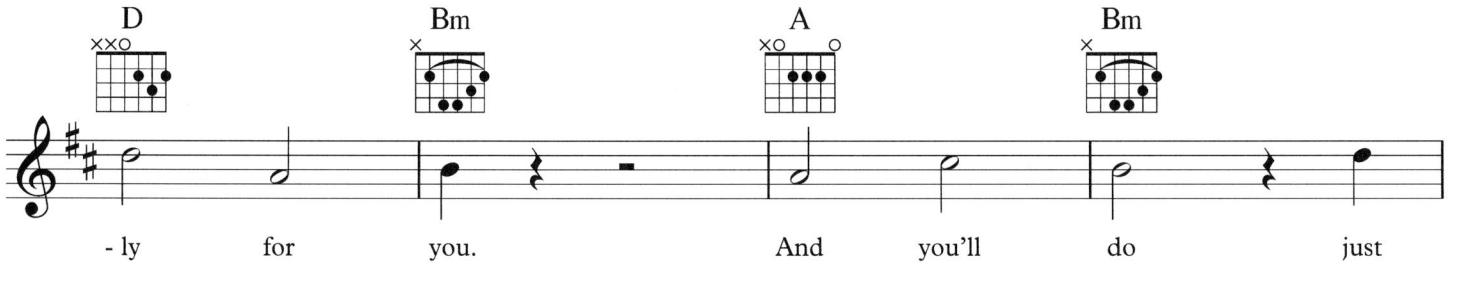

_____ all the times I've wait - ed pa - tient -

- ly for you. And you'll do just

what you choose to do;__ And I will__ be___

___ a lone a gain to night,___ my dear.

Interlude

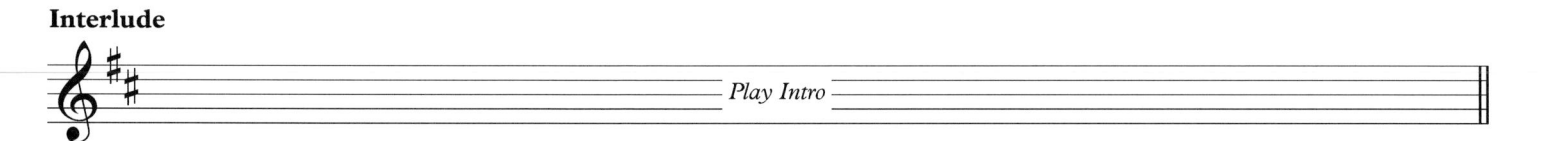

Play Intro

7

Interlude (as Intro)

To Coda
G
Gmaj7
Cm7(♭5)
F♯m
Em6/9
F♯m
Em6/9
F♯m
Em6/9
D.S. al Coda
Coda
Cm7(♭5)
Em6/9
Cm7(♭5)

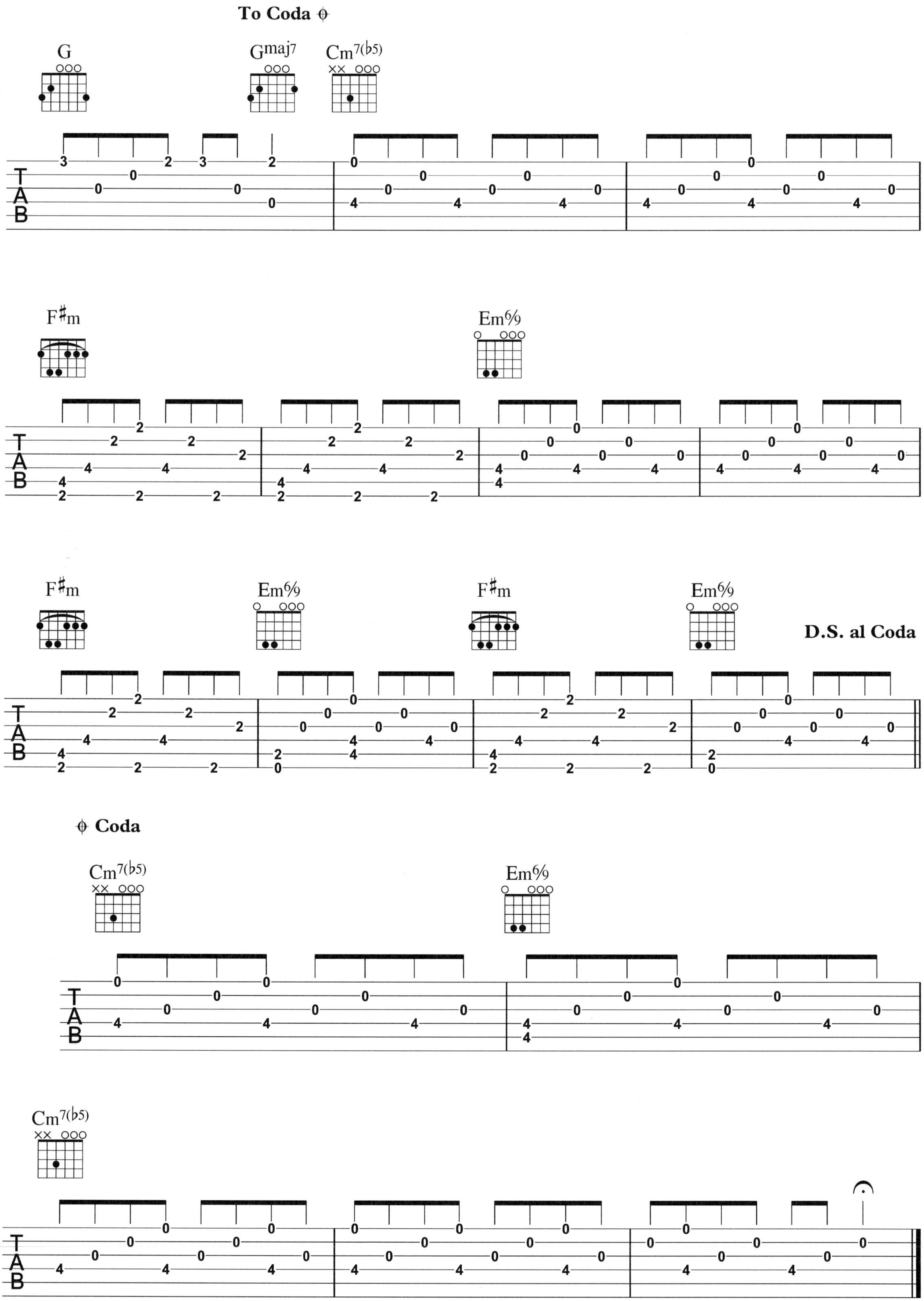

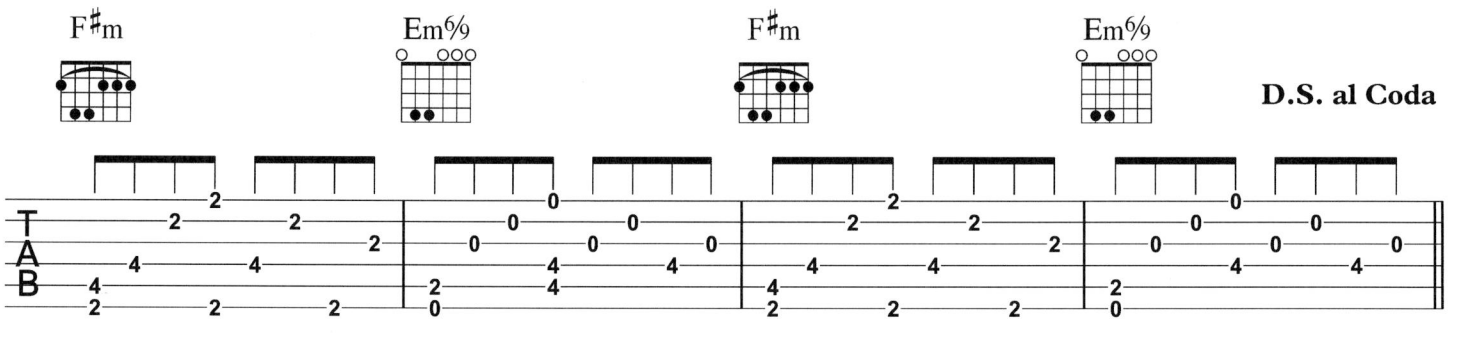

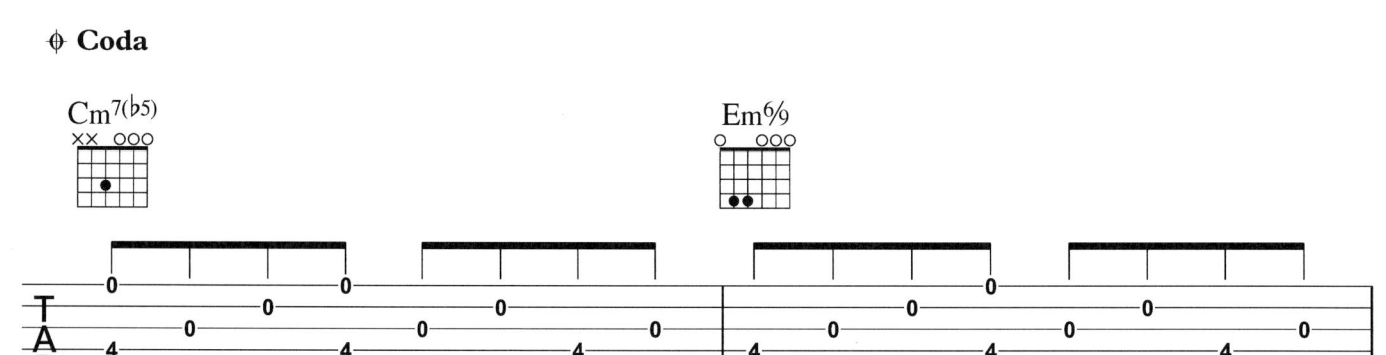

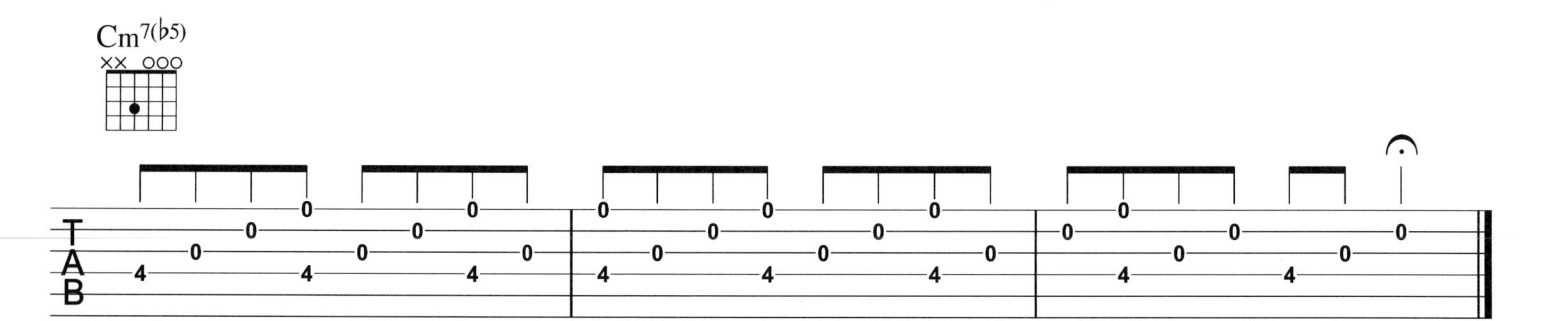

American Pie

Words & Music by Don McLean

© Copyright 1971 Songs Of Universal Incorporated/Benny Bird Company Inc.
Universal/MCA Music Limited.
All Rights Reserved. International Copyright Secured.

Strumming style:

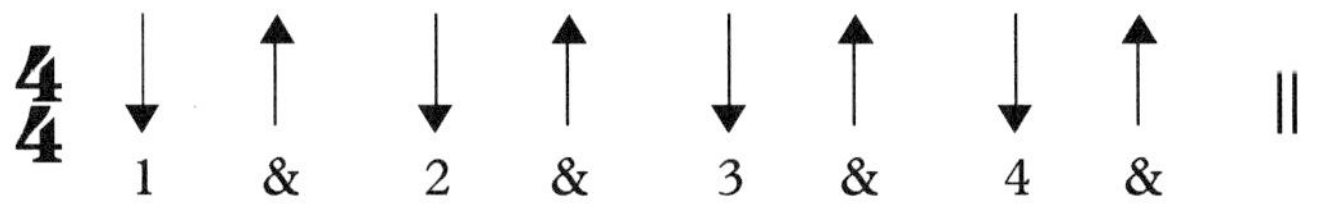

> This is a long song, but the structure's pretty simple.
> Memorising the repeating sections will make it easier.

Accompaniment: 4/4 Rhythm Freely

Verse

G   D/F♯   Em   Am   C

1. A long, long time a-go, I can still re-mem-ber how that
(6.) met a girl who sang the blues and I asked her for some hap-py news,

Em   D   G   D/F♯   Em

mu-sic used to make me smile.____ And I knew if I had my chance, that
she just smiled and turned a-way. I went down to the sa-cred store where

Am   C   Em   C   D

I could make those peo-ple dance and may-be they'd be hap-py for a while.
I'd heard the mu-sic years be-fore, But the man there said the mu-sic would-n't play. And

Em   Am   Em

But Feb-ru-a-ry made____ me shi-ver with ev-'ry pa-per I'd____
in the streets the chil-dren screamed, the lo-vers cried and the

whis-key and rye,___ sing-in' this-'ll be the day that I die,

To Coda ⊕

this-'ll be the day that I die.

Verse

3. Now for

2.   Did you___ write the book of love___ and do you___ have faith in
(3.) ten years we've been on our own___ and moss grows fat on a
4. Hel-ter skel-ter in___ a sum-mer___ swel-ter, the Byrds flew off with a
(Verse 5 see block lyrics)

God a - bove?___ If the bi-ble tells___ you so.___
rol-lin' stone,___ but___ that's not___ how it used to be.___
fall-out shel-ter, eight miles high and fall-ing fast.___

Now do you be-lieve in rock and roll___ and can
When the jes-ter sang___ for the King and Queen, in a
It land-ed___ foul on the grass, the

mu-sic save___ your___ mor-tal soul___ and___ can you teach me___
coat he bor-rowed from___ James Dean___ and a voice that came___
pla-yers tried___ for a for-ward pass___ with the jes-ter on the side-

how to dance_ real slow?_____ Well, I
from_ you and me. Oh and
- lines in a cast. Now the

know that you're_ in love with him_ 'cos I saw you danc - in'
while the King_ was look - ing down the jes - ter stole his
half - time air_ was sweet per - fume while ser - geants played a

in the gym._ You both kicked off your shoes_____ man, I
thor - ny crown. The cour - troom was ad - journed,_____ no
march - ing tune._ We all got up to dance,_____ oh but we

dig those rhy - thm 'n' blues._ I was a lone - ly teen - age
ver - dict was re - turned. And while Len - non read a book
ne - ver got the chance. 'cause the pla - yers tried to

bronc - in' buck with a pink car - na - tion and a pick - up truck_ but I
_ on Marx,_ the quar - tet prac - ticed in the park, and
take the field, the mar - ching band_ re - fused to yield._

knew I_____ was out of luck the day___
we sang dir - ges in the dark the day___
Do you re - call___ what was re - vealed the day___

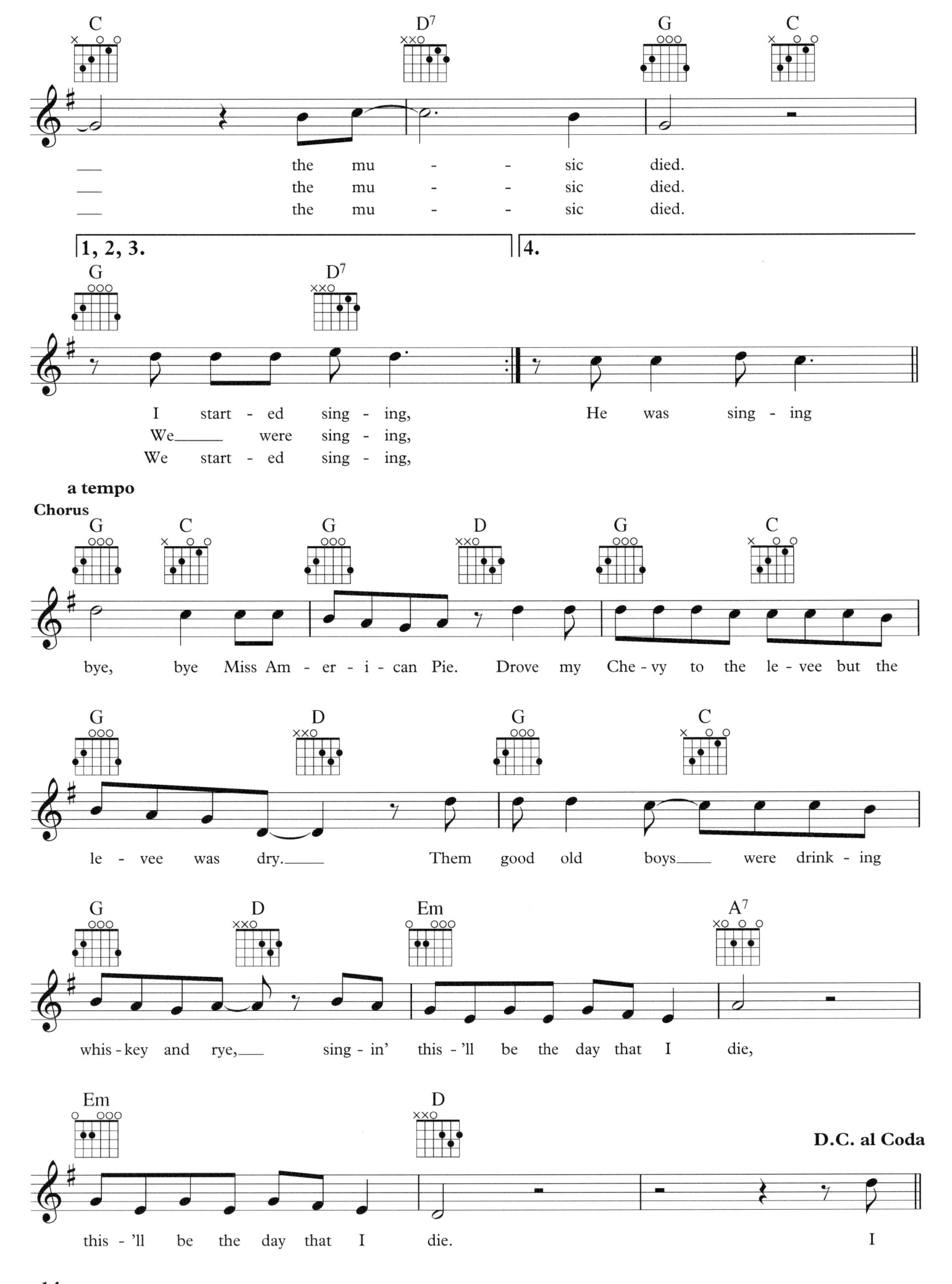

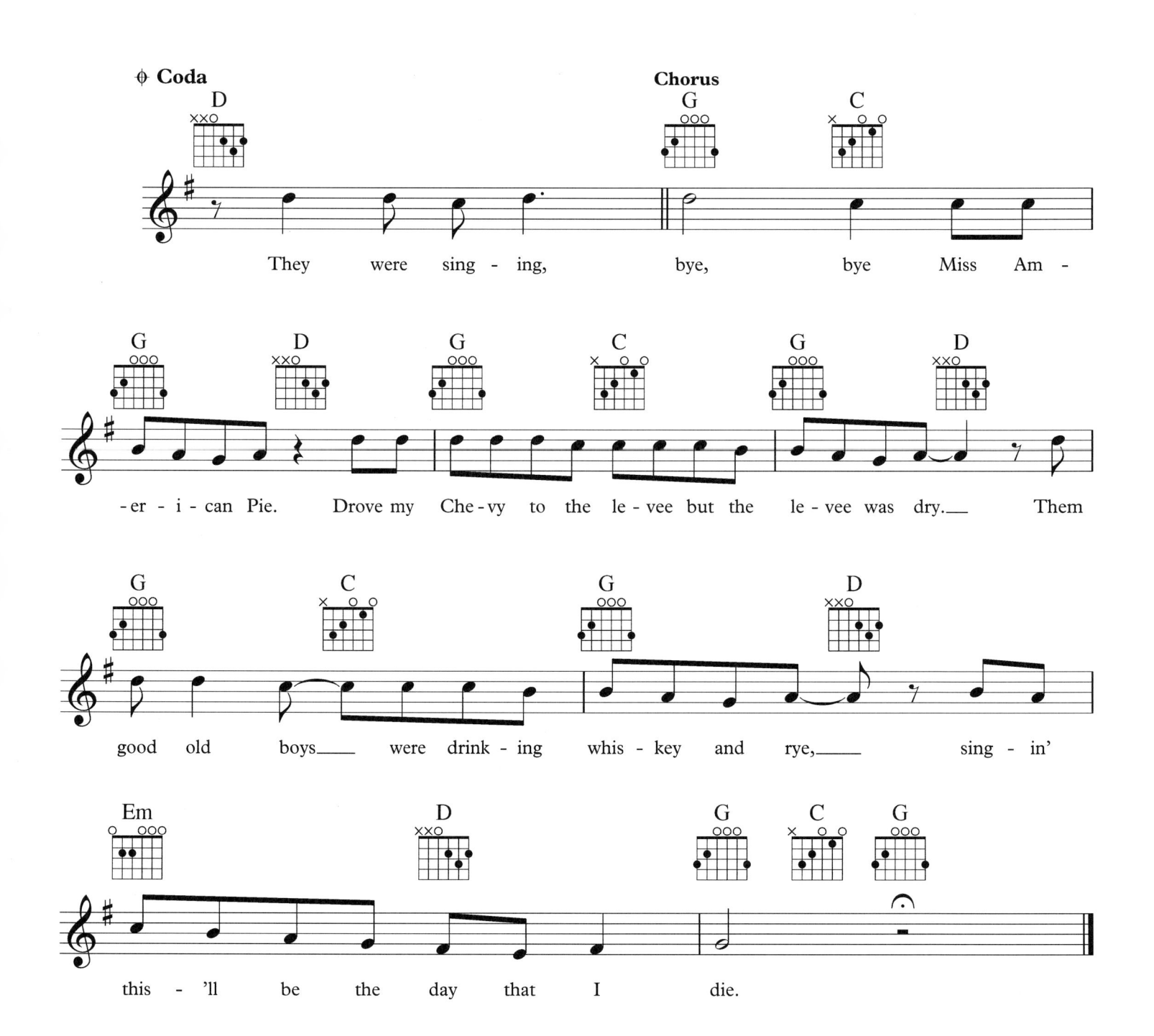

♦ Coda   **Chorus**

They were sing - ing, bye, bye Miss Am -

-er - i - can Pie. Drove my Che - vy to the le - vee but the le - vee was dry.___ Them

good old boys___ were drink - ing whis - key and rye,___ sing - in'

this - 'll be the day that I die.

Verse 5:
And there we were all in one place,
A generation lost in space
With no time left to start again.
So come on, Jack be nimble, Jack be quick
Jack Flash sat on a candlestick
Cause fire is the devil's only friend.

Oh, and as I watched him on the stage
My hands were clenched in fists of rage
No angel born in hell
Could break that Satan's spell.

And as the flames climbed high into the night
To light the sacrificial rite,
I saw Satan laughing with delight
The day the music died.
He was singing ...

Chorus

Angie

Words & Music by Keith Richards & Mick Jagger

© Copyright 1973 Promopub B.V.
Westminster Music Limited.
All Rights Reserved. International Copyright Secured.

Strumming style:

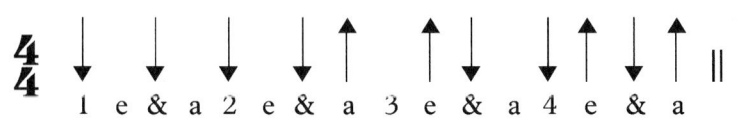

> The strumming is based on sixteenth-notes (four per beat). Leaving out certain strums, as shown, creates an interesting rhythm.

Intro

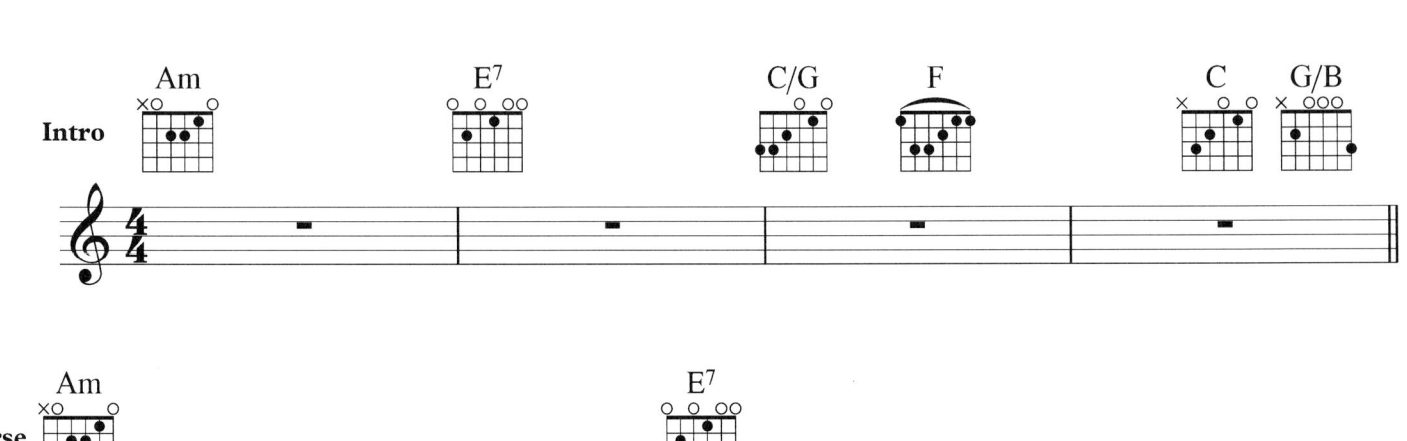

Verse

1. An - gie,_____ oh An - gie_____
2. An - gie,_____ you're beau - ti - ful,_____

(3. Instrumental)

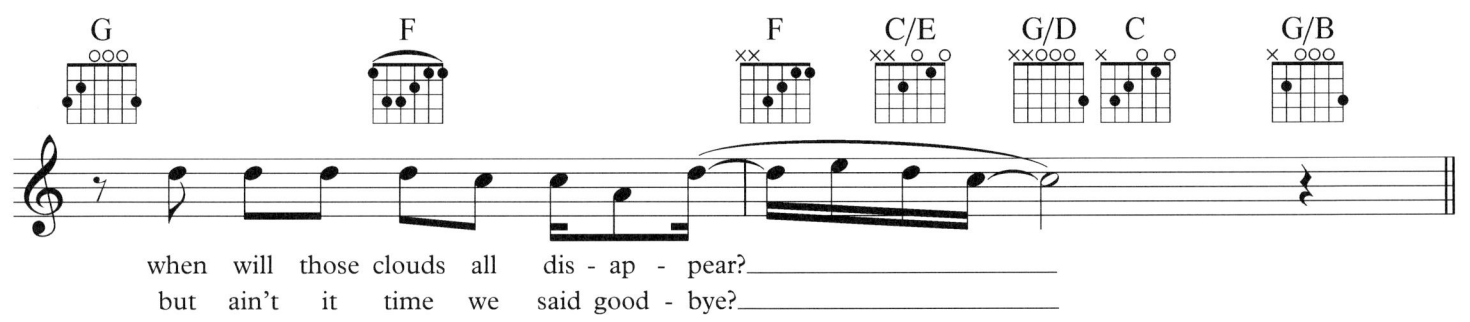

when will those clouds all dis - ap - pear?_____
but ain't it time we said good - bye?_____

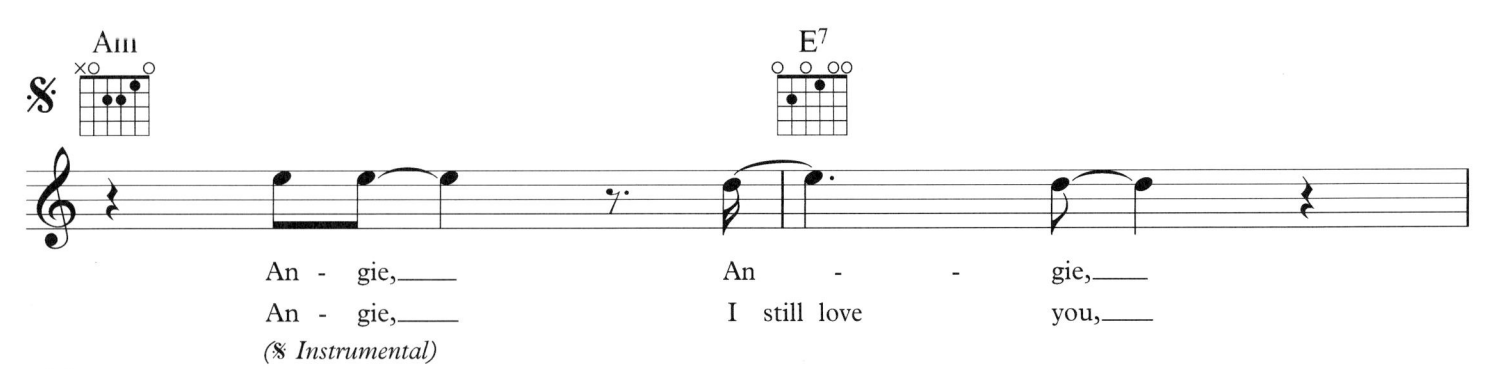

An - gie,____ An - - gie,____
An - gie,____ I still love you,____

(% Instrumental)

17

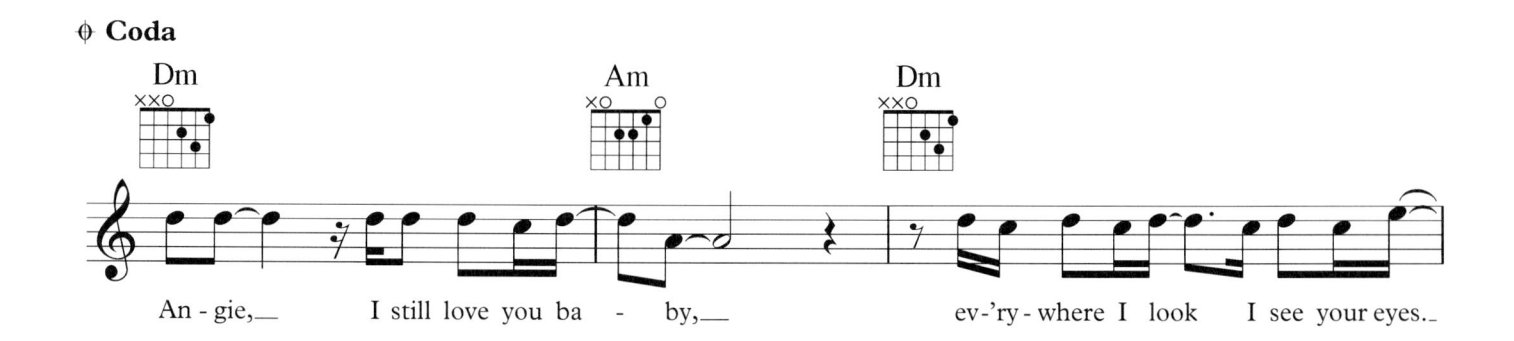

An - gie,__ I still love you ba - by,__ ev'ry-where I look I see your eyes._

_____ There ain't a wo - man who__ comes close to you,

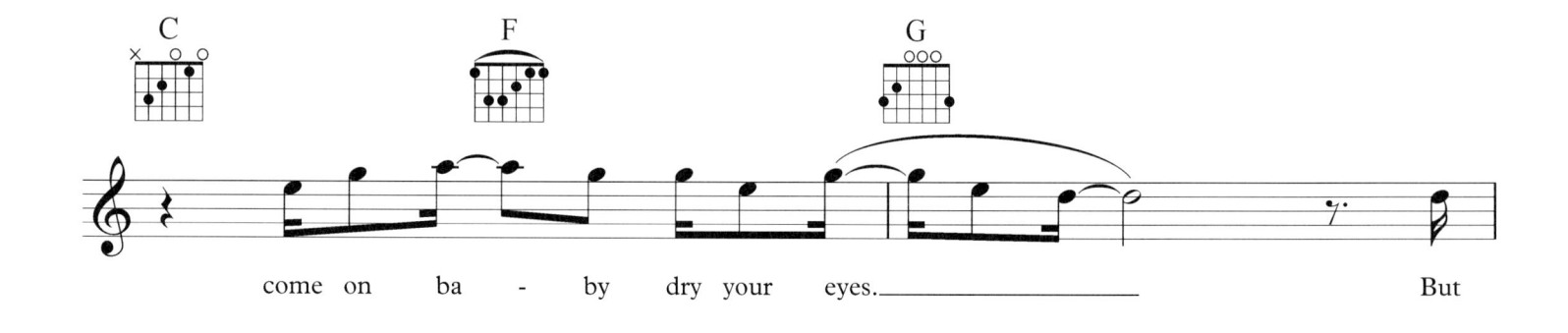

come on ba - by dry your eyes._____ But

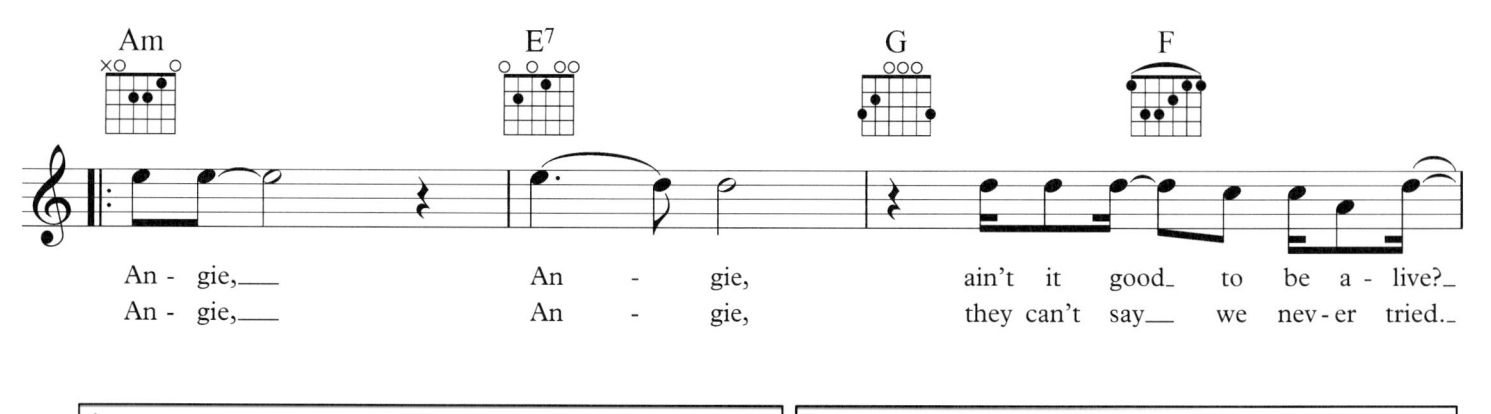

An - gie,___ An - gie, ain't it good__ to be a - live?
An - gie,___ An - gie, they can't say__ we nev - er tried.__

1. **2.**

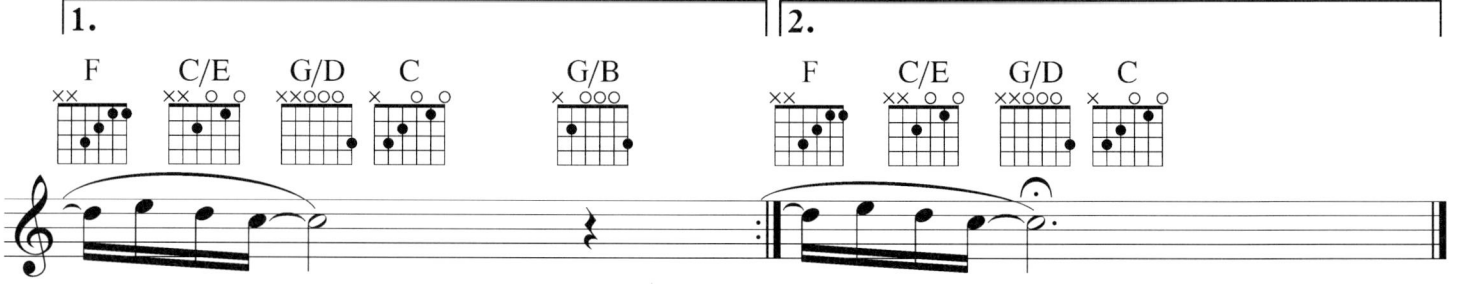

Blackbird

Words & Music by John Lennon & Paul McCartney

© Copyright 1968 Sony/ATV Music Publishing.
All Rights Reserved. International Copyright Secured.

Take a careful look at the tab for the intro: pairs of lower and higher notes are picked along with the open G string. Pick—or strum—in a similar fashion throughout the song.

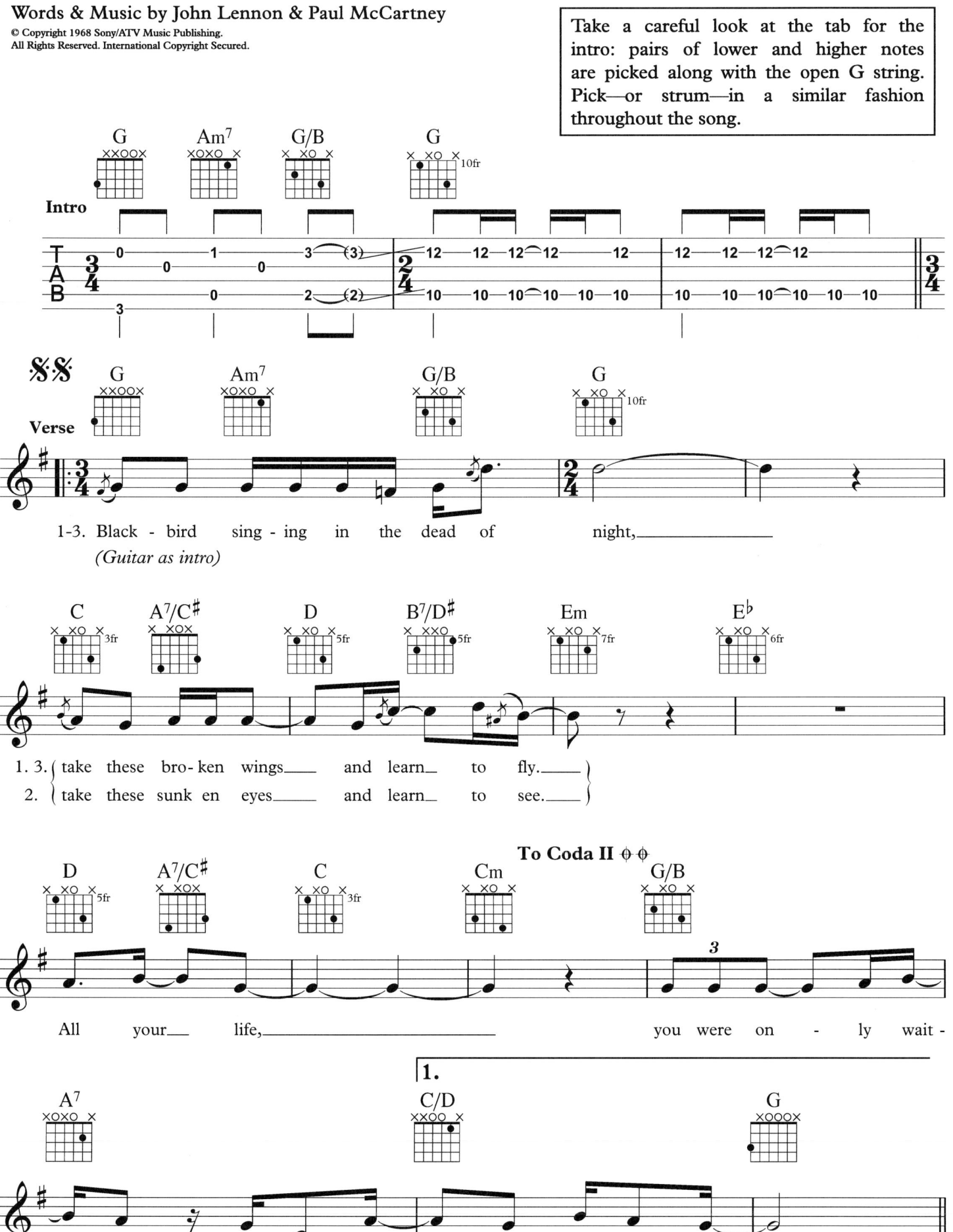

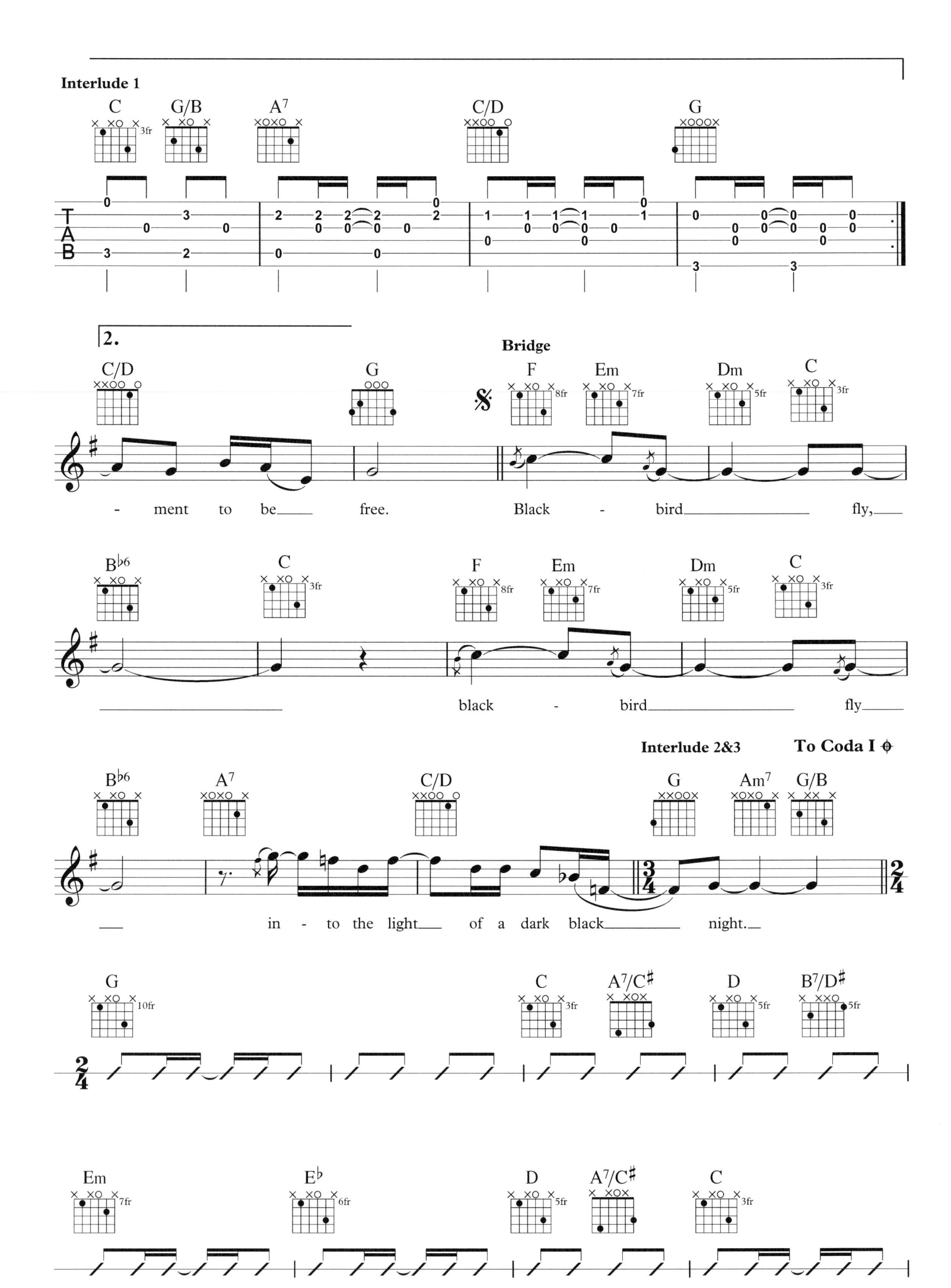

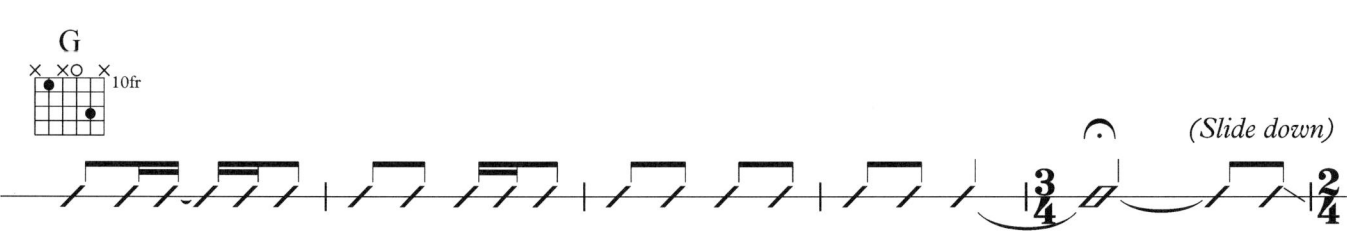

⊕ Coda I

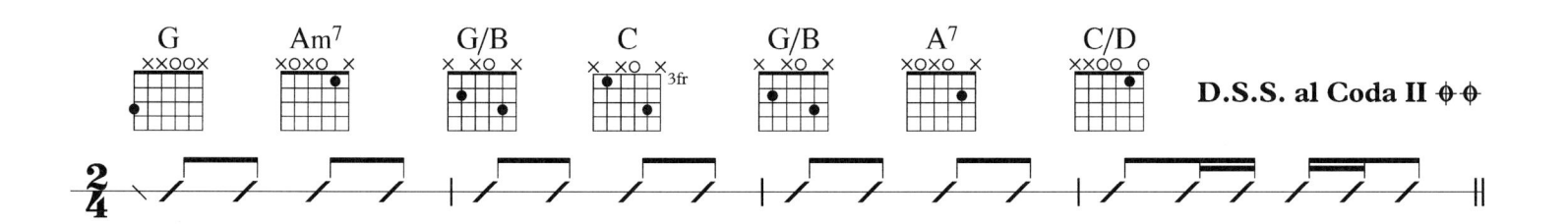

(Slide down)

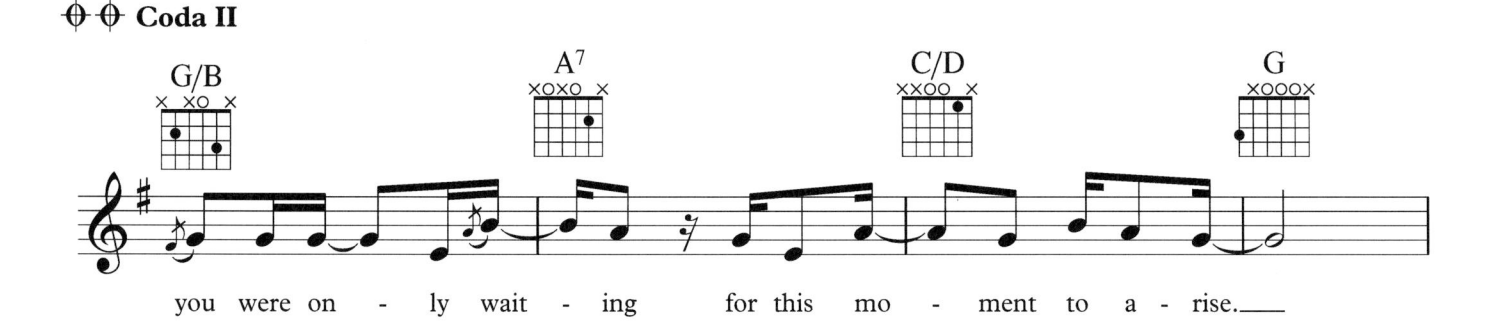

D.S.S. al Coda II ⊕ ⊕

⊕ ⊕ Coda II

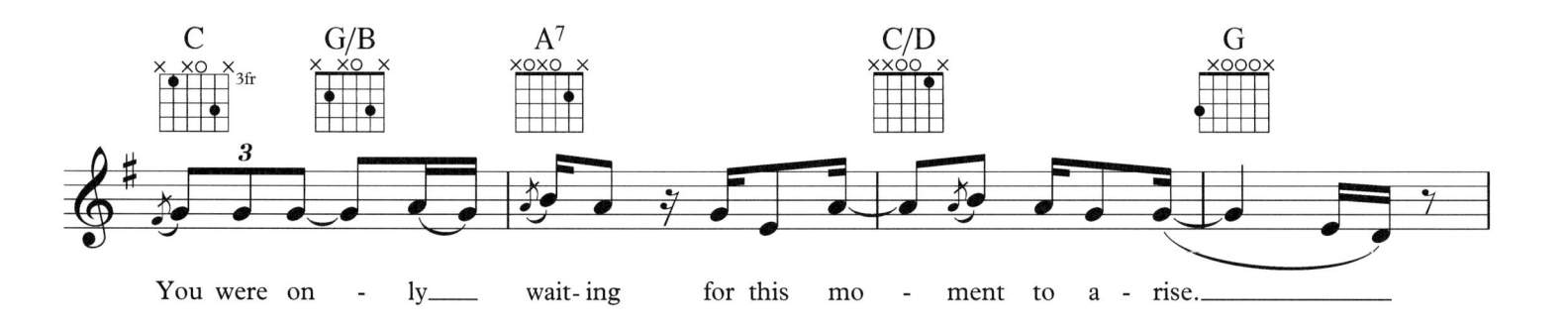

you were on - ly wait - ing for this mo - ment to a - rise.___

You were on - ly___ wait - ing for this mo - ment to a - rise._____

(Pat strings with fingers of right hand)

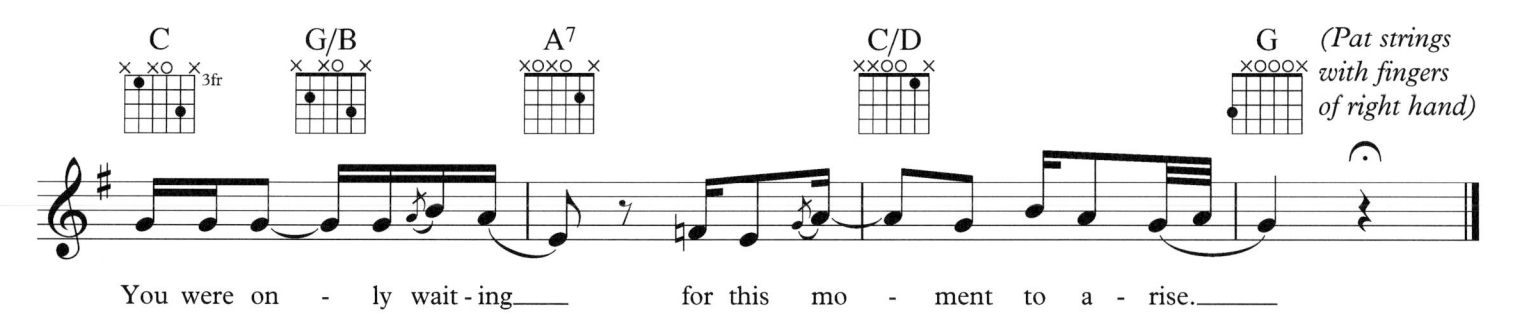

You were on - ly wait - ing___ for this mo - ment to a - rise._____

Budapest

Words & Music by George Ezra Barnett & Joel Laslett Pott

© Copyright 2013 BMG Rights Management (UK) Limited, a BMG Chrysalis company/Chrysalis Music Limited, a BMG Chrysalis Company.
All Rights Reserved. International Copyright Secured.

Picking style:

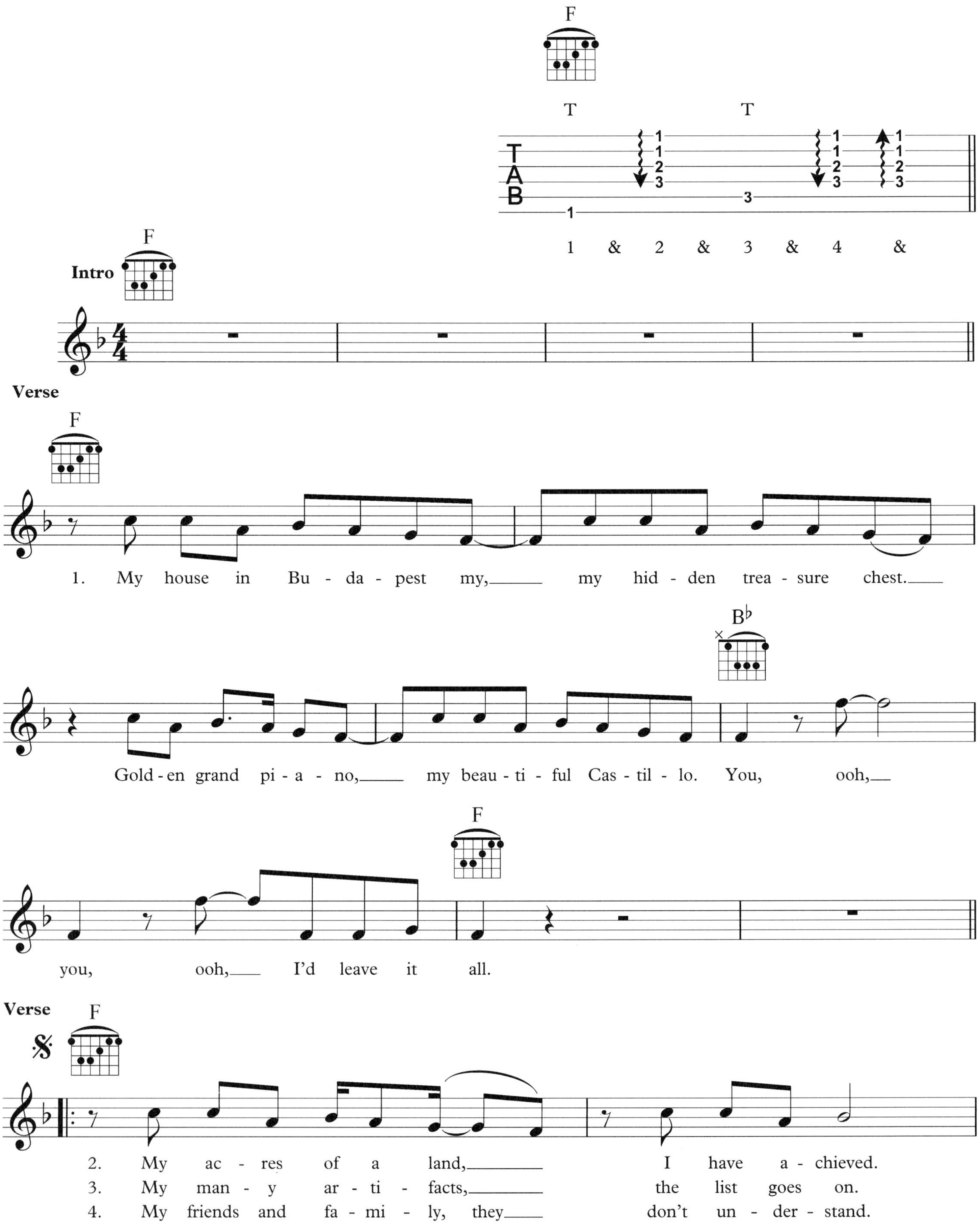

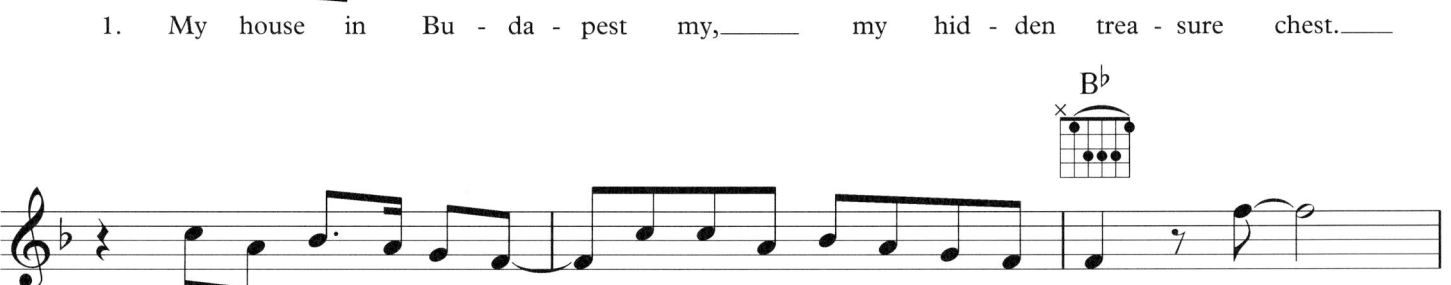

Intro

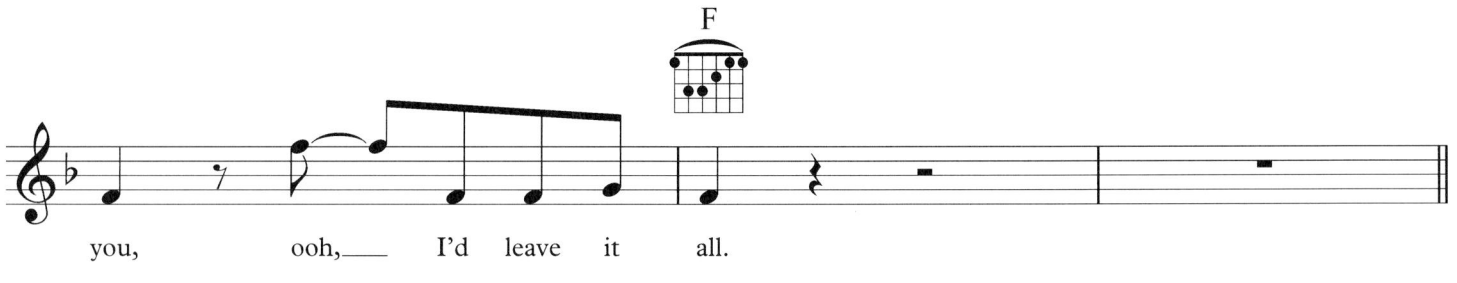

Verse

1. My house in Bu - da - pest my,_____ my hid - den trea - sure chest._____

Gold - en grand pi - a - no,_____ my beau - ti - ful Cas - til - lo. You, ooh,_____

you, ooh,_____ I'd leave it all.

Verse

2. My ac - res of a land,_____ I have a - chieved.
3. My man - y ar - ti - facts,_____ the list goes on.
4. My friends and fa - mi - ly, they_____ don't un - der - stand.

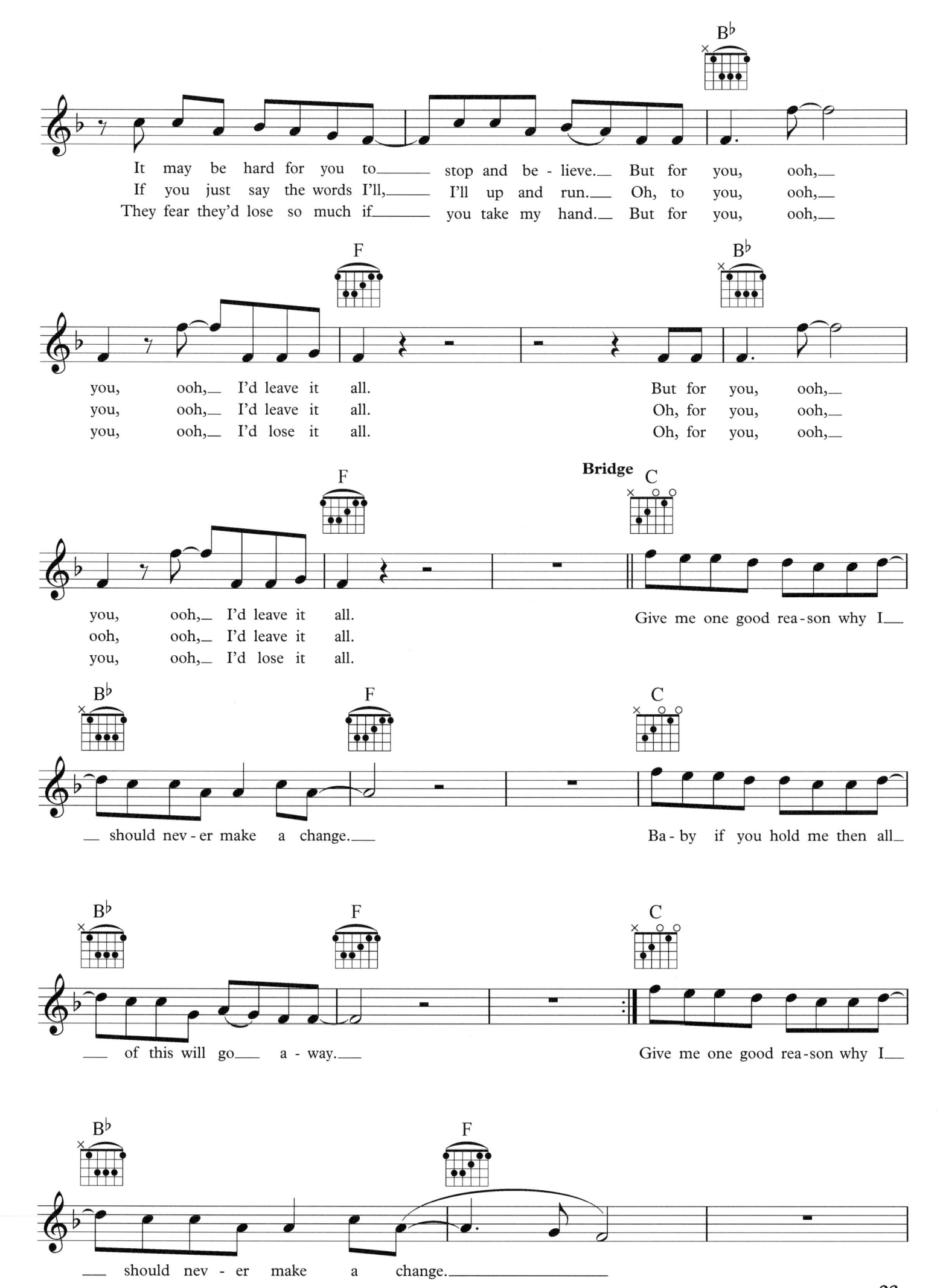

Ba-by if you hold me then all_____ of this will go___ a - way.___

(Ah

Interlude

ooh.)

(Ah

ooh.)

ϕ Coda

5. My house in Bu-da-pest my,___ my hid-den trea-sure chest. Gold-en grand pi-a - no,_

___ my beau-ti - ful Cas-til - lo. You, ooh,_ you, ooh,_ I'd leave it all.

Oh, for you, ooh,_ you, ooh,_ I'd leave it all.

Catch The Wind

Words & Music by Donovan Leitch

© Copyright 1965 Donovan (Music) Limited.
All Rights Reserved. International Copyright Secured.

Picking style:

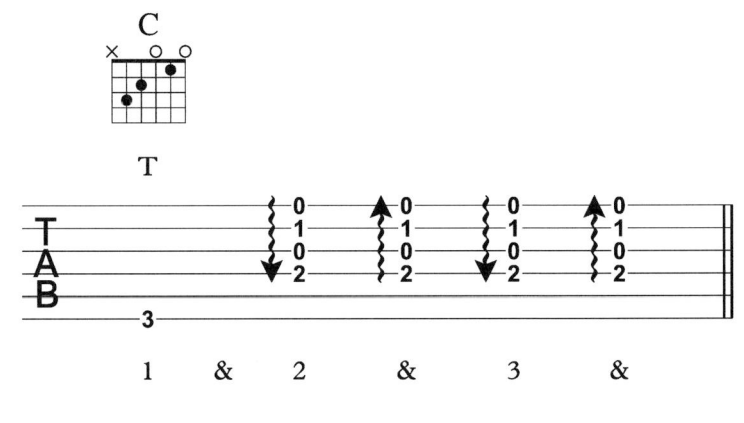

Capo: Fret 3

Intro

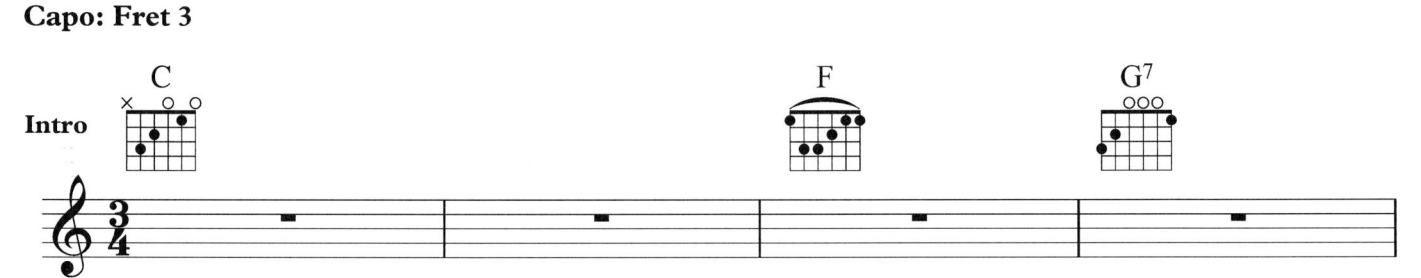

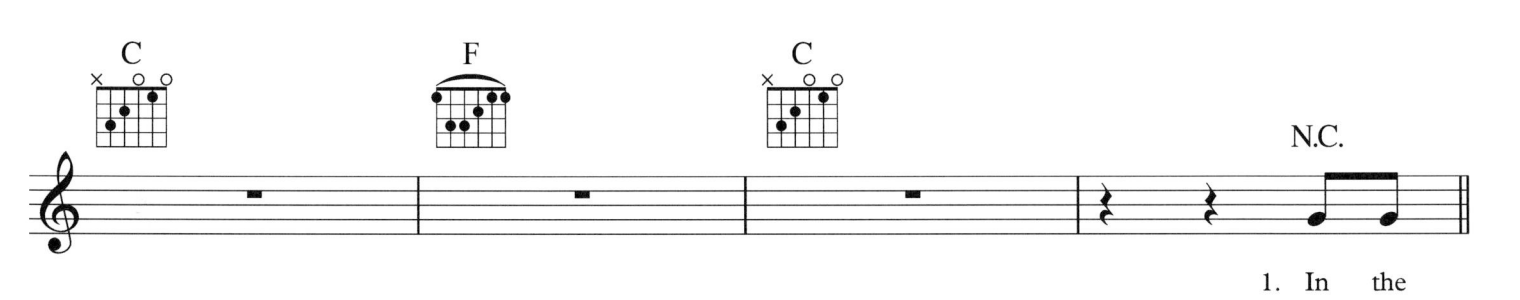

1. In the

Verse

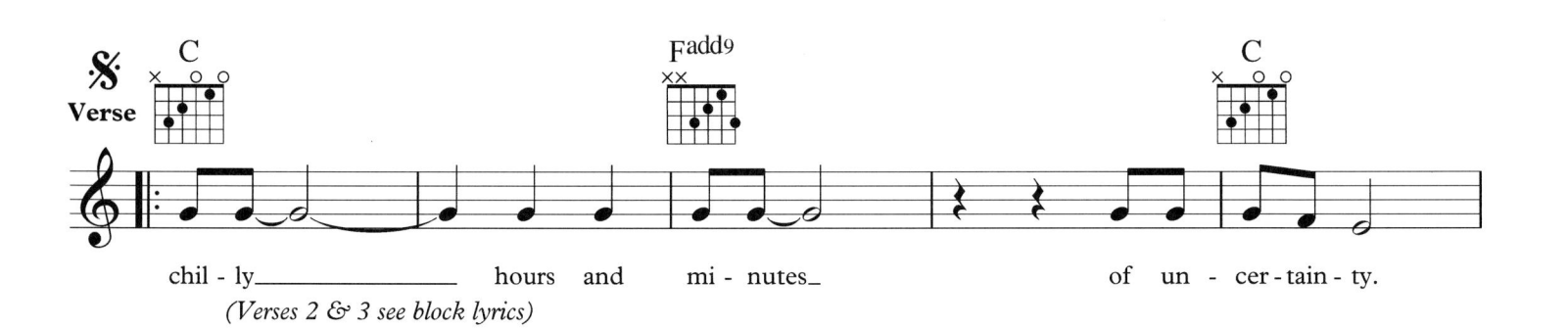

chil - ly_____ hours and mi - nutes_ of un - cer - tain - ty.

(Verses 2 & 3 see block lyrics)

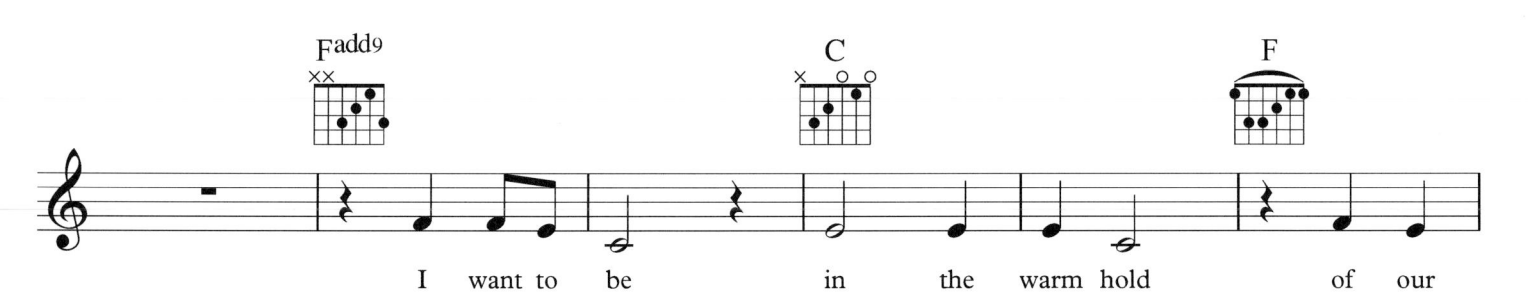

I want to be in the warm hold of our

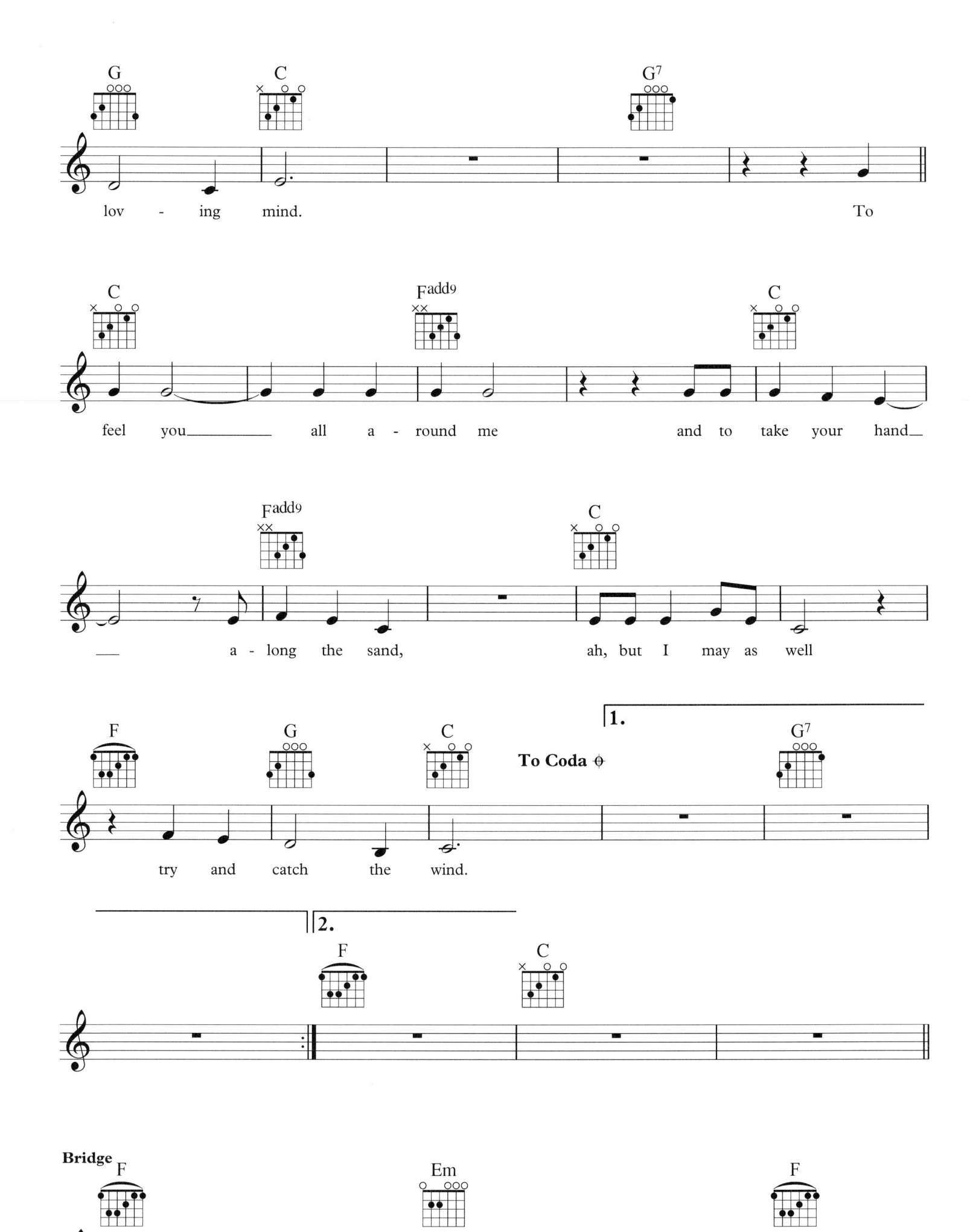

lov - ing mind.   To

feel you_____ all a - round me   and to take your hand__

__ a - long the sand,   ah, but I may as well

1.

To Coda ⊕

try and catch the wind.

2.

Bridge

Did - dy_____ di di di di di di di di,__   di di di__

26

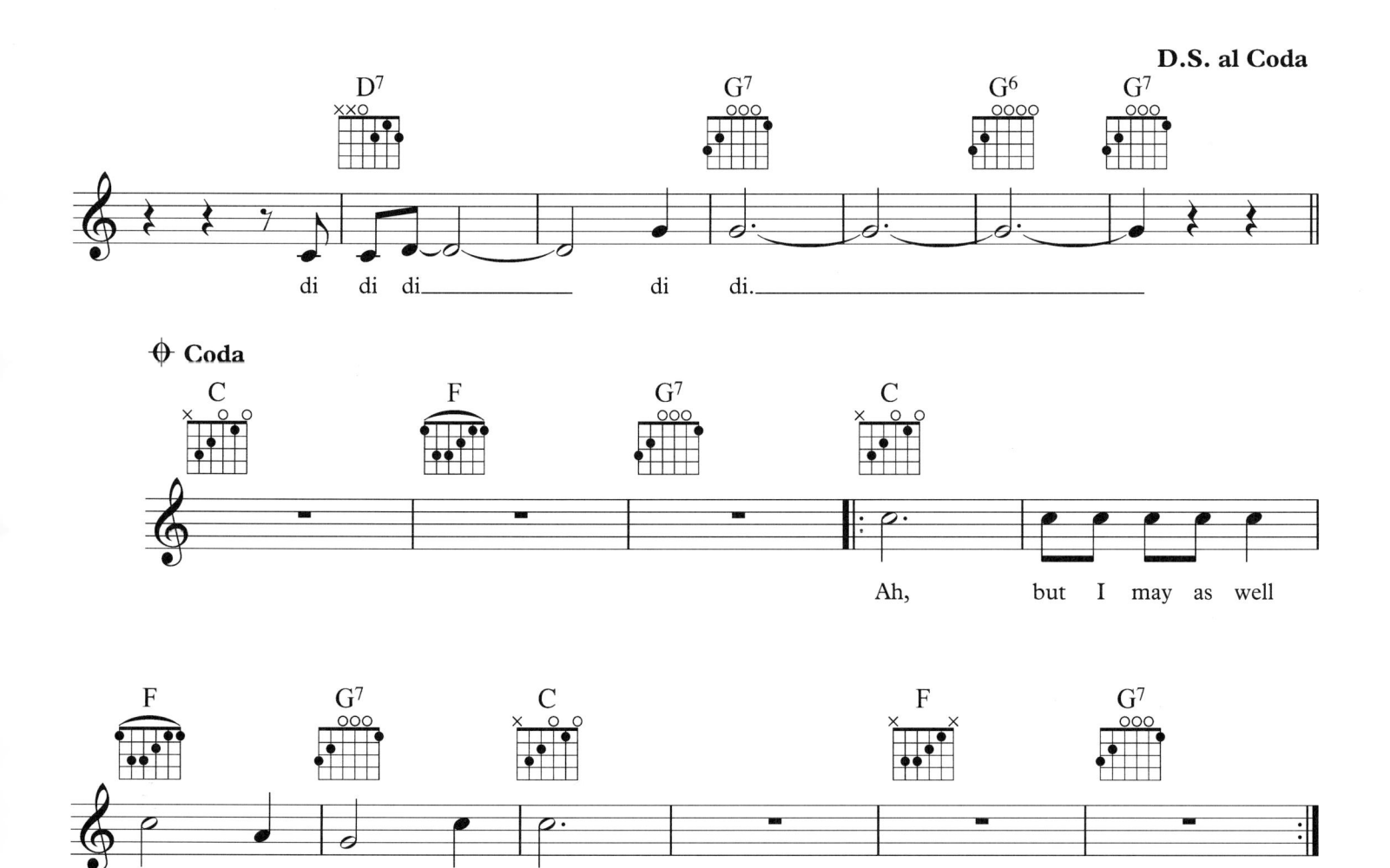

di di di_____ di di._____

 Coda

Ah, but I may as well

try and catch the wind.

Repeat ad lib. to fade

Verse 2
When sundown pales the sky
I want to hide awhile
Behind your smile,
And everywhere I'd look, your eyes I'd find.

For me to love you now
Would be the sweetest thing
'Twould make me sing
Ah but I may as well try and catch the wind.

Verse 3
When rain has hung the leaves with tears
I want you near
To kill my fears
To help me to leave all my blues behind.

For standing in your heart
Is where I want to be
And long to be
Ah but I may as well try and catch the wind.

Coat Of Many Colors

Words & Music by Dolly Parton

© Copyright 1969 Velvet Apple Music, USA.
Carlin Music Corporation.
All Rights Reserved. International Copyright Secured.

Picking style:

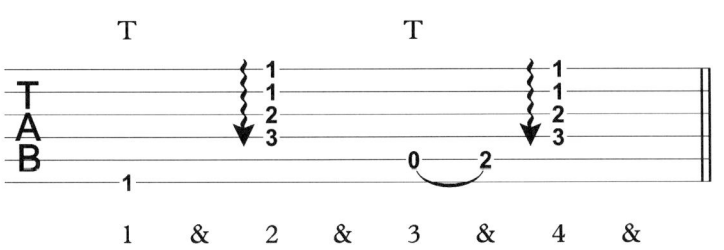

Play a hammer-on in the bass on the 3rd beat of each bar to achieve the insistent, rhythmic feel of the original.

Capo: Fret 3

Intro

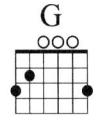

Verse

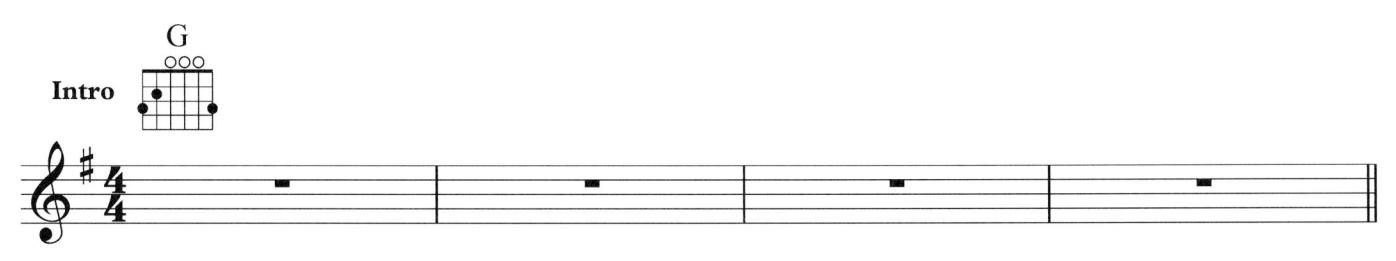

1. Back through the years____ I go wan - d'rin' once_ a - gain.

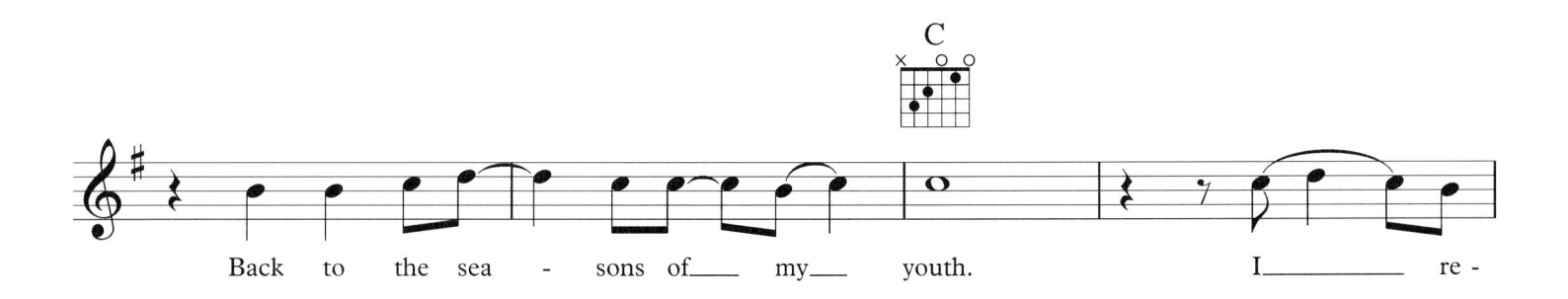

Back to the sea - sons of__ my__ youth. I_____ re -

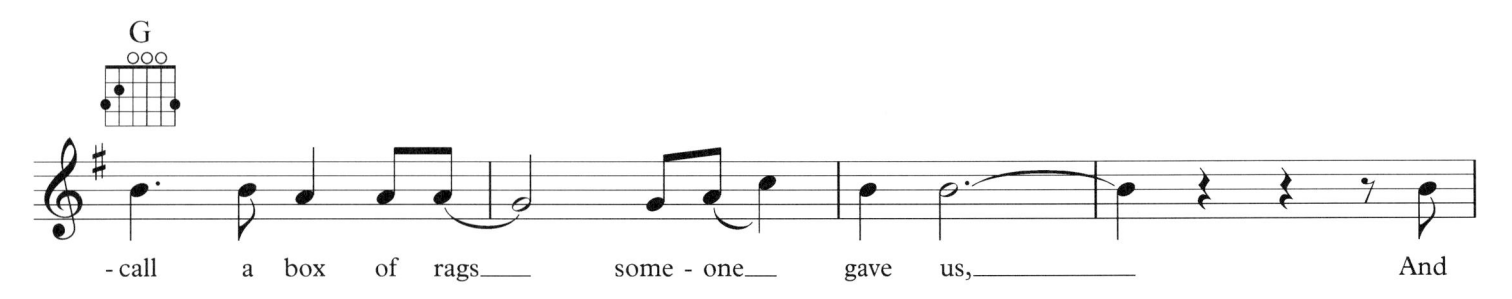

-call a box of rags____ some - one__ gave us,_____ And

how my Ma-ma put___ the rags___ to use.___ There were

rags of ma-ny co-lors. Ev-'ry piece___ was small and I

did-n't have___ a coat.___ And it was way down___ in___ the fall. Ma-ma

sewed the rags to-geth-er. Sew-in' ev-'ry piece with love. She made my___

coat of ma-ny col-ors,___ that I was so___ proud___ of.___

2. As she sewed she told a sto-ry from the bi-ble she had

read, a-bout a coat of ma-ny col-ors Jo-seph

C

rich as I____ could be_____ in my coat of ma - ny

D **G**

col - ors my Ma - ma made_ for me.___

E⁷ **Verse** **A**

3. So with patch - es on my britch - es and
(4.) could - n't un - der - stand it for

holes in both__ my shoes, in my coat of ma - ny co - lors I
I felt I____ was rich. And I told them 'bout the love my Ma - ma

E **A**

hur - ried off to school, just to find the o - thers laugh - ing and
sewed in ev - 'ry stitch. And I told them all the stor - ies Ma - ma

D **A**

mak - ing fun of me.____ and my coat of ma - ny col - ors my
told me why she sewed__ and how my coat of ma - ny col - ors was worth

31

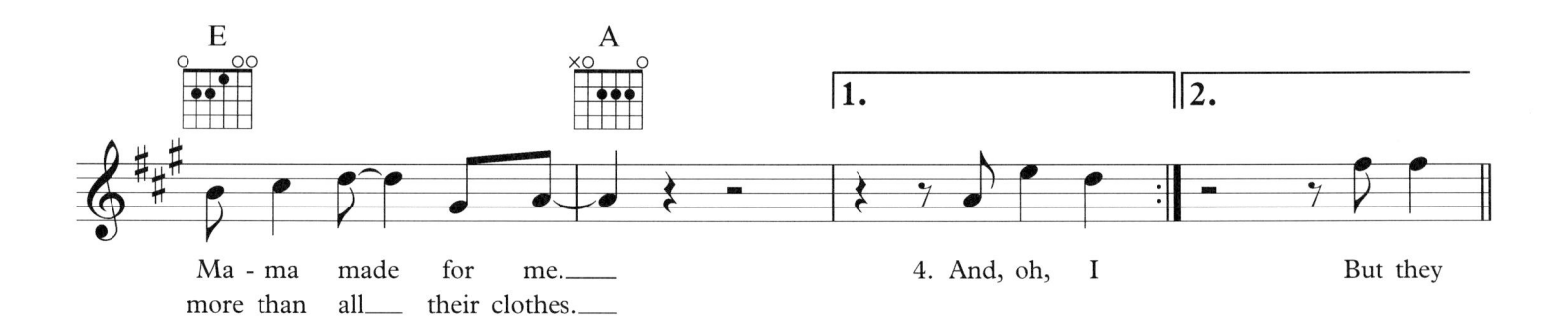

Ma - ma made for me.____ 4. And, oh, I But they

more than all__ their clothes.__

Chorus

did-n't un-der - stand it and I tried to make_ them see.__ That one is on-ly poor_

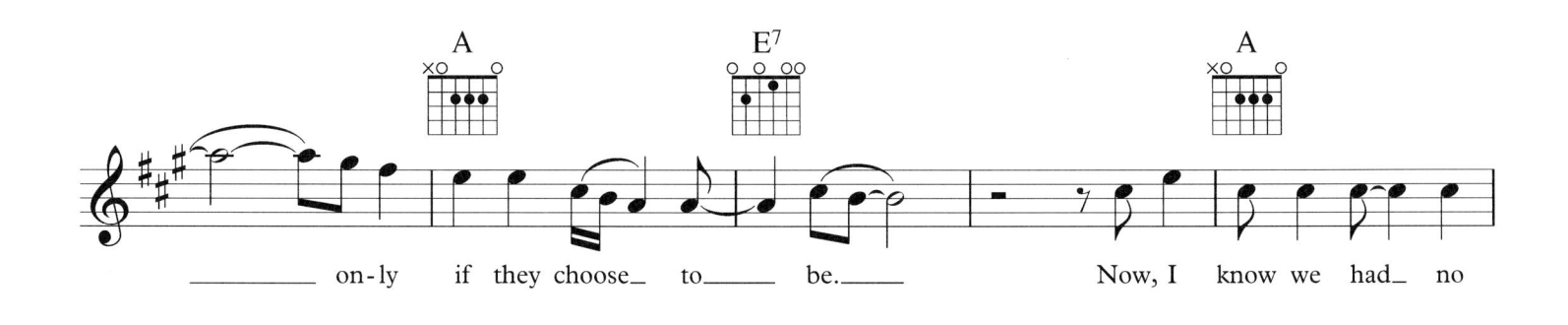

_____ on-ly if they choose_ to____ be.____ Now, I know we had_ no

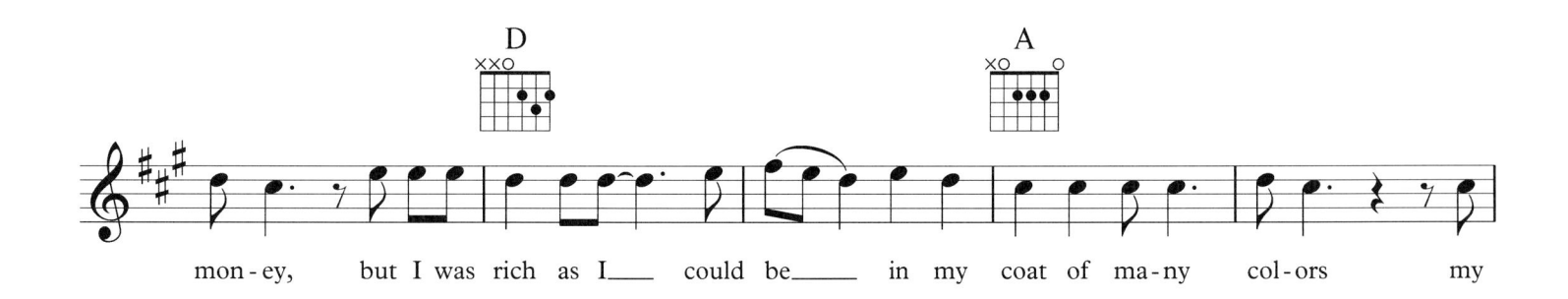

mon-ey, but I was rich as I___ could be____ in my coat of ma-ny col-ors my

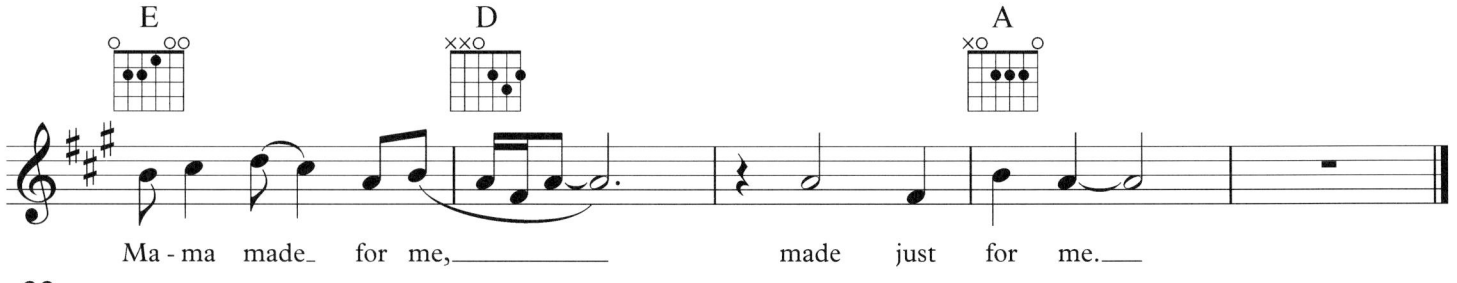

Ma - ma made_ for me,_____ made just for me.__

Crazy Little Thing Called Love

Words & Music by Freddie Mercury

© Copyright 1979 Queen Music Limited.
EMI Music Publishing Limited.
All Rights Reserved. International Copyright Secured.

> This song has a *swing* feel, meaning that the strums on the off-beat occur later than half-way through the beat, so delay the up-strums by a little. More delay = more swing!

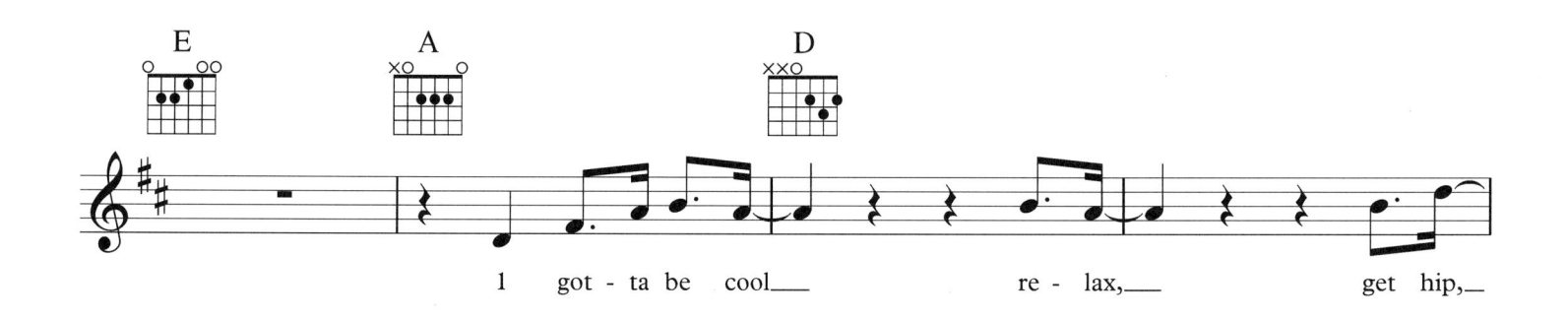

I got-ta be cool___ re-lax,___ get hip,___

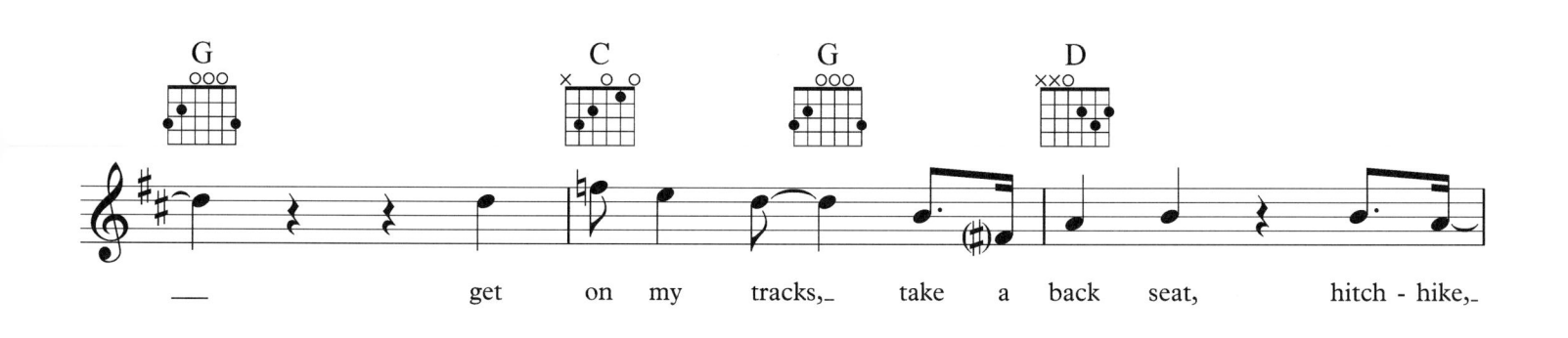

___ get on my tracks,___ take a back seat, hitch-hike,___

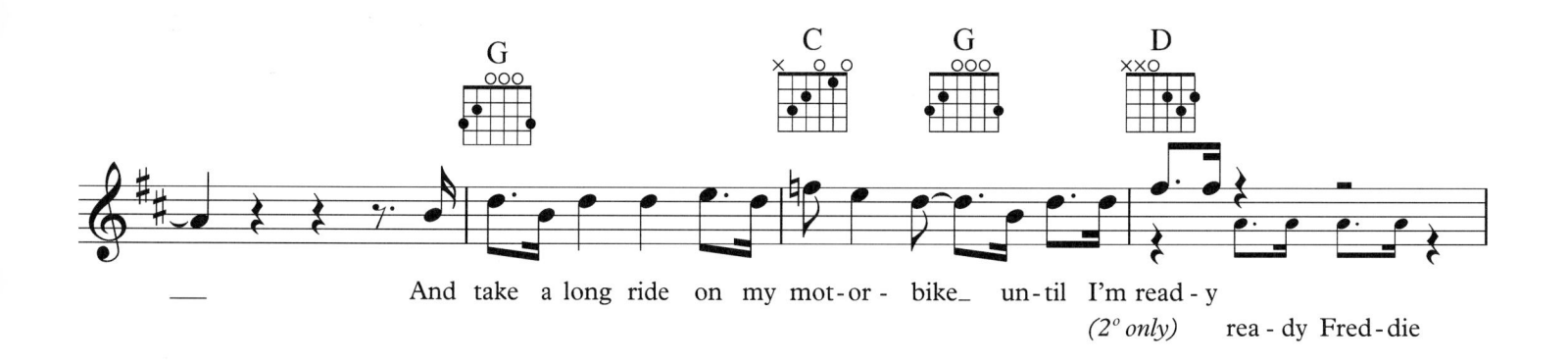

___ And take a long ride on my mot-or-bike_ un-til I'm read-y
(2° only) rea-dy Fred-die

1. **2.**

D.S. al Coda

cra-zy lit-tle thing called love___ There goes my This thing_

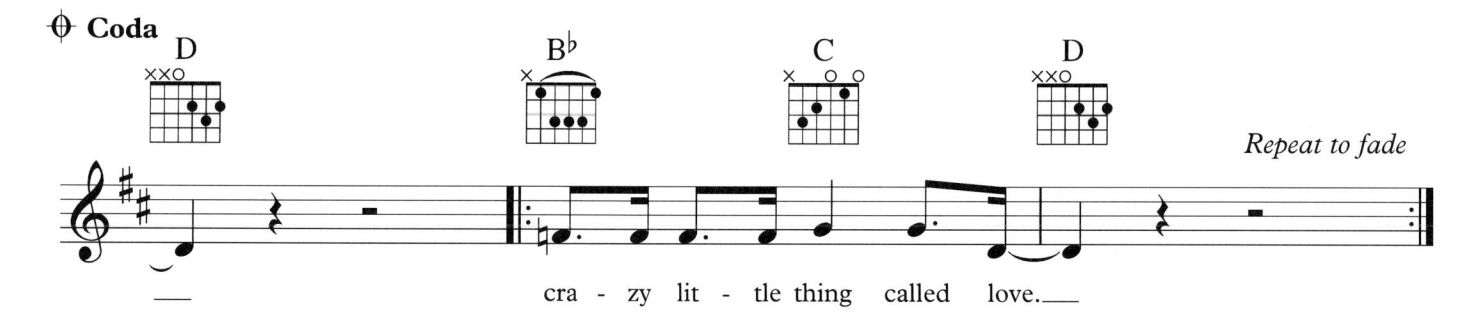

Coda

Repeat to fade

___ cra-zy lit-tle thing called love.___

Creep

Words & Music by Albert Hammond, Mike Hazlewood, Thom Yorke, Jonny Greenwood, Colin Greenwood, Ed O'Brien & Phil Selway

© Copyright 1992 Warner/Chappell Music Limited/Imagem Songs Limited.
All Rights Reserved. International Copyright Secured.

Picking style:

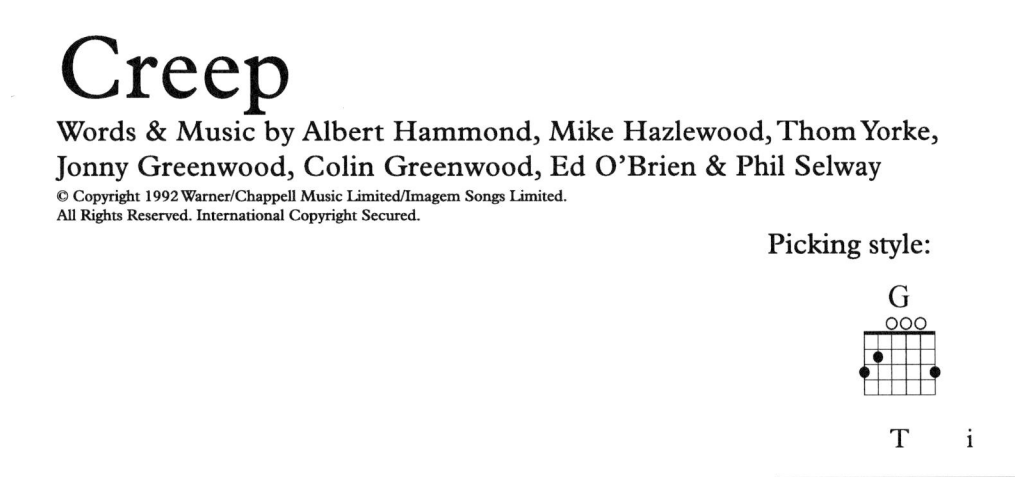

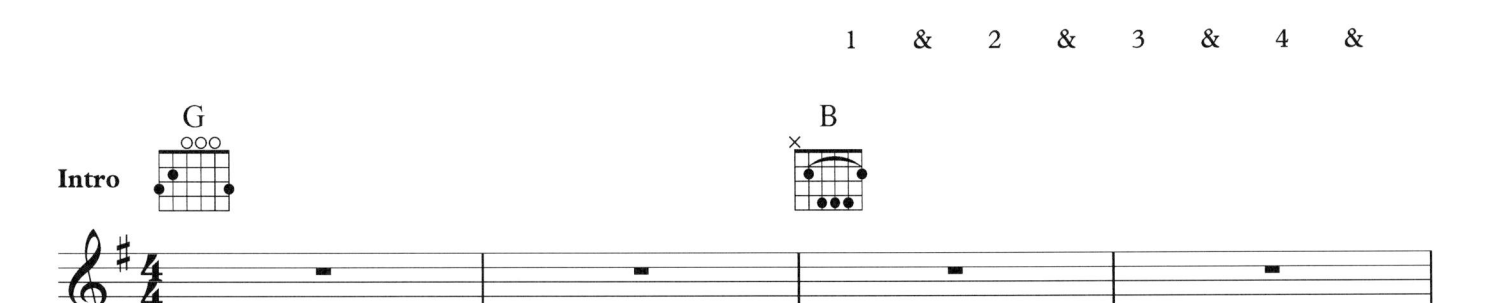

1. When you were here be-fore,

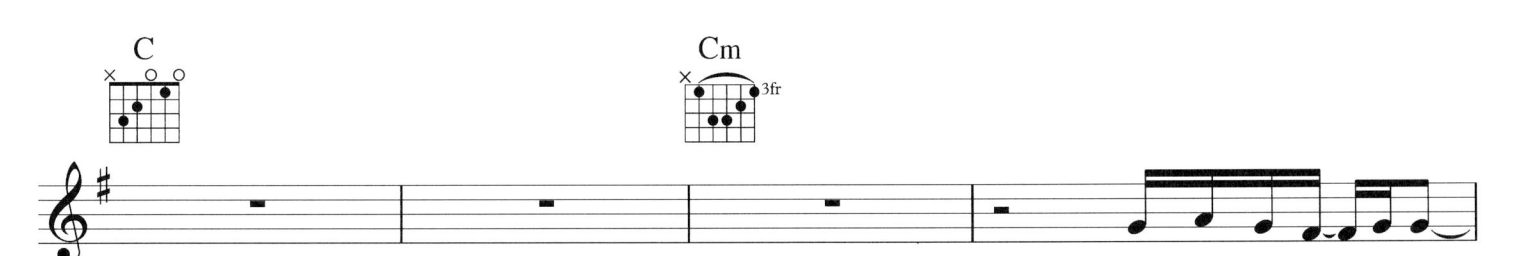

Verse

could-n't look you in___ the eye.___
I wanna have_ con - trol.___

You're just like an an - gel,
I wanna per-fect bod - y,

your skin makes me cry.___
I wanna per - fect soul.___

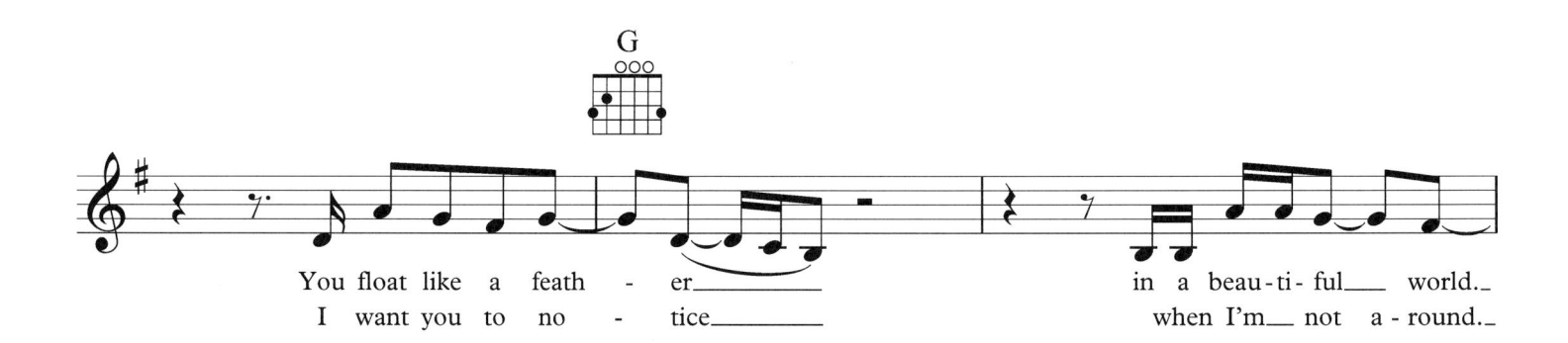

You float like a feath - er_____ in a beau - ti - ful___ world._
I want you to no - tice_____ when I'm___ not a - round._

___ I wish I was spe - cial,
___ You're so fuck - ing spe - cial,

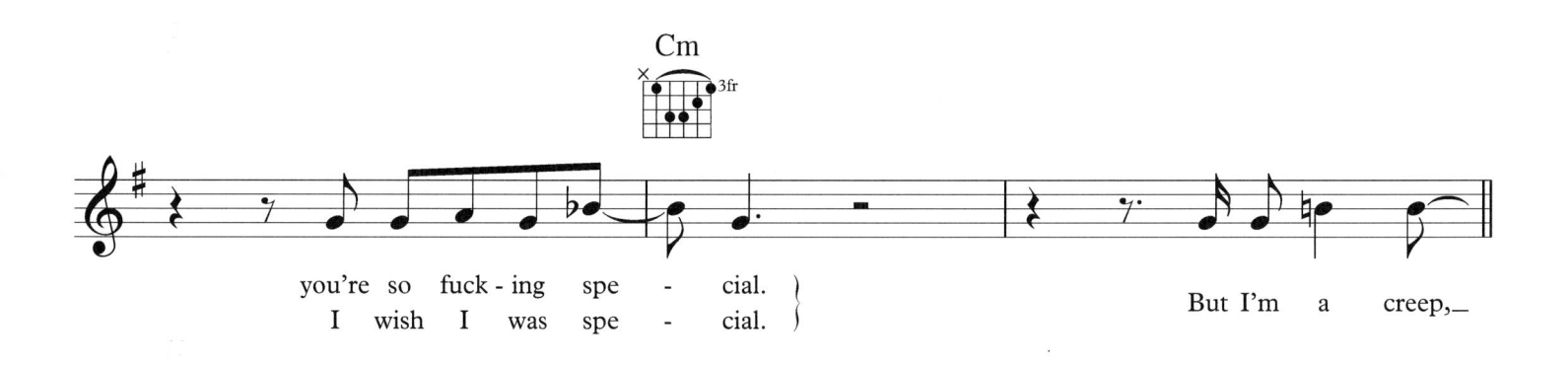

you're so fuck - ing spe - cial.
I wish I was spe - cial. But I'm a creep,_

Chorus

___ I'm a weir - do,_____

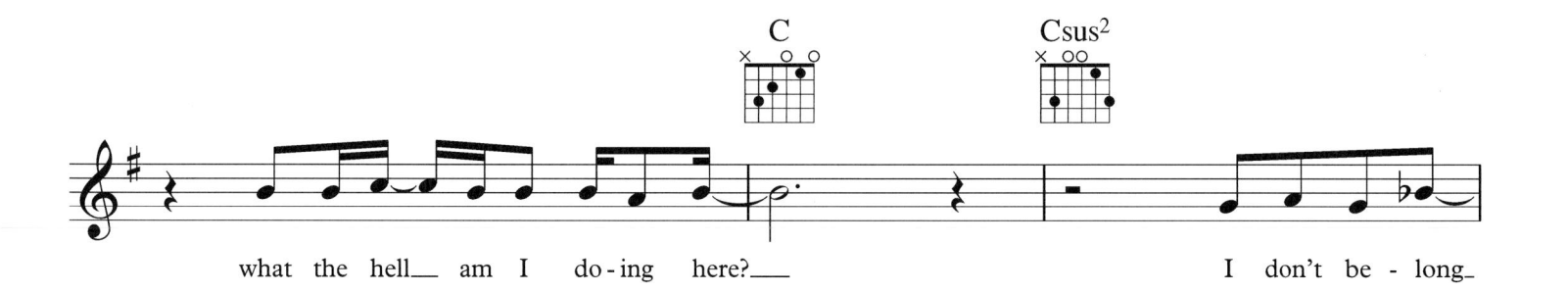

what the hell___ am I do - ing here?___ I don't be - long_

here.

2. I don't care if it hurts, Oh, oh.

She's run - ning out the door.

She's run - ning out, she run, run, run, run.

Run.

What - ev - er makes you hap - py,

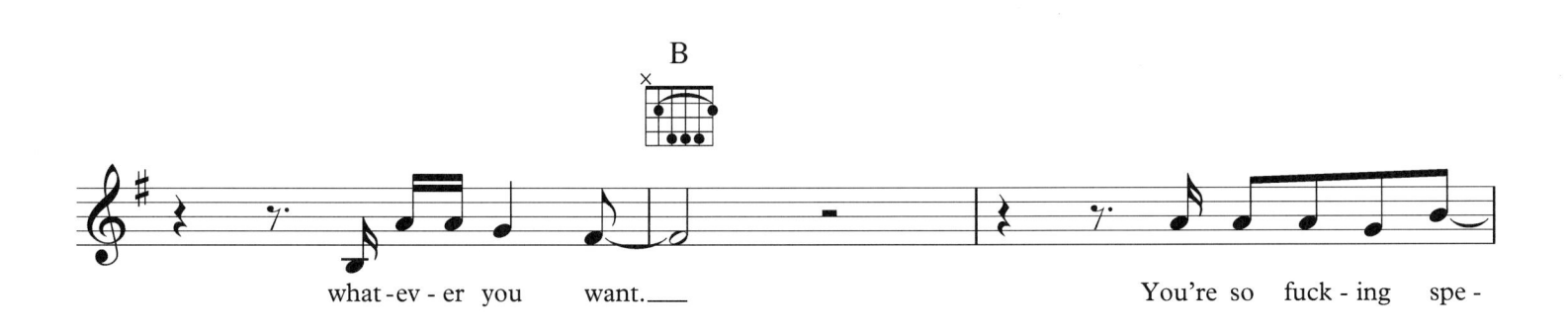

what-ev-er you   want.___   You're so fuck-ing spe-

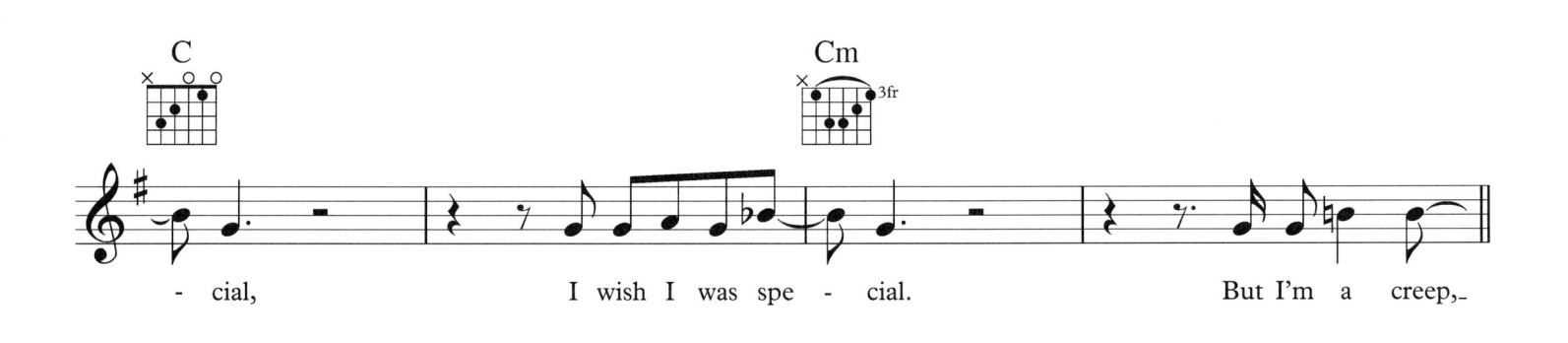

- cial,   I wish I was spe - cial.   But I'm a creep,_

___   I'm a   weir - do,_____

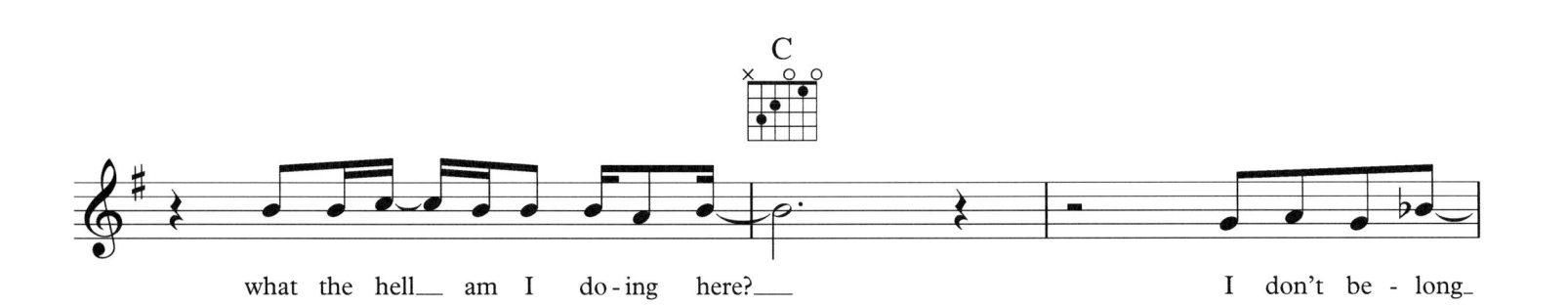

what the hell__ am I do-ing here?___   I don't be-long_

___ here.   I don't be-long___ here.

The First Time Ever I Saw Your Face

Words & Music by Ewan MacColl

© Copyright 1962 & 1972 Stormking Music Incorporated, USA.
Harmony Music Limited.
All Rights Reserved. International Copyright Secured.

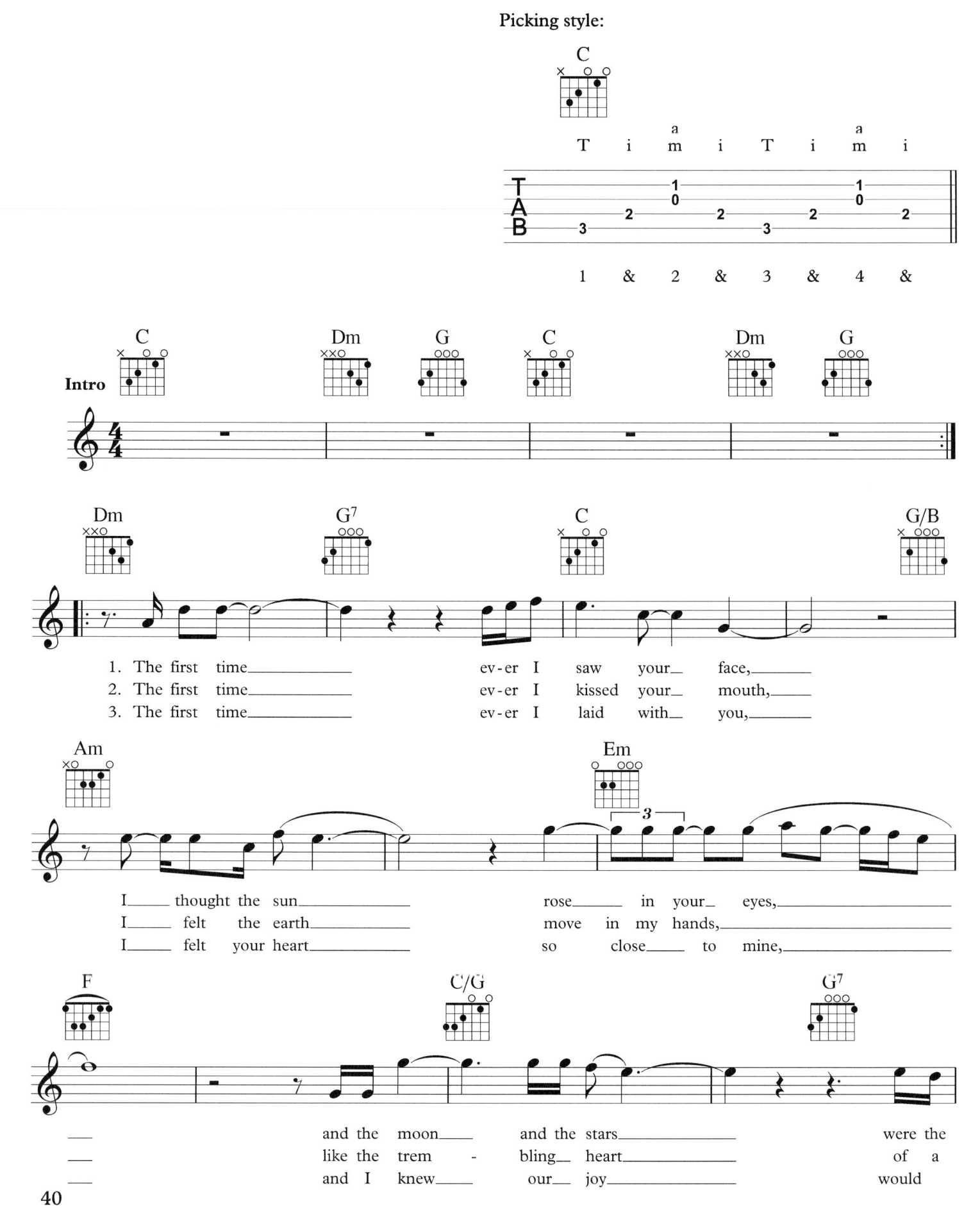

Picking style:

Intro

1. The first time ____ ev-er I saw your ____ face, ____
2. The first time ____ ev-er I kissed your ____ mouth, ____
3. The first time ____ ev-er I laid with ____ you, ____

I ____ thought the sun ____ rose ____ in your ____ eyes, ____
I ____ felt the earth ____ move in my hands, ____
I ____ felt your heart ____ so close ____ to mine, ____

____ and the moon ____ and the stars ____ were the
____ like the trem - bling ____ heart ____ of a
____ and I knew ____ our joy ____ would

gifts   you gave   to the   dark_____   and the end - less
cap - tive bird   that was   there_____   at my__ com -
fill   the earth   and__ last_____   till the end of

skies,_____   my__ love;   to the   dark_____   and the end -less
- mand,_____   my__ love;   that was   there_____   at my__ com -
time,_____   my__ love; and it would last_____   till the end of

1, 2.   **3.**

skies,_____   time,_____   my__ love.
- mand,_____

The first   time_____   ev - er I   saw_____

__   your face,   your face,

your face,_____   your   face.

Hold Back The River

Words & Music by Iain Archer & James Bay

© Copyright 2014 Kobalt Music Services Limited/B Unique Music.
Kobalt Music Publishing Limited.
All Rights Reserved. International Copyright Secured.

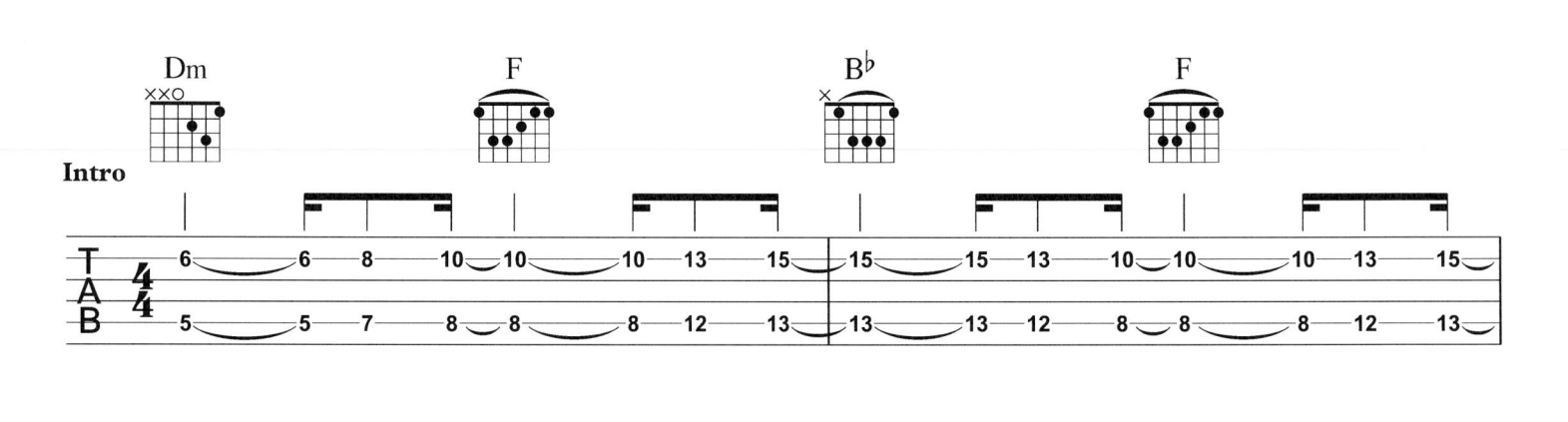

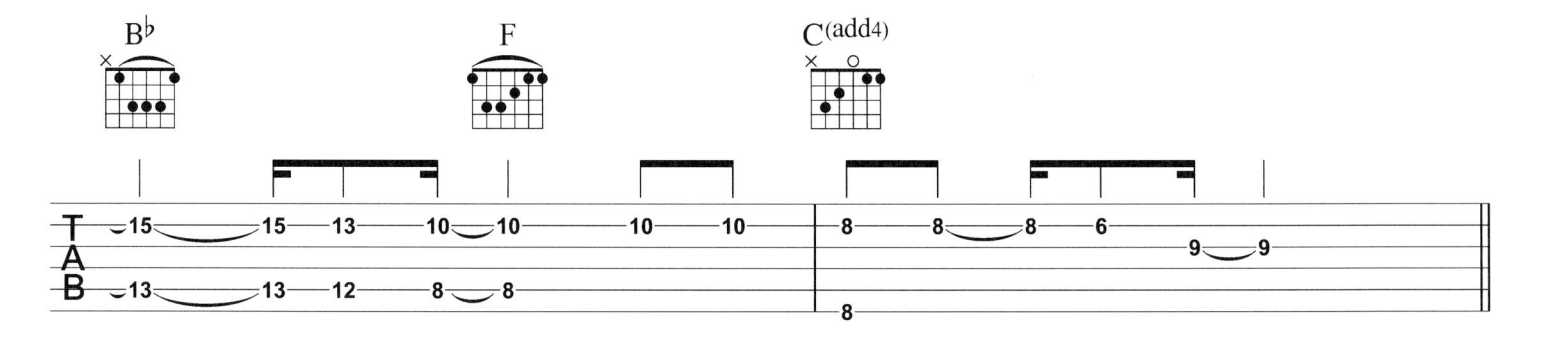

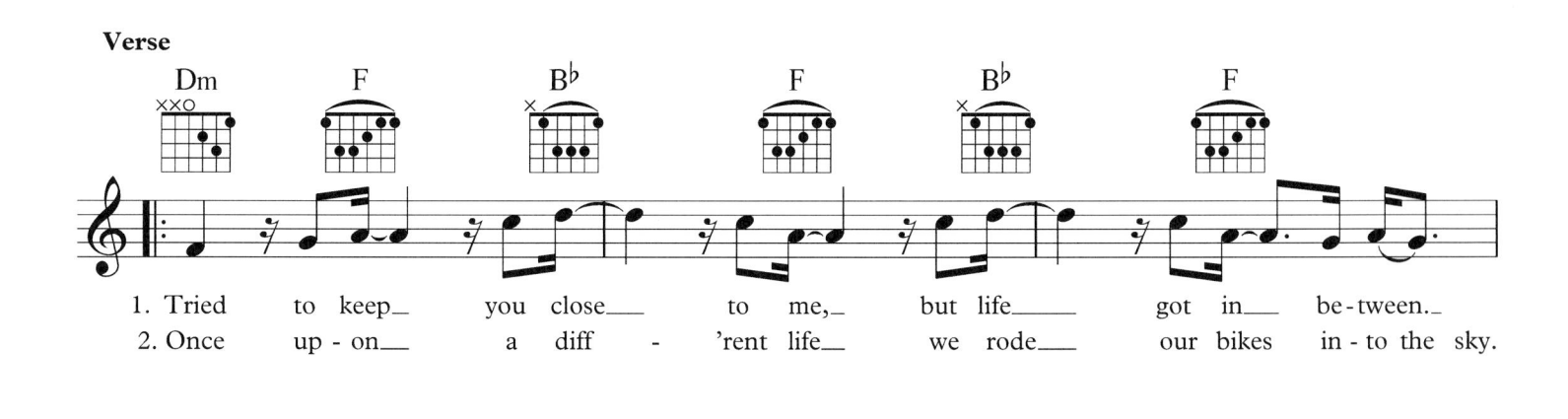

1. Tried to keep___ you close___ to me,___ but life_____ got in be-tween.___
2. Once up-on___ a diff - 'rent life___ we rode___ our bikes in-to the sky.

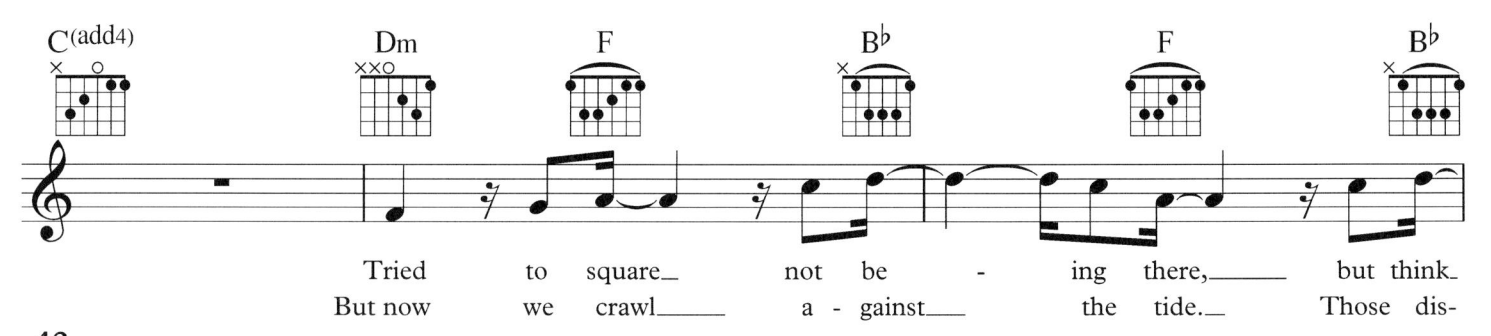

Tried to square___ not be - ing there,_____ but think__
But now we crawl___ a - gainst___ the tide.___ Those dis-

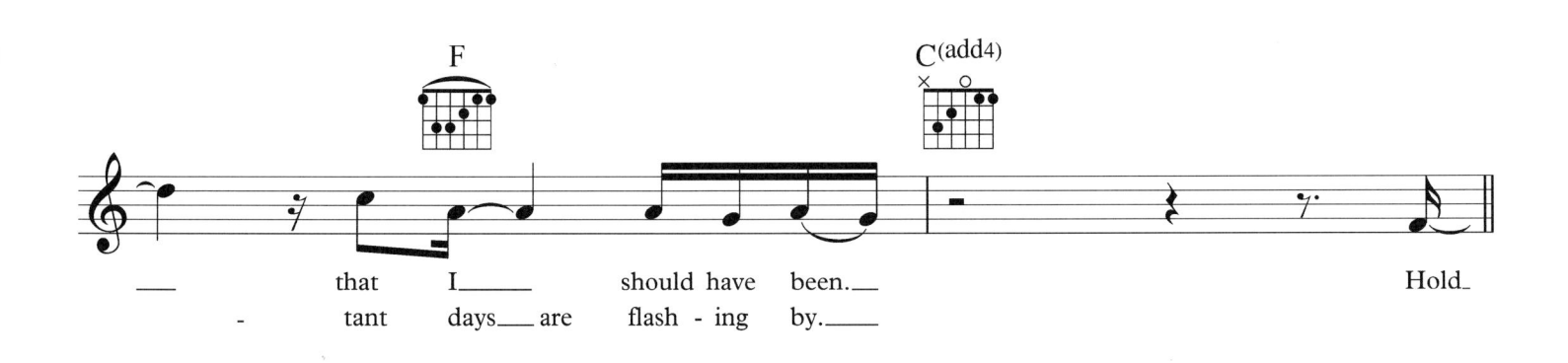

that I____ should have been.____ Hold___

-tant days___ are flash - ing by.___

Chorus

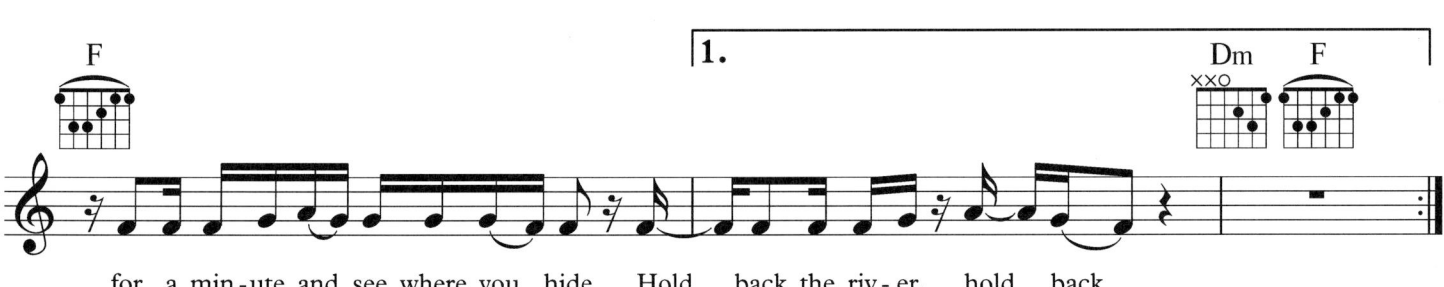

___ back the riv - er, let me look in your___ eyes. Hold____ back the riv - er so I_____ can stop

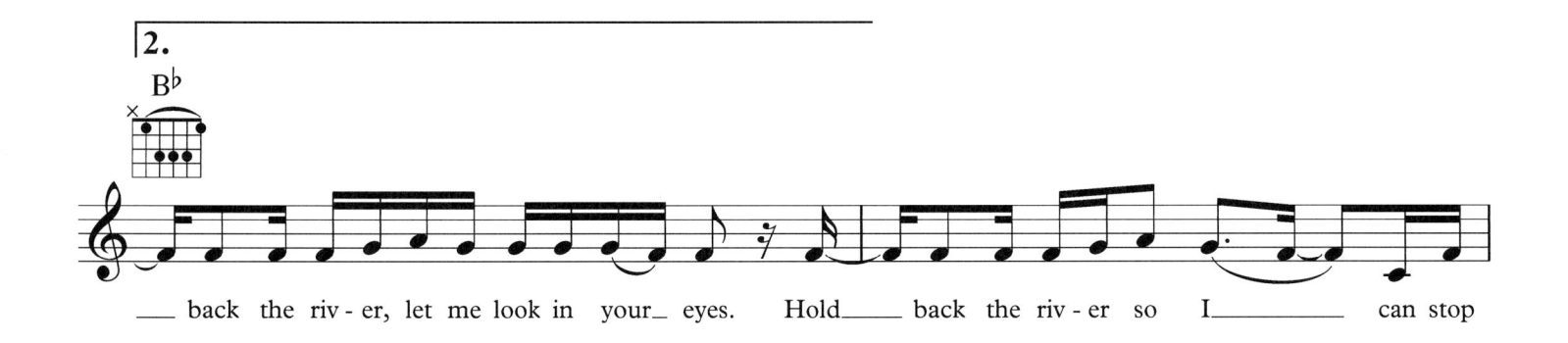

for a min - ute and___ see where you___ hide. Hold___ back the riv - er, hold___ back.___

(2°) be by your___ side.

2.

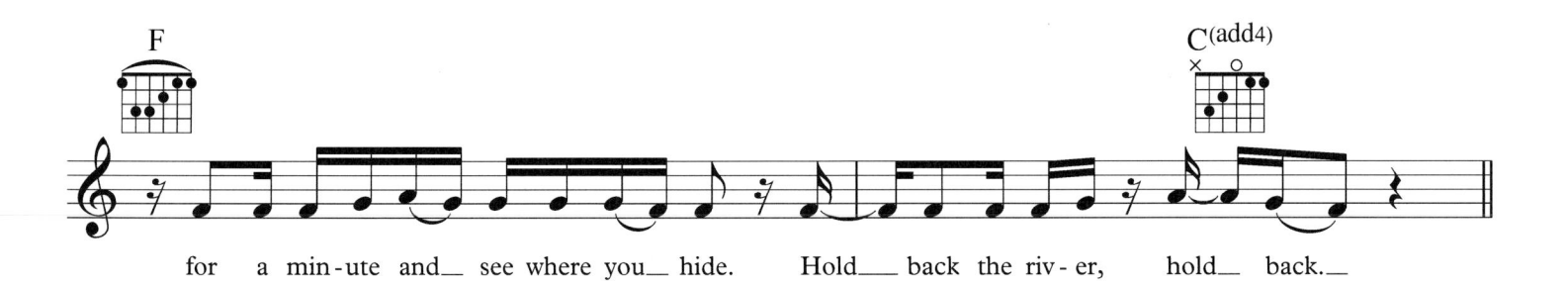

___ back the riv - er, let me look in your___ eyes. Hold____ back the riv - er so I_____ can stop

for a min - ute and___ see where you___ hide. Hold____ back the riv - er, hold___ back.___

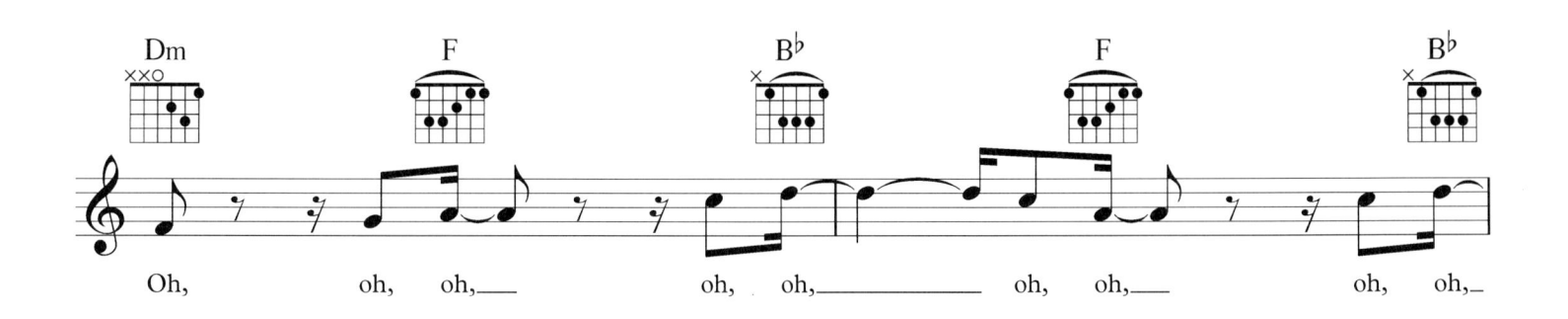

Oh,   oh,   oh,___   oh,   oh,_____   oh,   oh,___   oh,   oh,_

Bridge

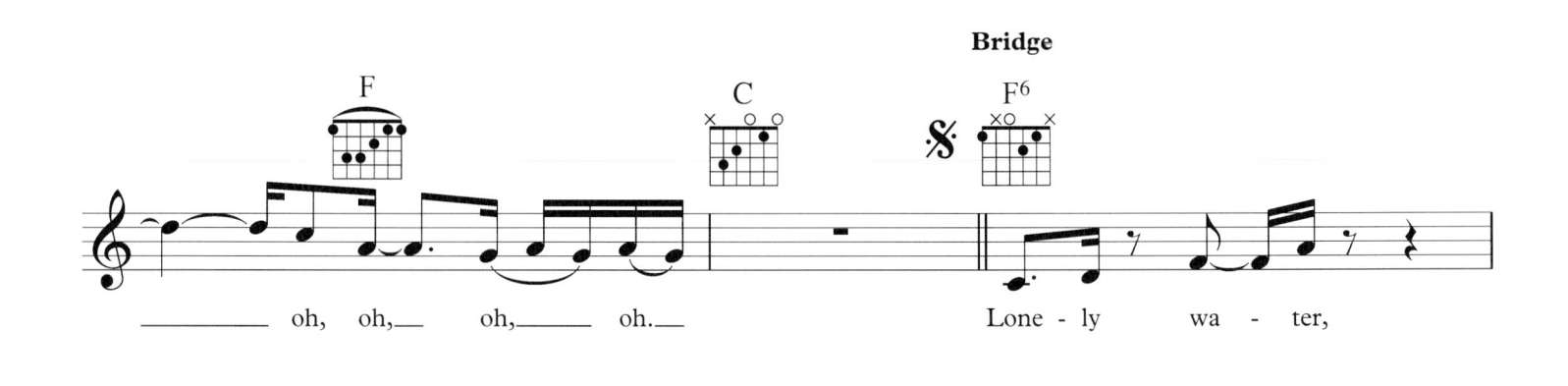

___   oh,   oh,__   oh,___   oh.__   Lone - ly   wa - ter,

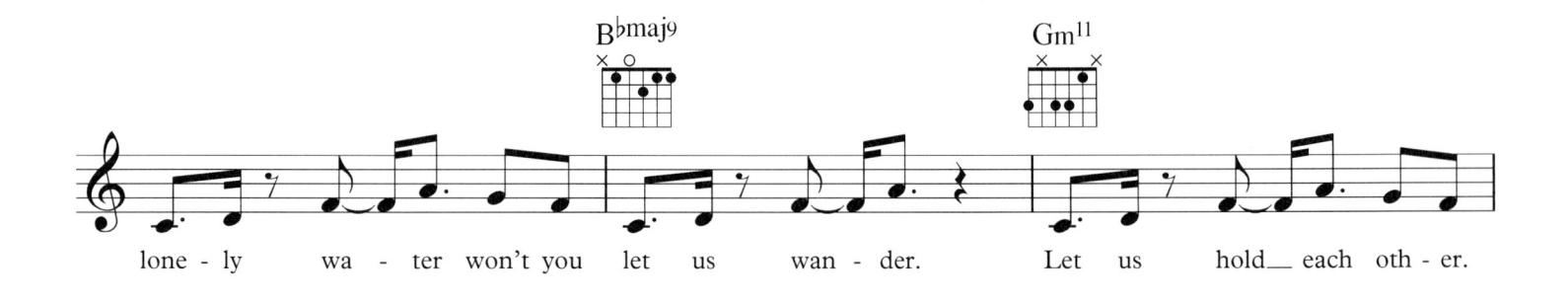

lone - ly   wa - ter won't you   let   us   wan - der.   Let   us   hold__ each oth - er.

To Coda

Lone - ly   wa - ter,   lone - ly   wa - ter won't you   let   us   wan - der.

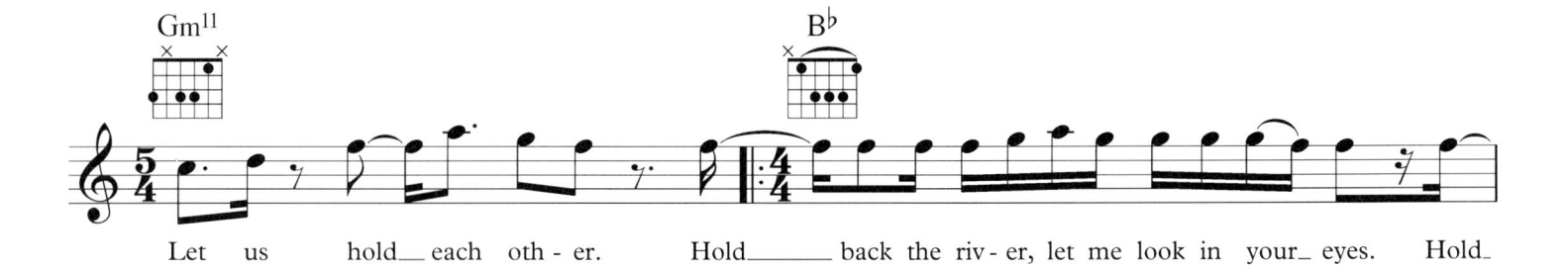

Let   us   hold__ each oth - er.   Hold_____ back the riv - er, let me look in your_ eyes.   Hold_

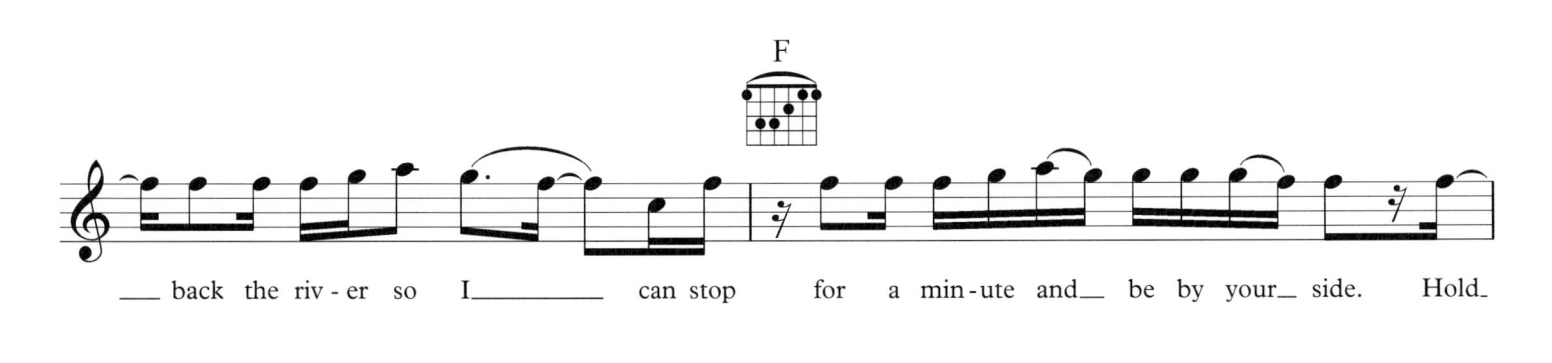

___ back the riv - er so I_____ can stop for a min - ute and__ be by your__ side. Hold_

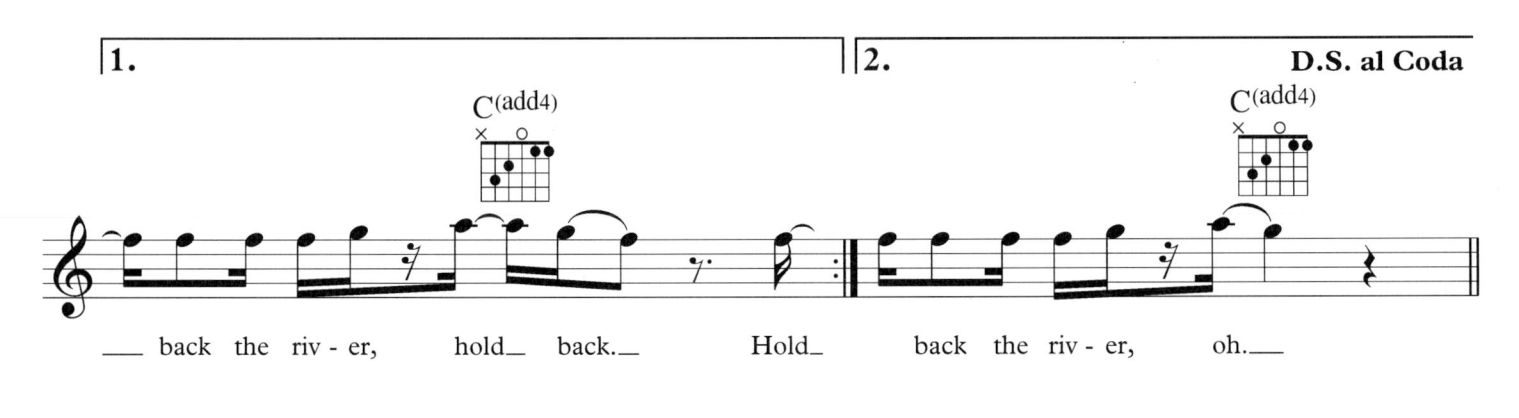

___ back the riv - er, hold__ back.__ Hold__ back the riv - er, oh.__

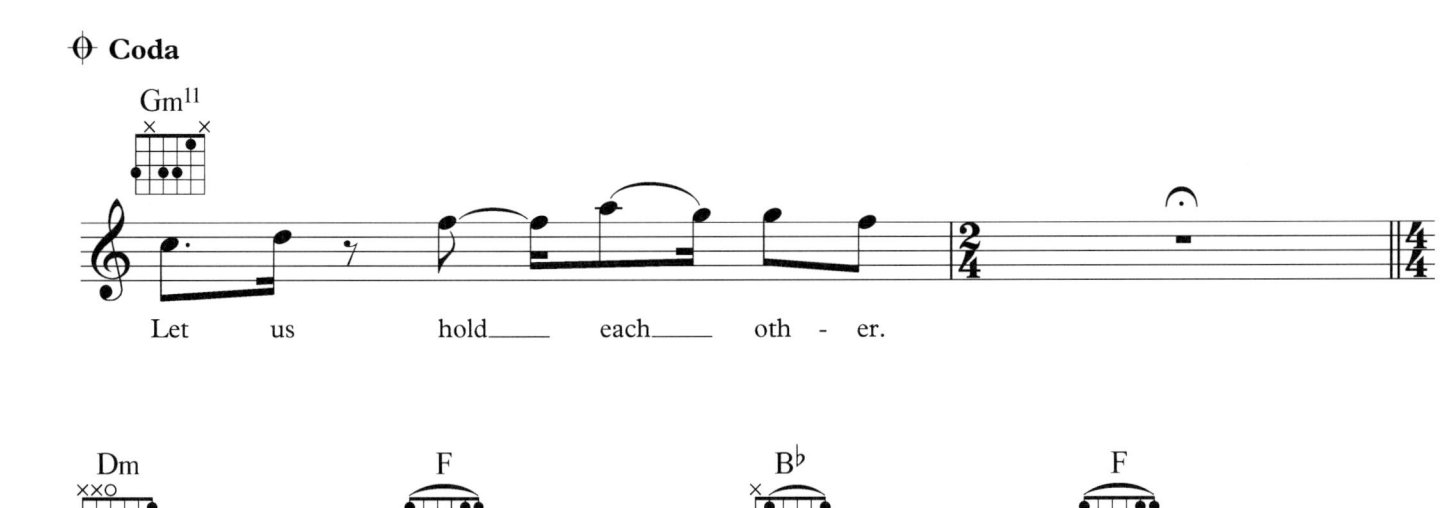

Let us hold_____ each_____ oth - er.

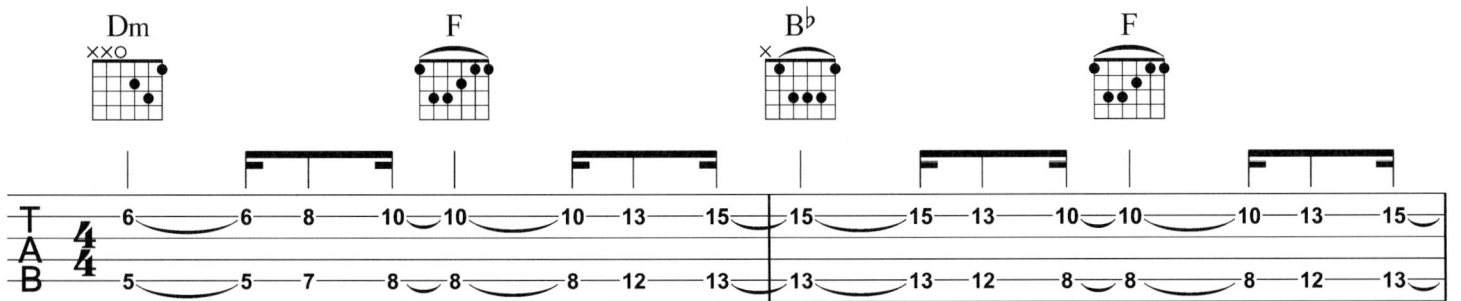

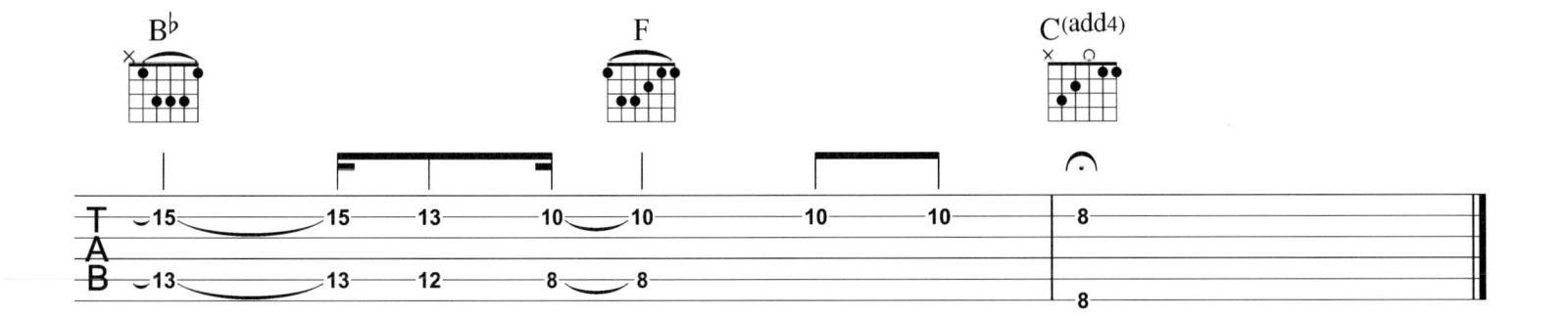

Free Fallin'

Words & Music by Tom Petty & Jeff Lynn

© Copyright 1989 Gone Gator Music, USA/EMI April Music Incorporated.
EMI Music Publishing Limited/Wixen Music UK Ltd.
All Rights Reserved. International Copyright Secured.

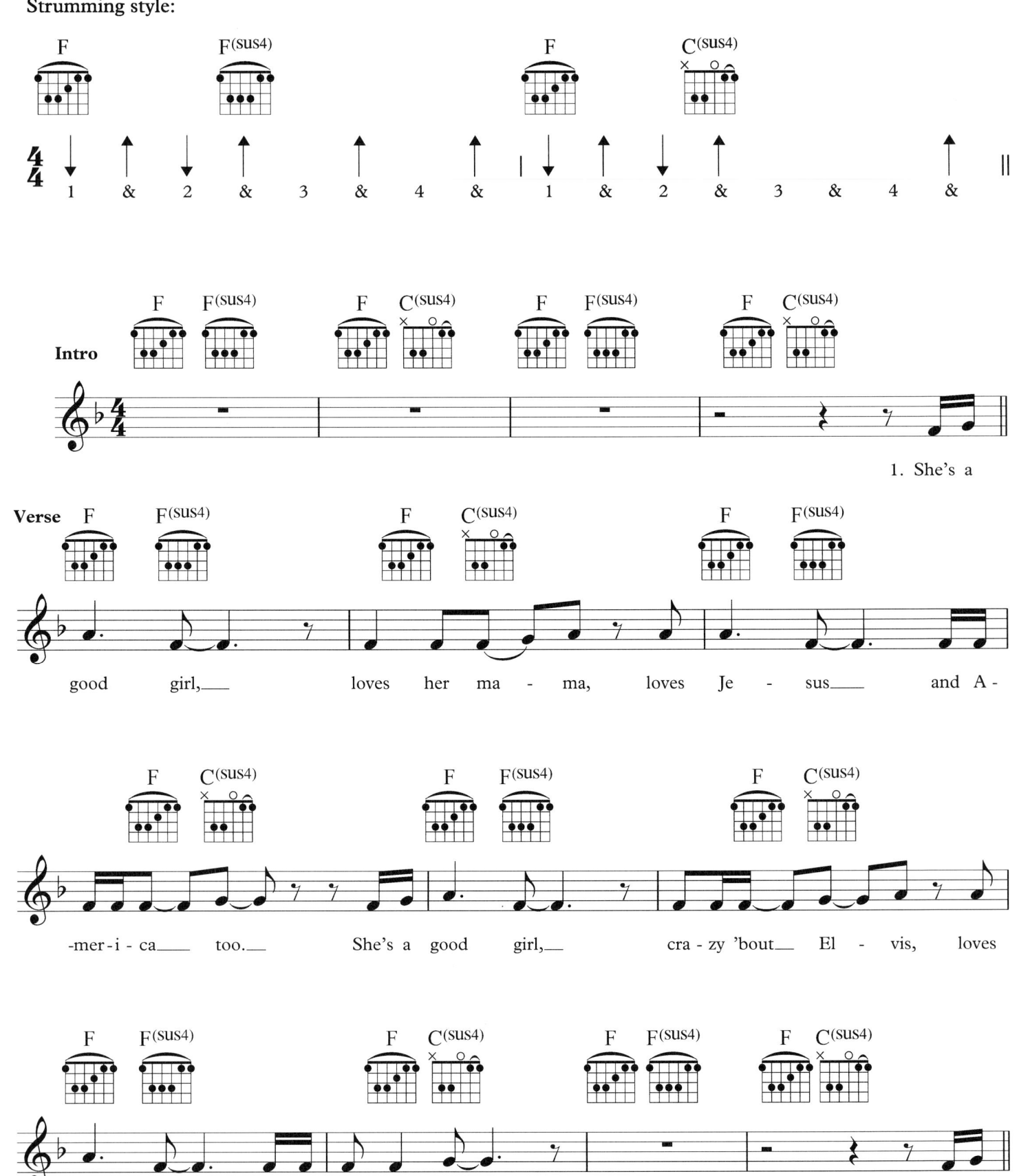

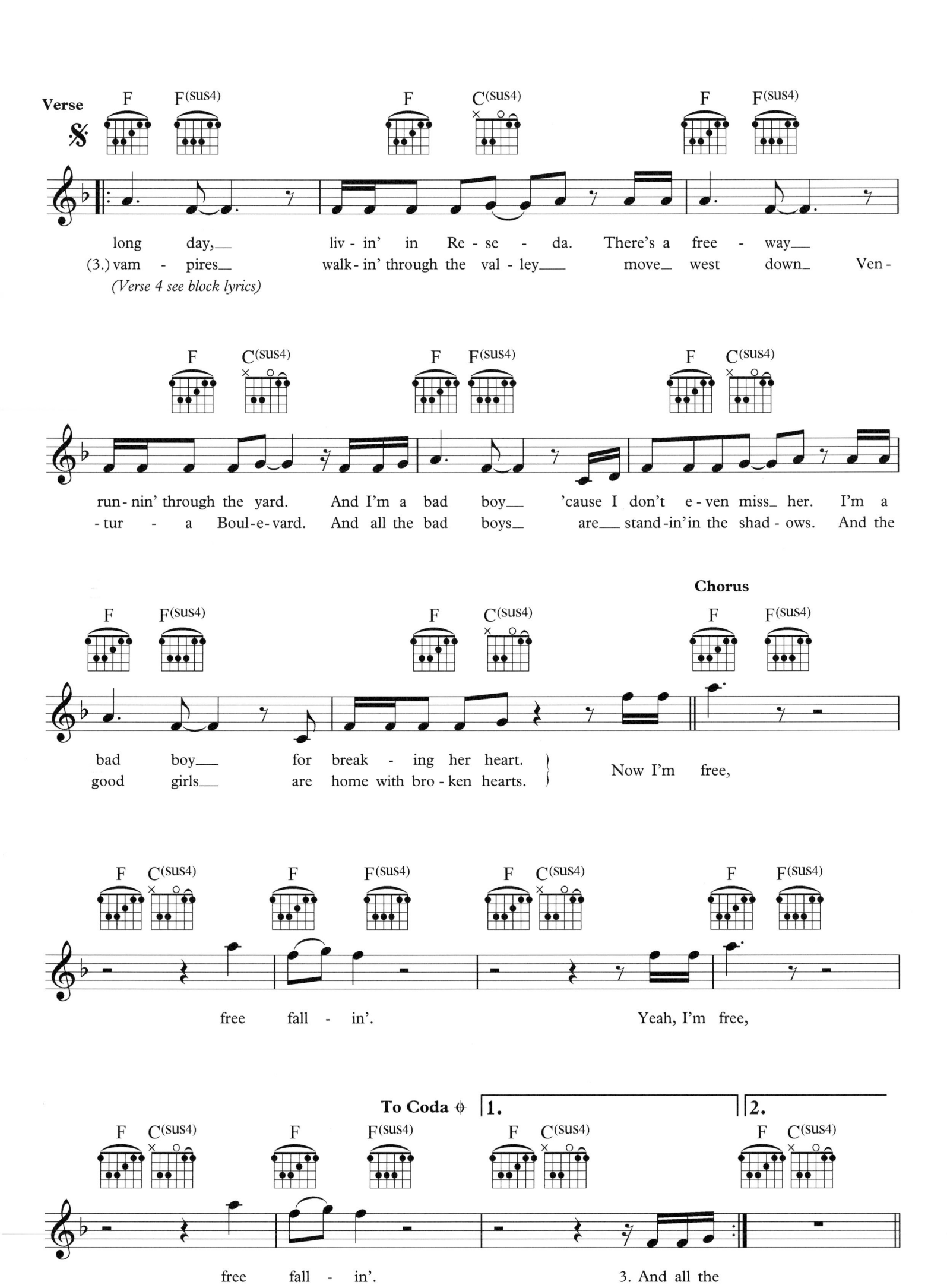

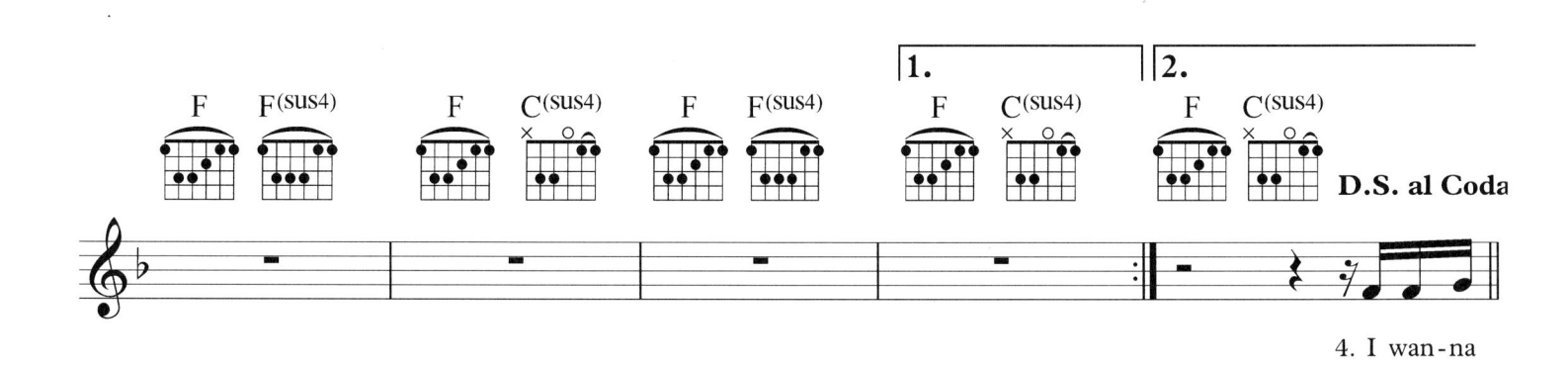

D.S. al Coda

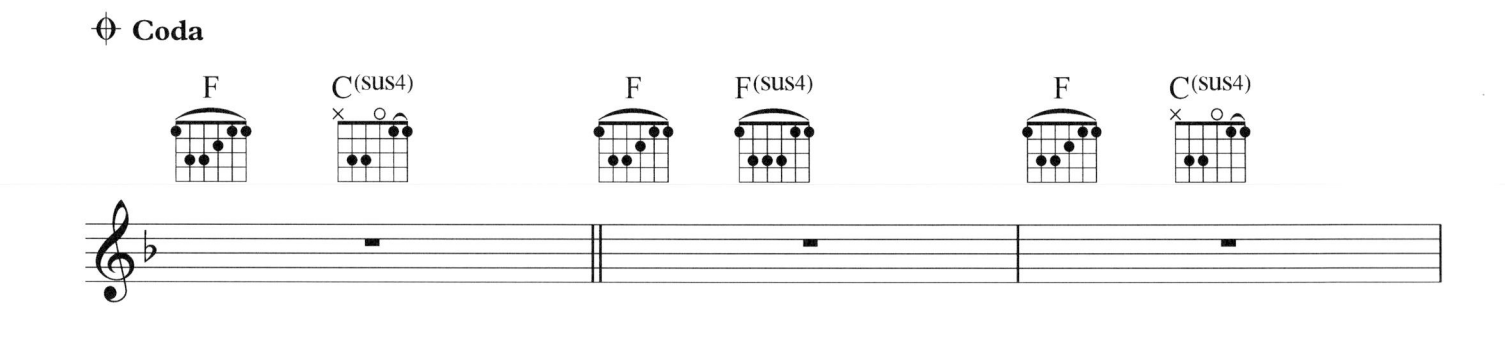

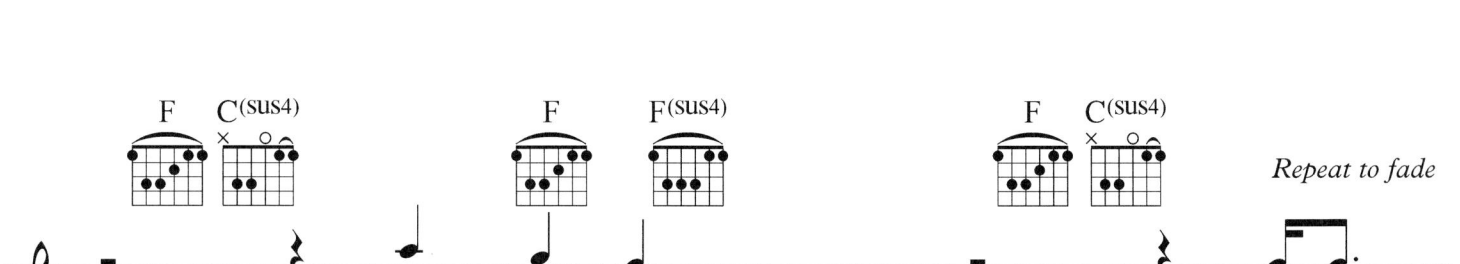

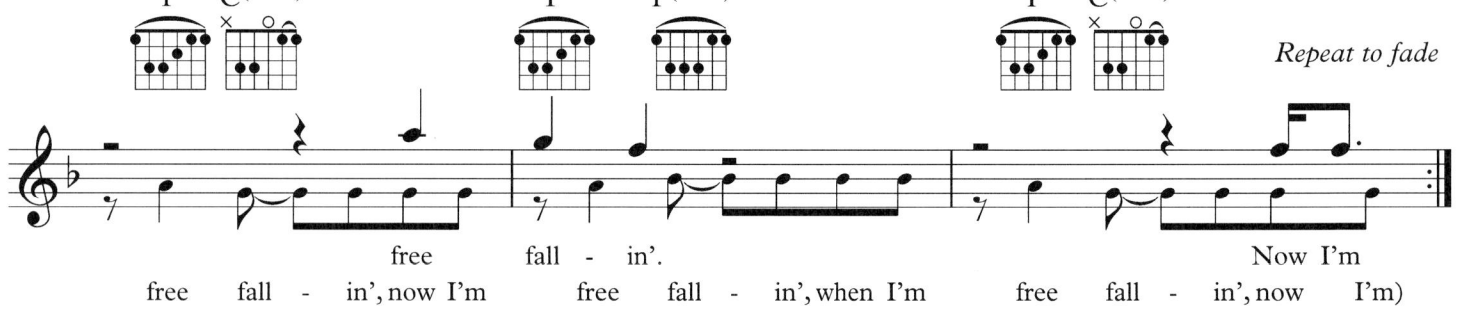

Repeat to fade

Verse 4
I wanna glide down over Mulholland,
I wanna write her name in the sky.
I'm gonna free fall out into nothing,
Gonna leave this world for a while.

The Girl From Ipanema

Words by Norman Gimbel & Vinicius De Moraes
Music by Antonio Carlos Jobim

© Copyright 1963 Songs Of Universal Inc/Fox-Gimbel Productions Inc.
Universal/MCA Music Limited/Imagem Music.
All Rights Reserved. International Copyright Secured.

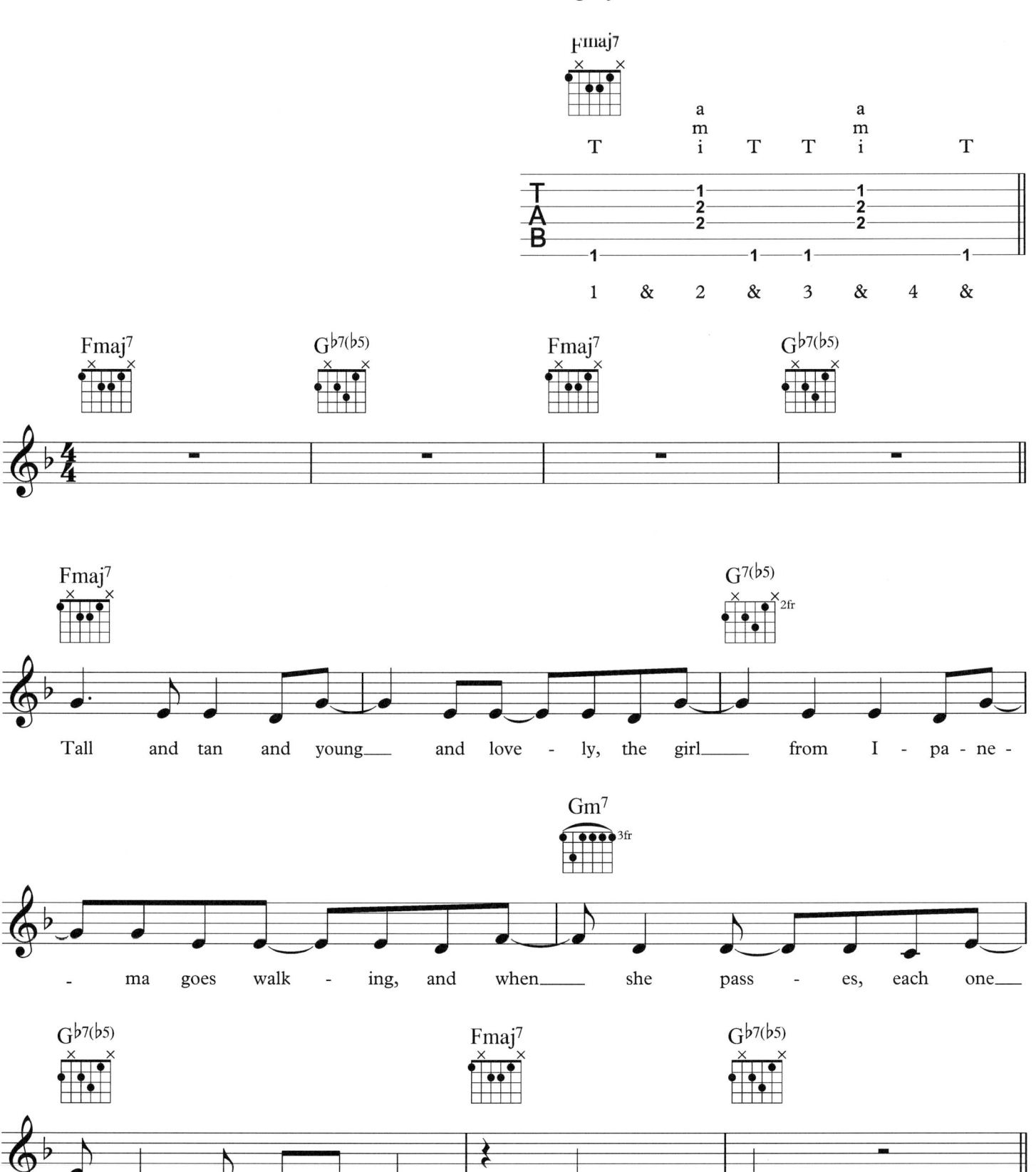

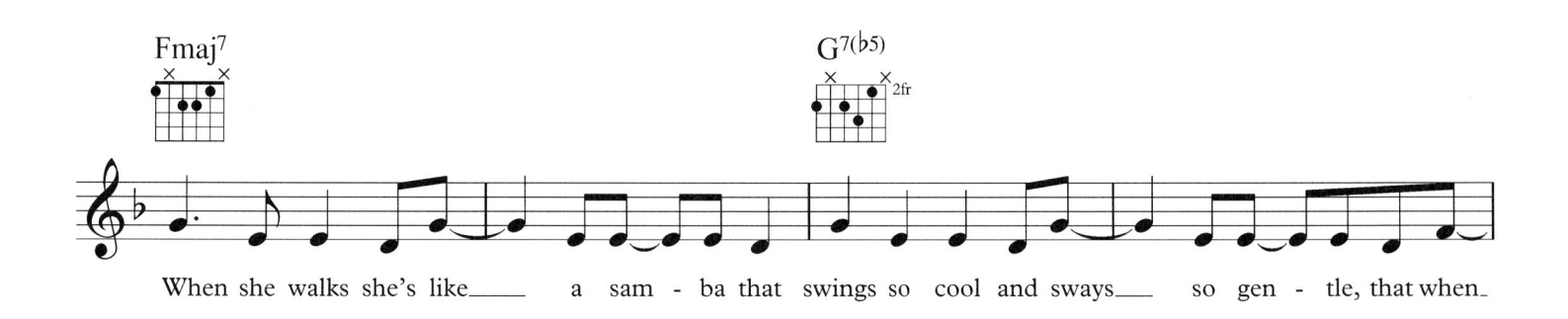

When she walks she's like____ a sam - ba that swings so cool and sways____ so gen - tle, that when____

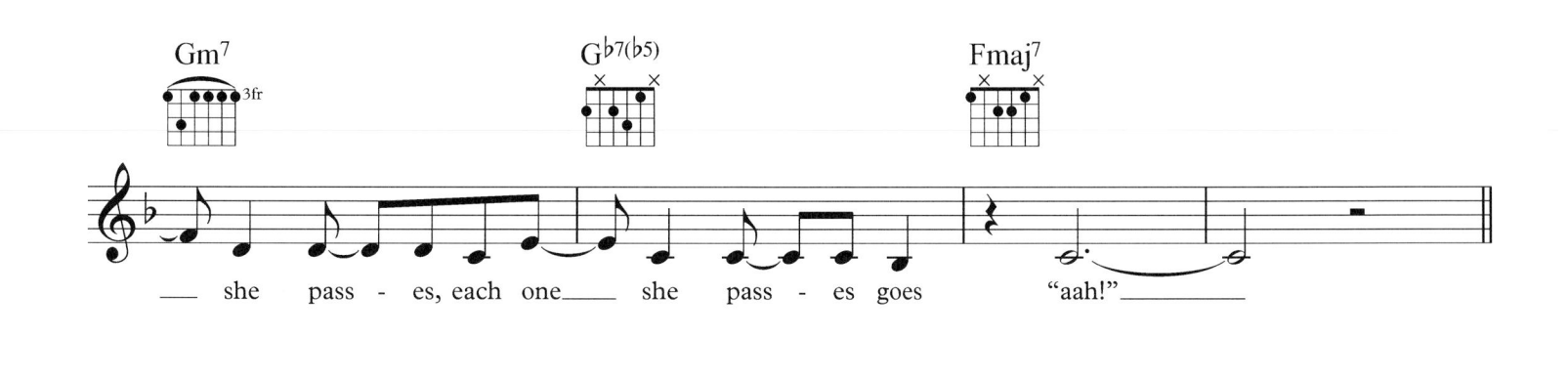

____ she pass - es, each one____ she pass - es goes "aah!"_____

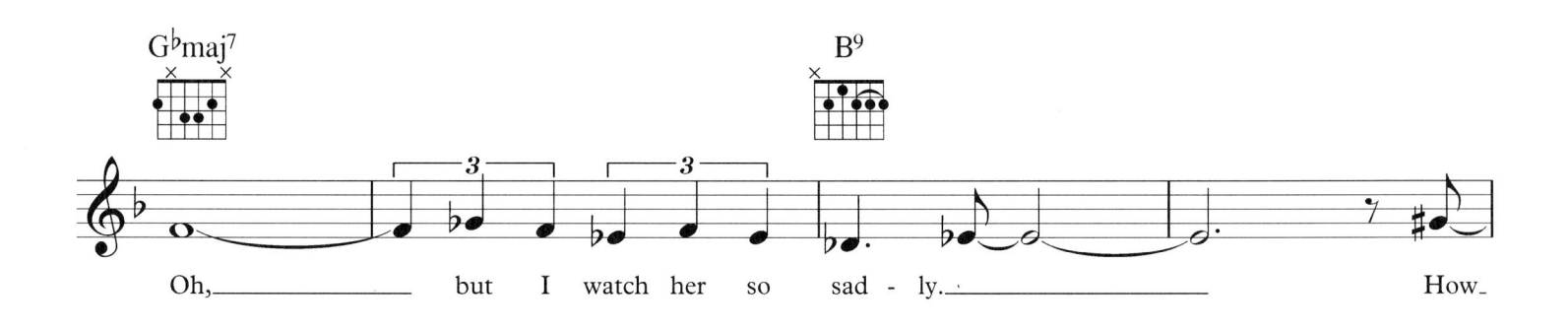

Oh,_____ but I watch her so sad - ly._____ How____

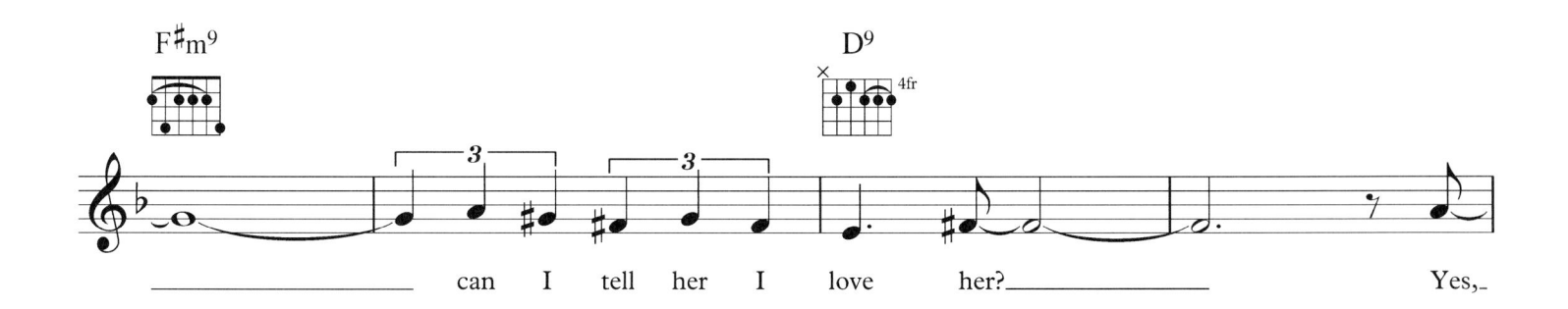

_____ can I tell her I love her?_____ Yes,____

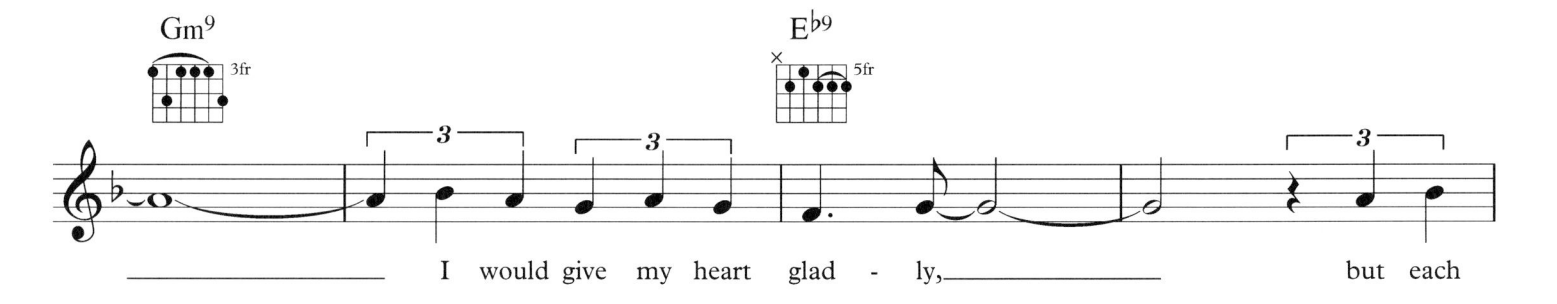

_____ I would give my heart glad - ly,_____ but each

I Am A Man Of Constant Sorrow

Words & Music by Carter Stanley

© Copyright 1953 Peer International Corporation, USA.
Peermusic (UK) Limited.
All Rights Reserved. International Copyright Secured.

The *dropped D* tuning allows the natural resonant qualities of the acoustic guitar to be heard clearly. Note the unusual shape for the G5 chord on account of the tuning.

Capo: Fret 3

6th String to D

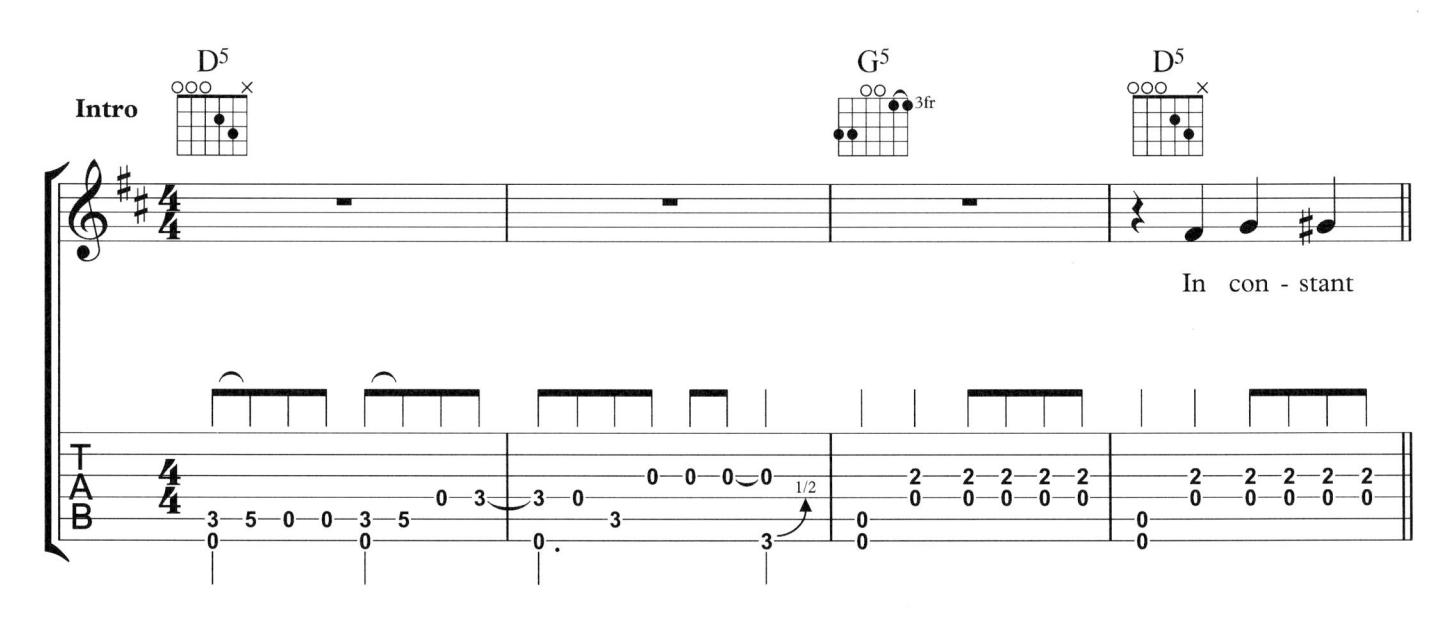

In con - stant

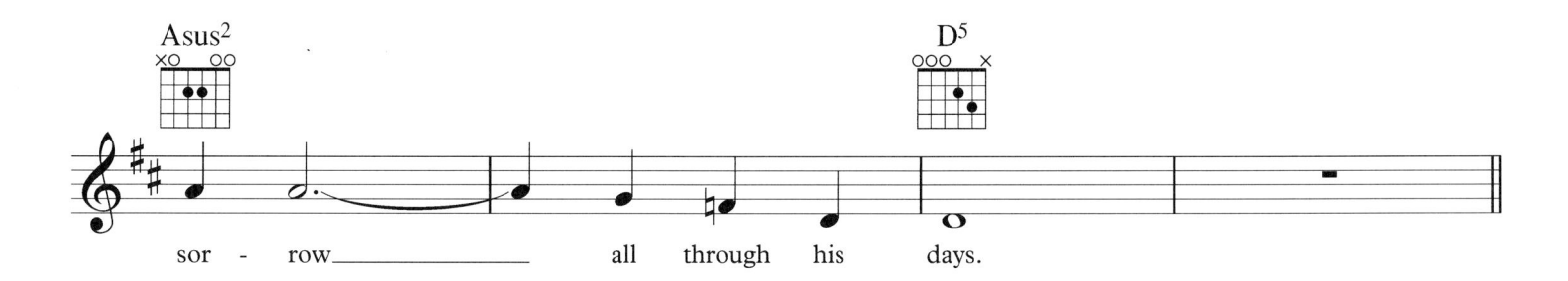

sor - row____ all through his days.

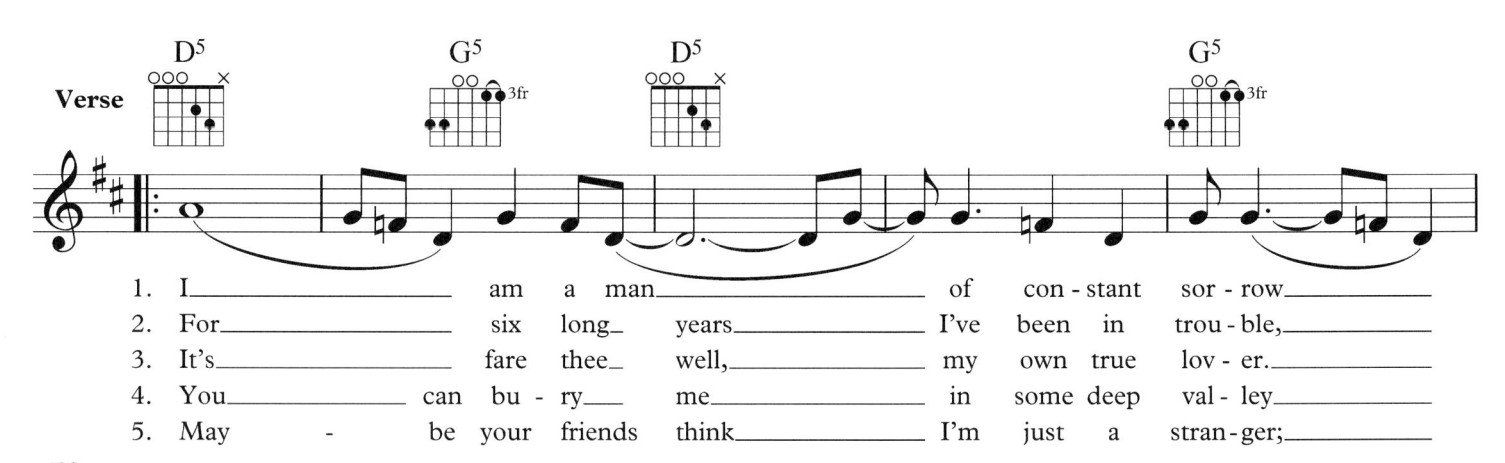

1. I____ am a man____ of con - stant sor - row____
2. For____ six long_ years____ I've been in trou - ble,____
3. It's____ fare thee well,____ my own true lov - er.
4. You____ can bu - ry____ me in some deep val - ley____
5. May - be your friends think____ I'm just a stran - ger;____

I Have A Dream

Words & Music by Benny Andersson & Björn Ulvaeus

© Copyright 1979 Universal/Union Songs Musikforlag AB.
Universal Music Publishing Limited.
All Rights Reserved. International Copyright Secured.

If you'd prefer to strum through instead of playing the original keyboard melody in the intro and interlude, strum steady, constant eighth-notes throughout.

Capo: Fret 3

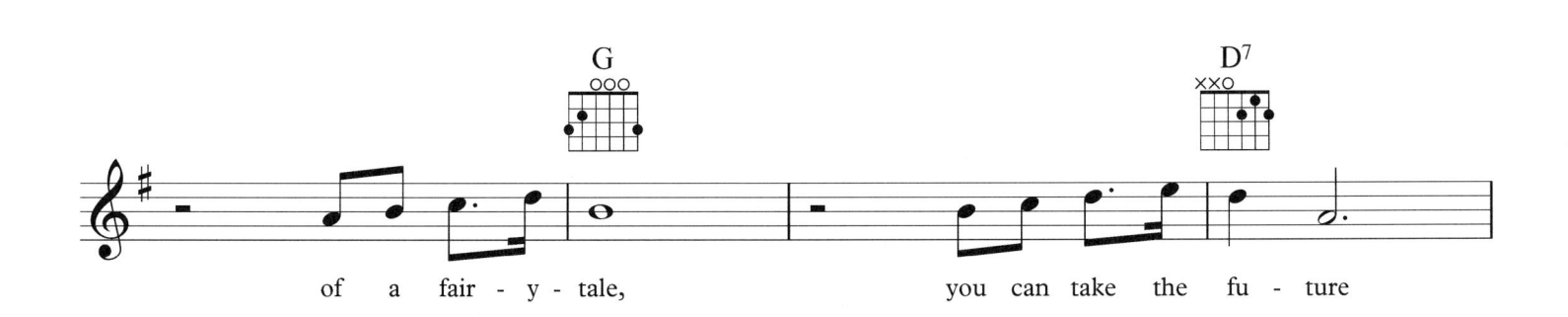

of a fair - y - tale, you can take the fu - ture

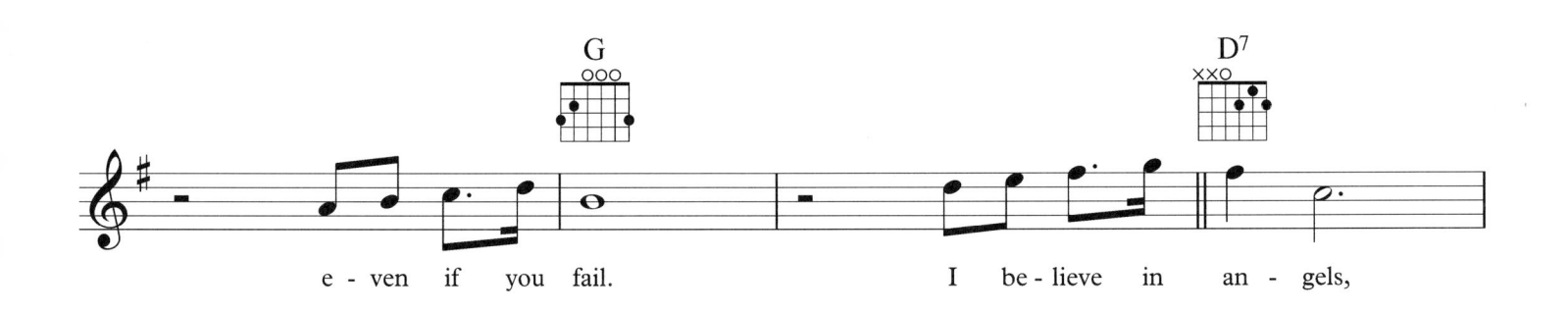

e - ven if you fail. I be - lieve in an - gels,

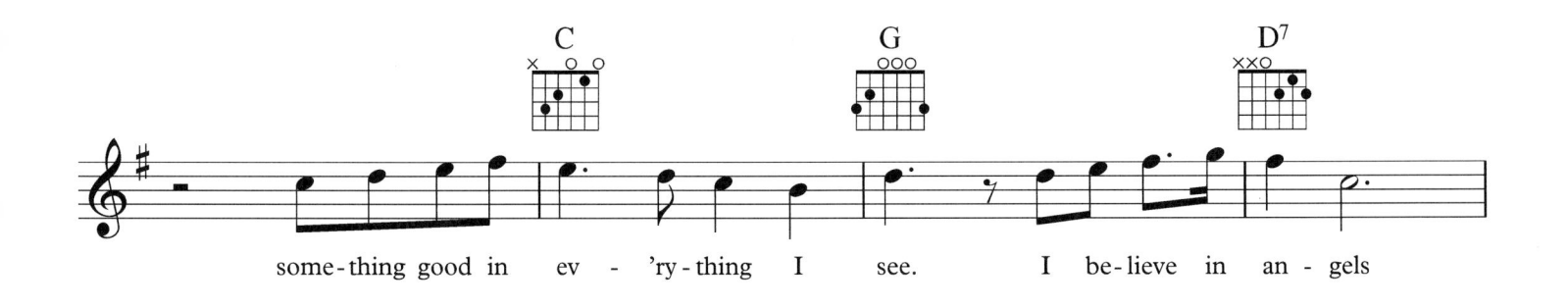

some - thing good in ev - 'ry - thing I see. I be - lieve in an - gels

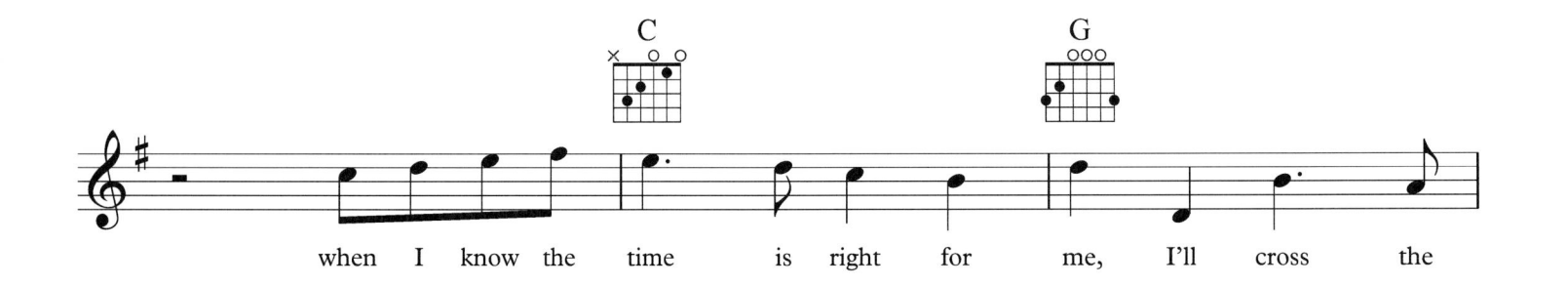

when I know the time is right for me, I'll cross the

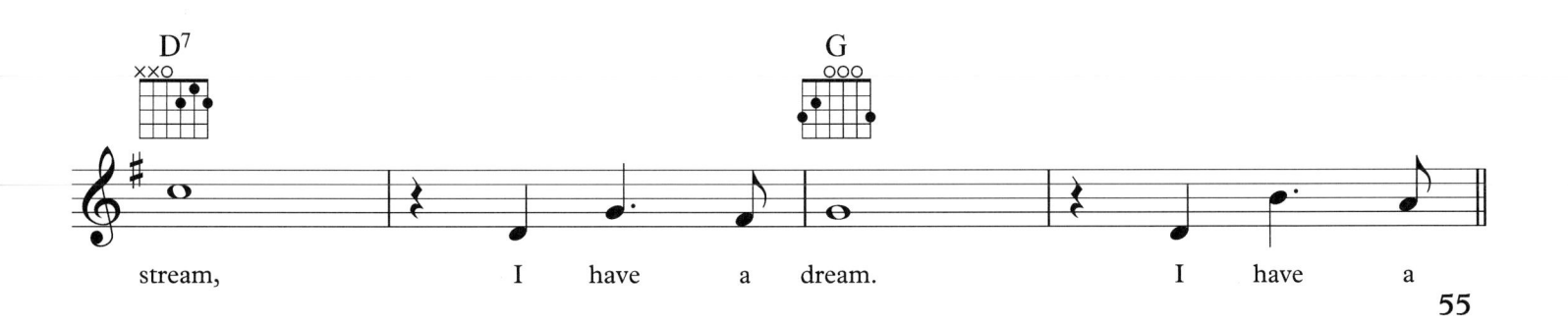

stream, I have a dream. I have a

dream,   a fan - ta - sy,   to help me
dream,   a song to sing,   to help me

through_____ re - al - i - ty.   And my des - ti -
cope_____ with an - y - thing.   If you see the

-na - tion   makes it worth the while,   push - ing through the
won - der   of a fair - y - tale,   you can take the

dark - ness   still an - oth - er mile.
fu - ture   e - ven if you fail.

I be - lieve_____ in an - gels,   some - thing good in

ev - 'ry - thing I see.   I be - lieve in an - gels   when I know the

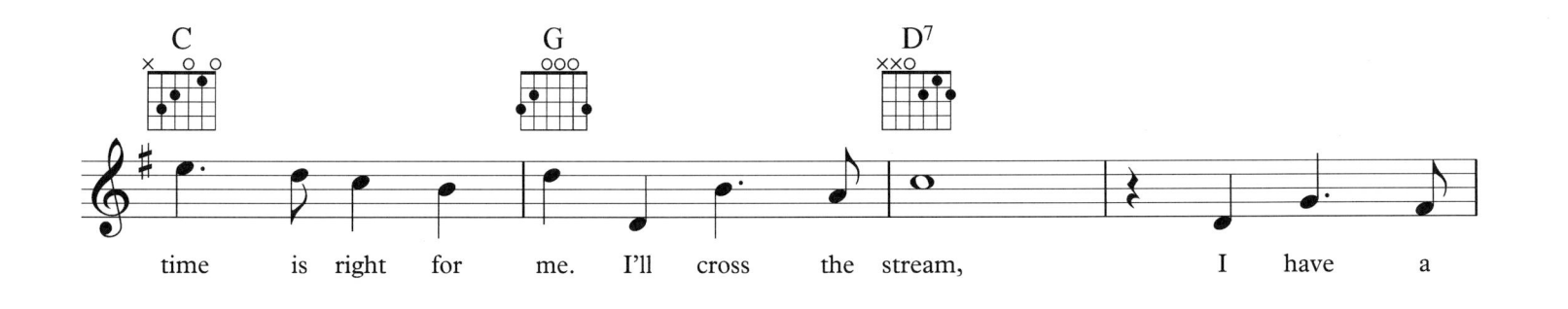

time   is   right   for   me.   I'll   cross   the   stream,   I   have   a

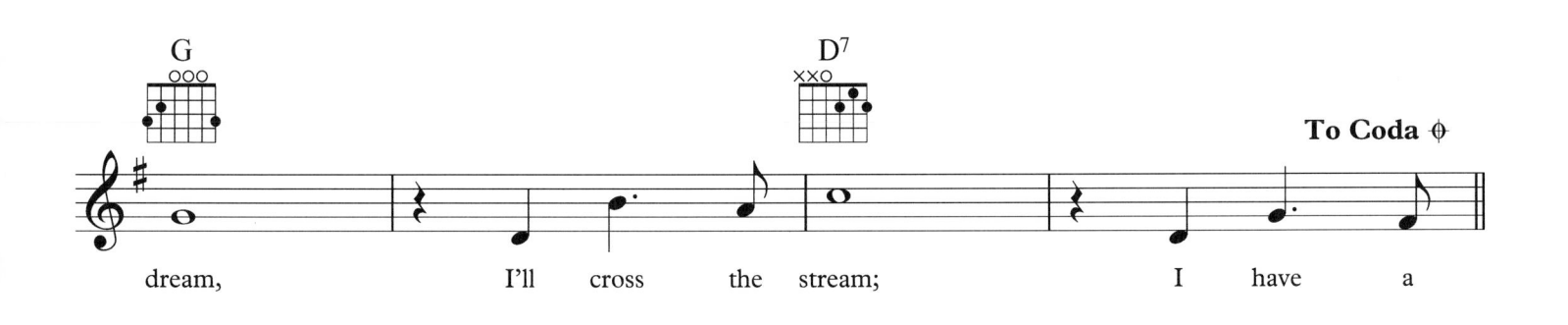

To Coda ⊕

dream,   I'll   cross   the   stream;   I   have   a

Interlude

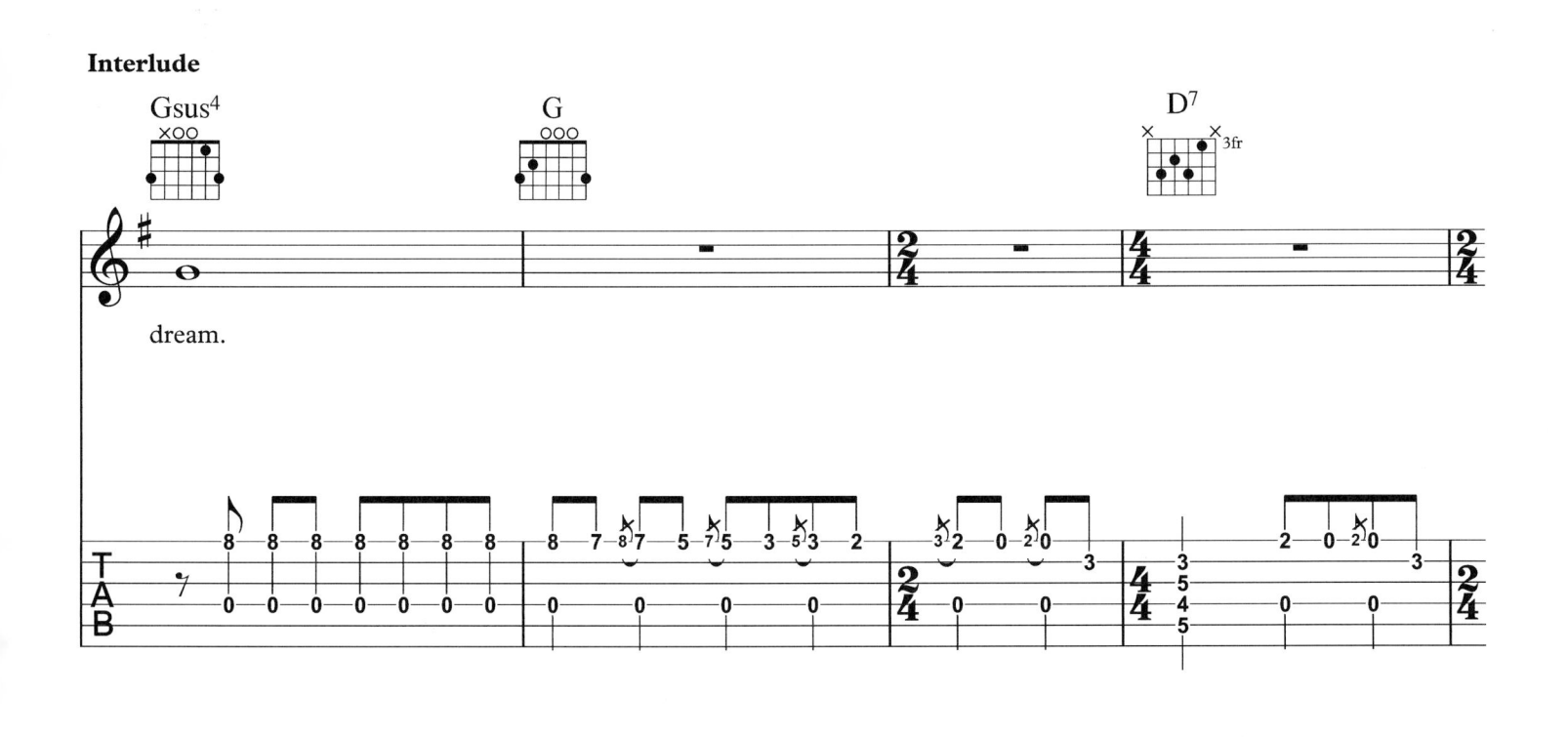

dream.

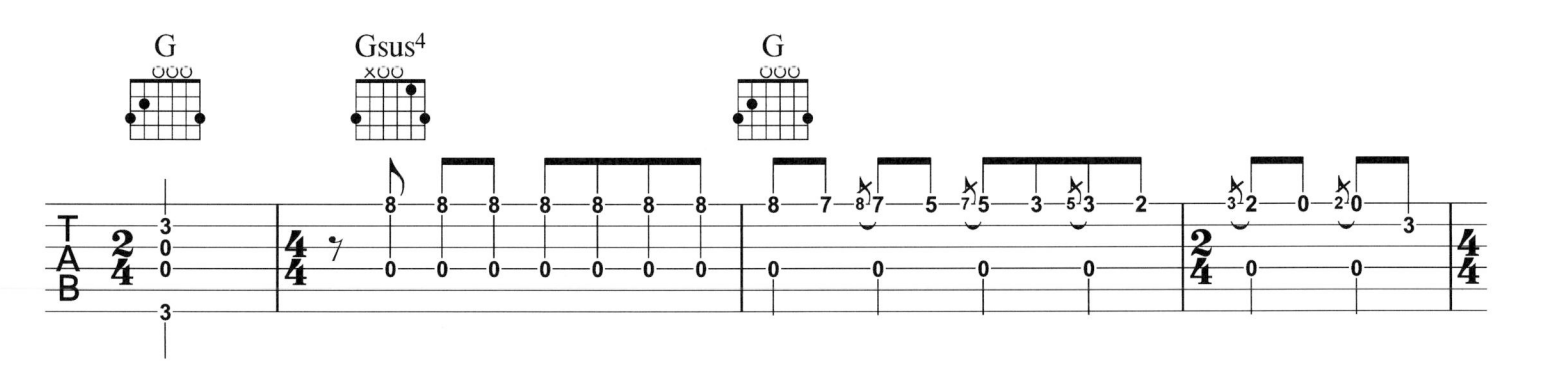

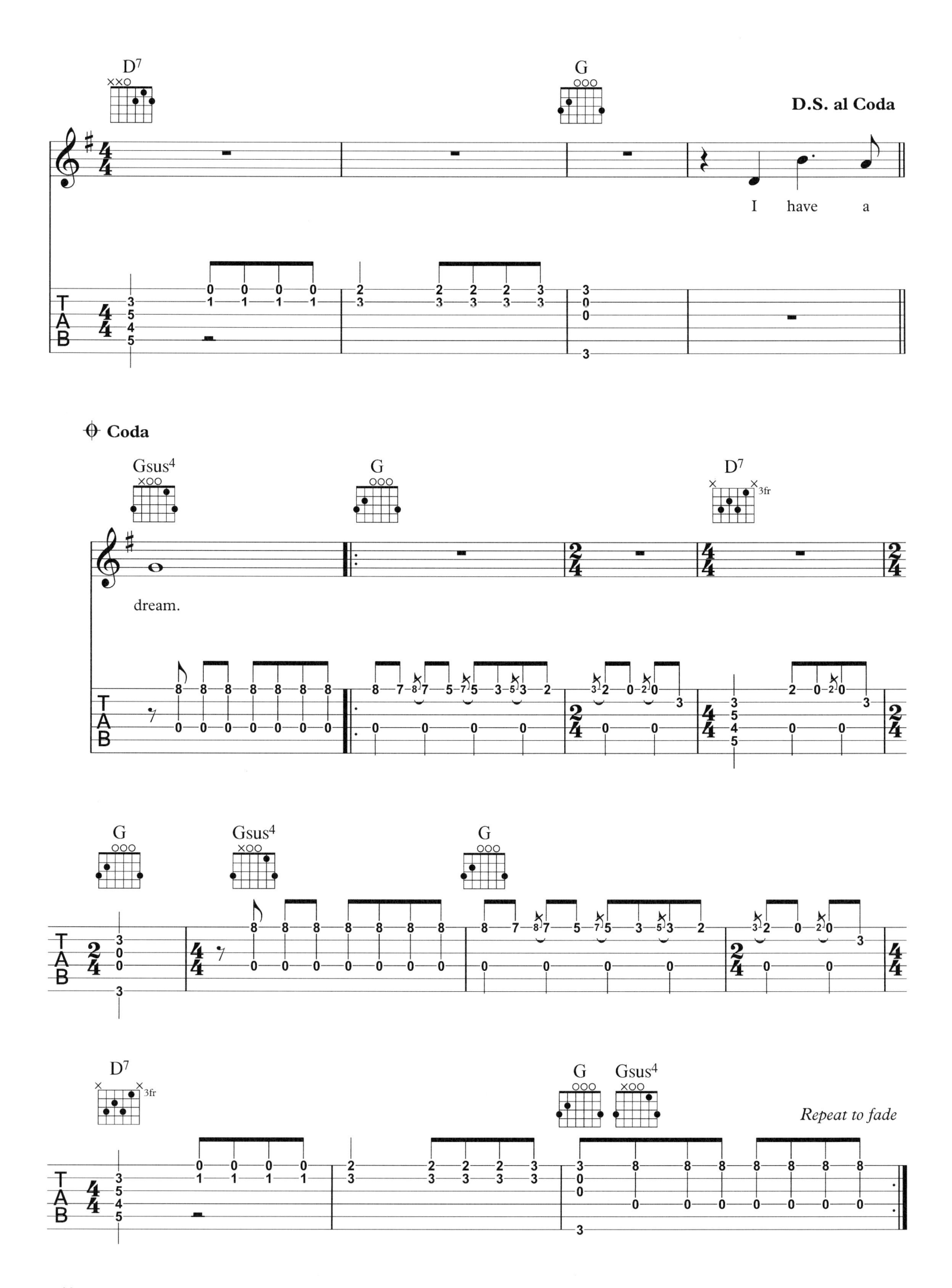

D.S. al Coda

I have a

Coda

dream.

Repeat to fade

58

I Say A Little Prayer

Words by Hal David
Music by Burt Bacharach

© Copyright 1966 New Hidden Valley Music Company
Warner/Chappell Music Publishing Limited/BMG Rights Management (US) LLC.
All Rights Reserved. International Copyright Secured.

Picking style:

This classic bossa nova style picking pattern is great for this song, but will need adapting for the three-beat bars.

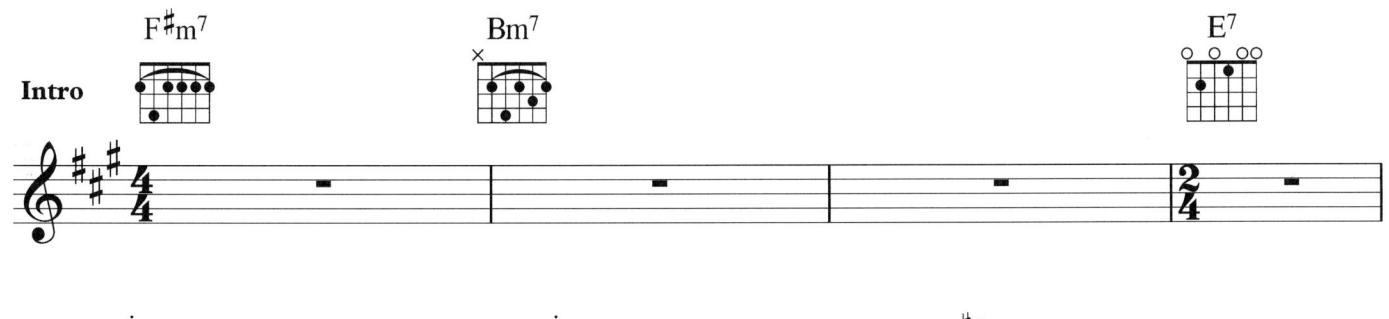

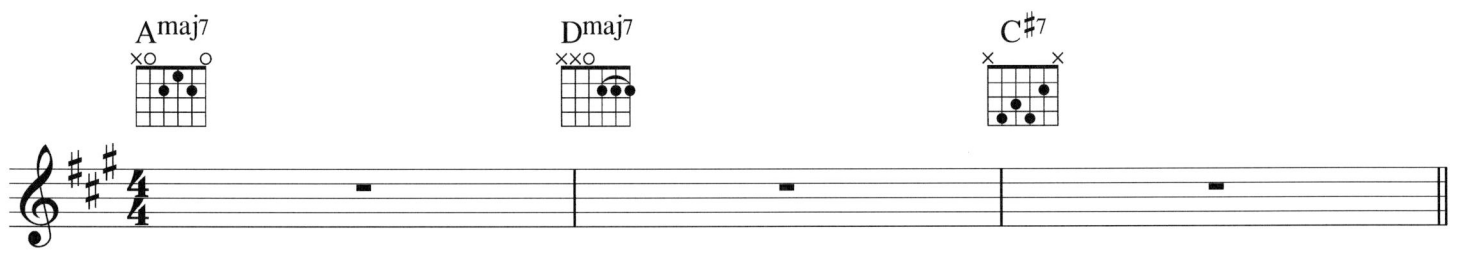

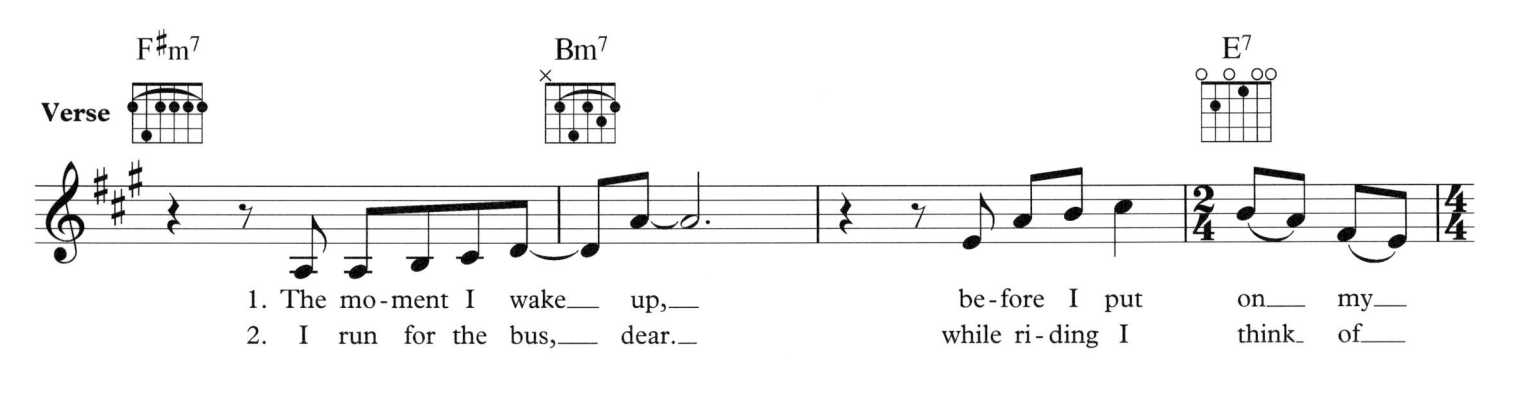

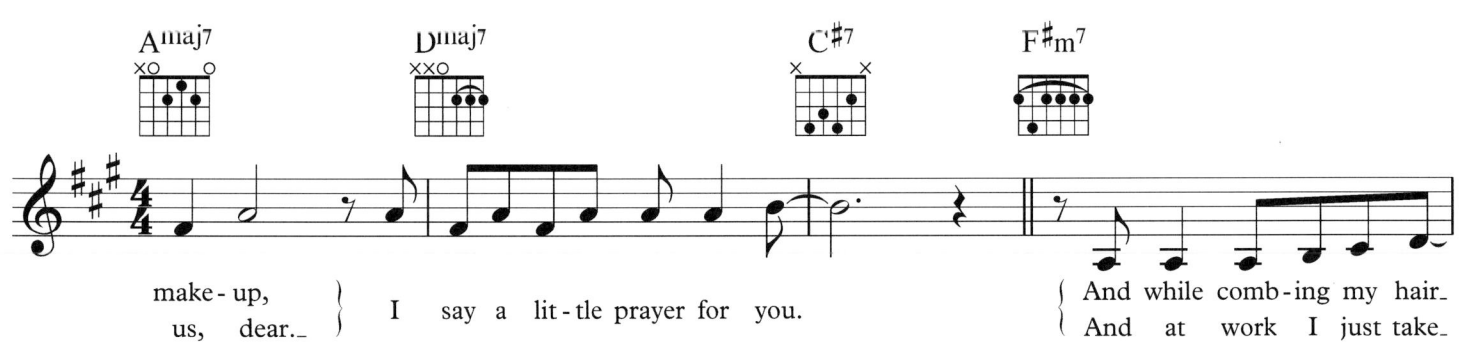

1. The mo-ment I wake__ up,__ be-fore I put on__ my__
2. I run for the bus,__ dear.__ while ri-ding I think__ of__

make-up,   }   I say a lit-tle prayer for you.
us, dear.__

{ And while comb-ing my hair__
{ And at work I just take__

now —
time, —
and won-d'ring what — dress — to —
and all through my — cof - fee —

wear, now,
break - time,
I say a lit-tle prayer for you. — For -

Chorus

-ev - er, and ev - er, you'll stay in my heart, — and I will love you, for -

-ev - er, and ev - er, we nev - er will part, — and how I'll love you, to -

- geth - er, to - ge - ther, that's how it must be — to live with - out you would

1.
on - ly mean heart-break for me. — —

2.
me. — —

It's All Over Now, Baby Blue

Words & Music by Bob Dylan

© Copyright 1965 Warner Brothers Incorporated.
© Copyright Renewed 1993 Special Rider Music.
All Rights Reserved. International Copyright Secured.

Strumming style:

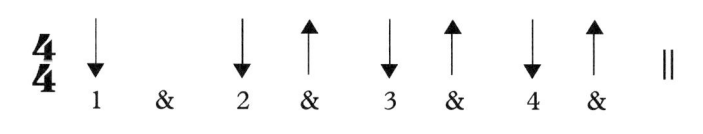

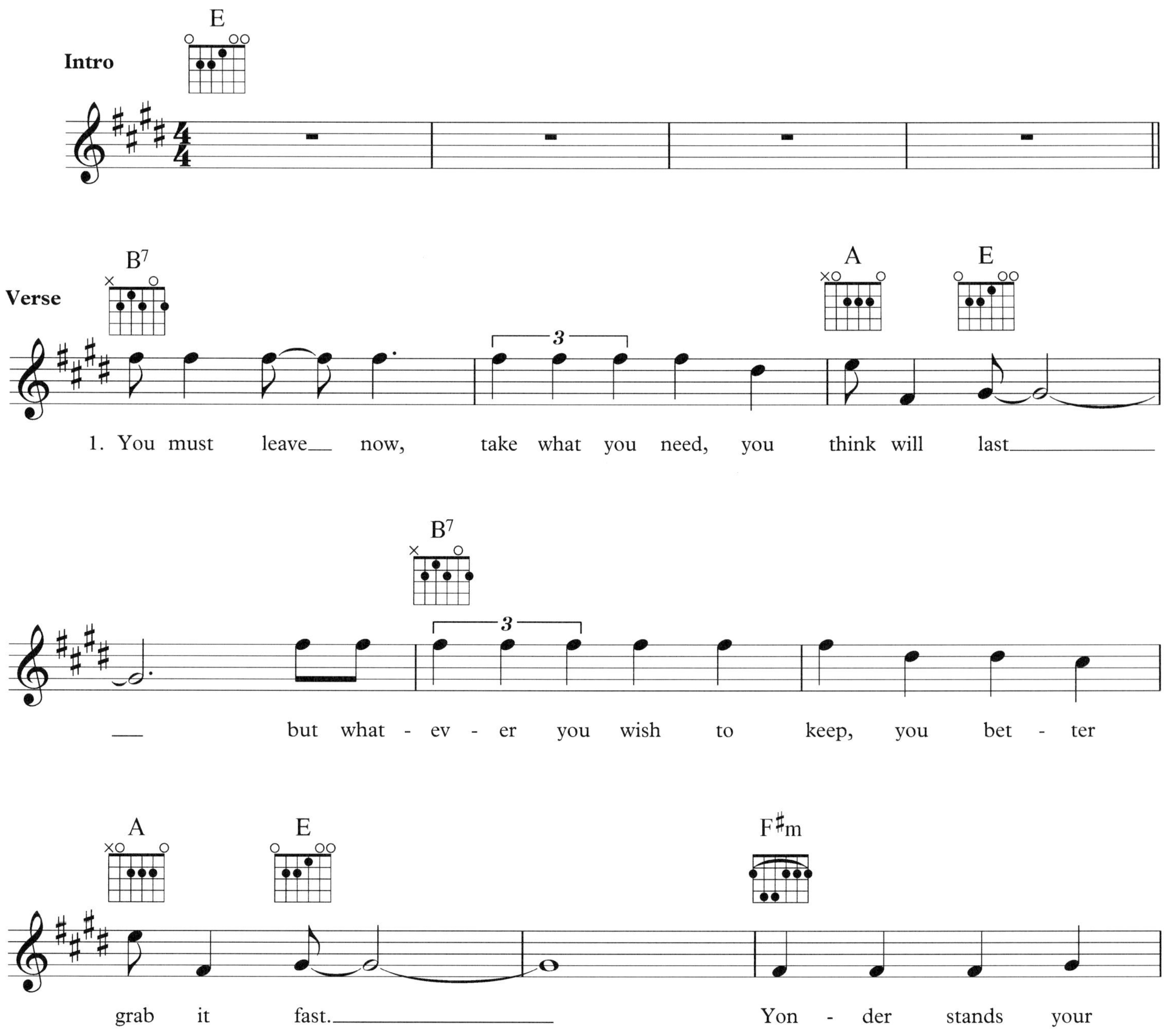

4
4
1 & 2 & 3 & 4 &

Intro
E
Verse
B7
A
E
1. You must leave__ now, take what you need, you think will last
B7
__ but what - ev - er you wish to keep, you bet - ter
A
E
F♯m
grab it fast.
Yon - der stands your

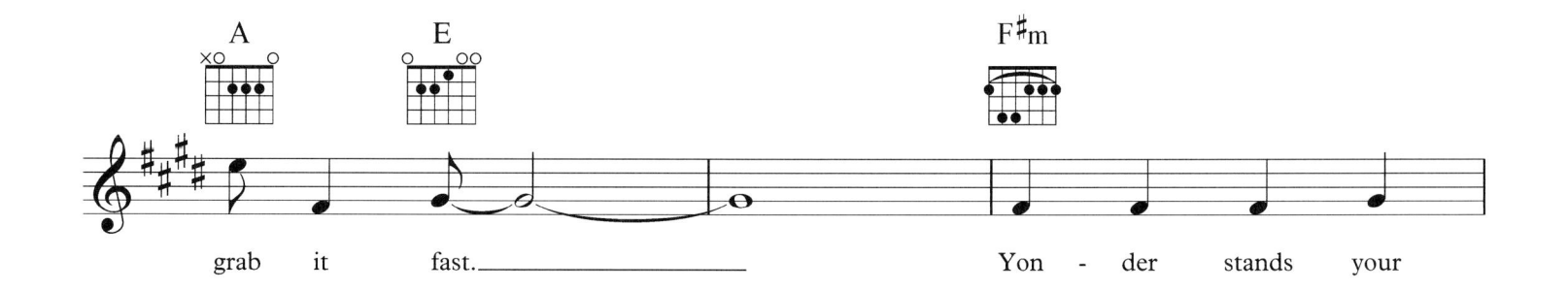

or - phan, with his gun,_____ cry - ing like a fire_____ in the sun,_____ ___ look out, the___ saints___ are com - ing___ through,_ and it's all o - ver now, Ba - by Blue.

Verse 2
The highway is for gamblers, better use your sins
Take what you have gathered from coincidence
The empty handed painter from your streets
Is drawing crazy patterns on your sheets
This sky too, is folding under you
And it's all over now, Baby Blue.

Verse 3
All your seasick sailors, they are rowing home
Your empty-handed armies, are all going home.
Your lover who just walked out the door
Has taken all his blankets from the floor
The carpet too, is moving under you
And it's all over now, Baby Blue.

Verse 4
Leave your stepping stones behind, something calls for you
Forget the dead you've left, they will not follow you
The vagabond who's rapping at your door
Is standing in the clothes that you once wore
Strike another match, go start anew
And it's all over now, Baby Blue.

I'm Yours

Words & Music by Jason Mraz

© Copyright 2006 Goo Eyed Music.
Fintage Publishing B.V.
All Rights Reserved. International Copyright Secured.

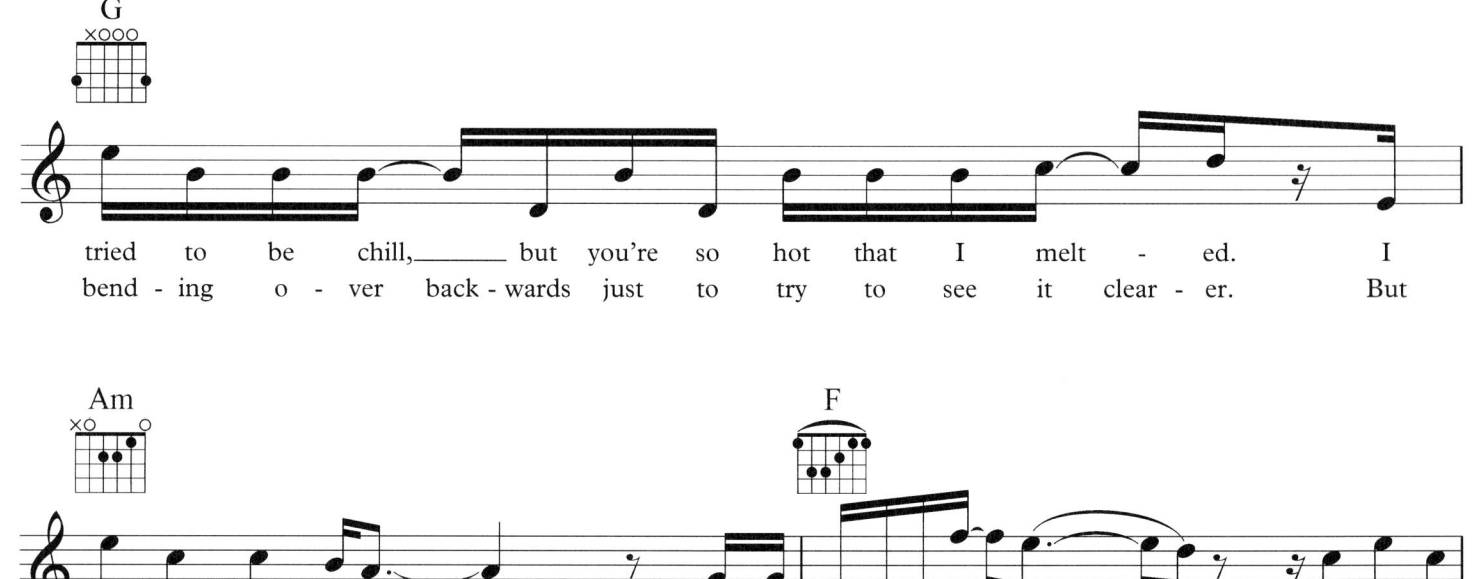

Strumming style:

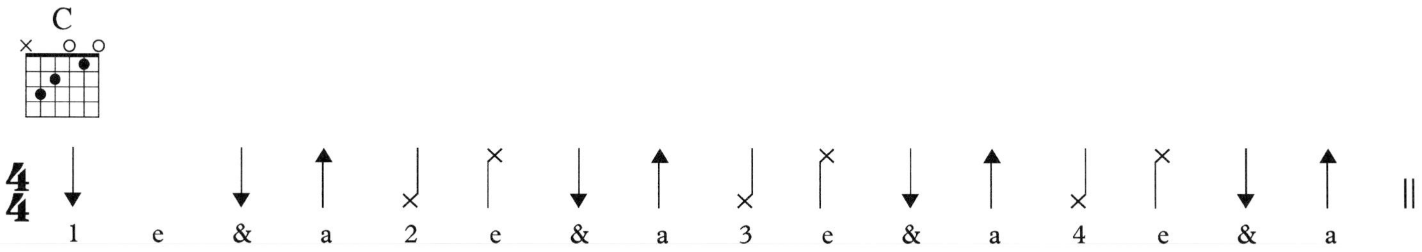
C
4/4
1 e & a 2 e & a 3 e & a 4 e & a

To match recording, tune down one semitone

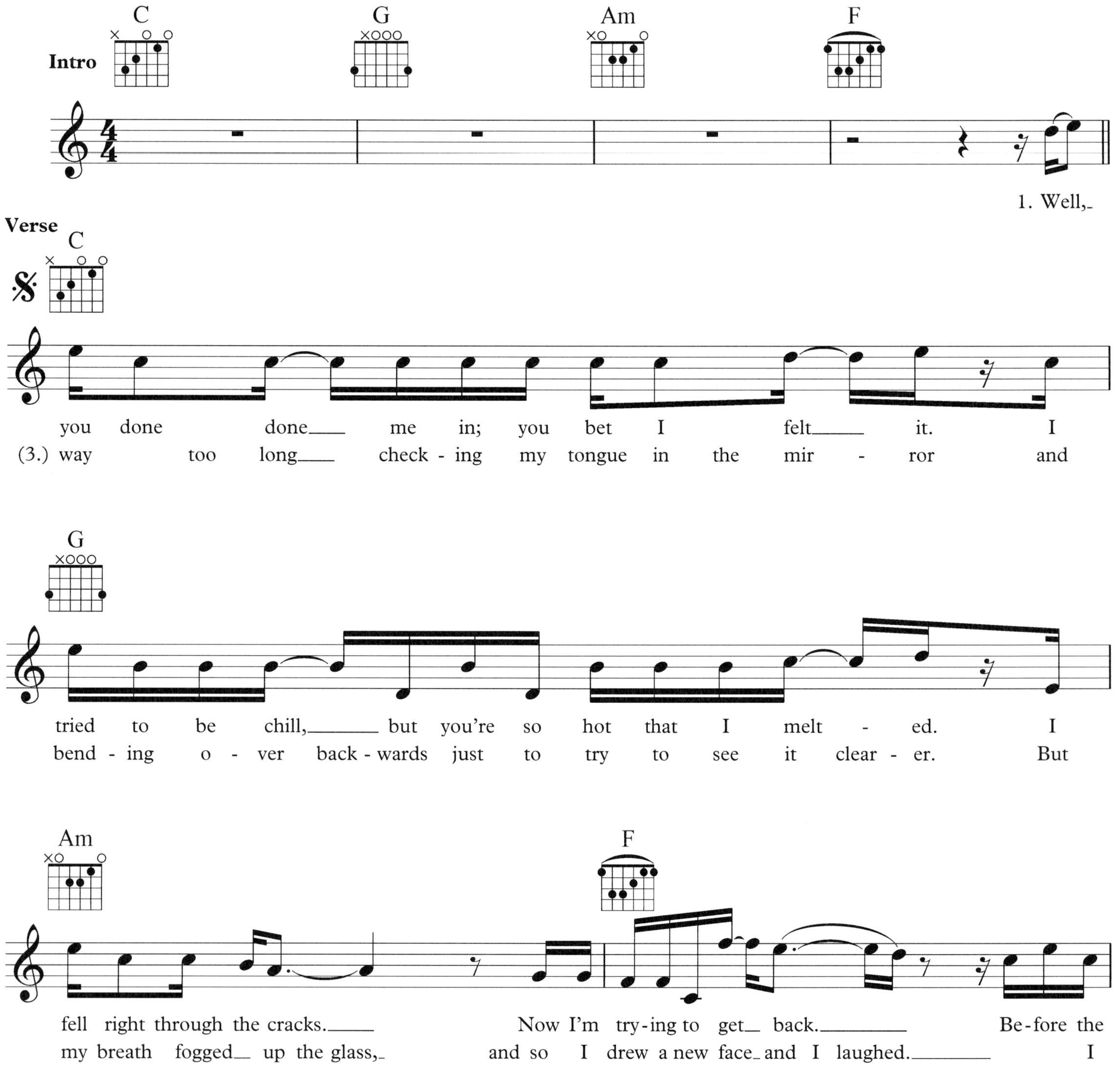
C
G
Am
F
Intro
1. Well,
Verse
C
you done done me in; you bet I felt it. I
(3.) way too long check - ing my tongue in the mir - ror and
G
tried to be chill, but you're so hot that I melt - ed. I
bend - ing o - ver back - wards just to try to see it clear - er. But
Am
F
fell right through the cracks. Now I'm try-ing to get back. Be-fore the
my breath fogged up the glass, and so I drew a new face and I laughed. I

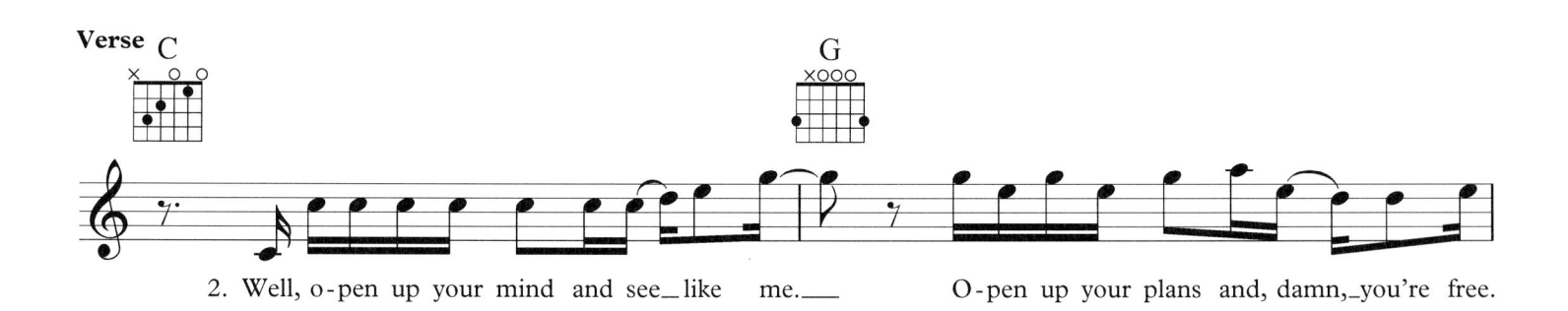

Verse

2. Well, o-pen up your mind and see_like me._ O-pen up your plans and, damn,_you're free.

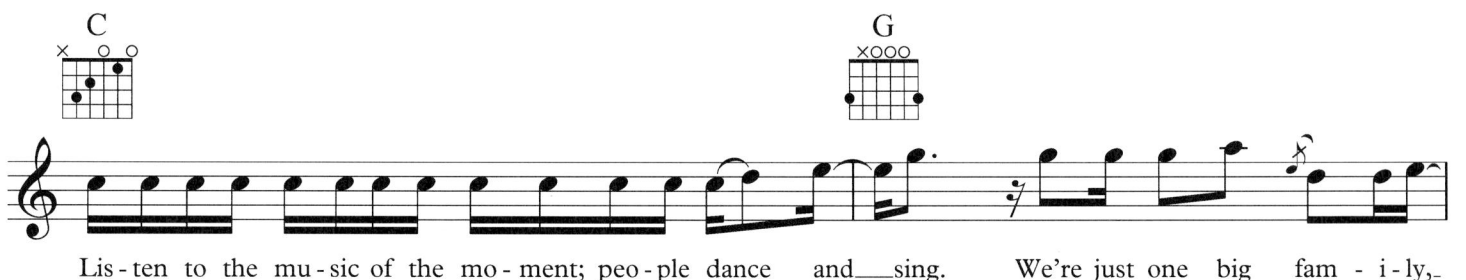

Look in-to your heart_ and you'll_ find love, love,_____love, love.

Lis-ten to the mu-sic of the mo-ment; peo-ple dance and_sing. We're just one big fam-i-ly,_

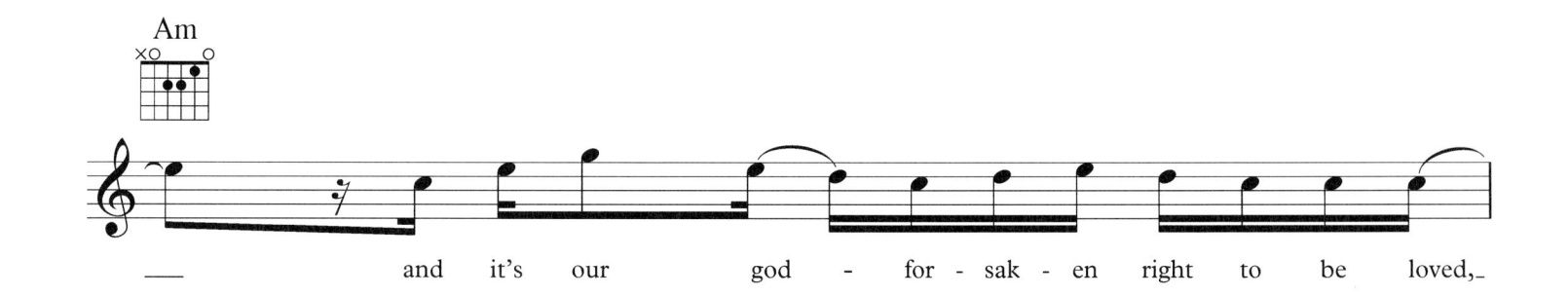

_ and it's our god - for - sak - en right to be loved,_

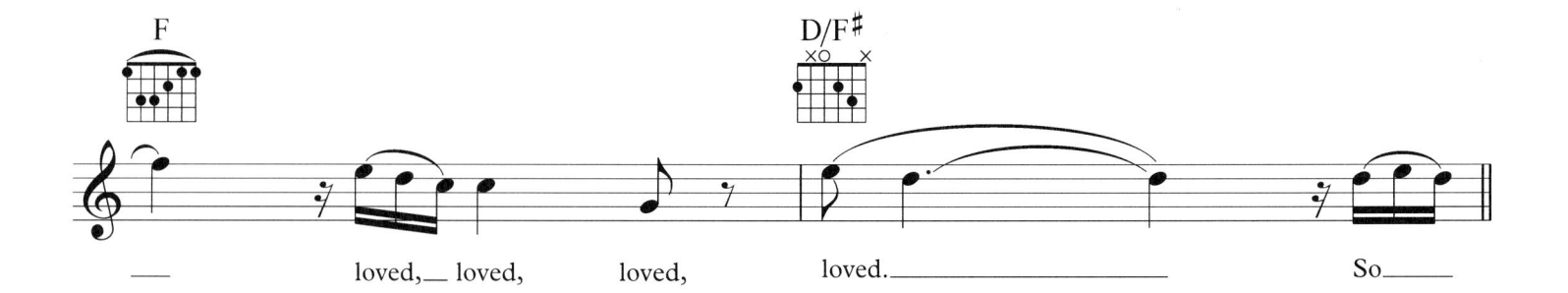

_ loved,_ loved, loved, loved._____ So_

Chorus

I____ won't hes - i - tate no more,_ no_____ more. It can - not

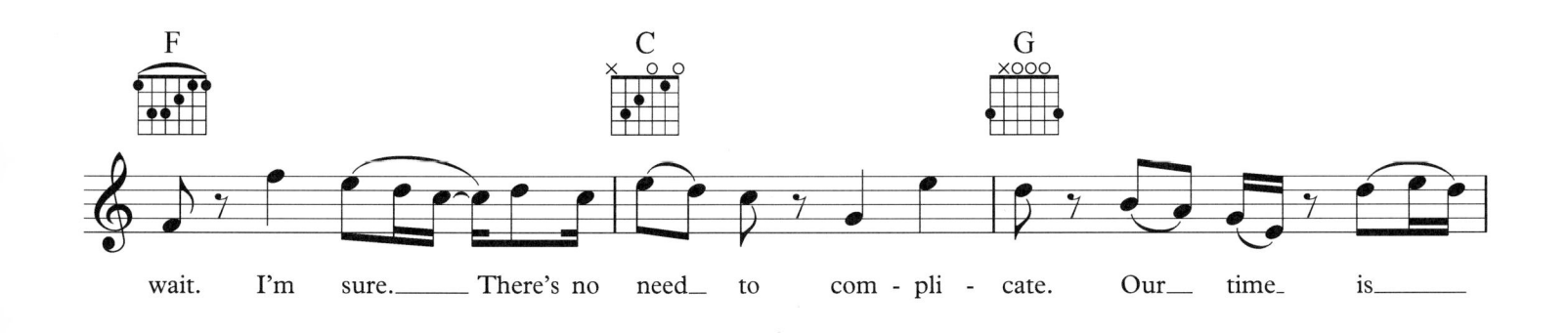

wait. I'm sure._____ There's no need_ to com - pli - cate. Our__ time_ is_____

short._ This is our fate. I'm yours._____ *Scat sing…*

Skooch on o - ver clos - er, dear, and I will nib - ble your ear._____ *Scat sing…*

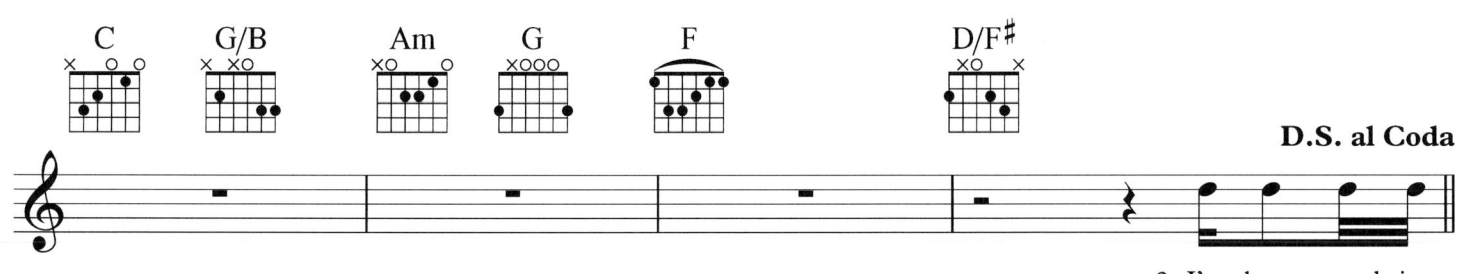

D.S. al Coda

3. I've been spend - ing

67

⊕ **Coda**

C

G

O-pen up your mind   and see like me.___   O-pen up your plans and, damn, you're free.__
(I   won't   hes - i - tate   no   more,   no

Am

F

___   Look in - to your heart_ and you'll   find_ that   the   sky__   is   yours._____   So
more.   It   can - not   wait.   I'm   sure._____   No

C

G

please don't, please don't, please   don't... There's no   need_ to   com - pli - cate   'cause our   time_
need   to   com - pli - cate.   Our   time   is

Am

F

D/F♯

___   is   short.___   This is, this is, this is our   fate.   I'm   yours._____   *Scat sing…*
short.   This   is   our   fate.   I'm   yours.)_____

C

G

Am

F

Repeat to fade

Layla

Words & Music by Eric Clapton & Jim Gordon

© Copyright 1970 E. P. Clapton.
All Rights Reserved. International Copyright Secured.

The instrumental intro, written out here in guitar tab, is in two sections: fi stly, one based around a sequence of power chords; and the other on a solo line high on the neck.
If the solo line isn't your thing, continue to play the chord shapes shown throughout the intro.

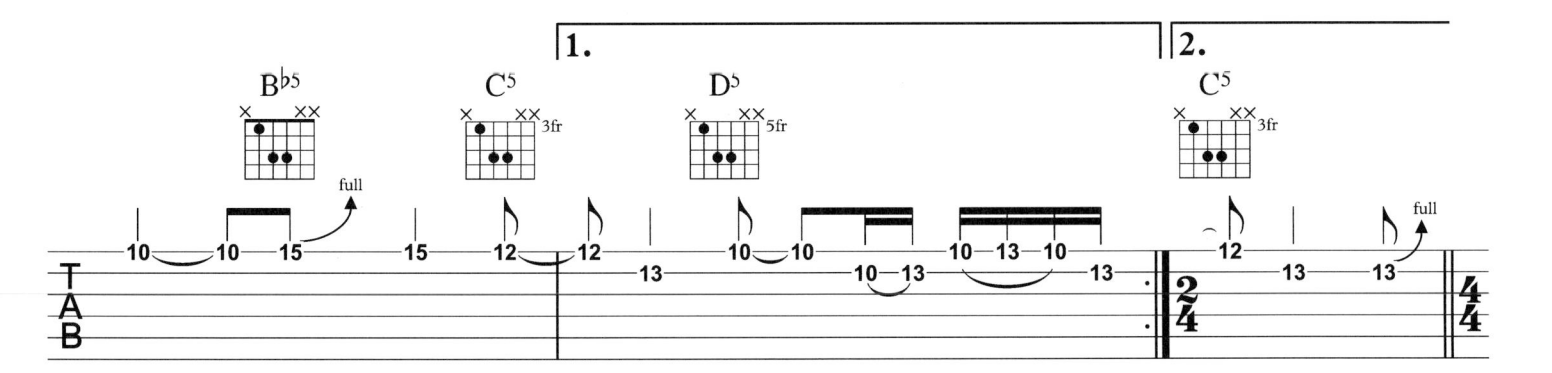

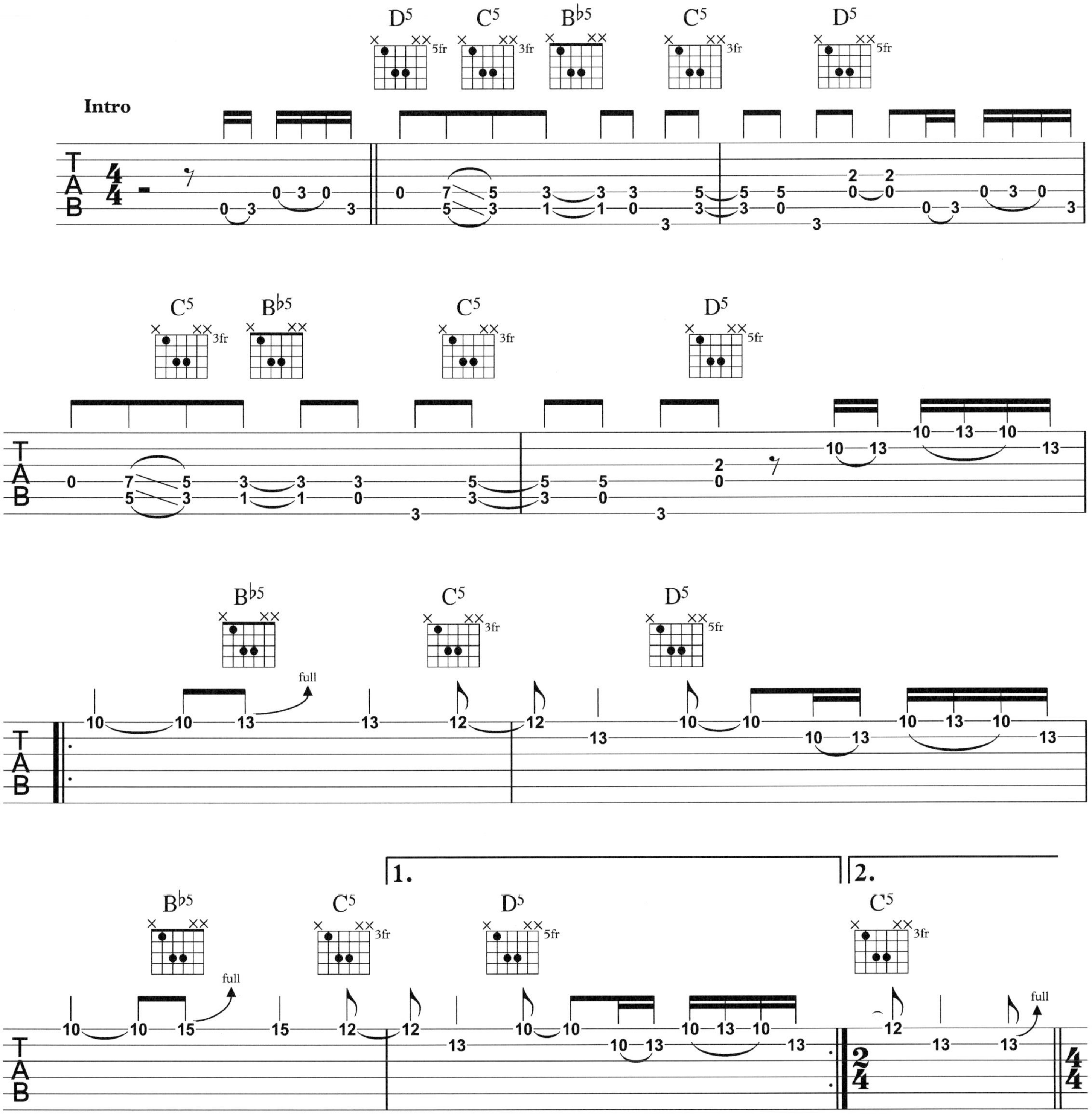

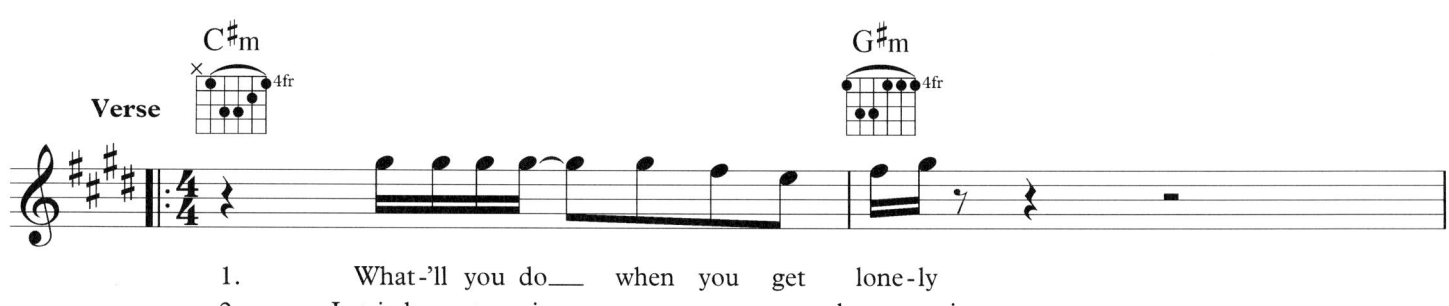

Verse

1.   What-'ll you do___ when you get lone-ly
2.   I tried   to give___ you con - so - la - tion,
3. Let's make   the best__ of the si - tu - a - tion,

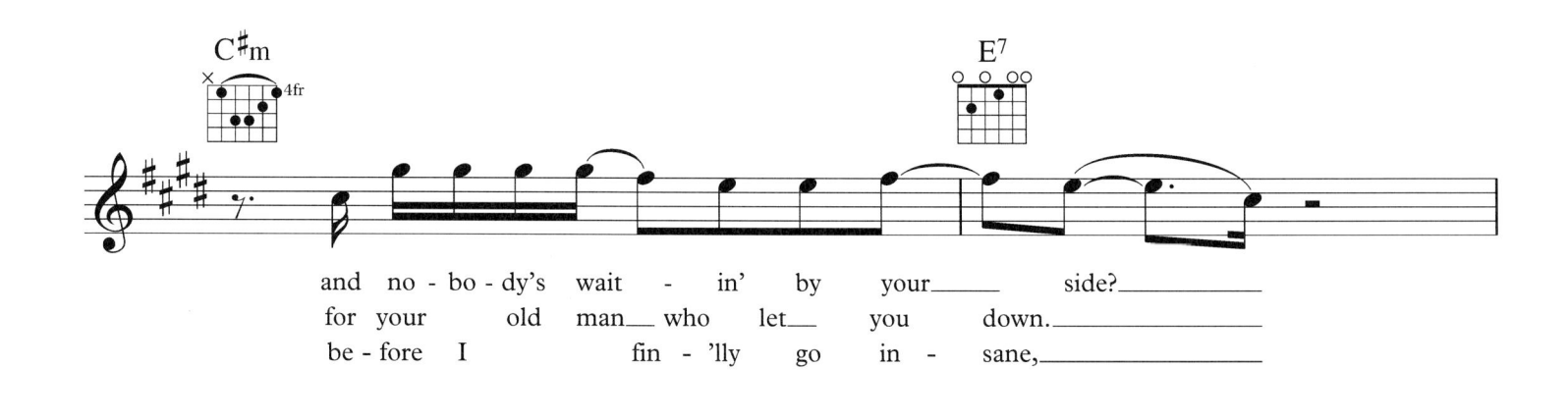

and no - bo - dy's wait - in' by your____   side?_____

for your   old man__ who let__   you   down._____

be - fore I   fin - 'lly go in - sane,_____

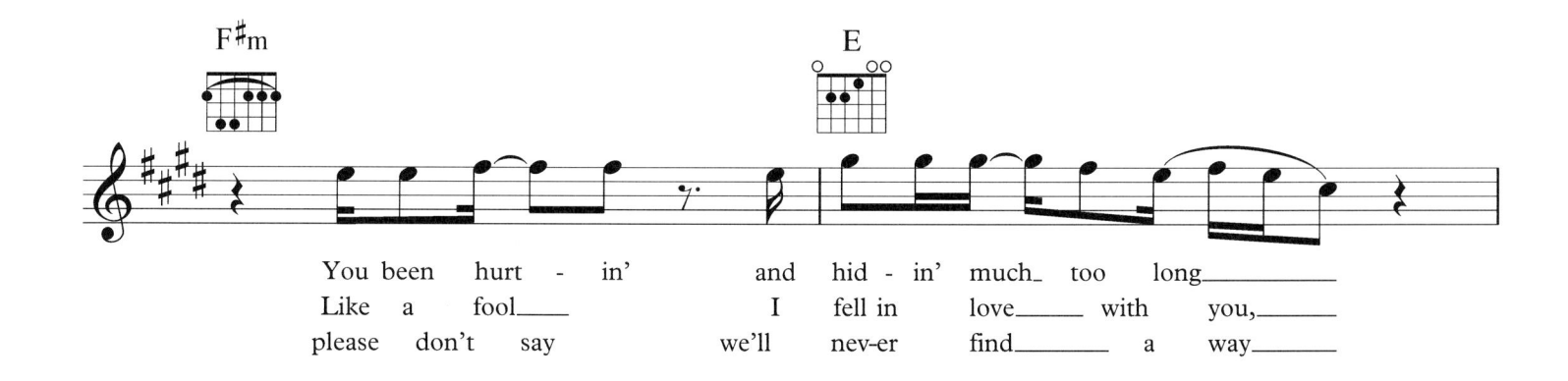

You been hurt - in'   and hid - in' much_ too long_____

Like a fool____   I fell in love____ with you,_____

please don't say   we'll nev-er find_____ a way_____

you know it's just___ your fool - ish pride.   Lay -

I turned my whole___ world up - side - down.   Lay -

and tell me all___ my love's___ in vain.   Lay -

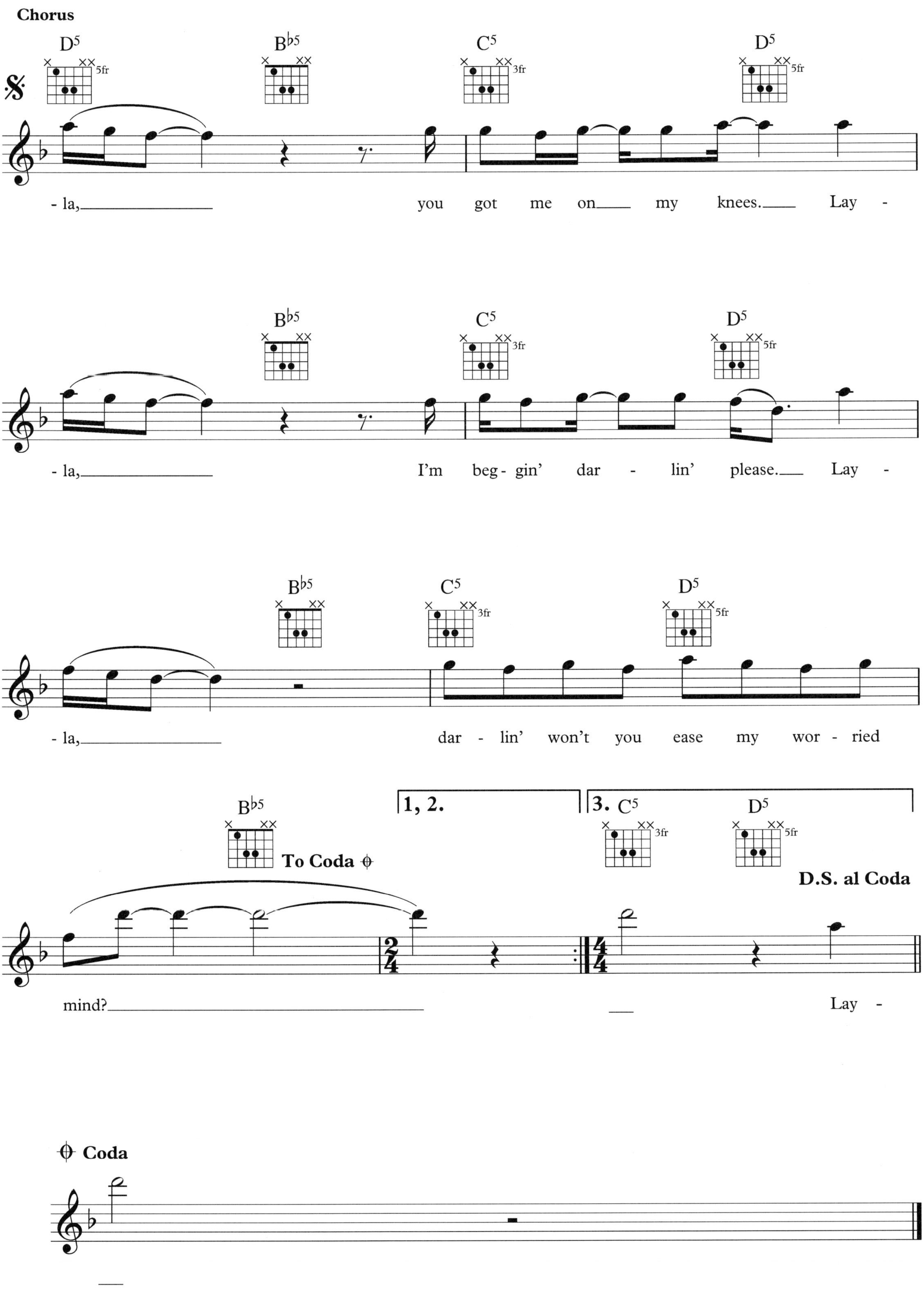

Chorus

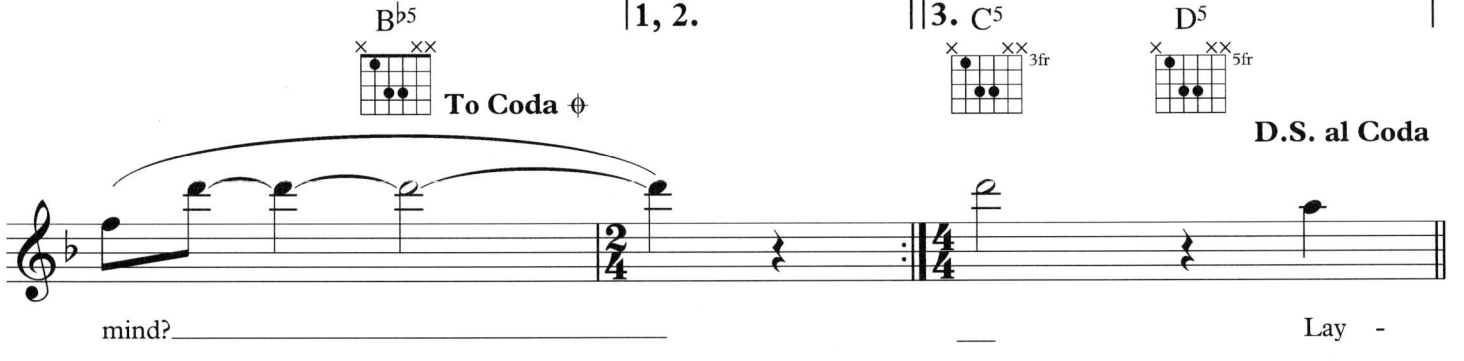

- la,_____ you got me on_____ my knees._____ Lay -

- la,_____ I'm beg-gin' dar - lin' please.____ Lay -

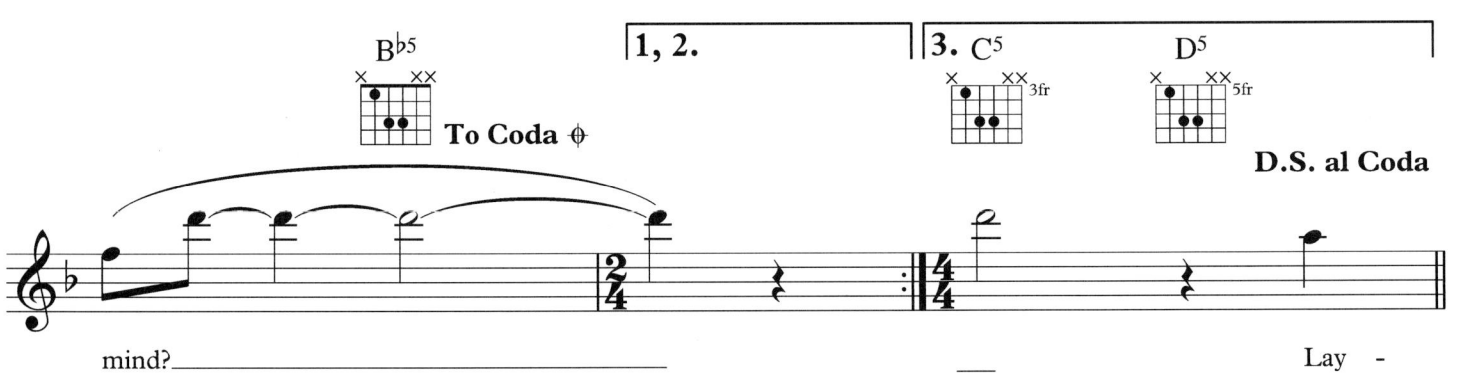

- la,_____ dar - lin' won't you ease my wor - ried

To Coda ⊕ **1, 2.** **3.** **D.S. al Coda**

mind?_____ Lay -

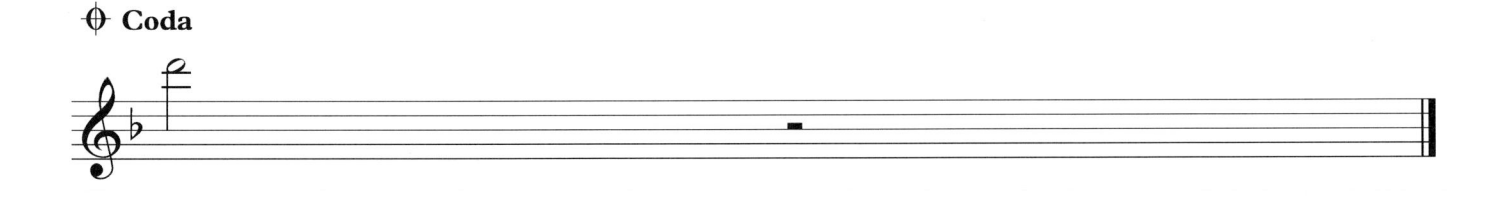

⊕ **Coda**

_____

Let Her Go

Words & Music by Michael Rosenberg

© Copyright 2012 Sony/ATV Music Publishing.
All Rights Reserved. International Copyright Secured.

Well, you on - ly need the light when it's burn - ing low. On - ly miss the

sun when it starts to snow._ On - ly know you love her when you let her go.

On - ly know_ you've been high when you're feel - ing low. On - ly hate the

Chorus

light when it's burn-ning low.　　On - ly miss the sun when it starts to snow.　　On - ly know you

love her when you let her go.　　On - ly know＿ you've been

high when you're feel-ing low.　　On - ly hate the road when you're miss-in' home.　　On - ly know you

To Coda ⊕　**1.**　**2.**

love her when you let her go.　　　　　　And you let her go.＿

＿　Oh,＿＿＿＿＿　oh＿ no.＿　And you let her go.＿

＿　Oh,＿＿＿＿＿　oh＿ no.＿　Well, you let her go.＿＿＿＿

Love The One You're With

Words & Music by Stephen Stills

© Copyright 1970 Gold Hill Music Incorporated, USA
Wixen Music UK Ltd.
All Rights Reserved. International Copyright Secured.

Strum in fast, light sixteenths, with an accent on the up-strums as shown here.

Strumming style:

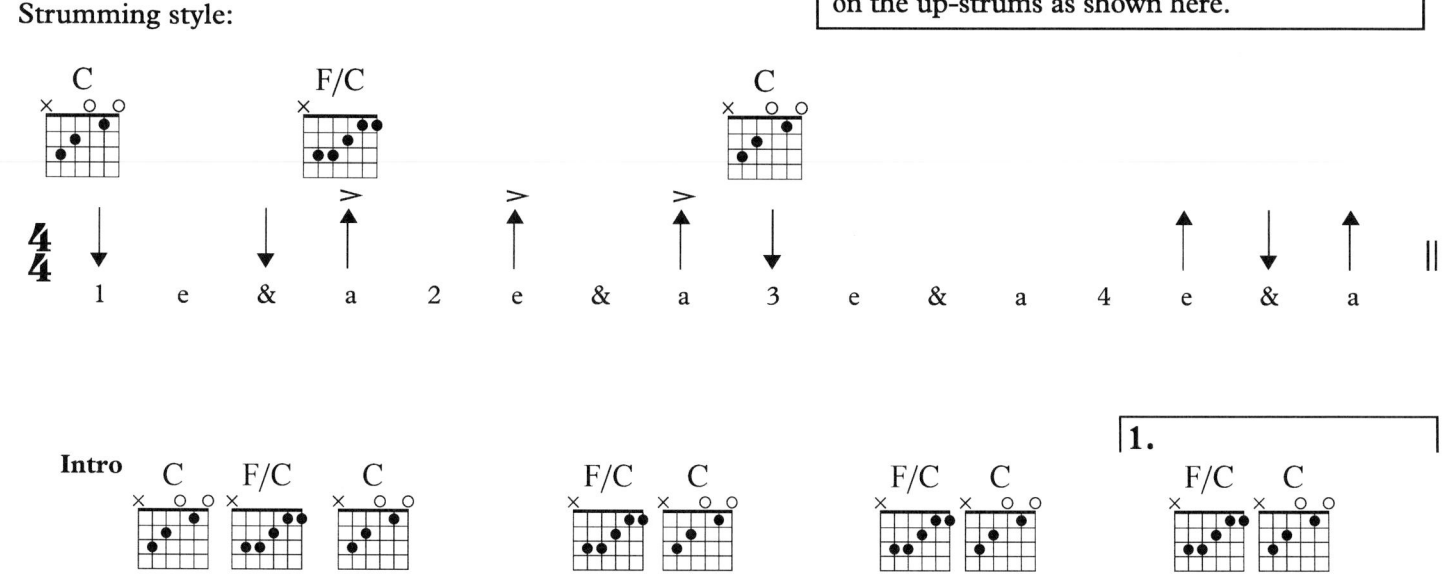

Intro

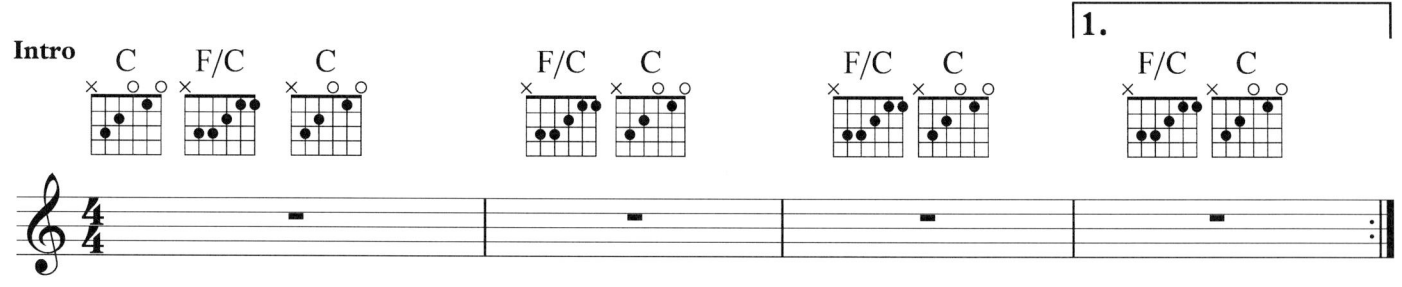

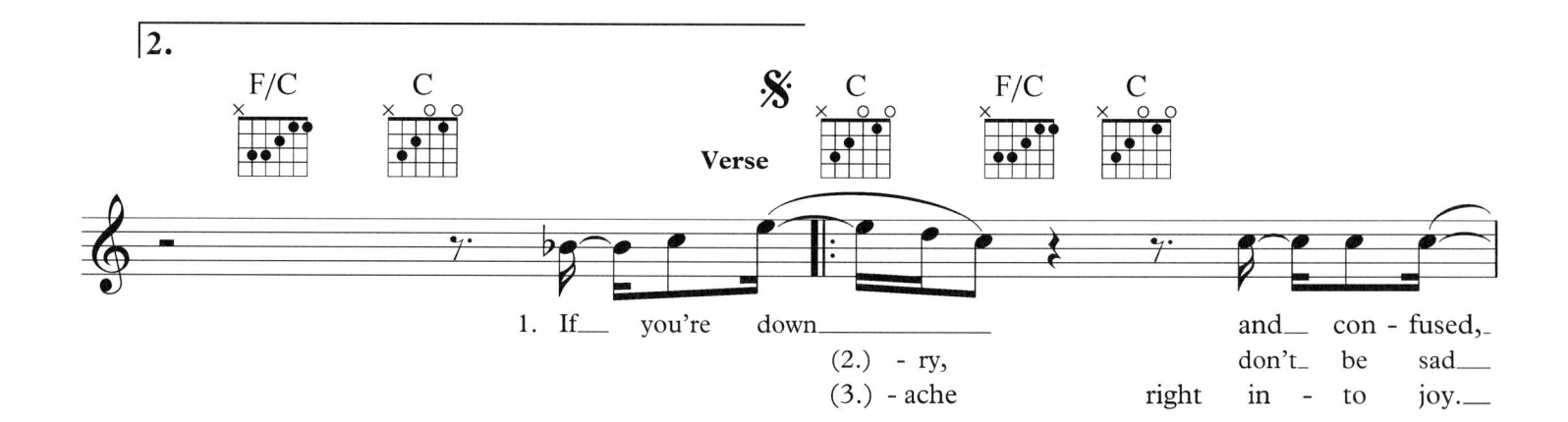

1. If you're down_____ and con-fused,
(2.) - ry, don't be sad_____
(3.) - ache right in-to joy._____

_____ and you don't re-mem-ber_____ who you're talk-ing to,_____
_____ don't sit cry-ing_____ ov-er good times you_____
_____ she's a girl_____ and you're a boy._____

76

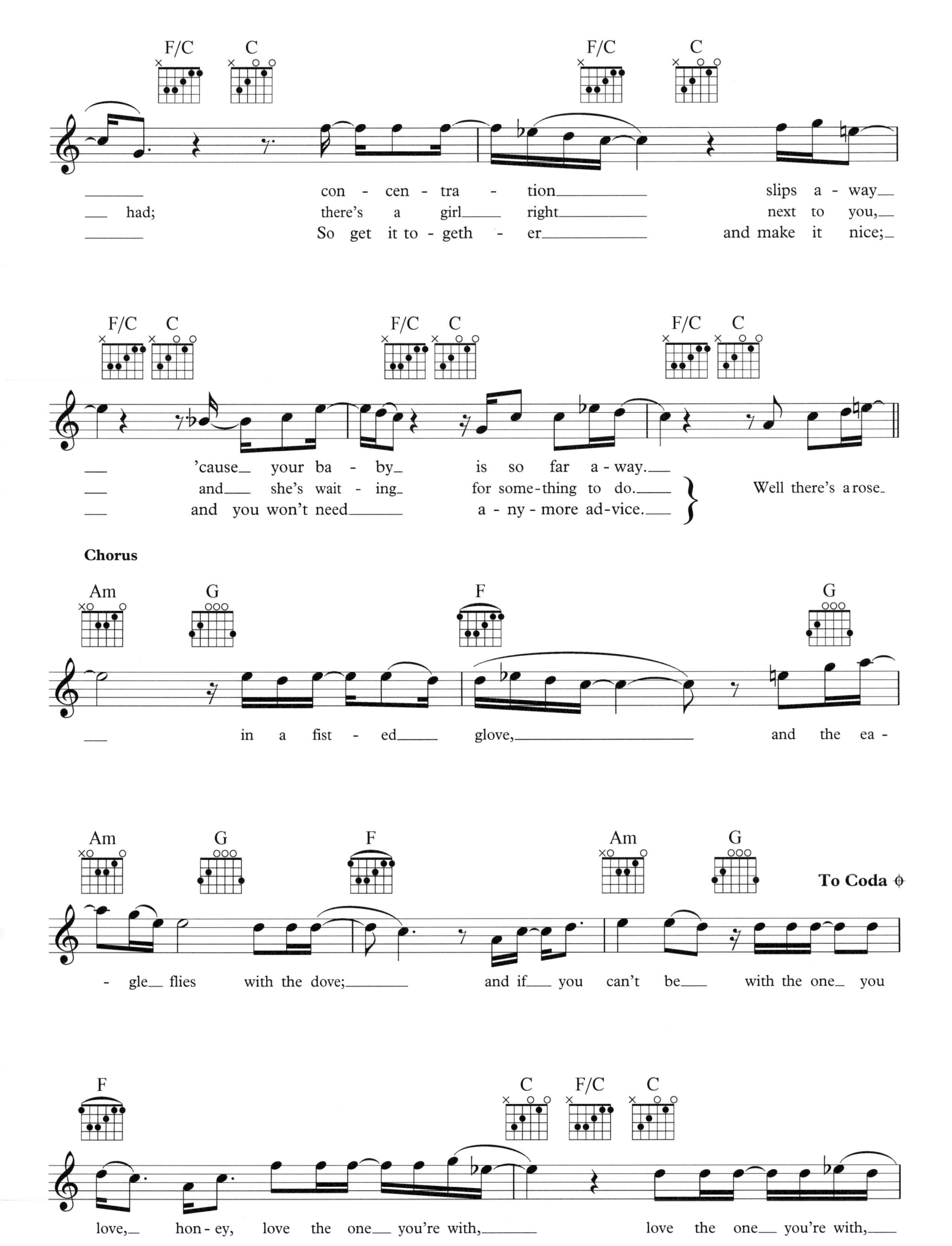

con - cen - tra - tion_____ slips a - way___
had; there's a girl____ right_____ next to you,___
So get it to - geth - er_____ and make it nice;___

'cause___ your ba - by___ is so far a - way.___
and___ she's wait - ing___ for some-thing to do.___
and you won't need_____ a - ny - more ad-vice.___

Well there's a rose___

Chorus

___ in a fist - ed____ glove,_____ and the ea -

- gle___ flies with the dove;_____ and if___ you can't be___ with the one___ you

love,___ hon - ey, love the one___ you're with,_____ love the one___ you're with,___

1.

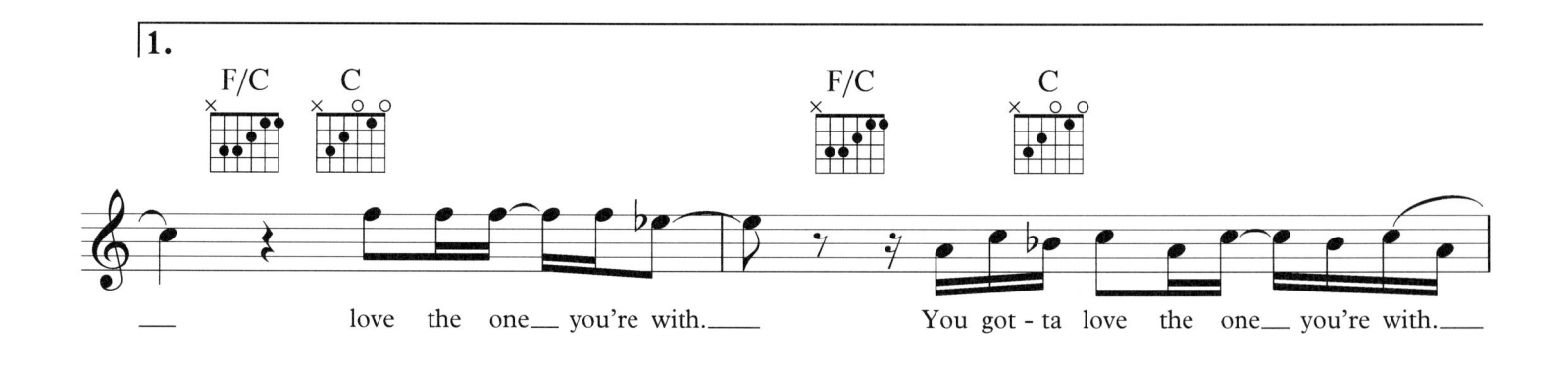

love the one___ you're with.___ You got-ta love the one___ you're with.

2.

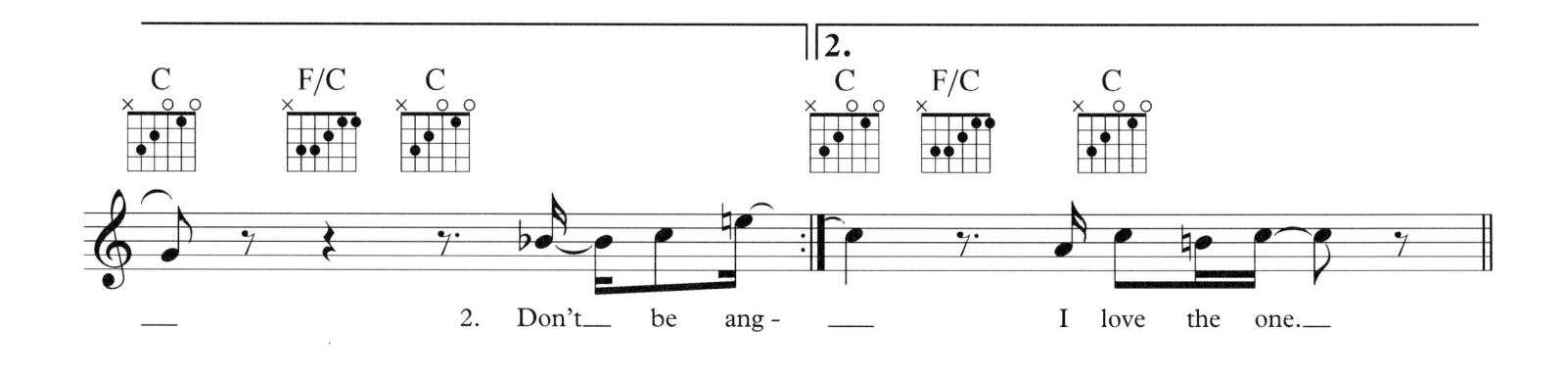

___ 2. Don't___ be ang - ___ I love the one.___

Bridge

Play 3 times

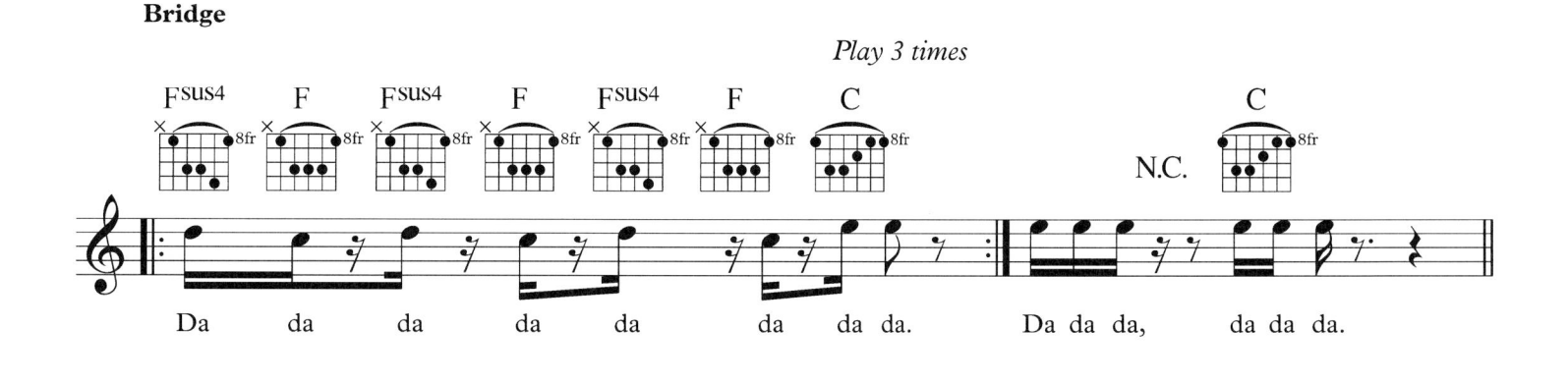

Da da da da da da da da. Da da da, da da da.

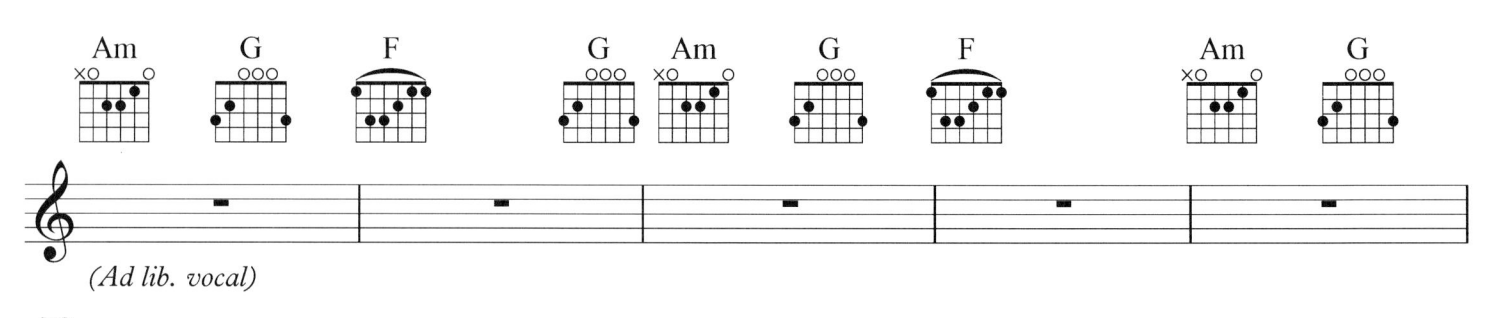

(Ad lib. vocal)

Love the one␣you're with,— love the one␣you're with,— and love the one␣you're␣

D.S. al Coda

with.— You got - ta love the one— you're with. 3. Turn your heart -

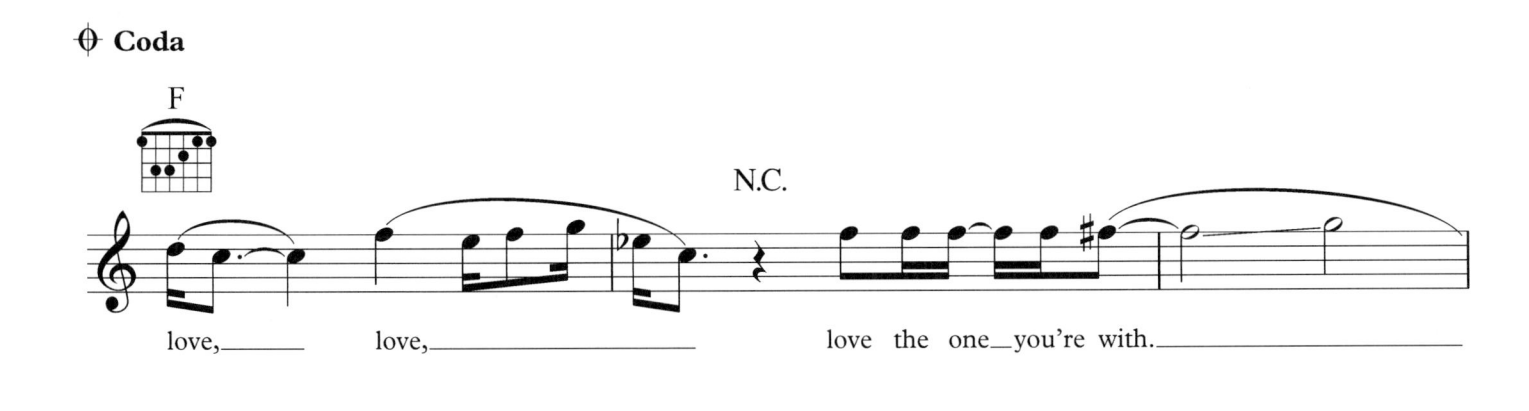

✛ **Coda**

N.C.

love,——— love,——————— love the one␣you're with.———————

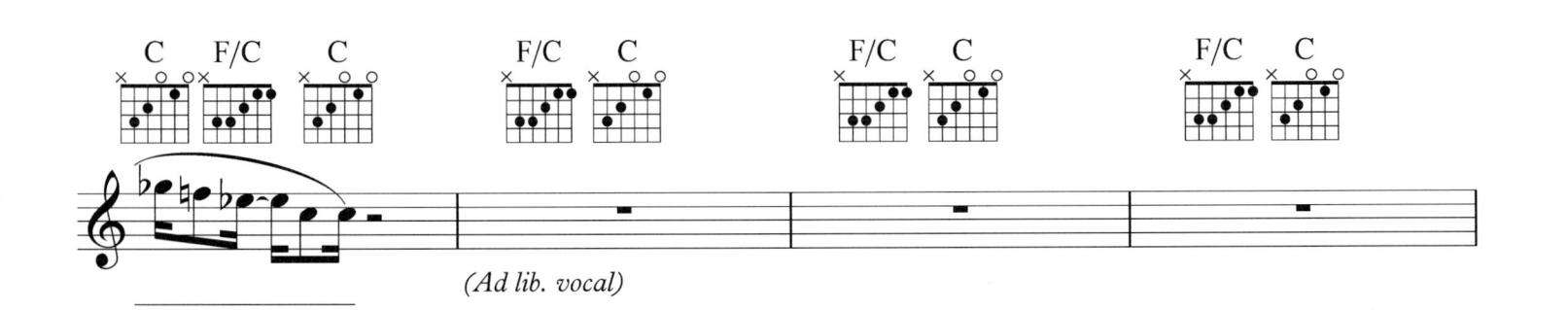

————————— *(Ad lib. vocal)*

Play 3 times

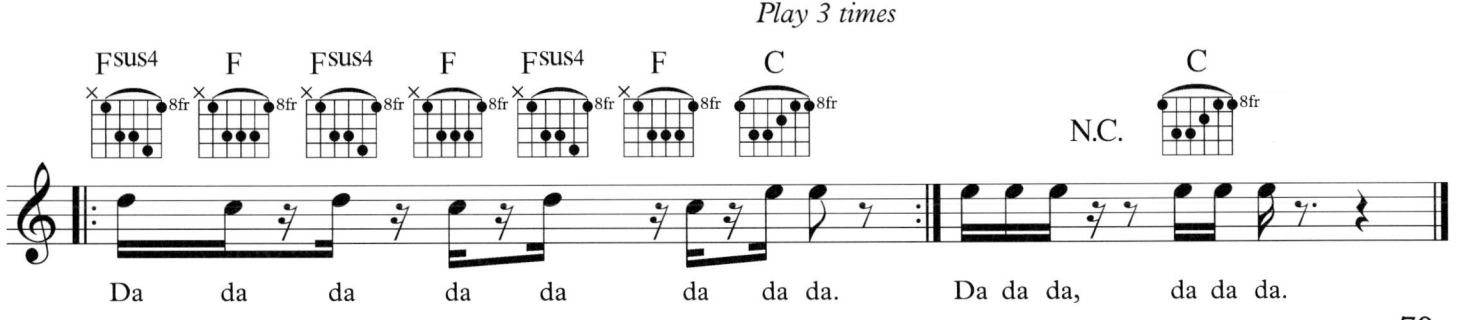

N.C.

Da da da da da da da da. Da da da, da da da.

Maggie May

Words & Music by Rod Stewart & Martin Quittenton

© Copyright 1971 (Renewed 1999) by Unichappell Music Inc./Rod Stewart/EMI Full Keel Music.
EMI Music Publishing Limited/Warner/Chappell North America Limited.
All Rights Reserved. International Copyright Secured.

Listen to the snare drum on the original recording and emulate it by strumming with a heavy accent on the 2nd and 4th beats—the so-called back-beat.

1. Wake up Mag-gie, I think I've got some-thing to say to you. It's
(2.) morn-ing sun,_ when it's in your face real-ly shows your age._ But
3. All I need-ed was a friend to lend a guid-ing hand. But you

late Sep-tem-ber and I real-ly should be back__
that don't wor-ry me none,____ in my eyes you're
turned in-to a lov-er and mo-ther, what a lov-er, you wore_

__ at__ school.
ev-'ry-thing.
__ me out.

I know I keep you a-mused__
I laugh at all of your jokes,_
All__ you did was wreck my bed,____

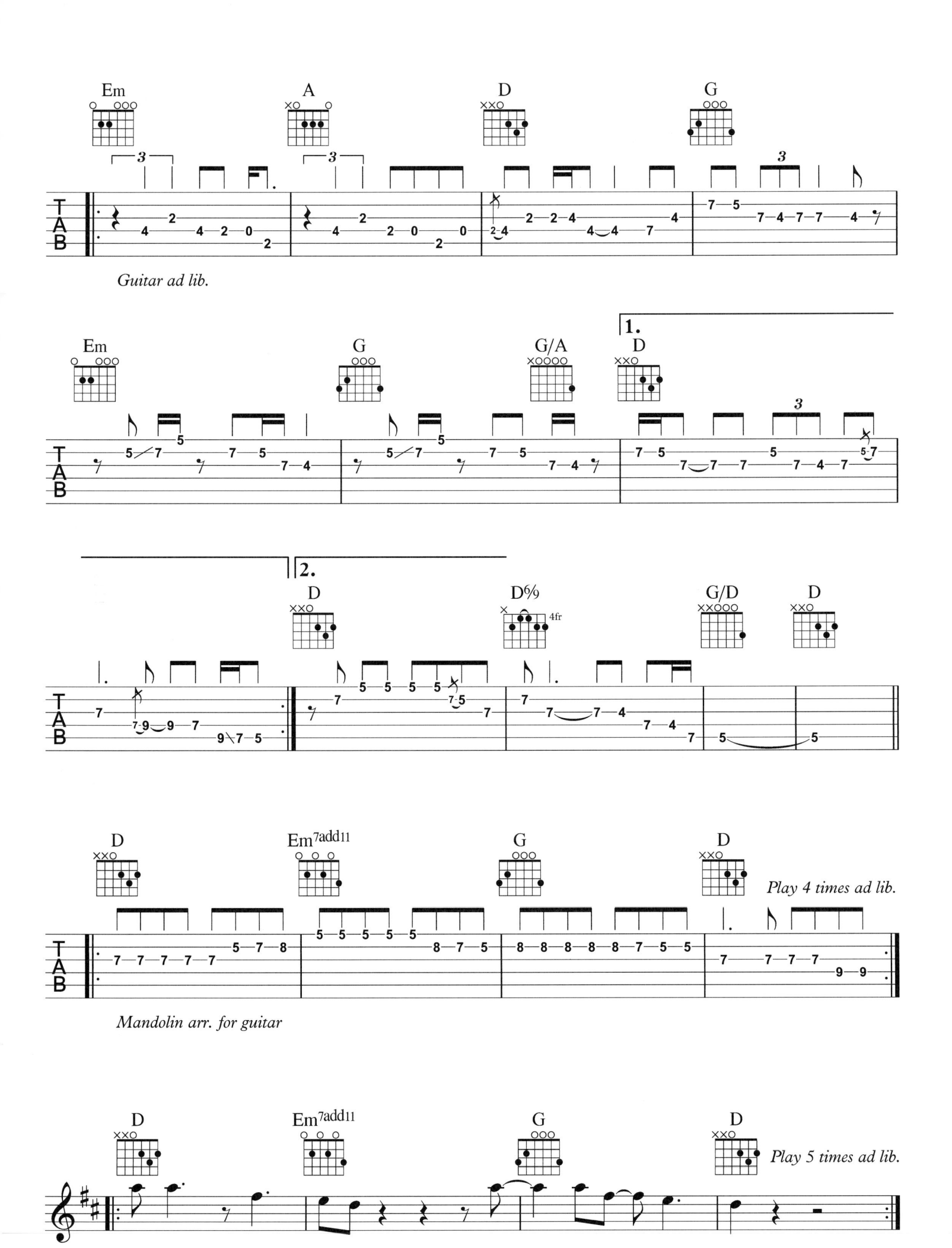

Guitar ad lib.

Mandolin arr. for guitar

Mag - gie, I wish I'd nev - er seen_ your face.
(Guitar sim.)

Lover, You Should've Come Over

Words & Music by Jeff Buckle

© Copyright 1994 Kobalt Music Publishing Limited.
All Rights Reserved. International Copyright Secured.

> The time signature, 6/8, is made up of two main beats in each bar, with each beat subdiving into three mini-beats.
> The arrows over the fi st line of strumming rhythm show how a constant down-&-up motion can be used to create the pattern shown.

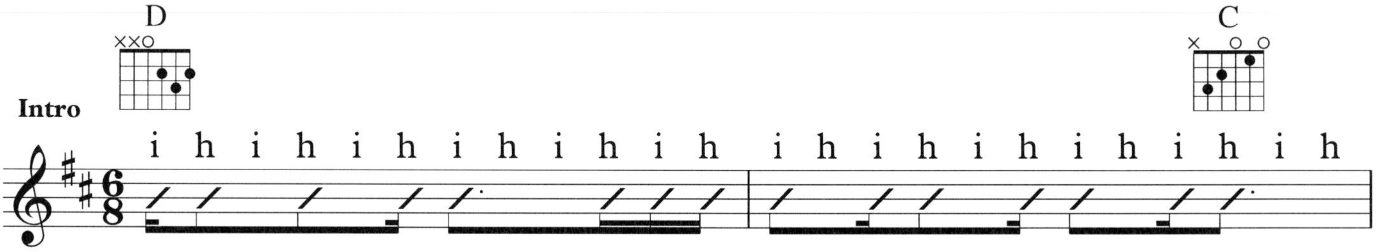

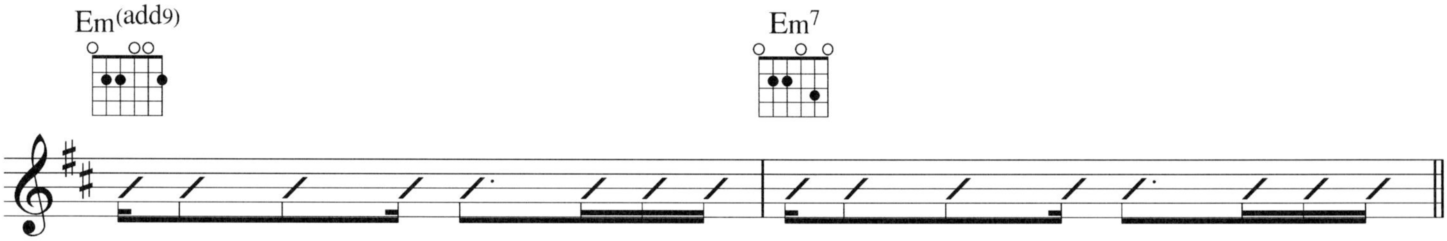

Intro

D · C

i h i h i h i h i h i h i h i h   i h i h i h i h i h i h i h i h

Em(add9) · Em⁷

Verse

D · C Em

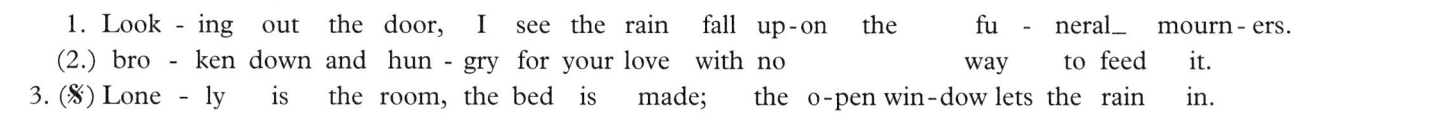

1. Look - ing out the door, I see the rain fall up-on the fu - neral_ mourn - ers.
(2.) bro - ken down and hun - gry for your love with no way to feed it.
3. (𝄋) Lone - ly is the room, the bed is made; the o-pen win-dow lets the rain in.

D · C Em

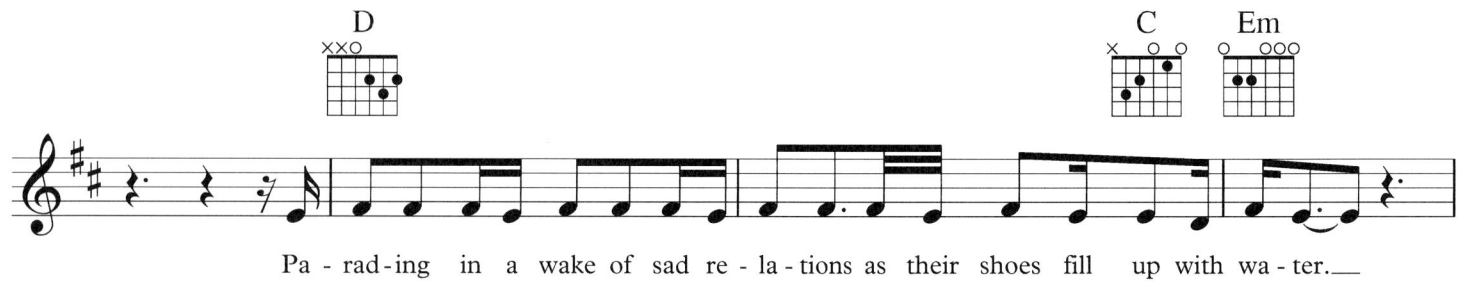

Pa - rad-ing in a wake of sad re - la - tions as their shoes fill up with wa - ter.__
Where_____ are you to-night, child, you know how much I need it?__
There burn-ing in the corn - er is the on - ly one who dreams he had you with him.__

84

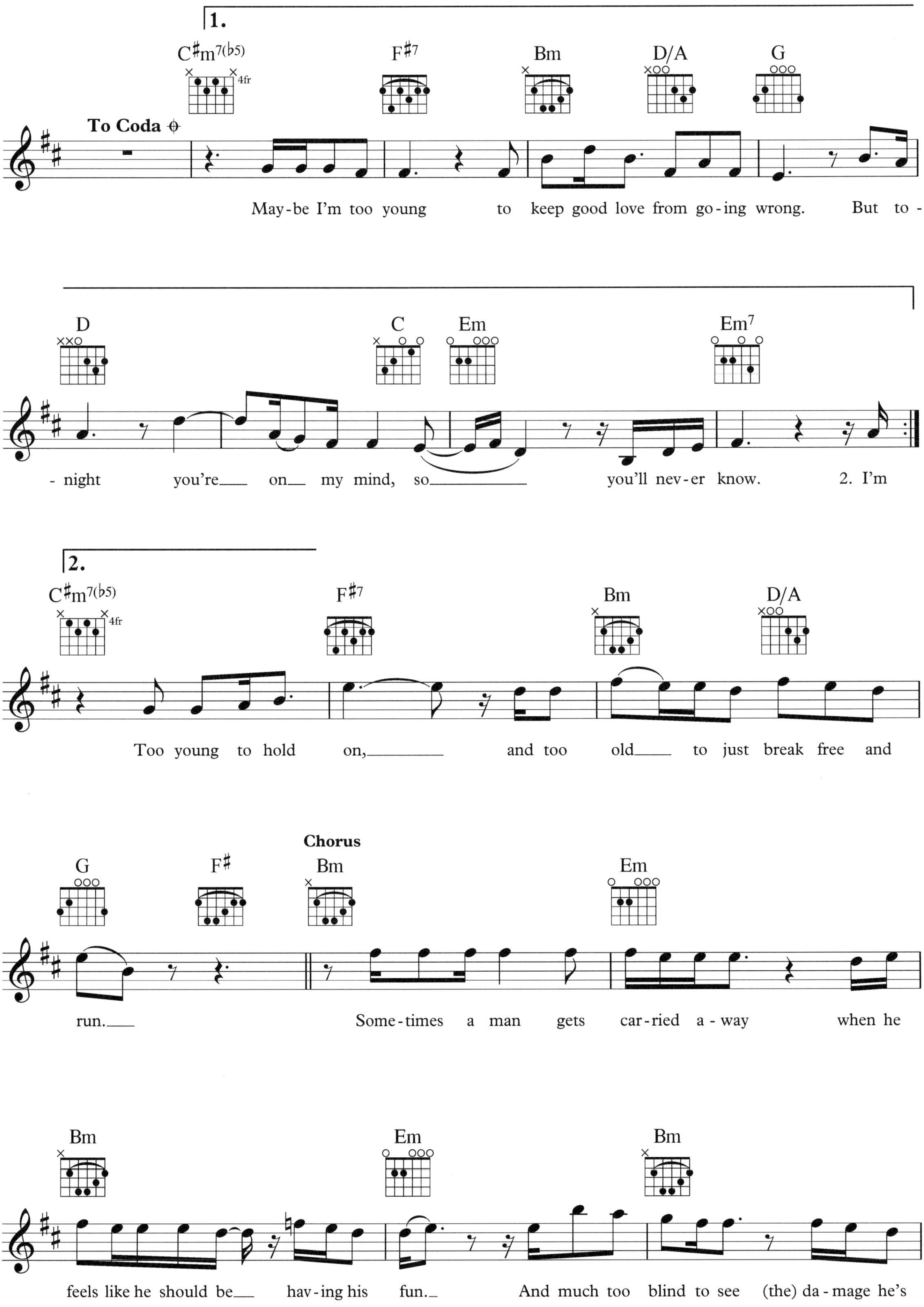

1.

C#m7(♭5)   F#7   Bm   D/A   G

To Coda ⊕

May-be I'm too young   to   keep good love from go-ing wrong.   But to-

D   C   Em   Em7

- night you're__ on__ my mind, so_____   you'll nev-er know.   2. I'm

2.

C#m7(♭5)   F#7   Bm   D/A

Too young to hold   on,_____   and too   old____ to just break free and

G   F#   **Chorus** Bm   Em

run.____   Some-times a man   gets car-ried a-way   when he

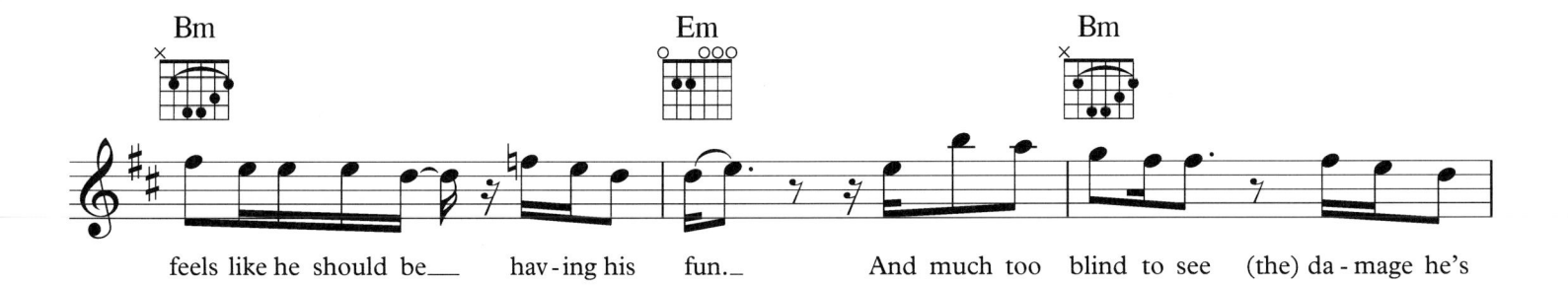

Bm   Em   Bm

feels like he should be____ hav-ing his fun.__   And much too blind to see (the) da-mage he's

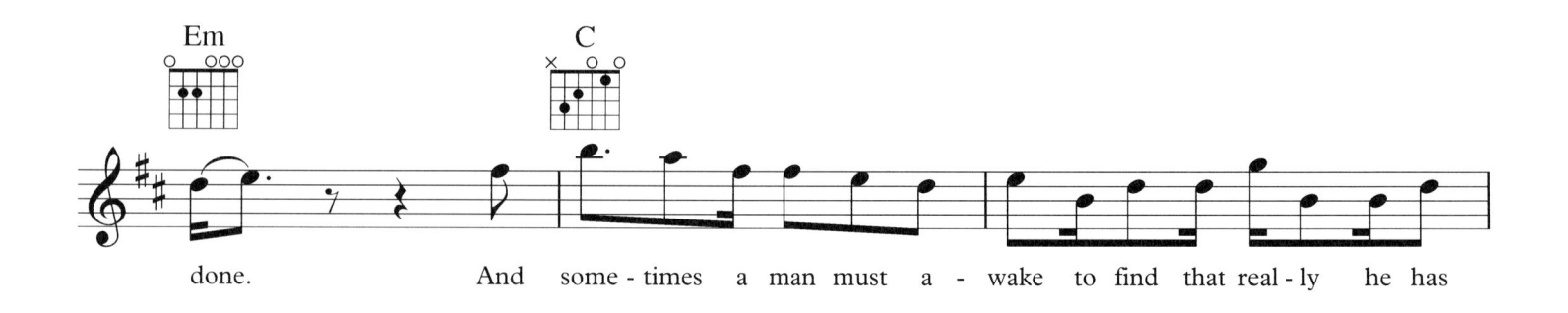

done. And some - times a man must a - wake to find that real - ly he has

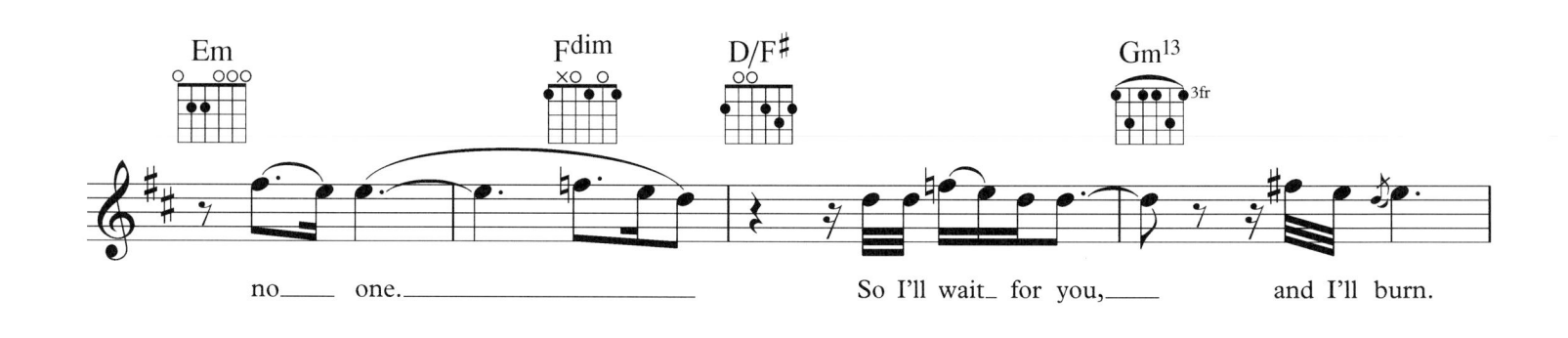

no____ one._____ So I'll wait_ for you,____ and I'll burn.

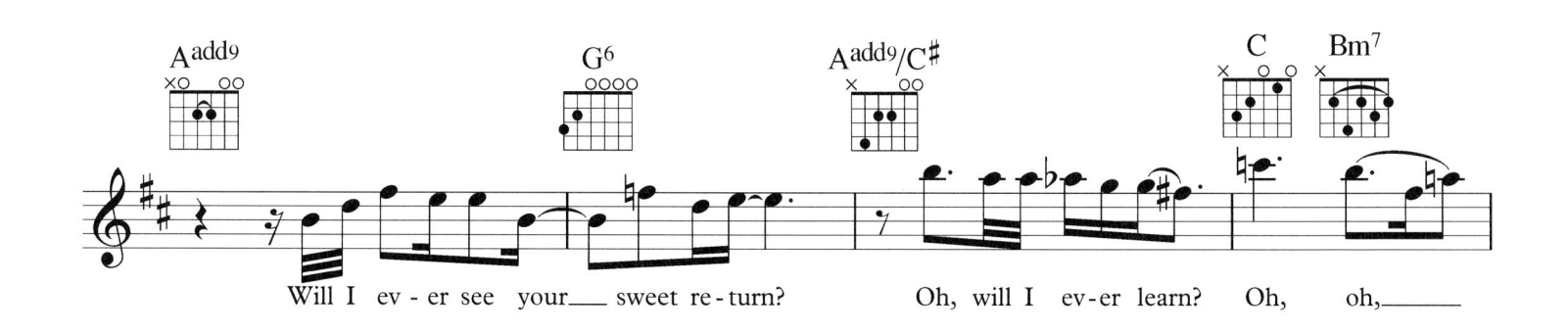

Will I ev - er see your___ sweet re - turn? Oh, will I ev - er learn? Oh, oh,____

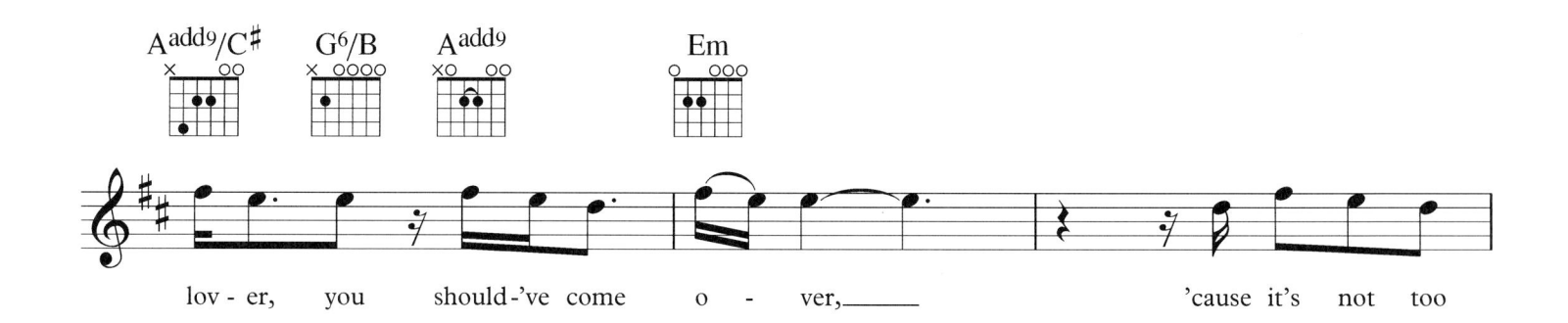

lov - er, you should - 've come o - ver,____ 'cause it's not too

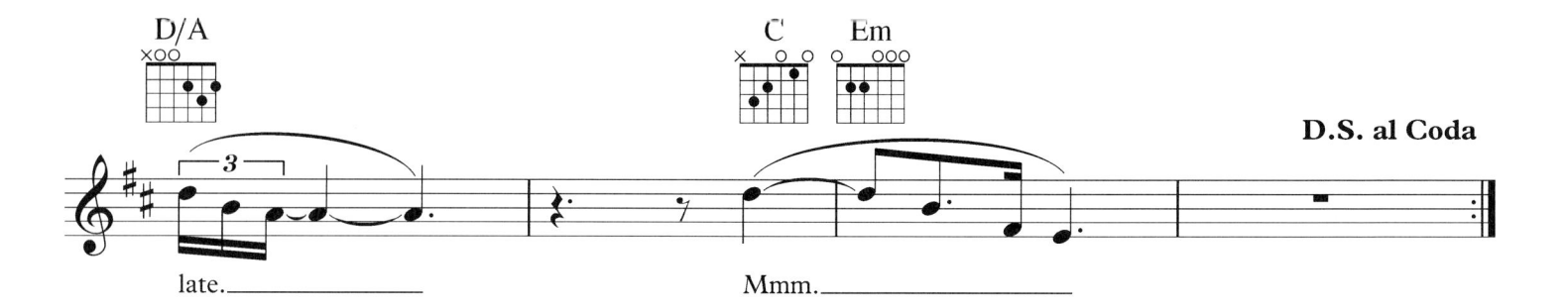

D.S. al Coda

late.____ Mmm._____

Coda
C♯m7(♭5)
4fr
F♯7
My bo - dy turns and yearns for a
Bm
D/A
G
Dm/F
D
sleep that won't ev - er come. It's nev - er o - ver, my
o - ver, all my
C
Em
king - dom for a kiss up - on her shoul - der. It's nev - er
blood for the sweet - ness of her laugh - ter. It's nev - er
D
C
Em
o - ver, all my rich - es for her smiles, when I slept so soft a - gainst her.
o - ver, she's a tear that hangs in - side my soul for ev - er.
1.
2.
Em7
Em7
C♯m7(♭5)
4fr
It's nev - er
Ah, but may - be I'm just too

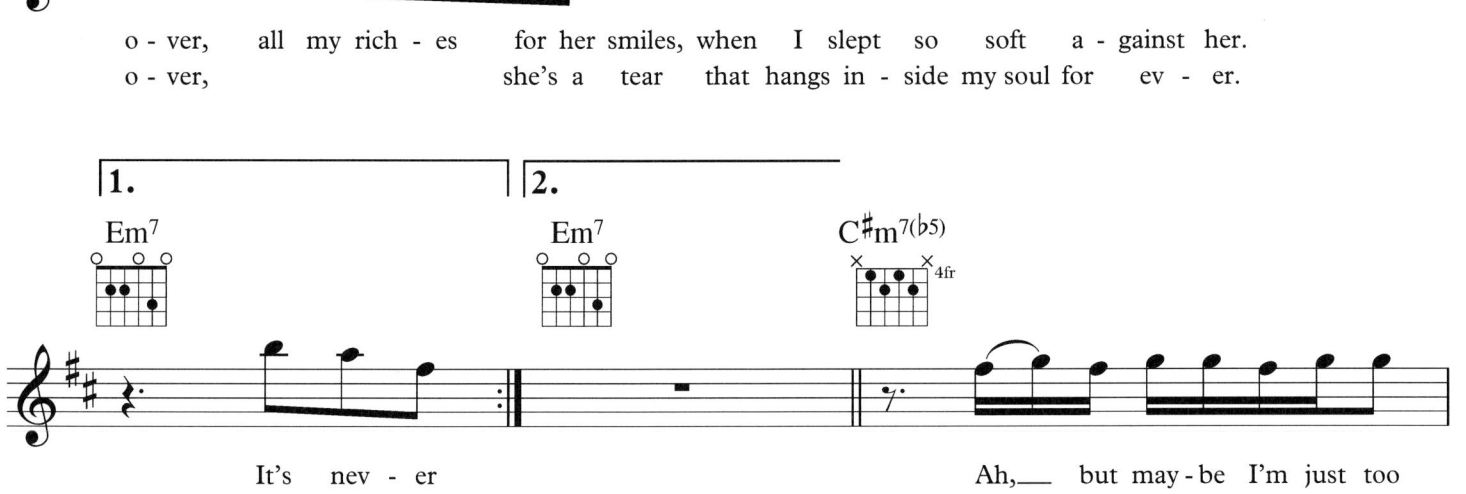

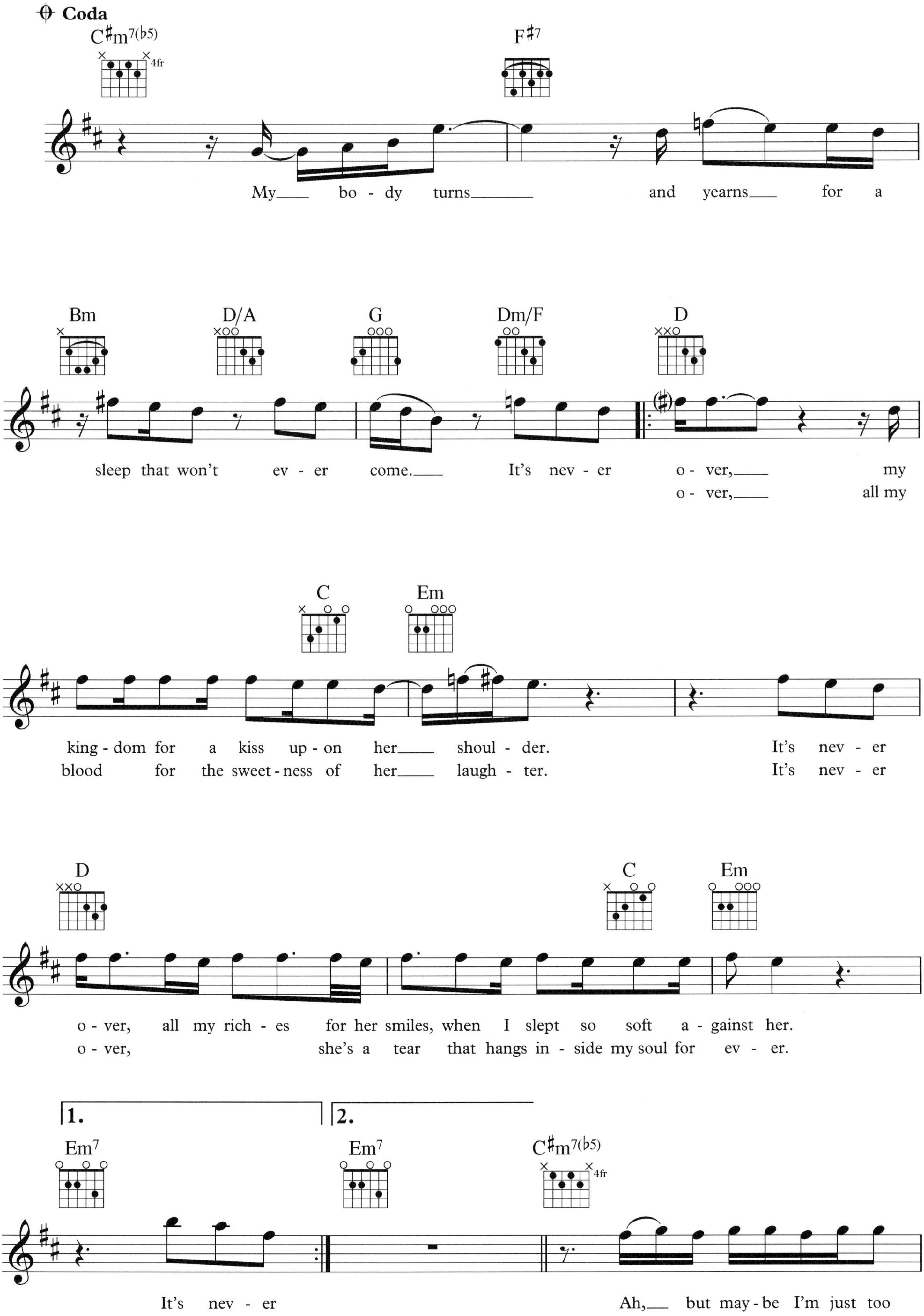

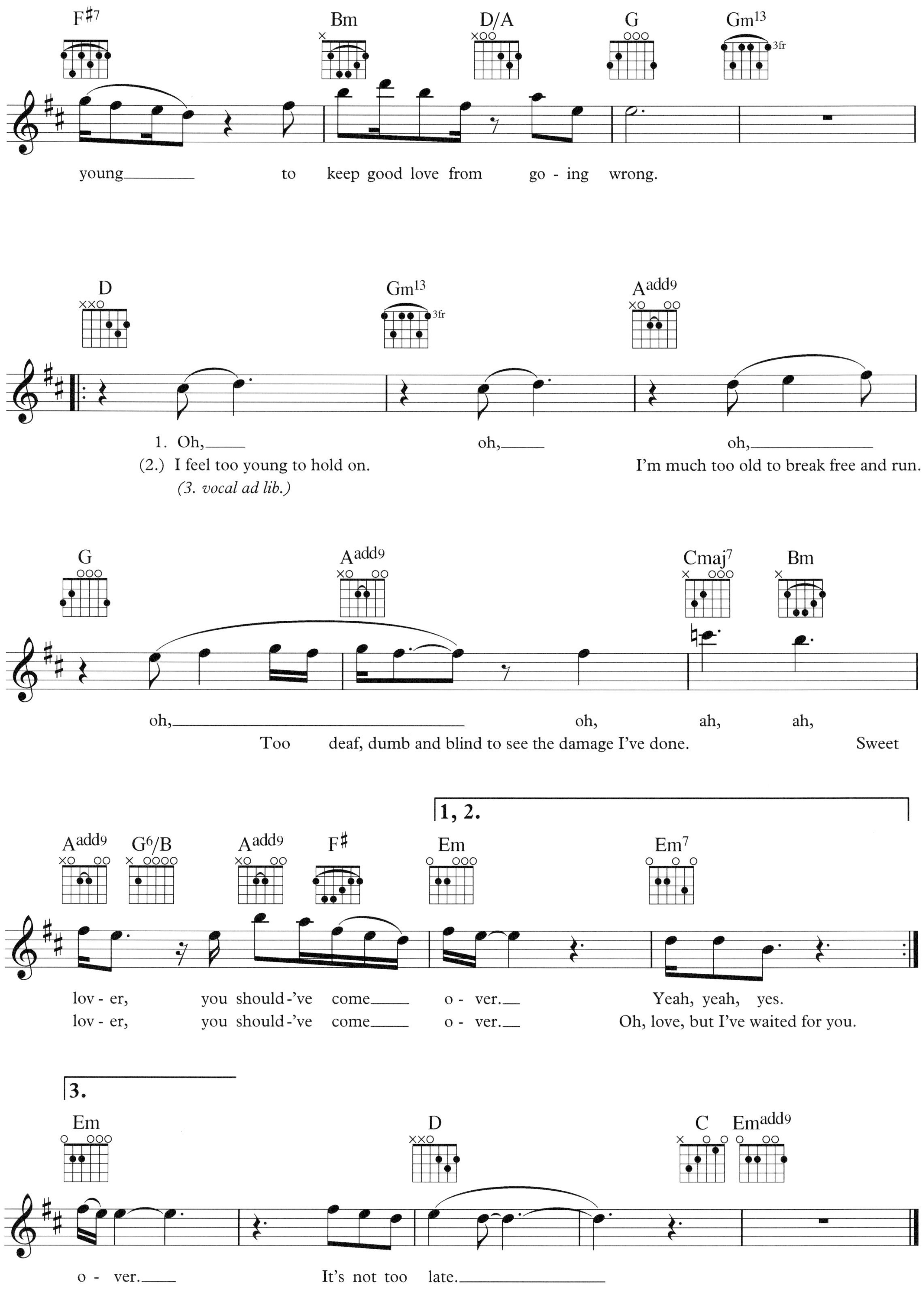

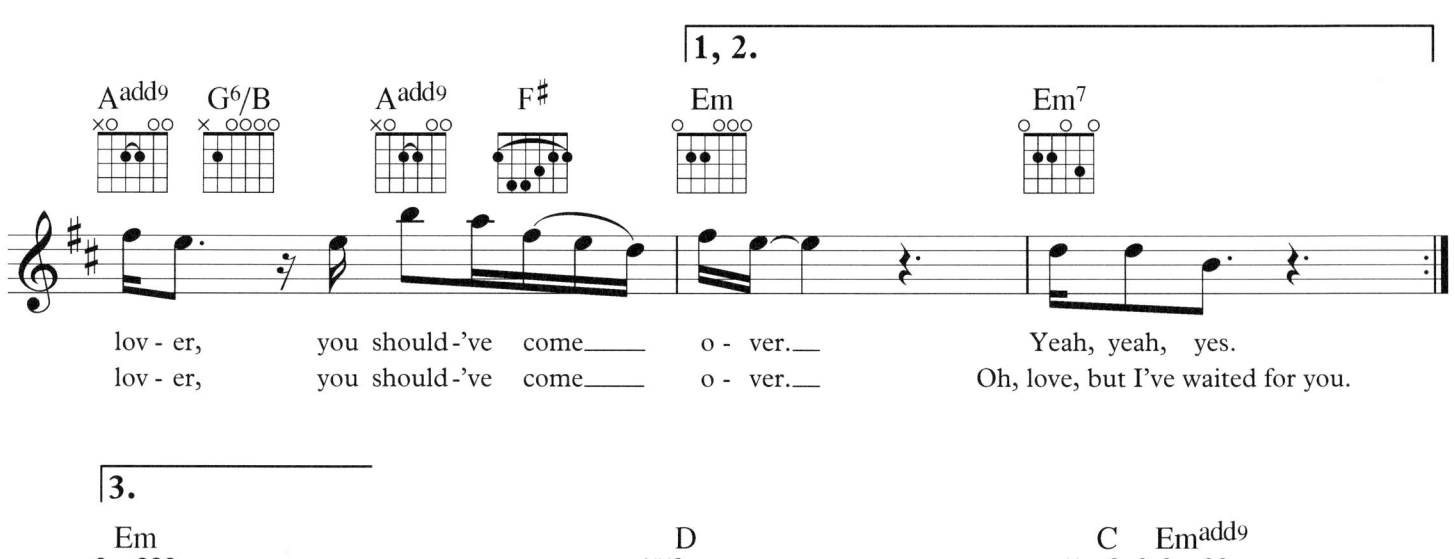

F♯7
Bm
D/A
G
Gm13
3fr
young
to
keep good love from
go - ing
wrong.
D
Gm13
3fr
Aadd9
1. Oh,
oh,
oh,
(2.) I feel too young to hold on.
I'm much too old to break free and run.
(3. vocal ad lib.)
G
Aadd9
Cmaj7
Bm
oh,
oh,
ah,
ah,
Too
deaf, dumb and blind to see the damage I've done.
Sweet
1, 2.
Aadd9
G6/B
Aadd9
F♯
Em
Em7
lov - er,
you should -'ve
come
o - ver.
Yeah, yeah, yes.
lov - er,
you should -'ve
come
o - ver.
Oh, love, but I've waited for you.
3.
Em
D
C
Emadd9
o - ver.
It's not too
late.

The Man Who Sold The World

Words & Music by David Bowie

© Copyright 1971 Tintoretto Music/Mainman-Saag Ltd New York.
Chrysalis Music Limited, a BMG Chrysalis Company/
RZO Music Limited/EMI Music Publishing Limited.
All Rights Reserved. International Copyright Secured.

> Play the solo line shown in the intro—and again in the interlude—or else strum in very even eighth-notes.

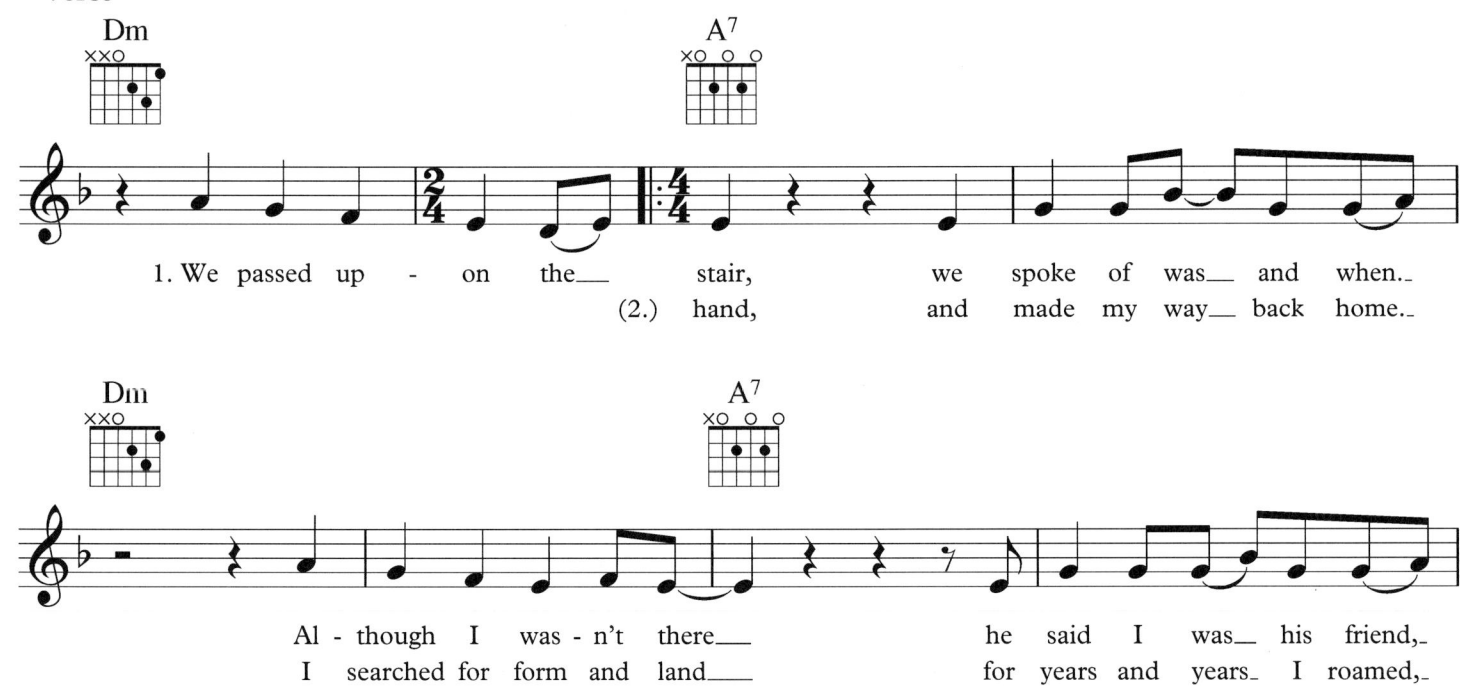

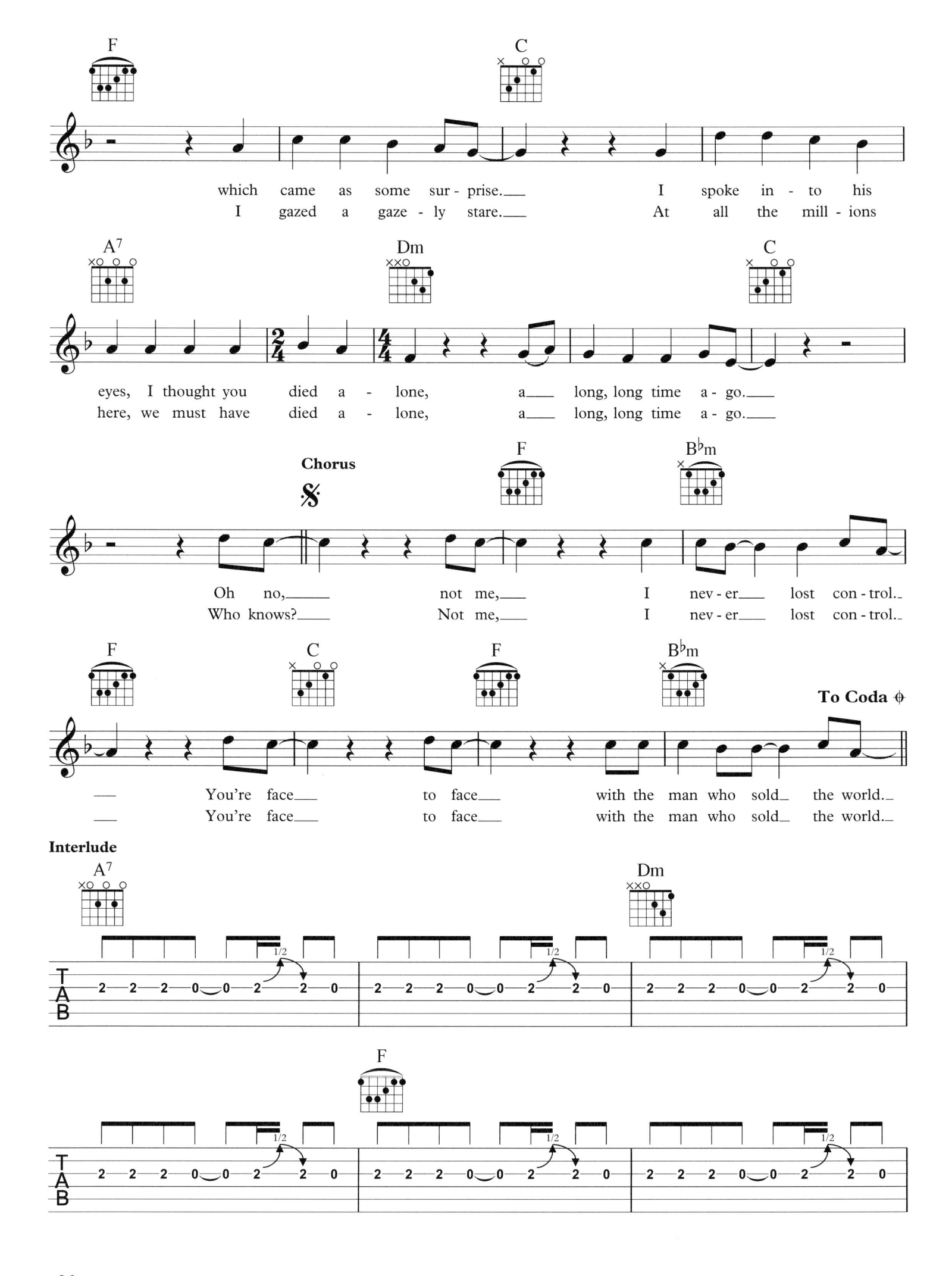

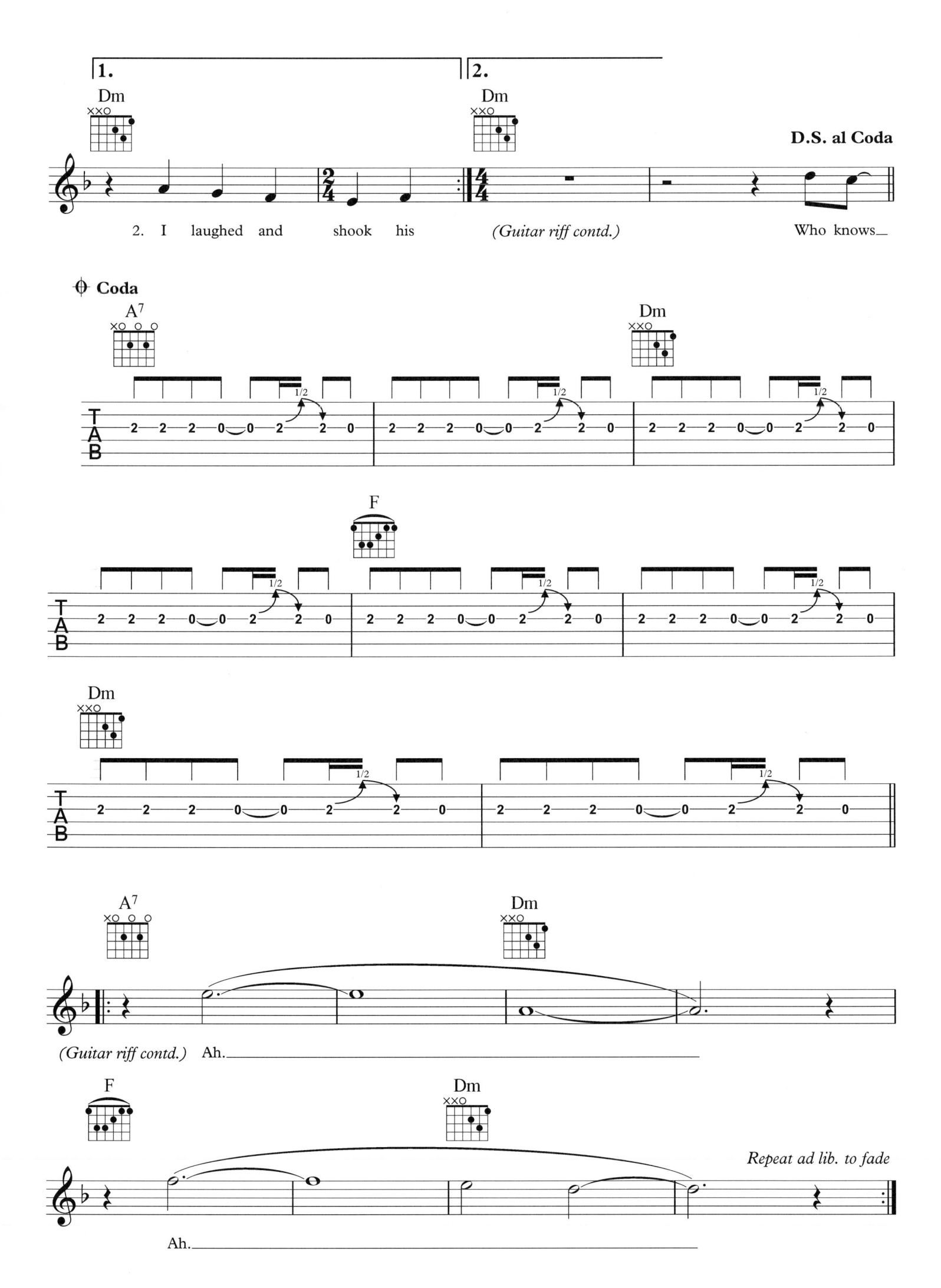

Me And Julio Down By The Schoolyard

Words & Music by Paul Simon

© Copyright 1971 Paul Simon (BMI).
All Rights Reserved. International Copyright Secured.

Notice in the intro that the second A chord comes just *before* the 3rd beat.
Keep the strums short and crisp, with the hand moving in even sixteenths.

Strumming style:

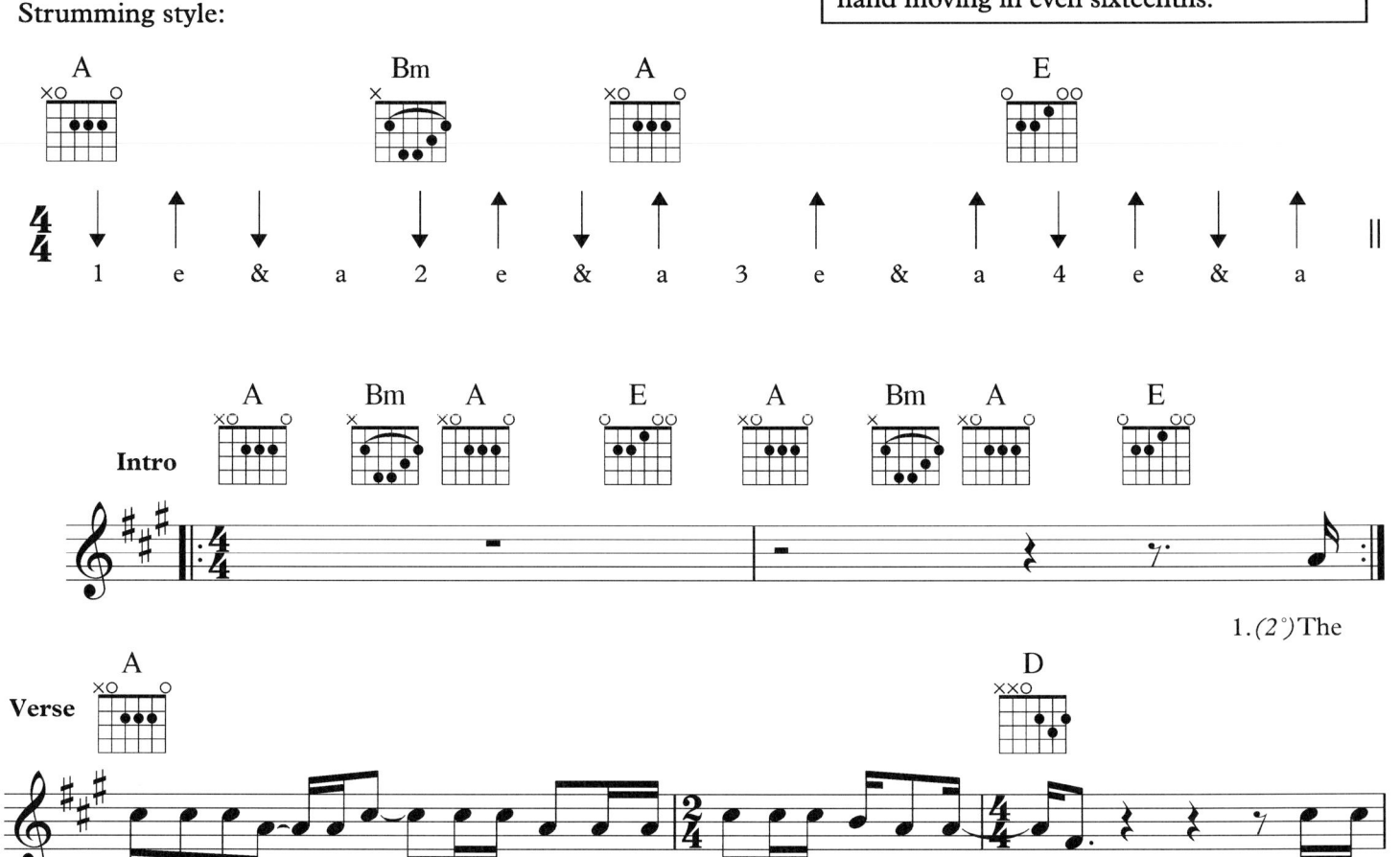

Intro

1.(2°) The

Verse

Ma-ma py-ja - ma rolled out-ta bed and she ran to the po-lice sta - tion. When the

Pa-pa found out he be-gan to shout__ and we start - ed the in-ves-ti-ga-

- tion. It's a-gainst the law,_____ it was a-gainst the law,_

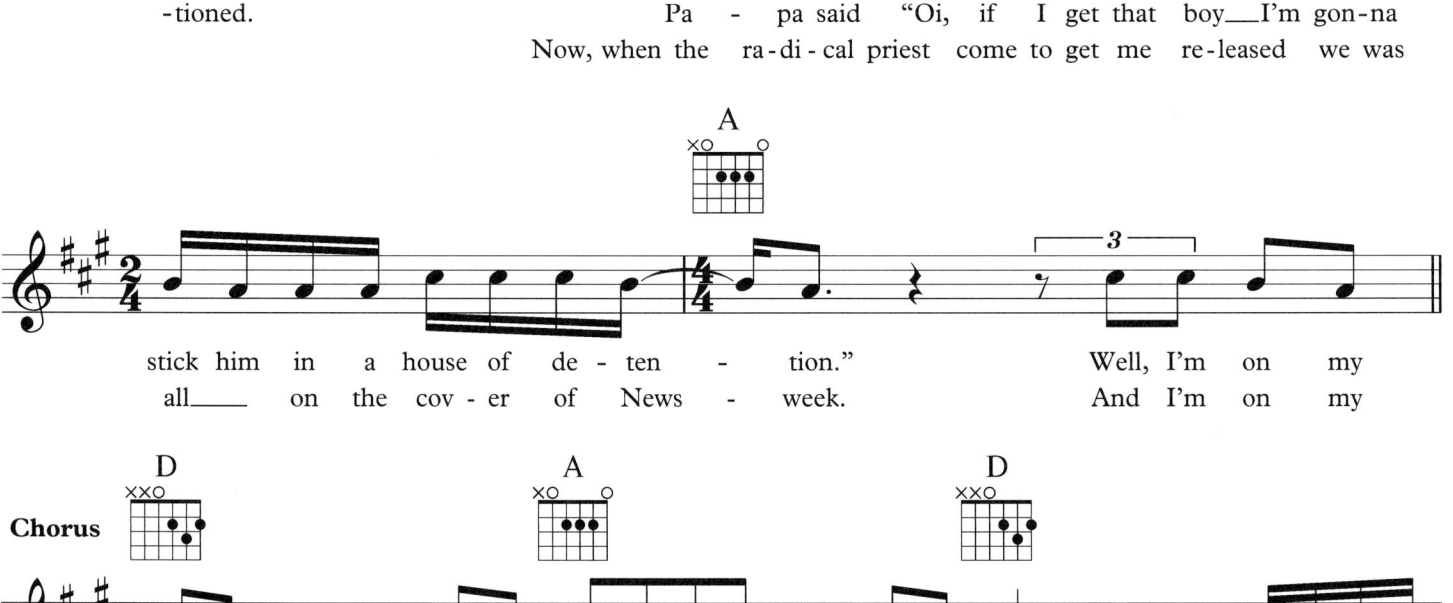

Verse 1

oh, what the Ma-ma saw,___ it was a-gainst the law.___ Ooh,

%

2. Ma - ma looked down and spit on the ground ev-'ry time my name_ gets men-
cou - ple of days they come and take me a - way, but the press let the sto - ry leak.

-tioned. Pa - pa said "Oi, if I get that boy__I'm gon-na
Now, when the ra-di-cal priest come to get me re-leased we was

stick him in a house of de - ten - tion." Well, I'm on my
all__ on the cov - er of News - week. And I'm on my

Chorus

way,_ I don't know where I'm go - in'.___ I'm on my way. I'm tak-in' my time_

(Whistle on repeat)

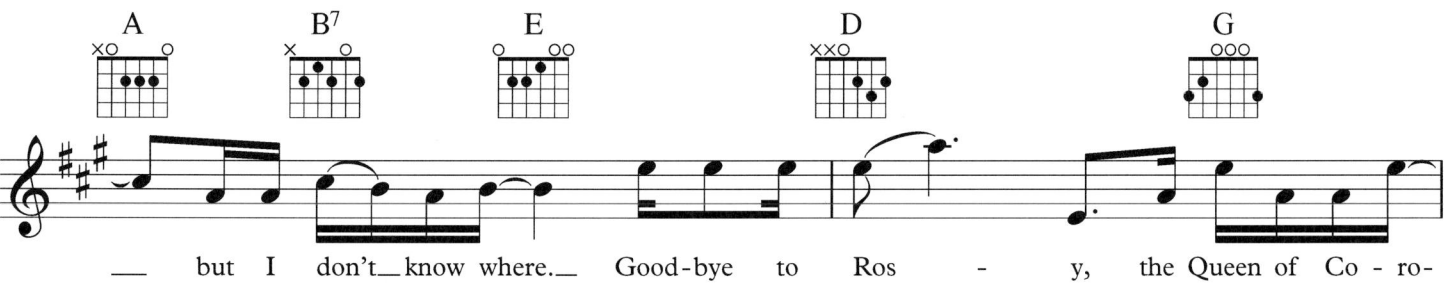

___ but I don't__know where.__ Good-bye to Ros - y, the Queen of Co - ro-

93

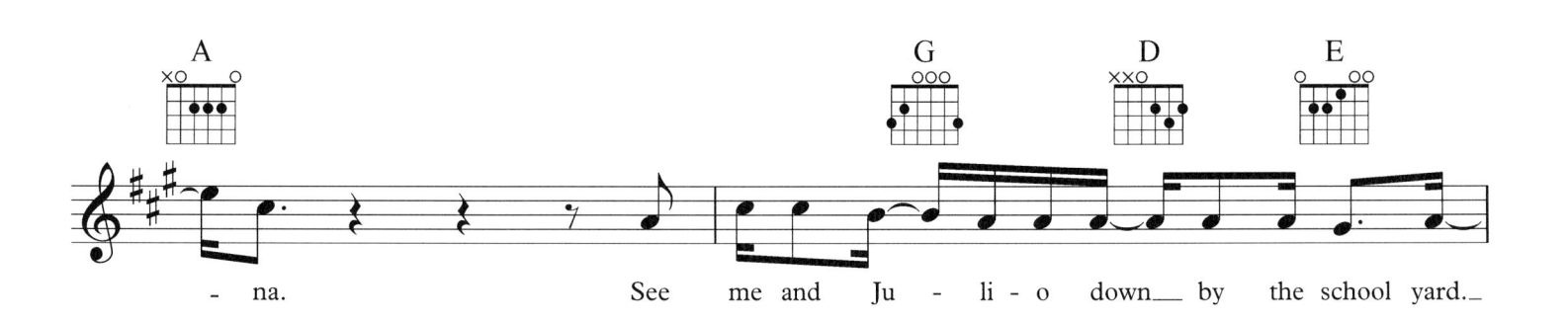

- na.   See me and Ju - li - o down__ by   the school yard.__

To Coda ⊕

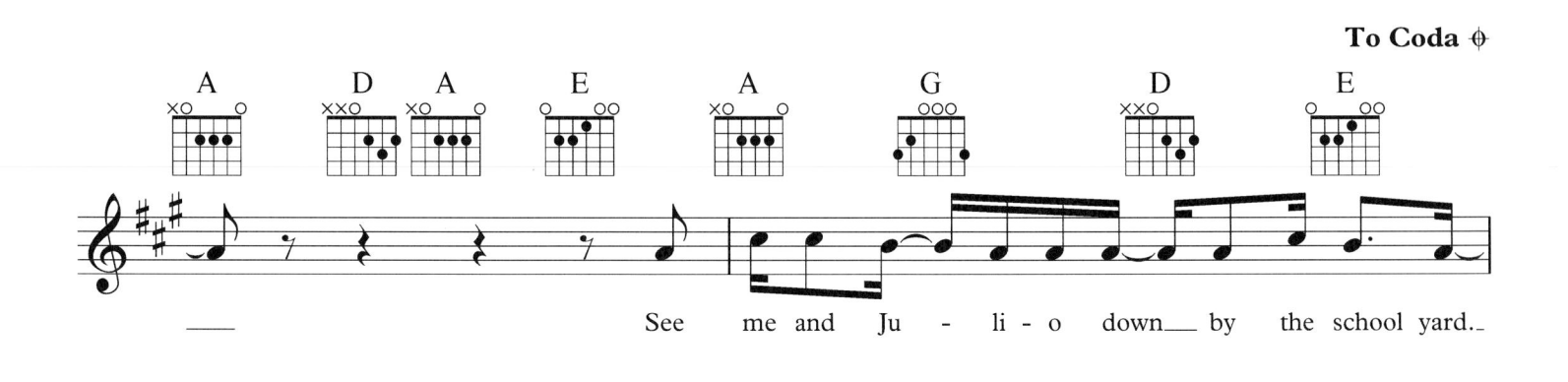

____   See me and Ju - li - o down__ by   the school yard.__

D.S. al Coda

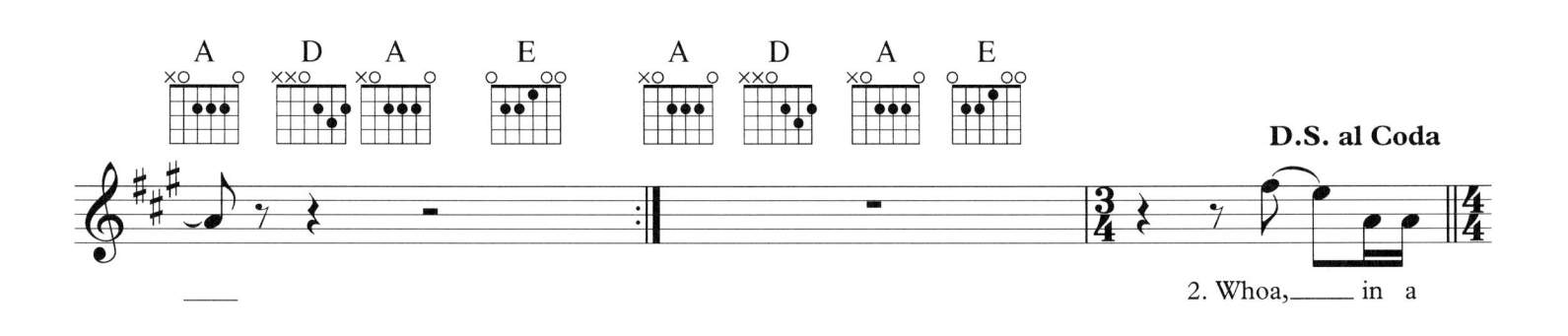

____   2. Whoa,____ in a

⊕ Coda

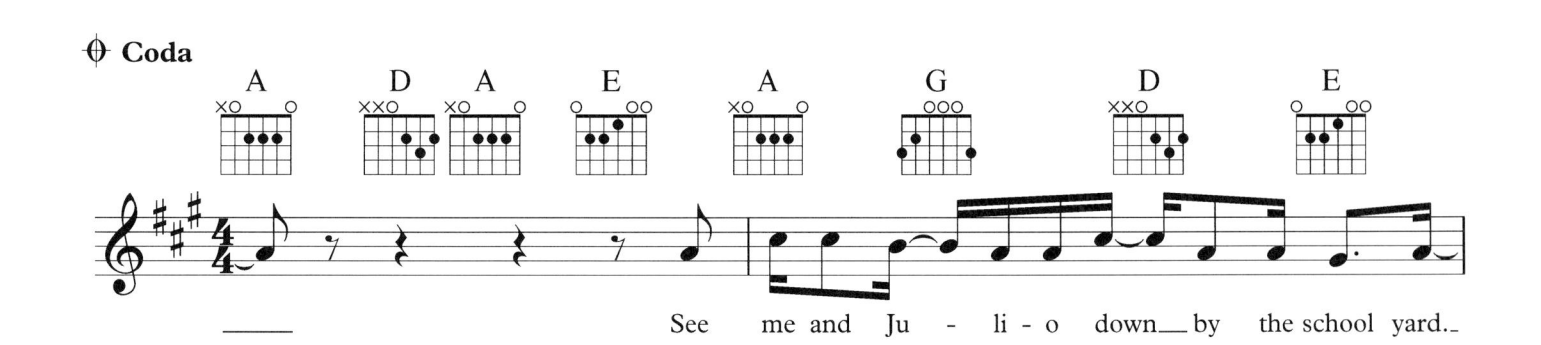

____   See me and Ju - li - o down__ by   the school yard.__

Repeat ad. lib. to fade

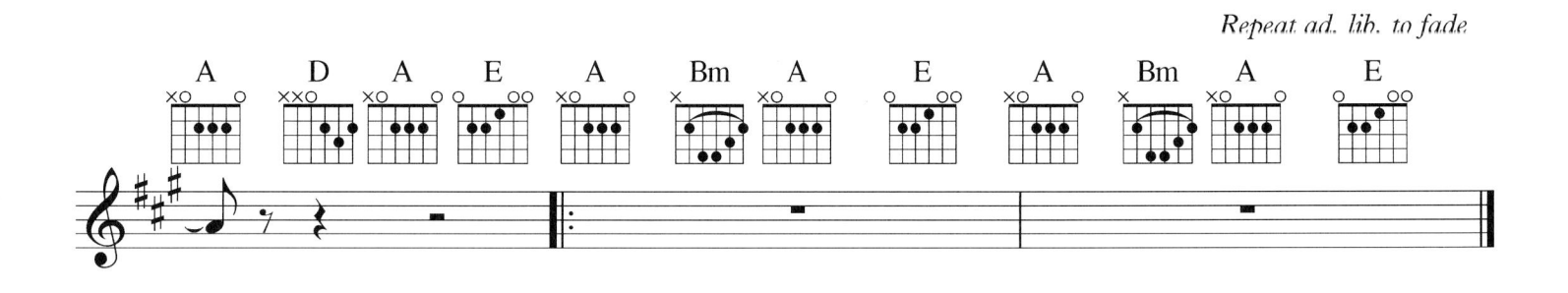

____

Moonshadow

Words & Music by Cat Stevens

© Copyright 1971 Cat Music Limited.
BMG Rights Management (UK) Limited, a BMG Chrysalis company.
All Rights Reserved. International Copyright Secured.

Picking style:

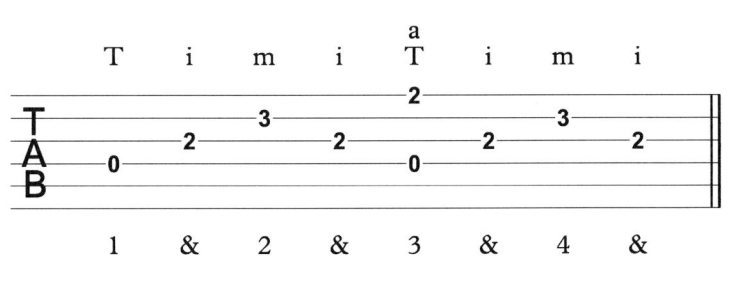

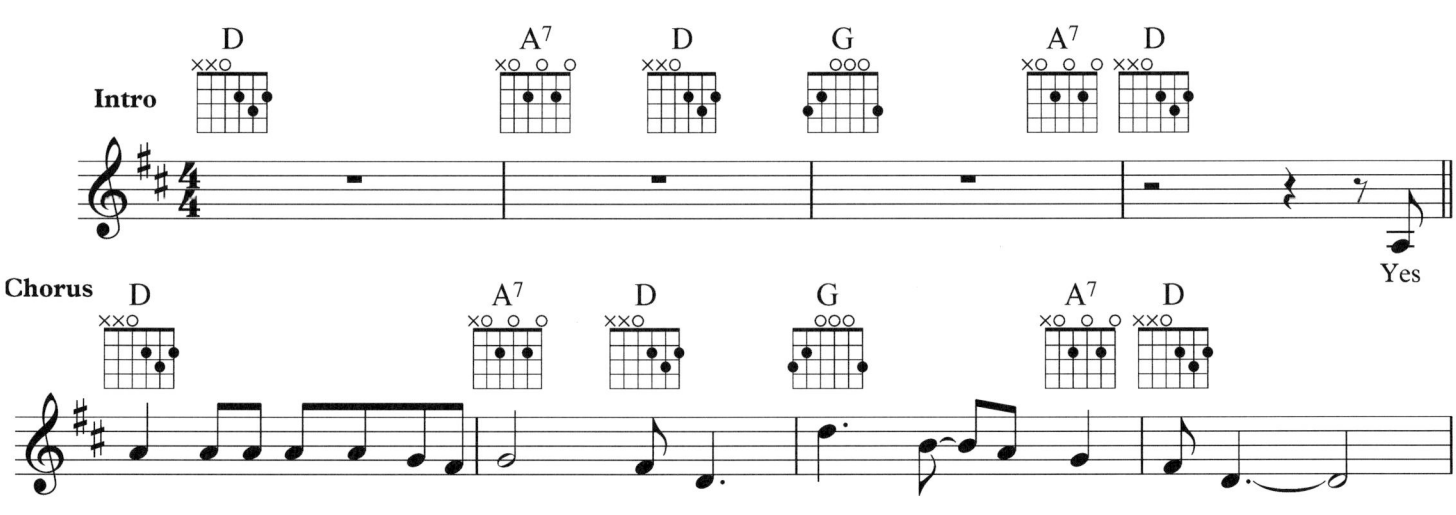

Intro

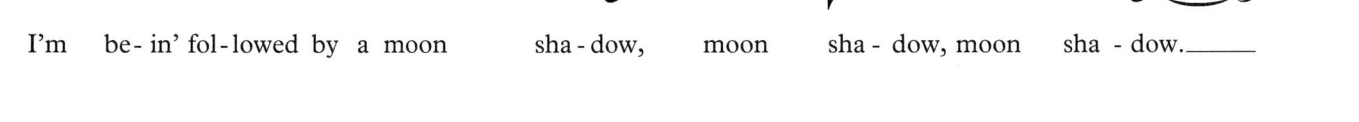

Yes

Chorus

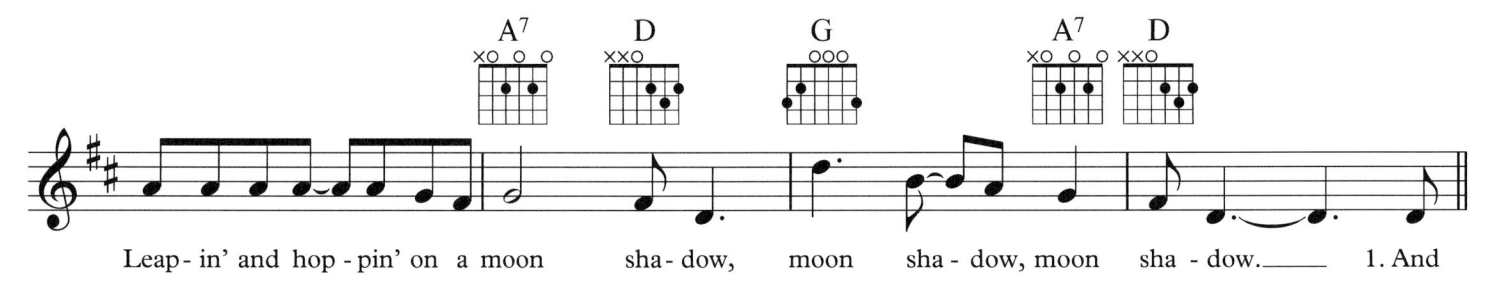

I'm be-in' fol-lowed by a moon sha-dow, moon sha-dow, moon sha-dow.____

Leap-in' and hop-pin' on a moon sha-dow, moon sha-dow, moon sha-dow.____ 1. And

Verse

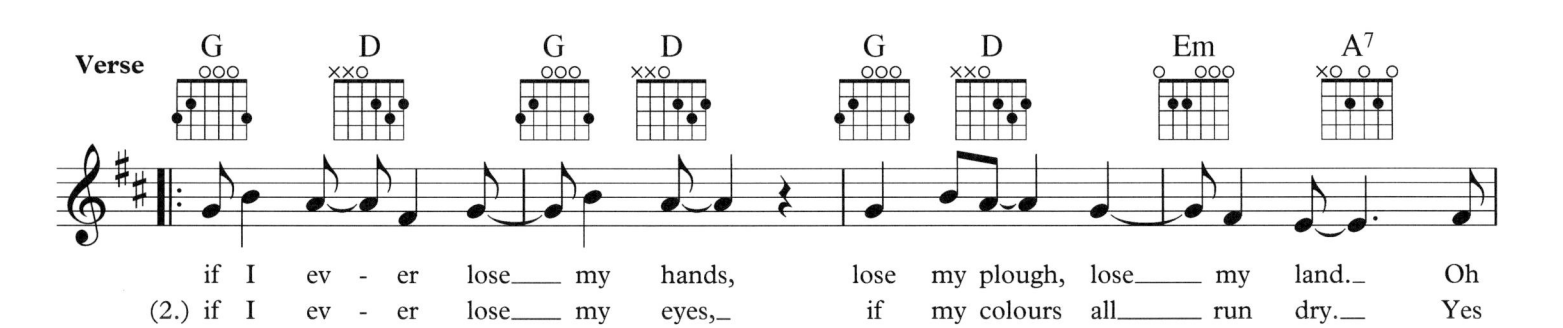

if I ev-er lose____ my hands, lose my plough, lose____ my land.__ Oh

(2.) if I ev-er lose____ my eyes,__ if my colours all____ run dry.__ Yes

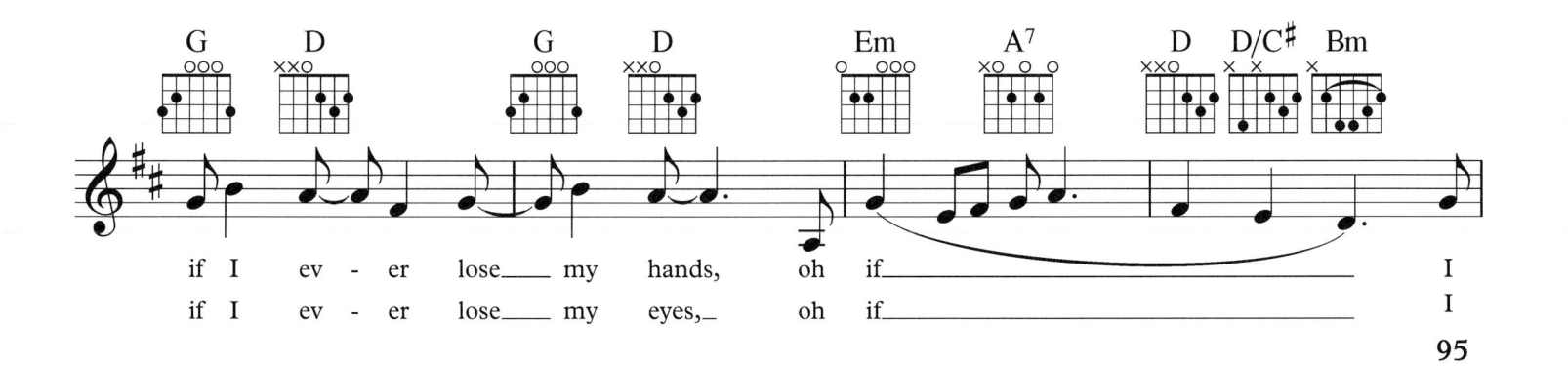

if I ev-er lose____ my hands, oh if_____ I

if I ev-er lose____ my eyes,__ oh if_____ I

95

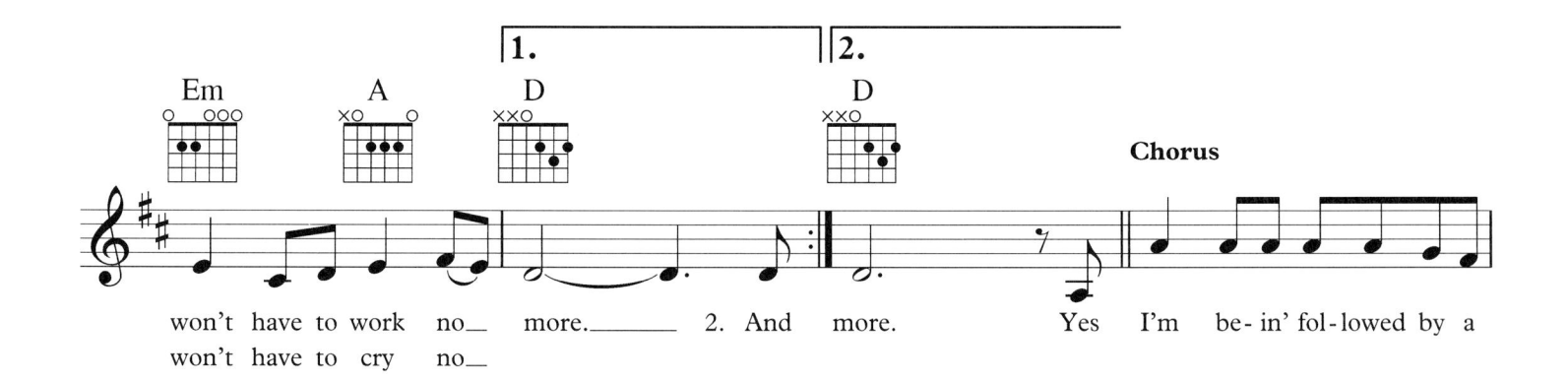

won't have to work no___ more._____ 2. And more.   Yes I'm be- in' fol-lowed by a
won't have to cry no___

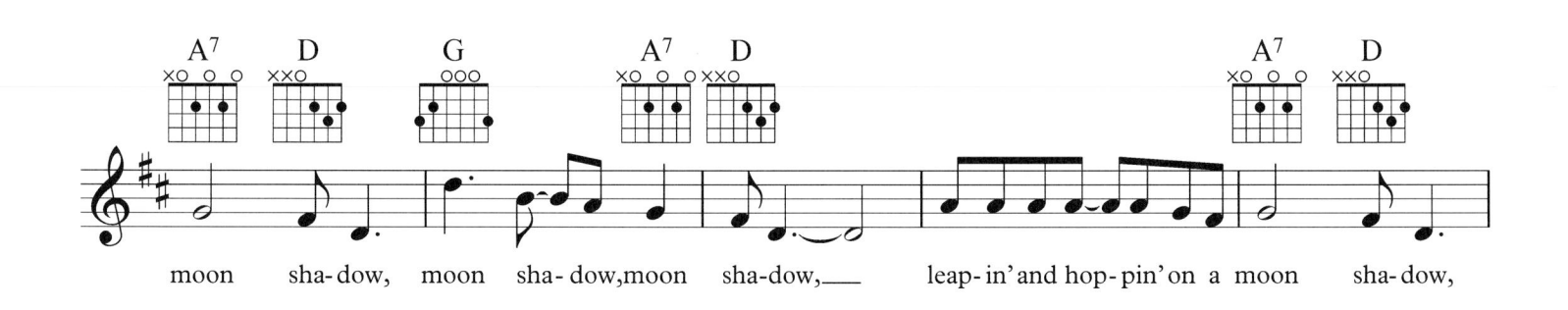

moon sha- dow, moon sha- dow, moon sha- dow,___   leap-in' and hop-pin' on a moon   sha- dow,

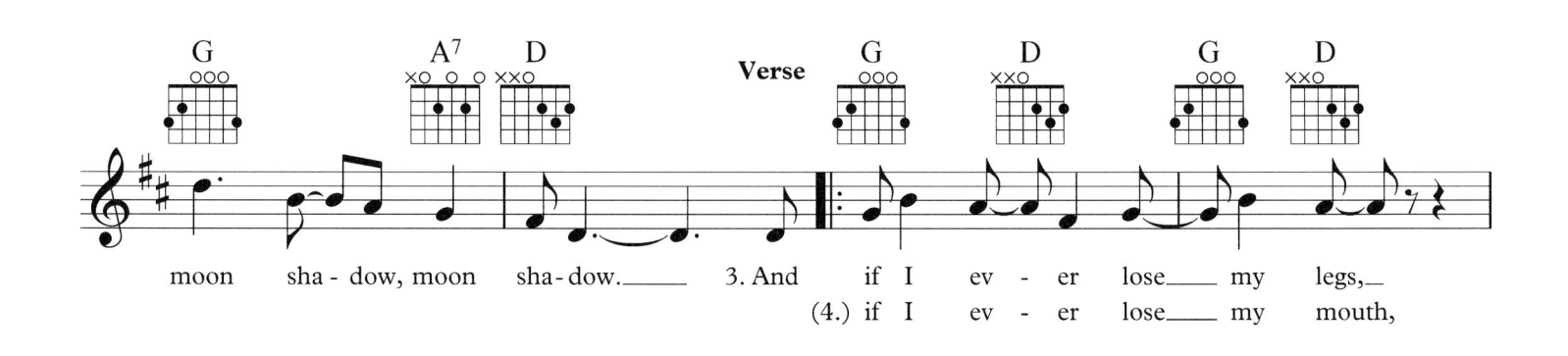

moon   sha - dow, moon   sha - dow.____   3. And   if I ev - er   lose___ my   legs,___   Oh
(4.) if I   ev - er   lose___ my   mouth,

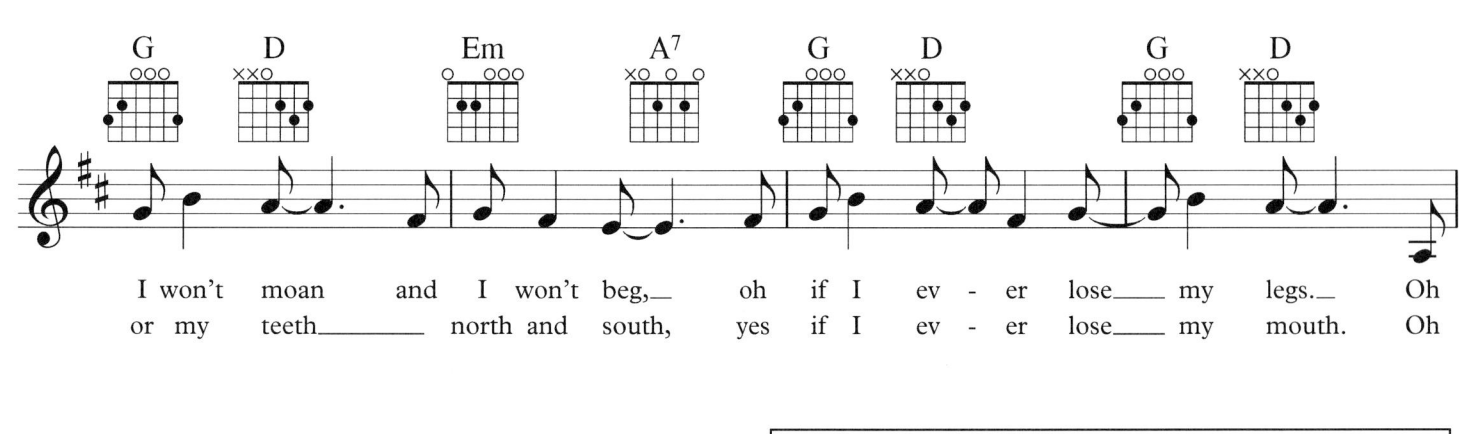

I won't moan   and I won't beg,___   oh if I ev - er lose___ my legs.___   Oh
or my   teeth_____ north and south,   yes if I ev - er lose___ my mouth.   Oh

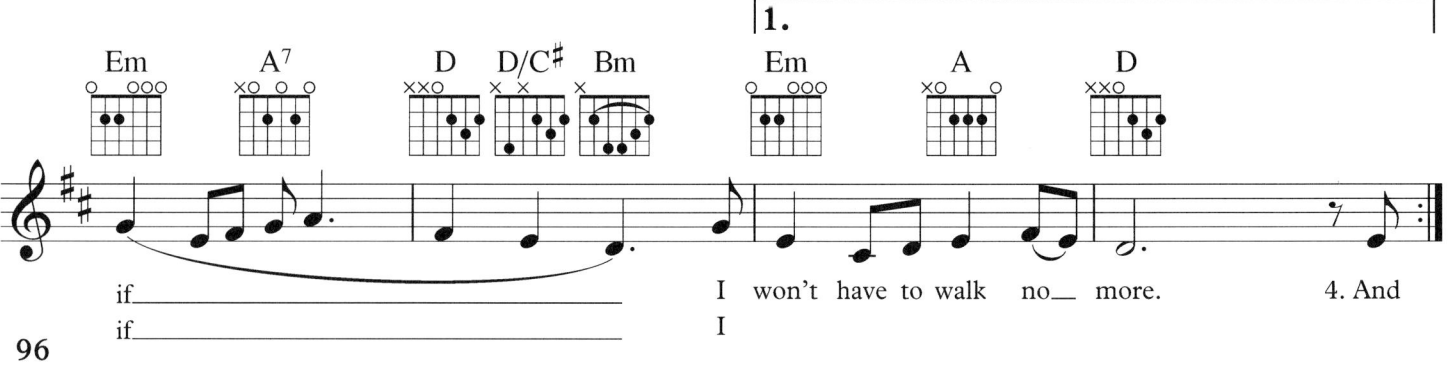

if_____   I won't have to walk no__ more.   4. And
if_____   I

96

won't have to talk.

Bridge

Did it take long to find___ me? I asked the faith - ful light.___

Did it take long to find___ me___ and are you gon-na stay the night?_____ Oh

Chorus

I'm be- ing' fol-lowed by a moon sha- dow, moon sha- dow, moon sha- dow,___

leap- in' and hop-pin' on a moon sha- dow, moon sha- dow, moon sha- dow,___

moon sha- dow, moon sha- dow,___ moon sha- dow, moon sha- dow.___

More Than Words

Words & Music by Nuno Bettencourt & Gary Cherone

© Copyright 1990 Color Me Blind Music, USA
Rondor Music International, Inc.
All Rights Reserved. International Copyright Secured.

The x symbols in the tab indicate a percussive knocking or slapping sound on beats 2 and 4. This is created by bringing the picking finge s down hard onto the strings.

To match recording, tune down one semitone

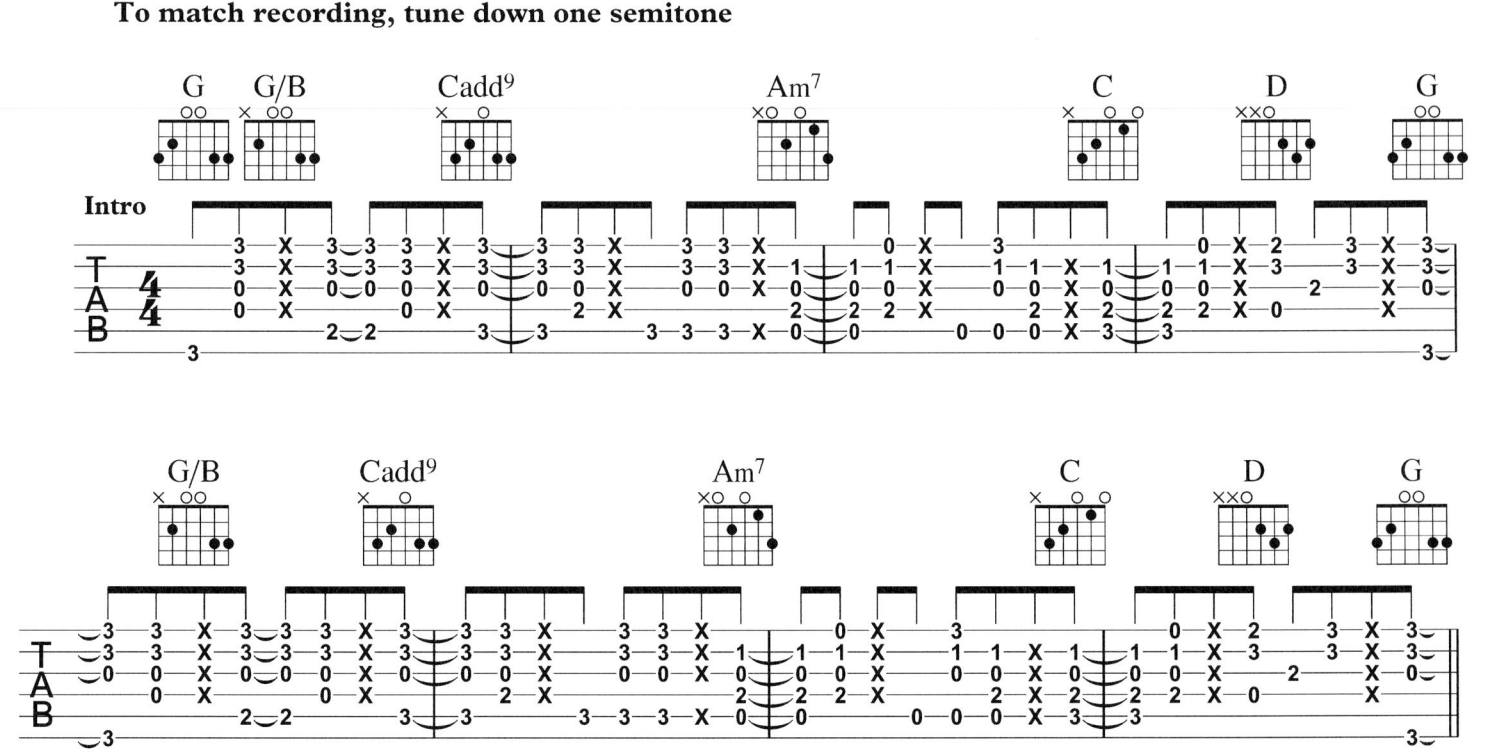

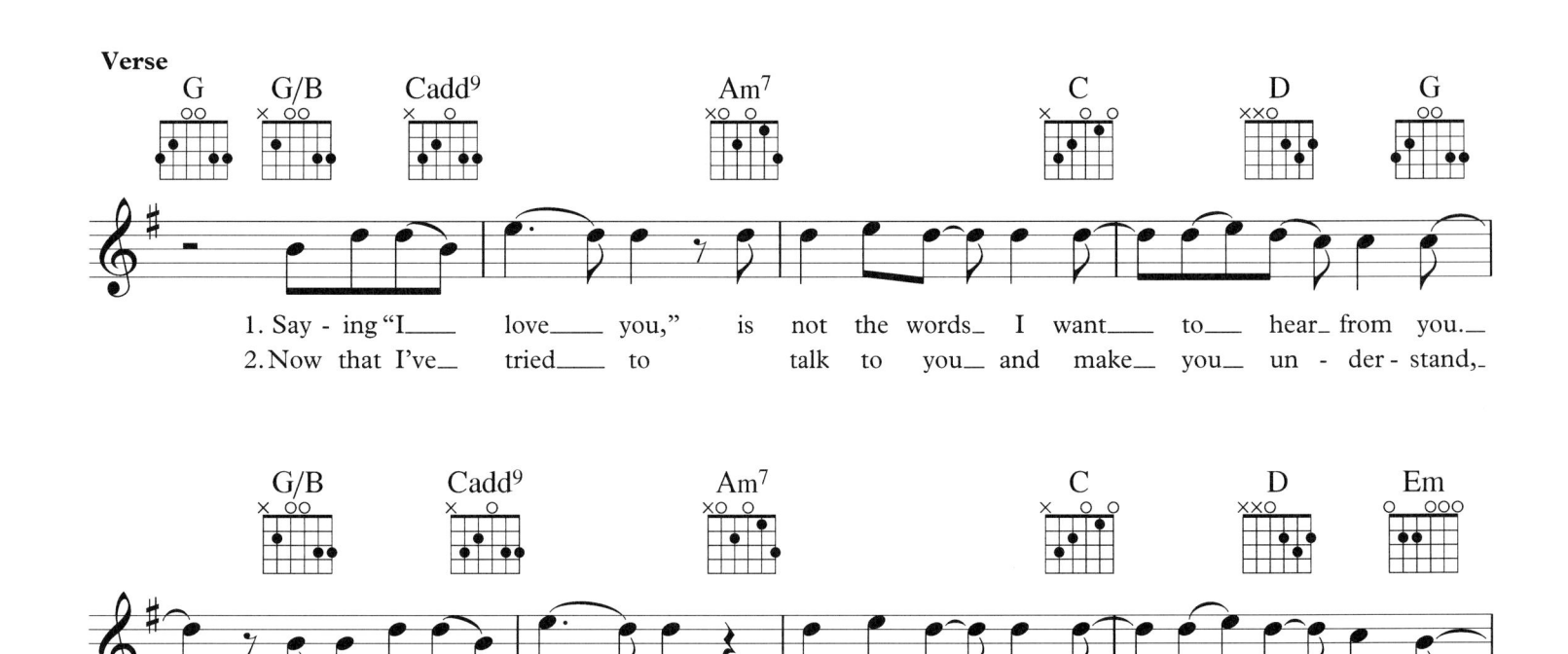

Verse

1. Say - ing "I____ love____ you," is not the words_ I want____ to__ hear_ from you._

2. Now that I've__ tried____ to talk to you_ and make__ you__ un - der - stand,_

____ It's not that I__ want____ you not to say,_ but if__ you__ on - ly knew_

____ all__ you__ have to do is close your eyes_ and just__ reach out__ your hand_

More than words to show you feel, that your love

for me is real. What would you say if I took

those words a - way? Then you could - n't make things new,

just by say - ing I love you.

La di da, la di da, la di da da da, more than words.

1.

La di da, la di da.

2.

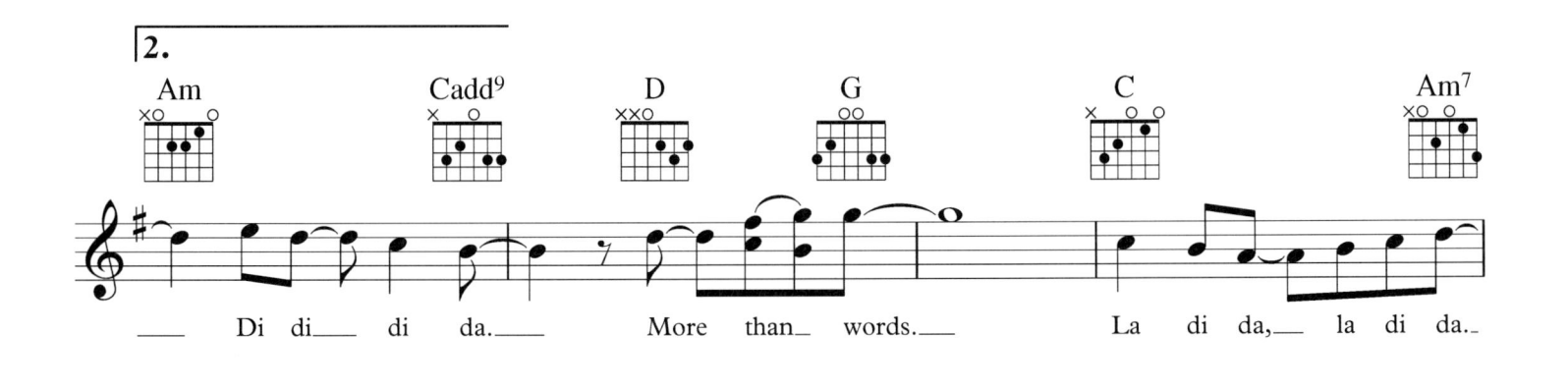

___ Di di___ di da.___ More than___ words.___ La di da,___ la di da.__

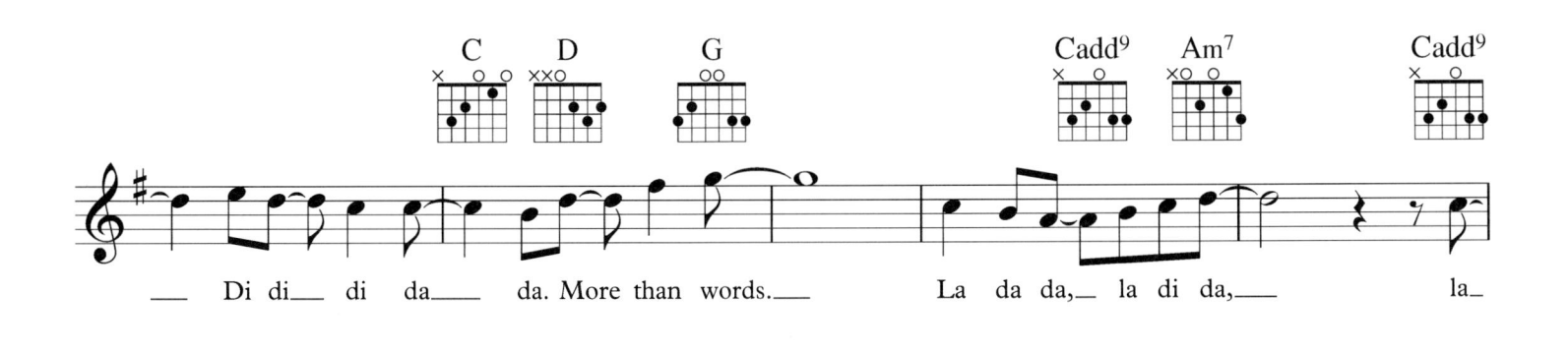

___ Di di___ di da___ da. More than words.___ La da da,___ la di da,___ la__

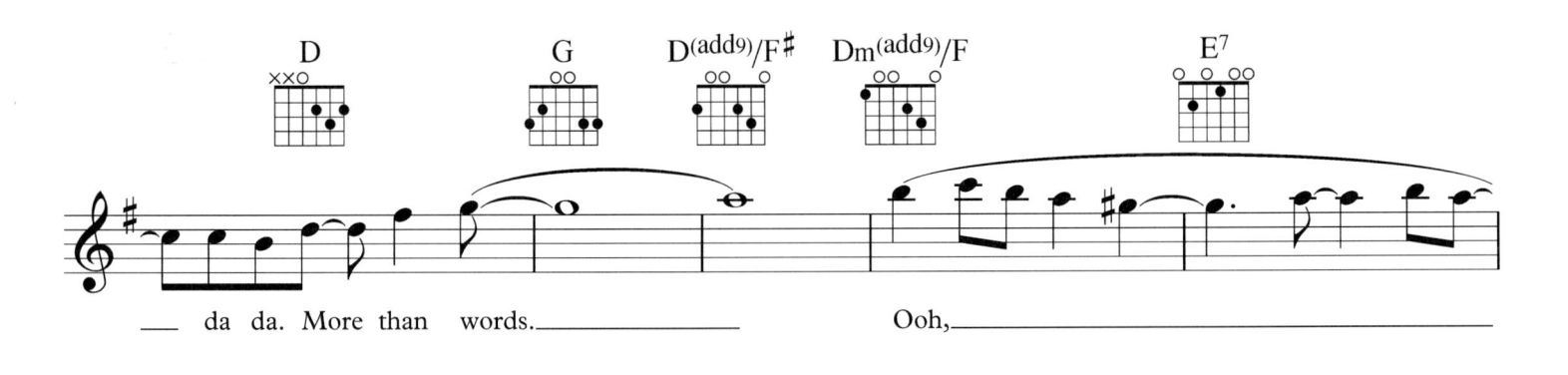

___ da da. More than___ words.___ Ooh,___

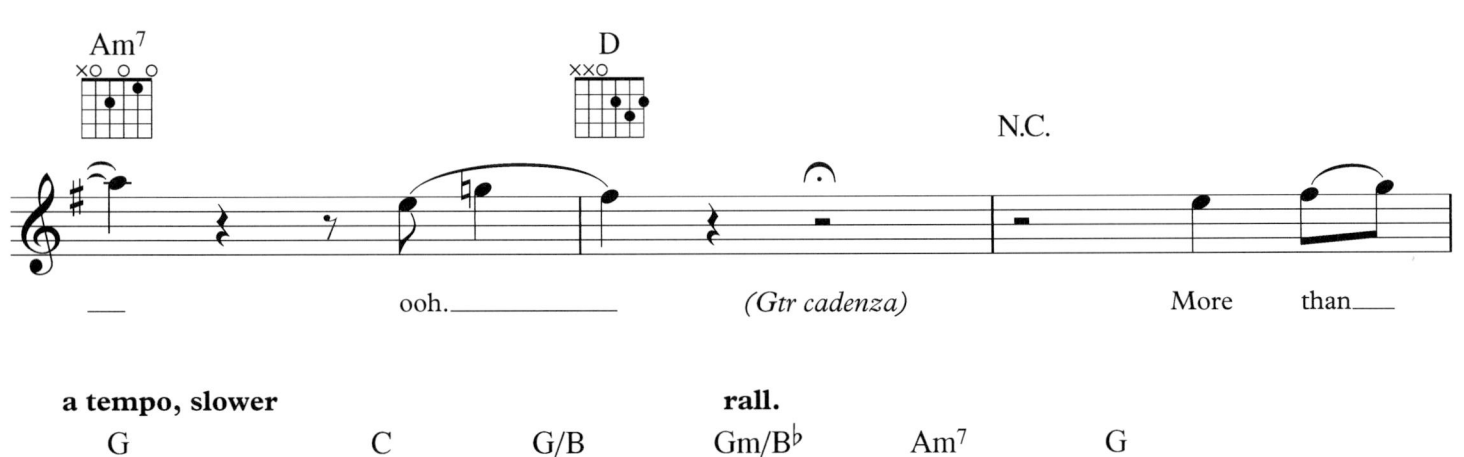

___ ooh.___ *(Gtr cadenza)* More than___

a tempo, slower   **rall.**

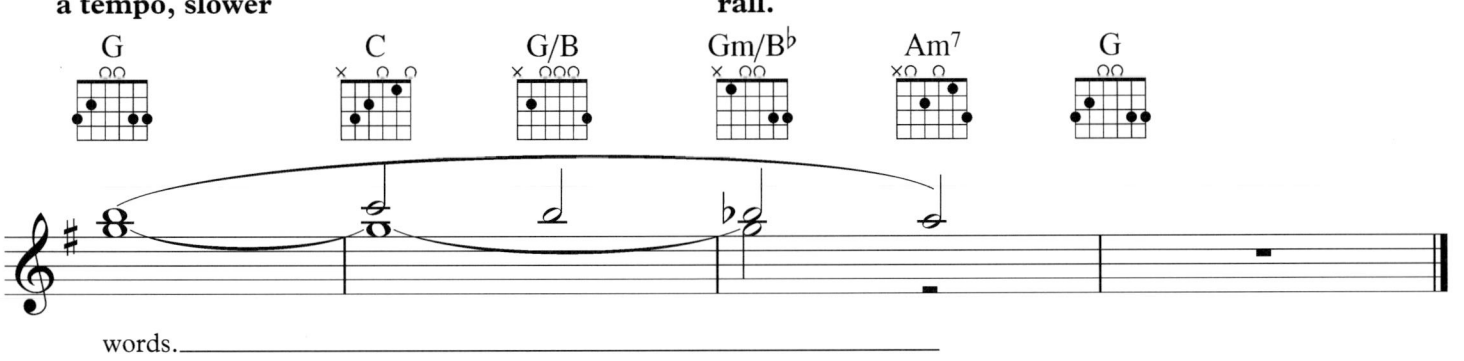

words.___

Ophelia

Words & Music by Jeremy Fraites & Wesley Schultz

© Copyright 2016 Kobalt Music Publishing Limited.
All Rights Reserved. International Copyright Secured.

(Piano arranged for guitar)

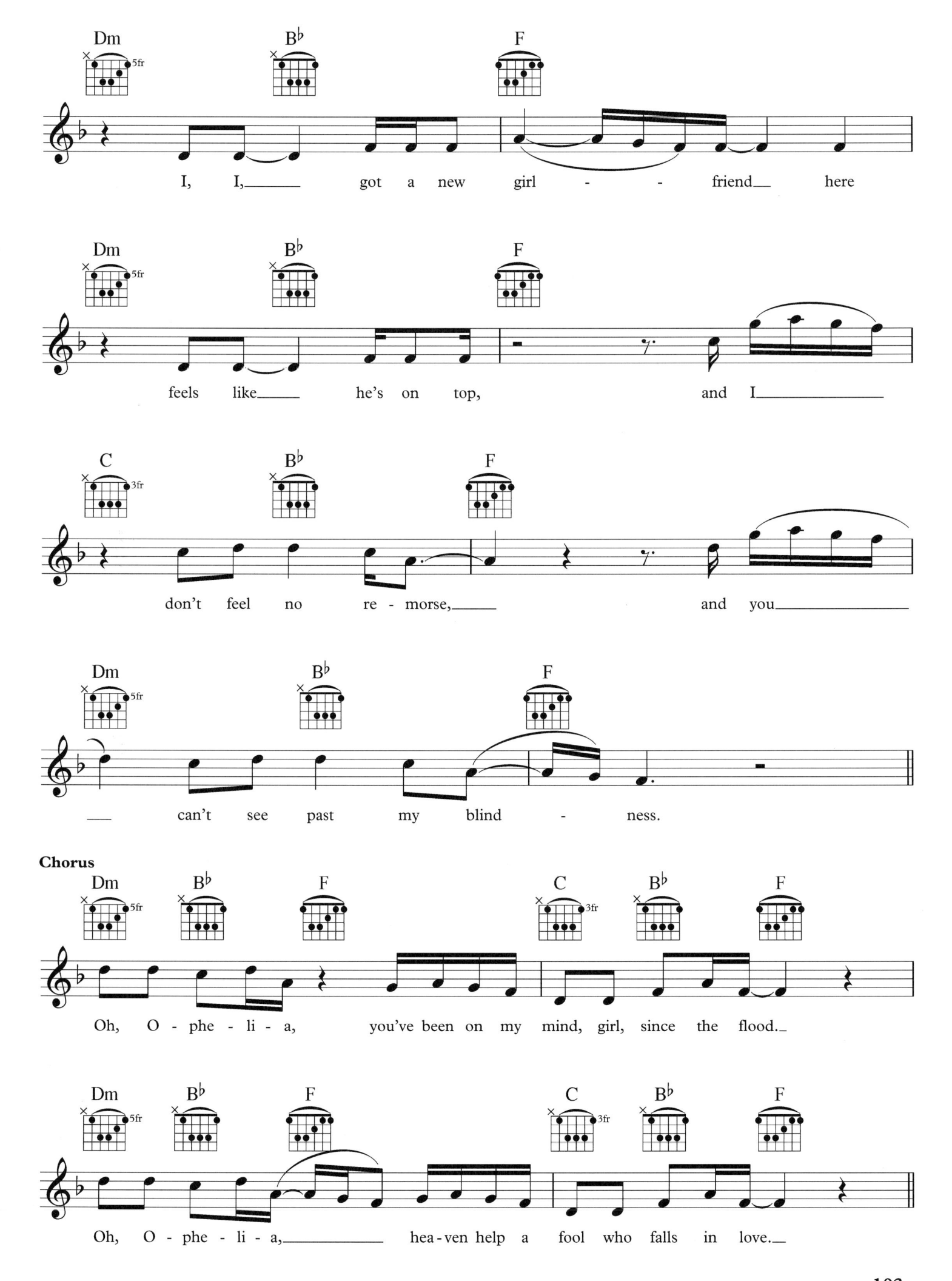

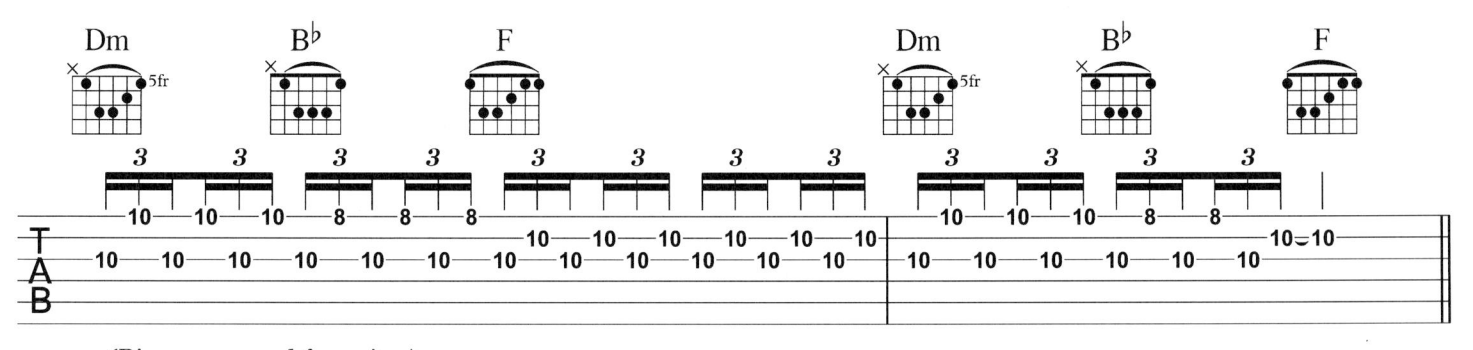

(Piano arranged for guitar)

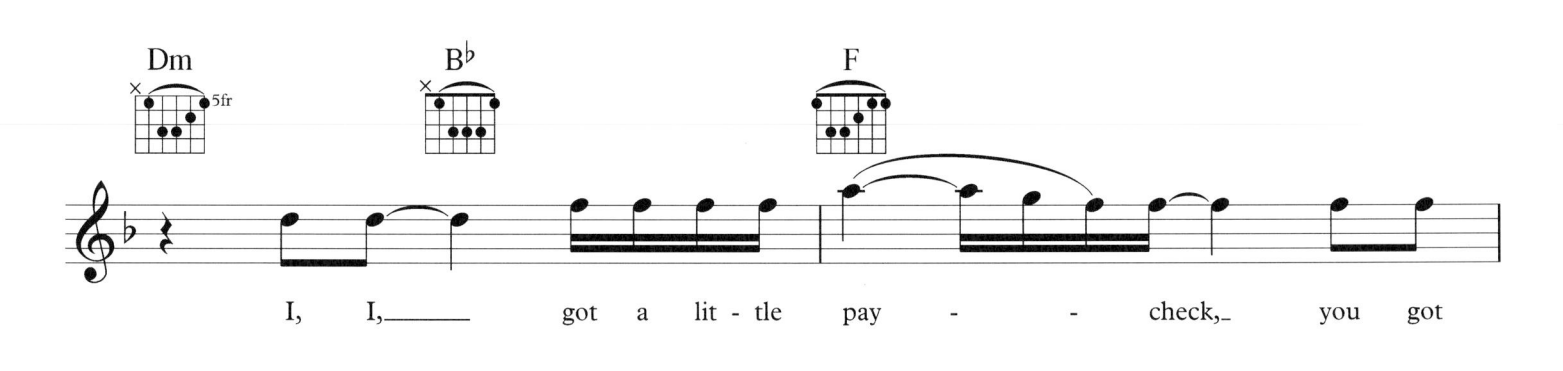

I, I,_____ got a lit - tle pay - - check,_ you got

big plans___ and you got - ta move,_____ and I_____

don't feel no - thing at all,___ and you_____ can't feel no - thing small._

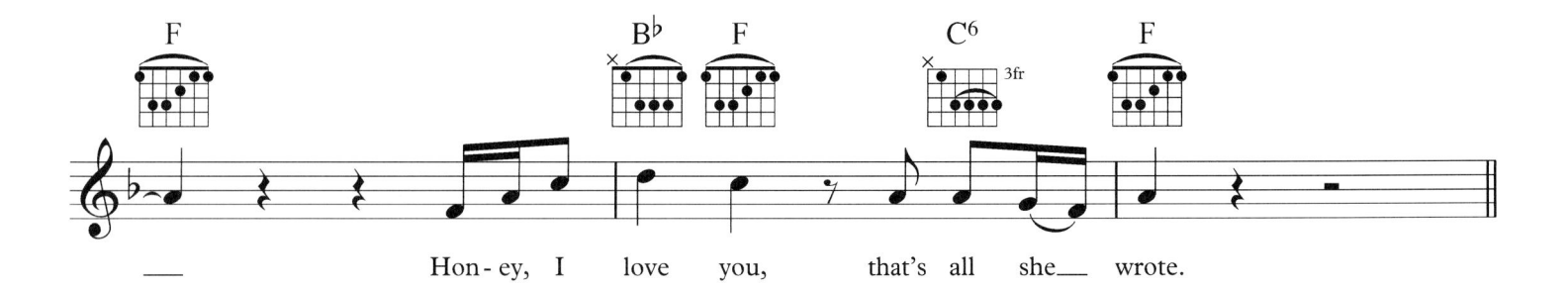

___ Hon - ey, I love you, that's all she__ wrote.

Chorus

Our House

Words & Music by Christopher Foreman & Cathal Smyth

© Copyright 1982 EMI Music Publishing Limited.
All Rights Reserved. International Copyright Secured.

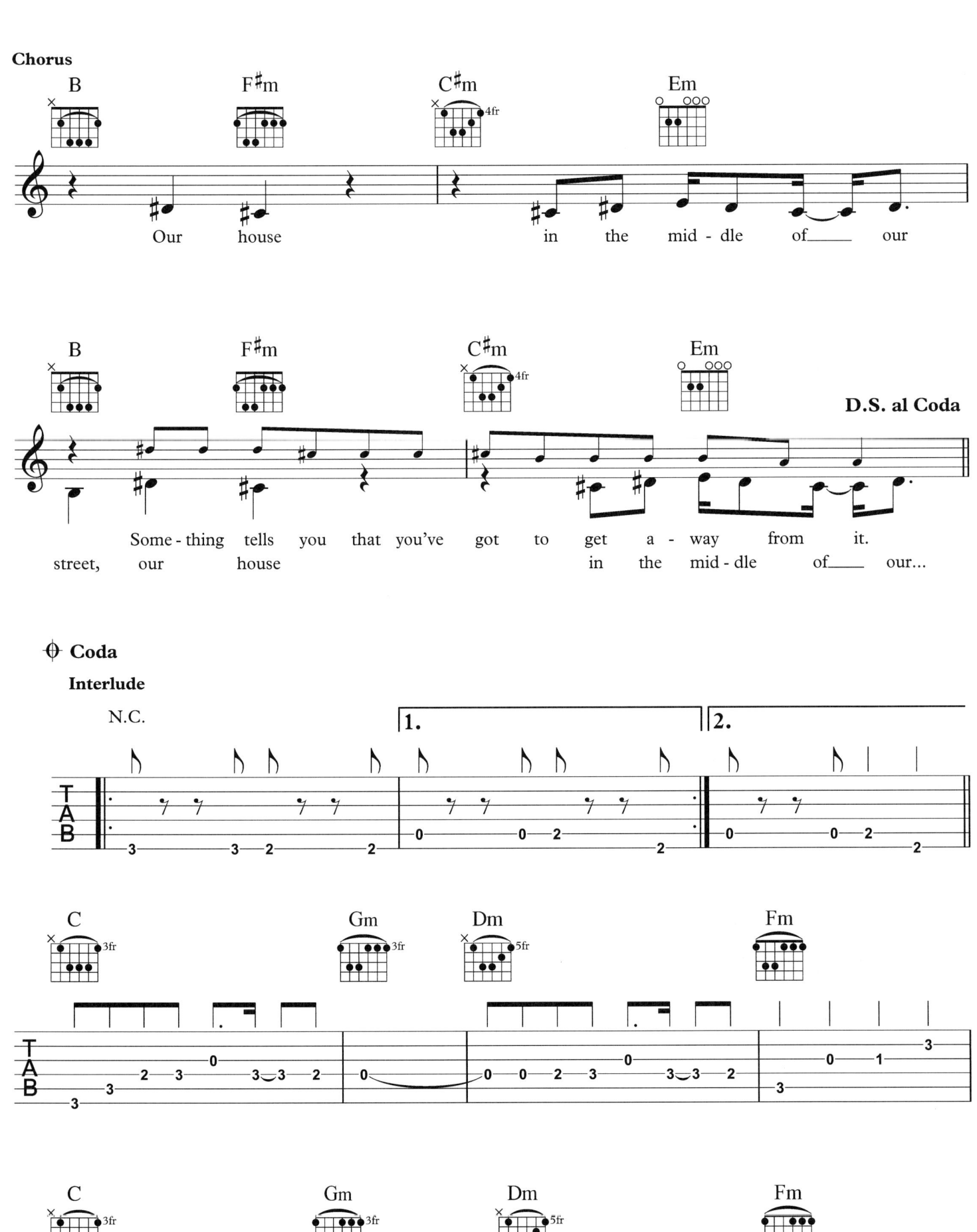

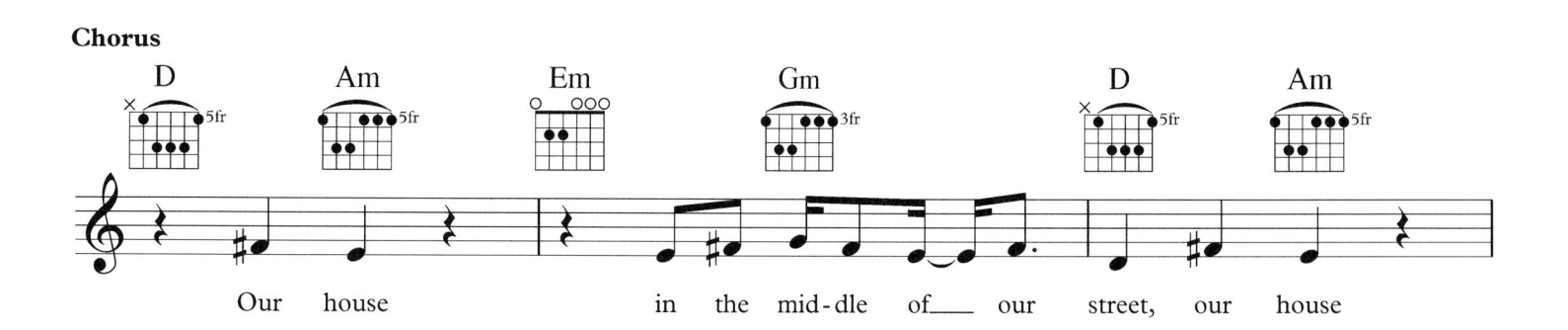

Our house   in the mid-dle of___ our   street, our house

Verse

in the mid-dle of___ our...   4. I re-mem-ber way back then, when ev-'ry-thing was true and when

5. Fa - ther wears_ his Sun-day

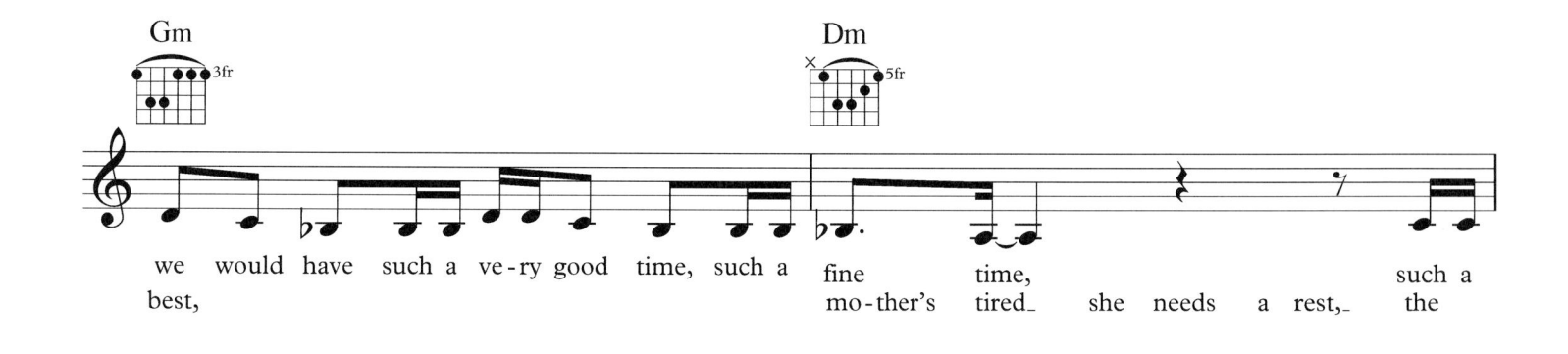

we   would have such a ve-ry good time, such a   fine   time,   such a

best,   mo-ther's tired_ she needs a rest,_ the

hap - py time.   And   I re-mem-ber how we'd play, sim-ply waste the day a-way,

kids are play-ing up_ down - stairs.   Sis - ter's sigh-ing in___ her

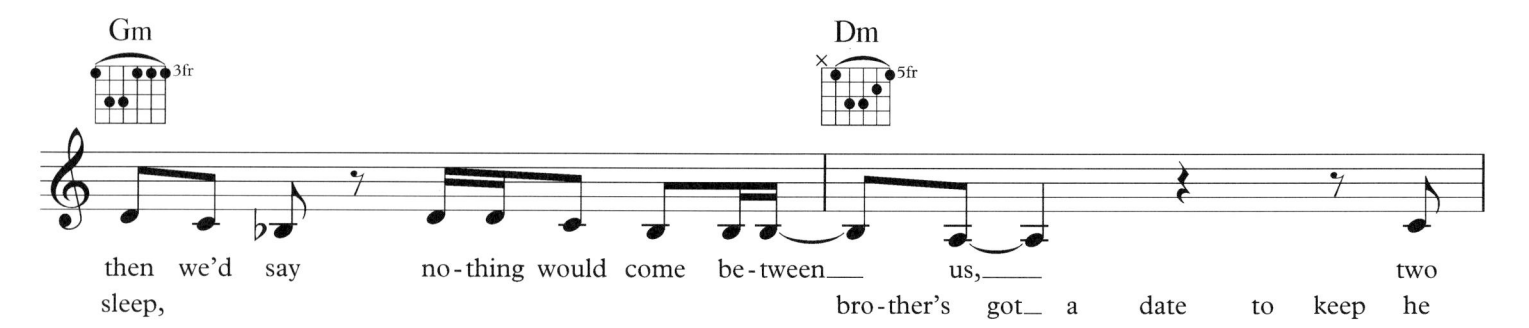

then we'd say   no-thing would come be-tween___ us,___   two

sleep,   bro-ther's got_ a date to keep he

Chorus

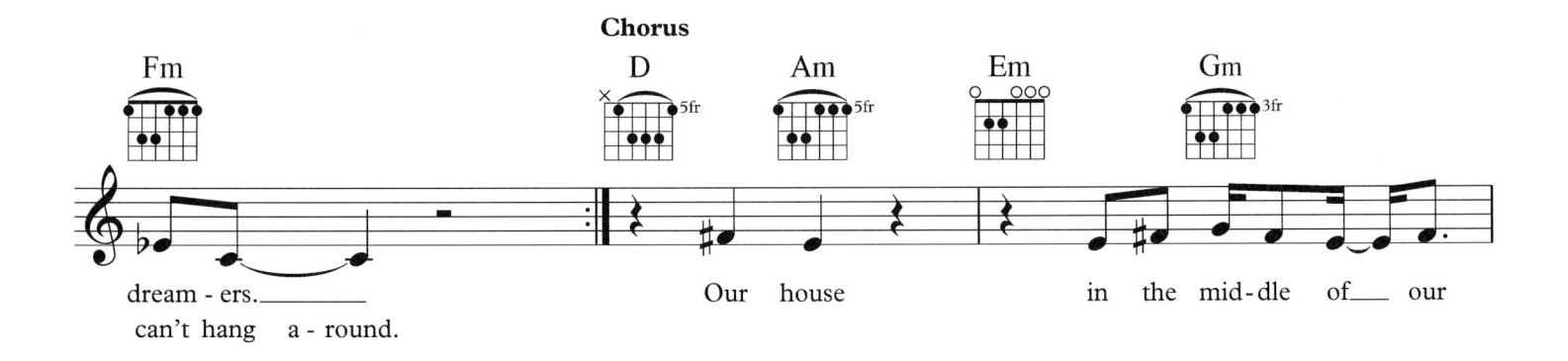

dream - ers._____
can't hang   a - round.

Our house   in the mid-dle of___ our

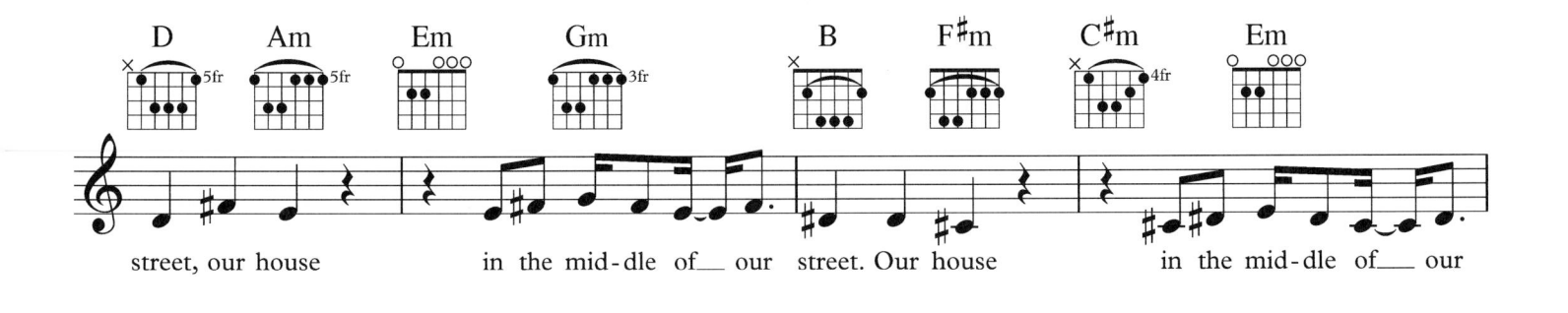

street, our house   in the mid-dle of___ our street. Our house   in the mid-dle of___ our

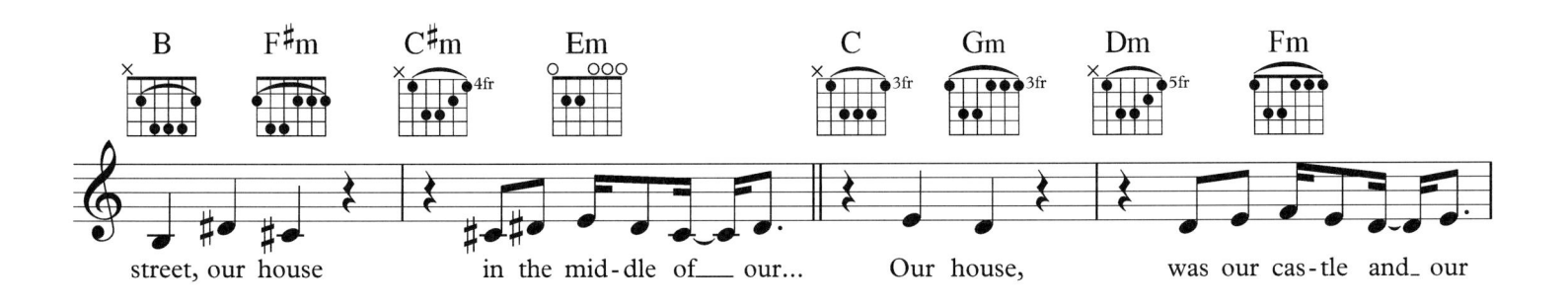

street, our house   in the mid-dle of___ our...   Our house,   was our cas-tle and_ our

Begin fade

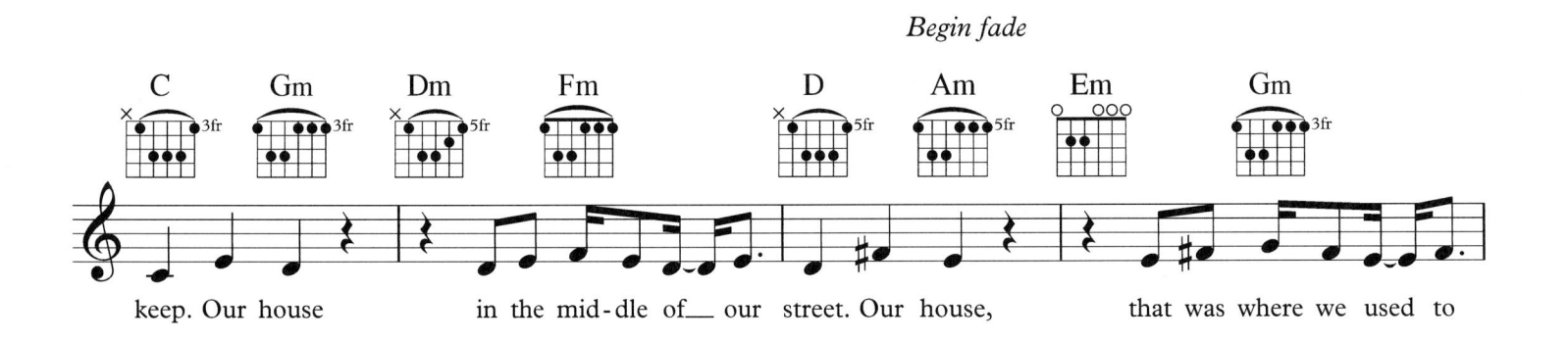

keep. Our house   in the mid-dle of___ our street. Our house,   that was where we used to

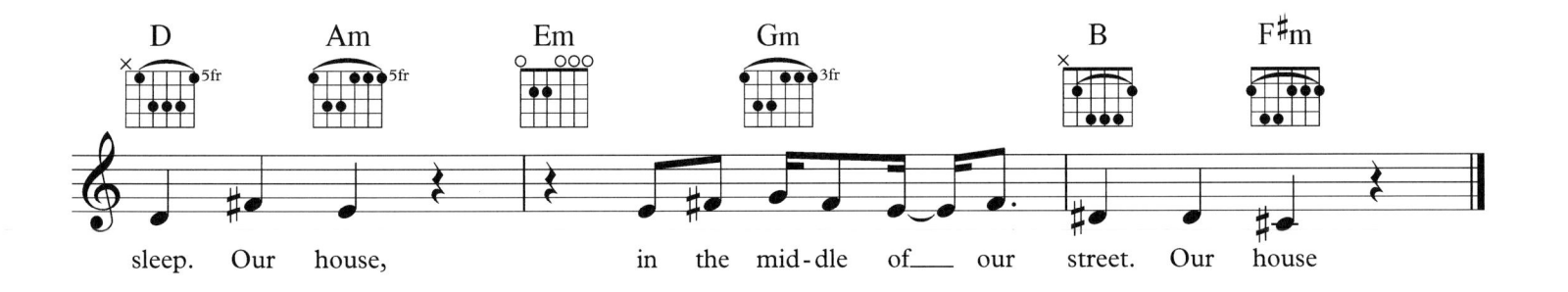

sleep. Our   house,   in the mid-dle of___ our   street. Our house

Rolling In The Deep

Words & Music by Paul Epworth & Adele Adkins

© Copyright 2010, 2011 Melted Stone Publishing Ltd.
Universal Music Publishing Limited/EMI Music Publishing Limited.
All Rights Reserved. International Copyright Secured.

Create the rock feel by strumming in constant eighths—but always with a short, palm-muted down-strum.

Capo: Fret 3

Intro B⁵

Verse

B⁵   F♯⁵

1. There's a_____ fire_____ start - ing in my_____ heart,
2. See how__ I'll__ leave with ev - 'ry piece of you.
3. (𝄋) Ba - by,__ I_____ have no sto - ry to be told. But

A⁵   F♯⁵   A⁵

reach - ing_____ a fe - ver pitch and it's bring-ing me out the dark.____
Don't un - der - es - ti - mate the things that I will do.____
I've heard_____ one on you now I'm gon - na make your head burn.

B⁵   F♯⁵

Fin - al - ly_____ I can see you crys - tal clear.
There's a_____ fire_____ start - ing in my heart,
Think of__ me_____ in the depths of your des - pair.

A⁵   F♯⁵   A⁵

Go a - head__ and sell me out and I'll lay your shit bare.
reach - ing_____ a fe - ver pitch and it's bring - ing me out the dark.
Make a_____ home down there as mine sure won't be shared.

Running Scared

Words & Music by Roy Orbison & Joe Melson

© Copyright 1961 (Renewed 1989) Roy Orbison Music Company/Barbara Orbison Music Company,
USA/Sony/ATV Acuff Rose Musi .
Kobalt Music Publishing Limited/Sony/ATV Music Publishing.
All Rights Reserved. International Copyright Secured.

C#m **E7**

scared,_____ you loved him so._____ Just run - ning

A **Bm**

scared,_____ a - fraid to lose._____ If he came

C#m **E7** **A** **A7** **D**

back,_____ which one would you choose? Then all at once,

he was stand-ing there, so sure of him-self; his head in the air.__

My heart was break - ing, which one would it be?

E7 **A**

You turned a - round and walked a - way with me.

Shape Of My Heart

Words & Music by Sting & Dominic Miller

© Copyright 1992 Magnetic Publishing Limited/Steerpike Limited.
EMI Music Publishing Limited.
All Rights Reserved. International Copyright Secured.

> The original guitar tab for the intro, shown here, can be played throughout the song. Alternatively strum the given chord shapes.

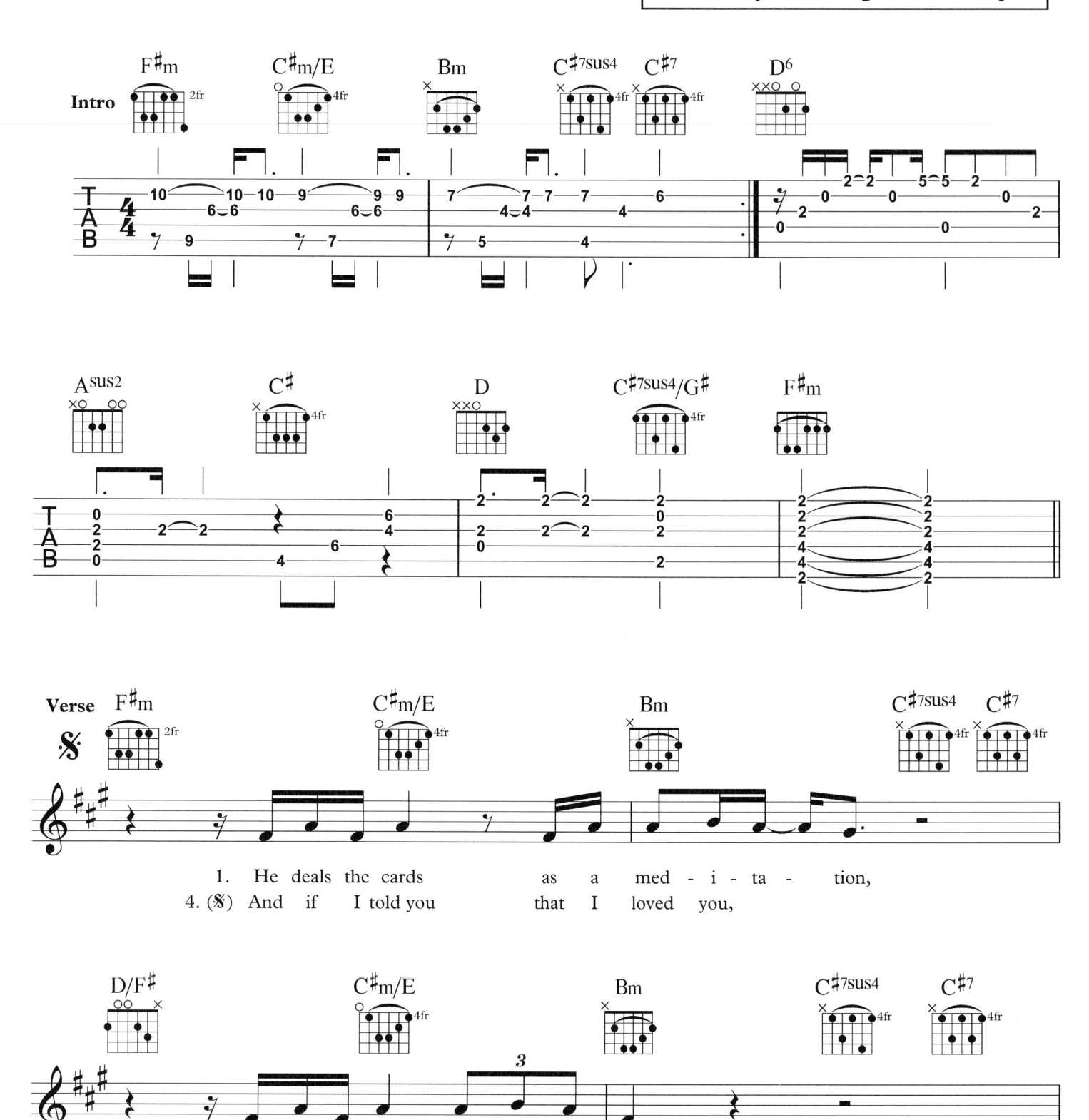

Verse

1. He deals the cards as a med - i - ta - tion,
4. (𝄋) And if I told you that I loved you,

and those he plays nev - er sus - pect.
you'd may - be think there's some - thing wrong.

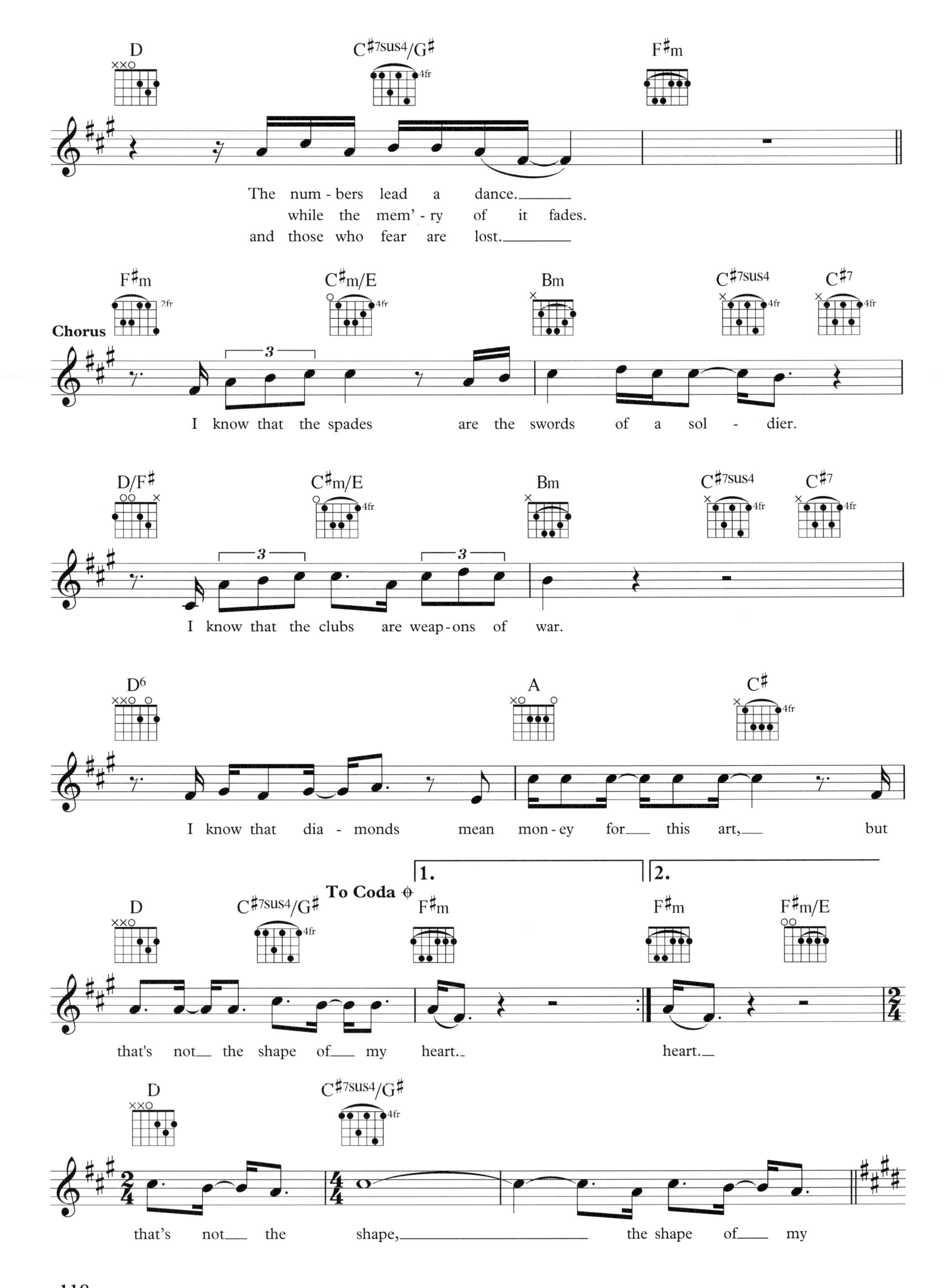

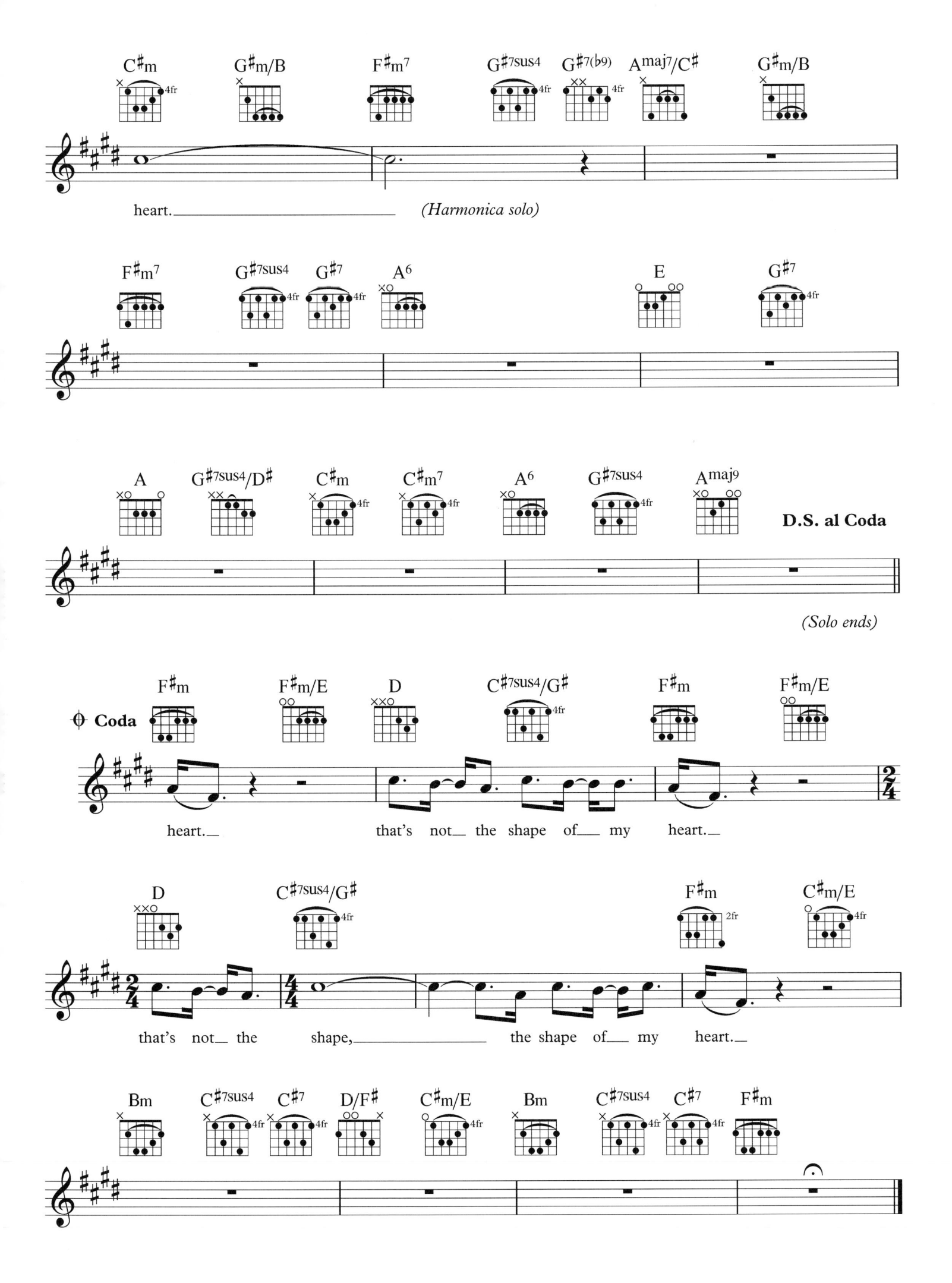

heart._____ *(Harmonica solo)*

D.S. al Coda

(Solo ends)

Coda

heart.__ that's not__ the shape of__ my heart.__

that's not__ the shape,_____ the shape of__ my heart.__

She's Always A Woman

Words & Music by Billy Joel

© Copyright 1977, 1978 Impulsive Music.
Rondor Music International.
All Rights Reserved. International Copyright Secured.

Verse

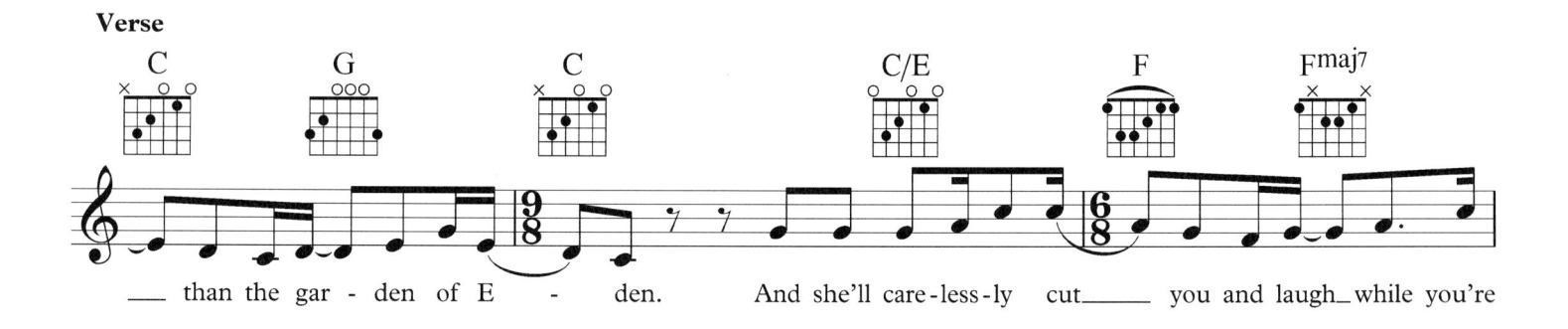

than the gar - den of E - den. And she'll care-less-ly cut___ you and laugh_ while you're

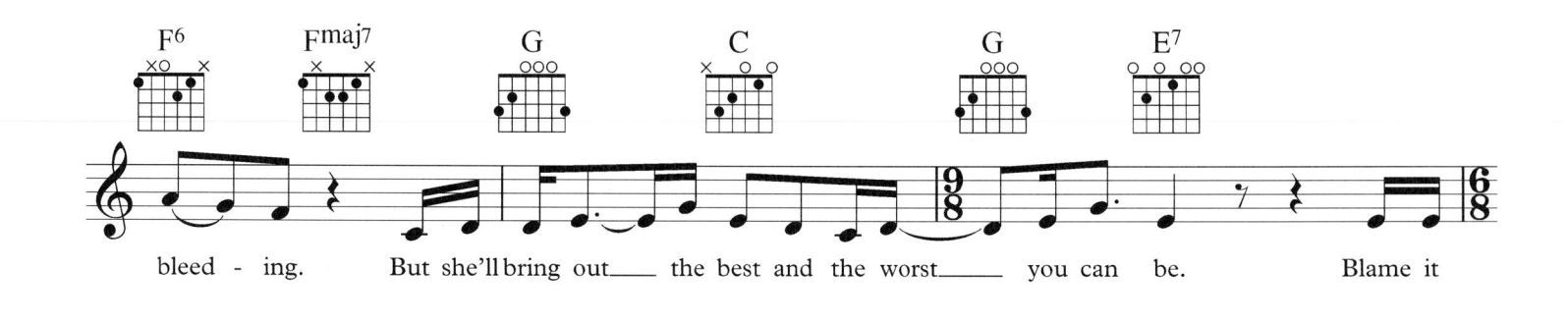

bleed - ing. But she'll bring out___ the best and the worst___ you can be. Blame it

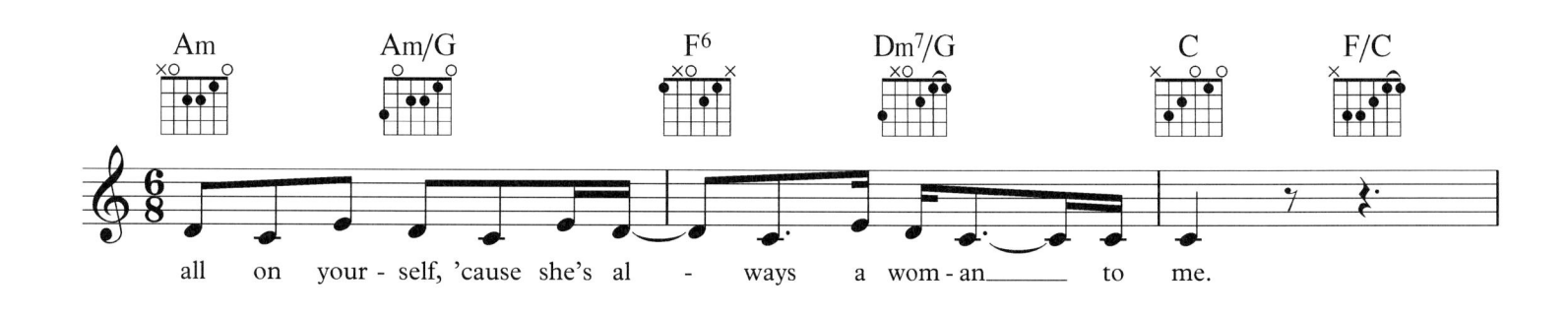

all on your - self, 'cause she's al - ways a wom - an_____ to me.

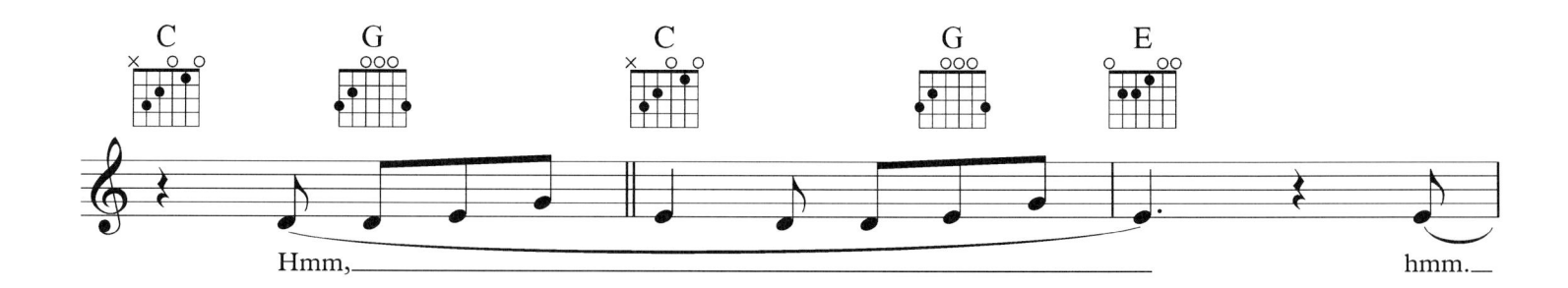

Hmm,_____ hmm._

D.S. al Coda

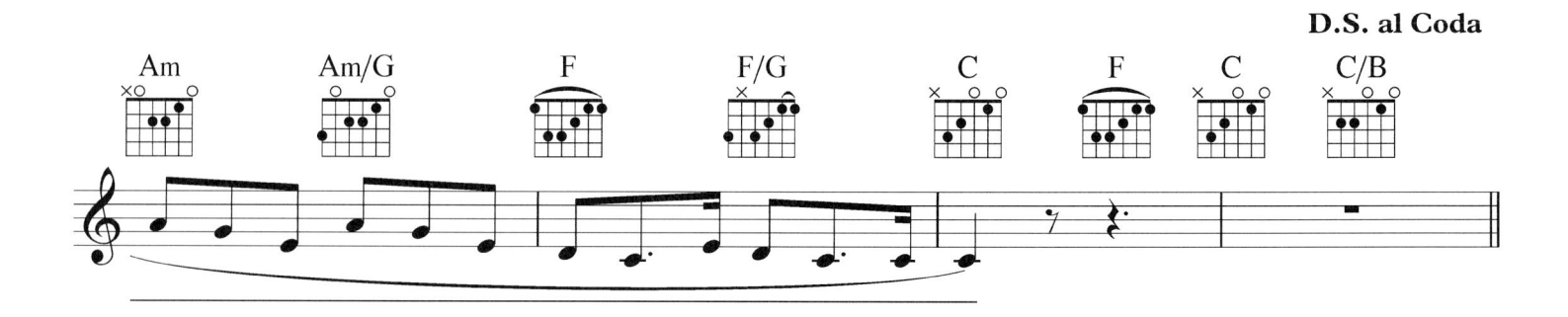

Verse

She is fre-quent-ly kind___ and she's sud-den-ly cruel.___ Well, she can do as she plea-

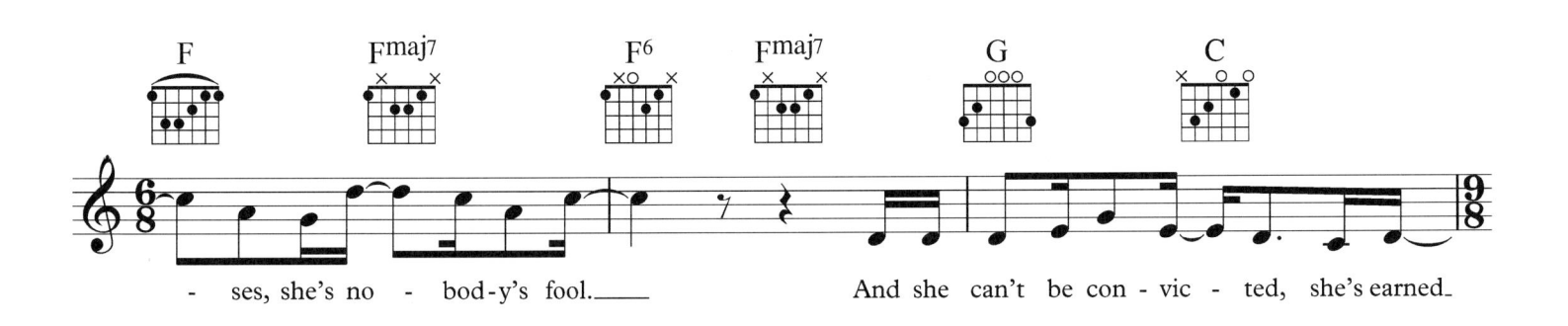

- ses, she's no - bod-y's fool.___ And she can't be con - vic - ted, she's earned_

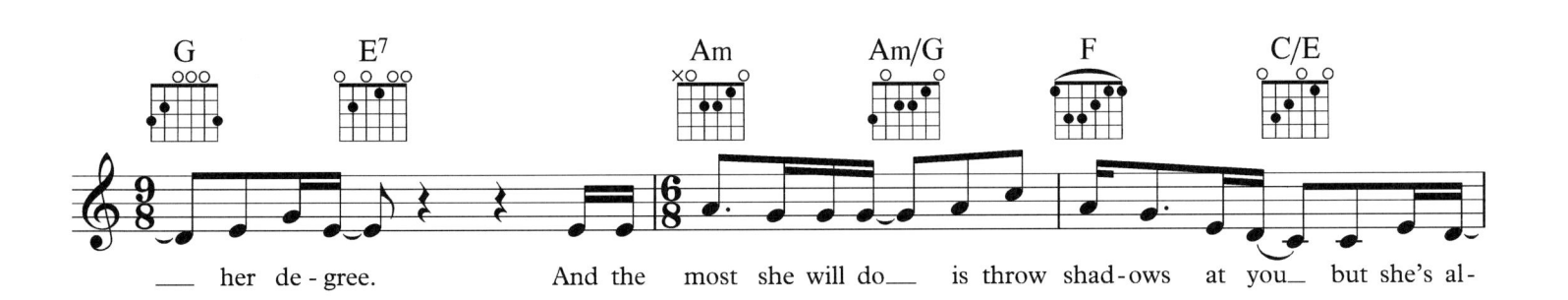

___ her de - gree. And the most she will do___ is throw shad-ows at you_ but she's al-

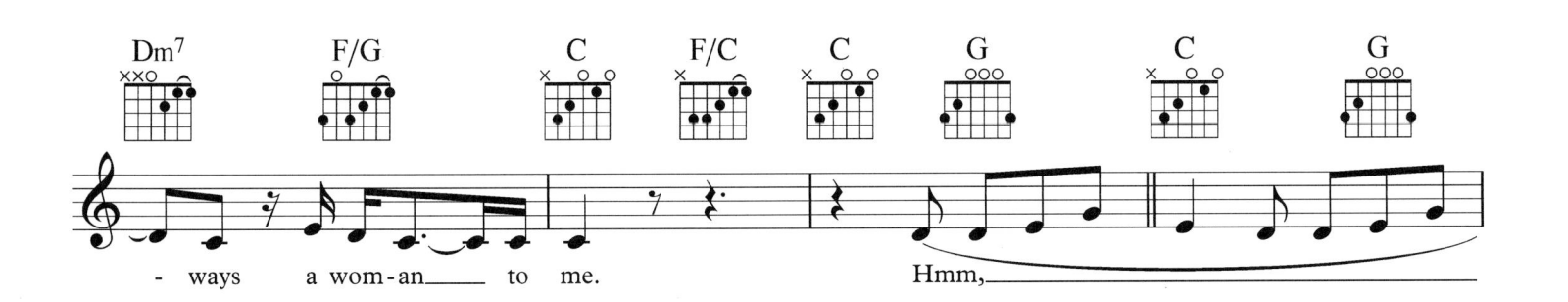

- ways a wom-an___ to me. Hmm,_____

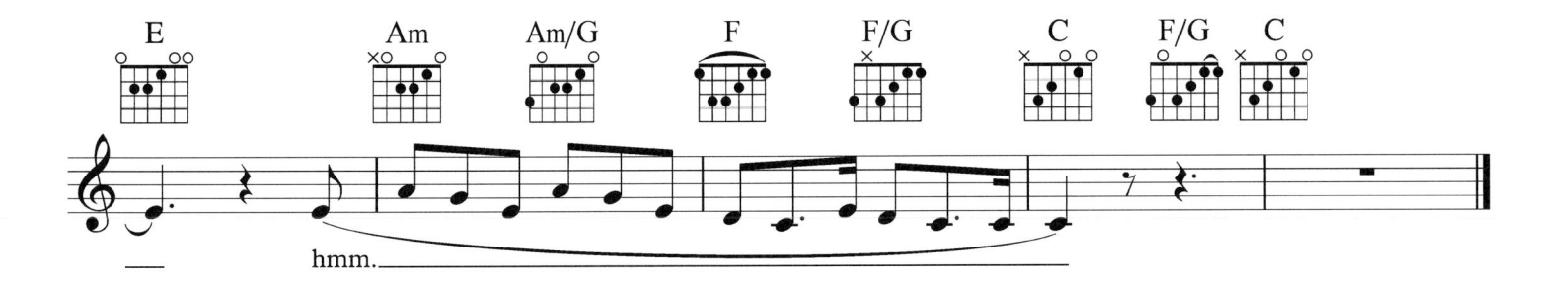

___ hmm._____

One Love (People Get Ready)

Words & Music by Bob Marley & Curtis Mayfiel

© Copyright 1977 Odnil Music Limited/Warner Tamerlane Publishing Corporation/Mijac Music.
Blue Mountain Music Limited/Warner/Chappell North America Limited/Sony/ATV Music Publishing.
All Rights Reserved. International Copyright Secured.

The typical *skank* rhythm heard in reggae and ska is played with muted chords on beats 2 and 4, occasionally followed by a ghosted up-strum.

Barre chords are easy to mute by relaxing the barring finger so try barre chord shapes too.

Strumming style:

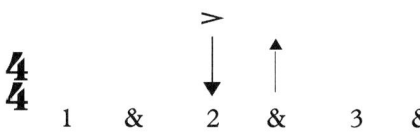

Capo: Fret 3

Intro

| G | D | C | G | D | D7 | G |

Verse

| G | D | C | G |

One love,—   one heart.—   Let's   get   to-geth - er and

| D | G |

feel   all   right.   Hear the chil-dren cry - ing. (One   love.)   Hear the chil-dren

As   it   was   in   the   be - gin-ning, (One   love.)   so shall it be   in   the

I'm   plead-ing to___ man - kind. (One   love.)   Oh,   Lord._____

To Coda ⊕

| D | C | G |

cry - ing. (One   heart.)   Say - in',

end.___ (One   heart.)   Al - right, "Give thanks and praise to the Lord,   and I will

_____ (One   heart.)   Whoa.

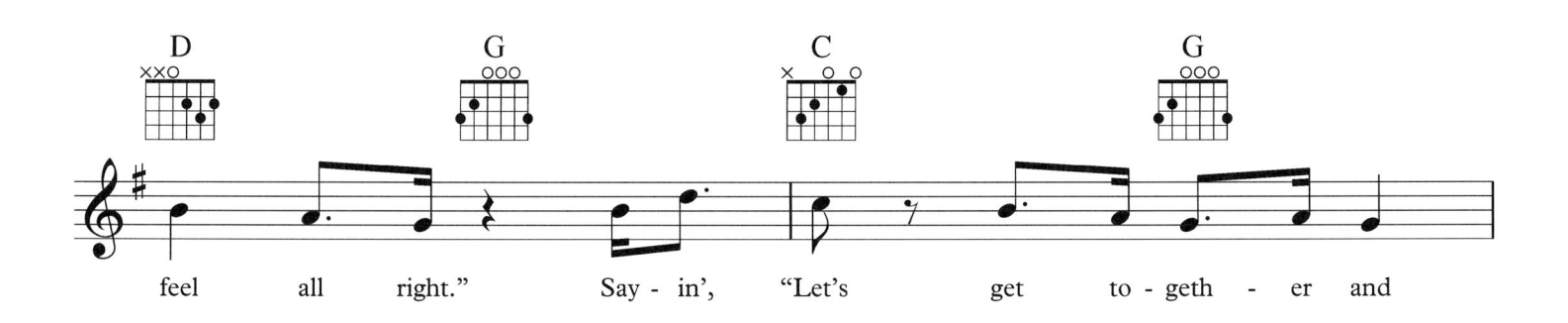

feel all right." Say - in', "Let's get to - geth - er and

feel all right." { Whoa, whoa, whoa, whoa. | Let them all pass all___ their
{ One more thing. | Let's get to - geth - er___ to

dir - ty re - marks. (One love.) There is one ques - tion I'd
fight this Ho - ly Ar - ma - ged - don, (One love.) so when the Man comes there

real - ly love to ask.___ (One heart.) Is there a place___ for the
will be no, no doom. (One song.) Have pi - ty on those___ whose chan -

hope - less sin - ner who has hurt all man - kind just to
- ces grow thin - ner. There ain't no hid - ing place from the

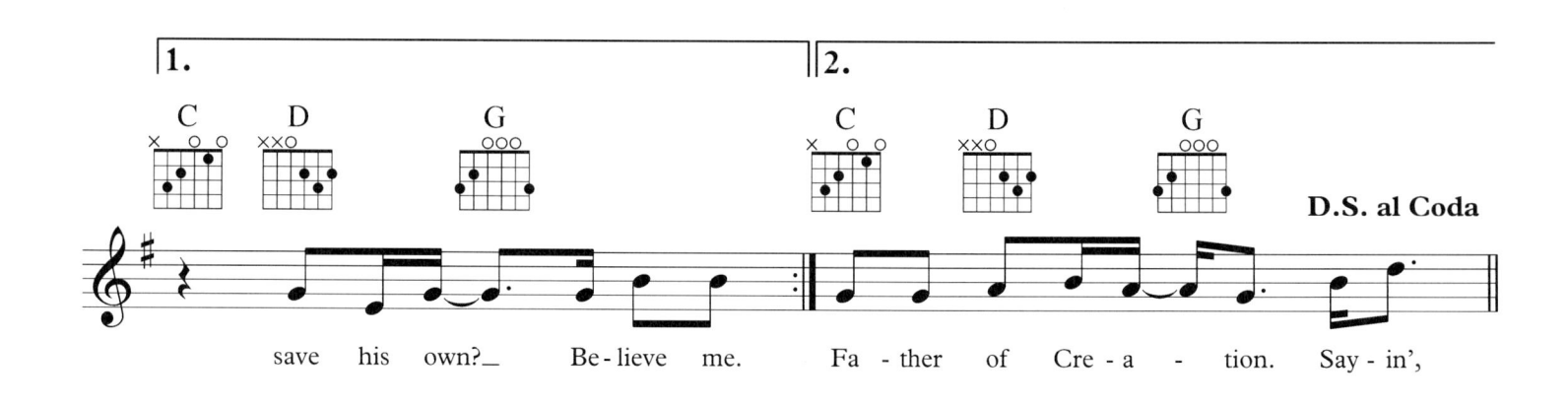

save his own?__ Be - lieve me. Fa - ther of Cre - a - tion. Say - in',

✛ **Coda**

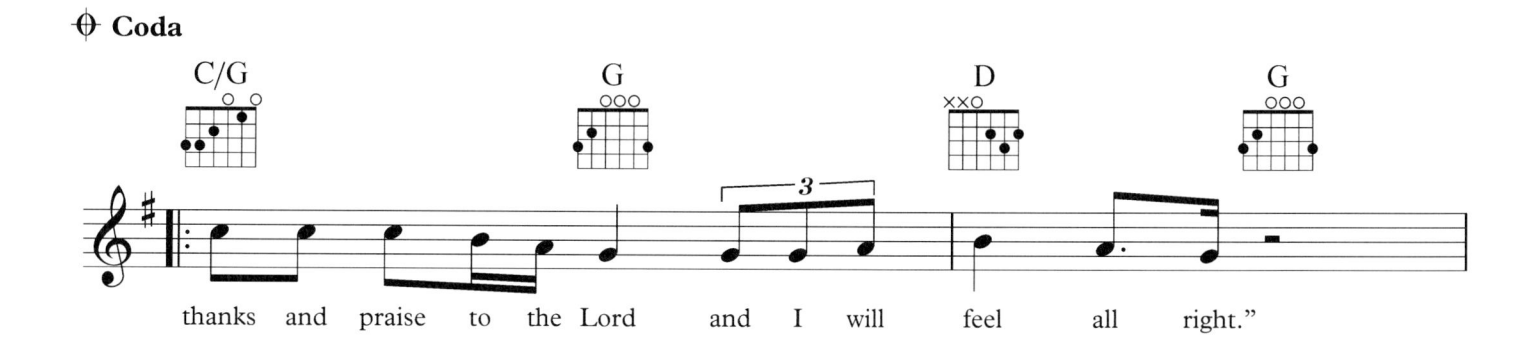

thanks and praise to the Lord and I will feel all right."

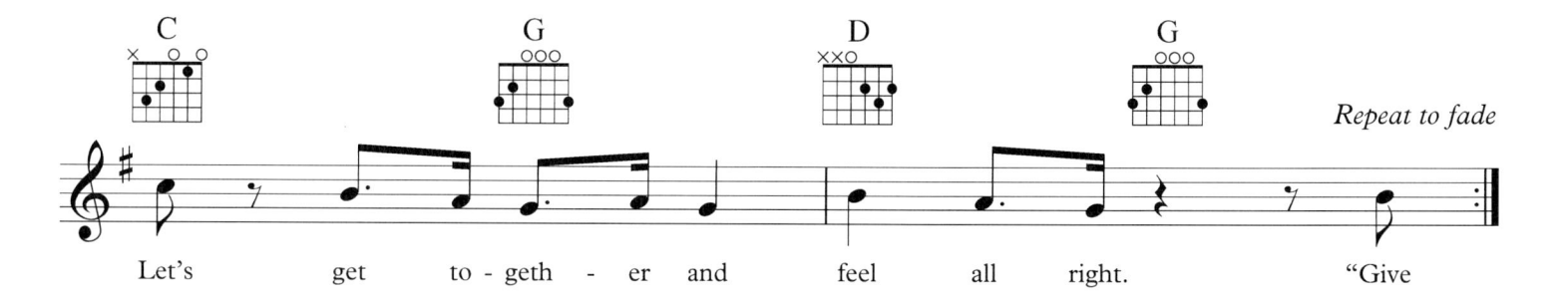

Let's get to - geth - er and feel all right. "Give

(Sittin' On) The Dock Of The Bay

Words & Music by Otis Redding & Steve Cropper

© Copyright 1967 Cotillion Music Incorporated, USA/Irving Music Corporation, USA.
Warner/Chappell Music Limited/Rondor Music International.
All Rights Reserved. International Copyright Secured.

Notice the barre chord shapes used for the intro, verse and chorus, contrasting with the open shapes for the bridge.
Strum in even eighth-notes, using the barre to create a muted sound. Emphasise beats 2 and 4.

Strumming style:

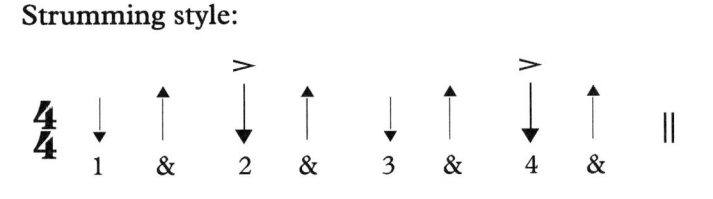

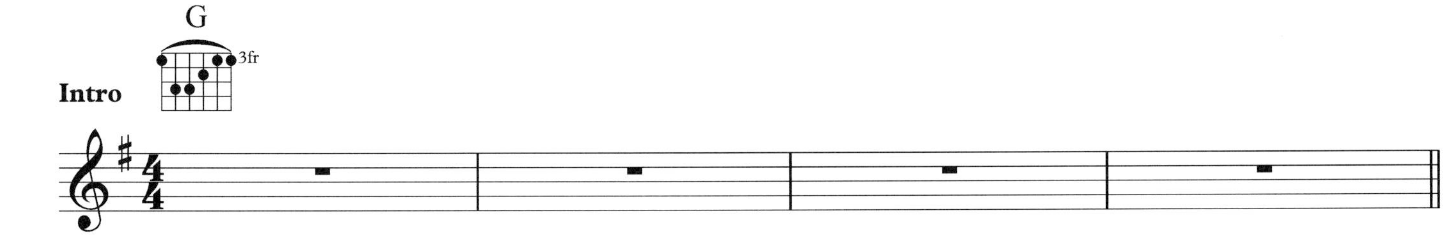

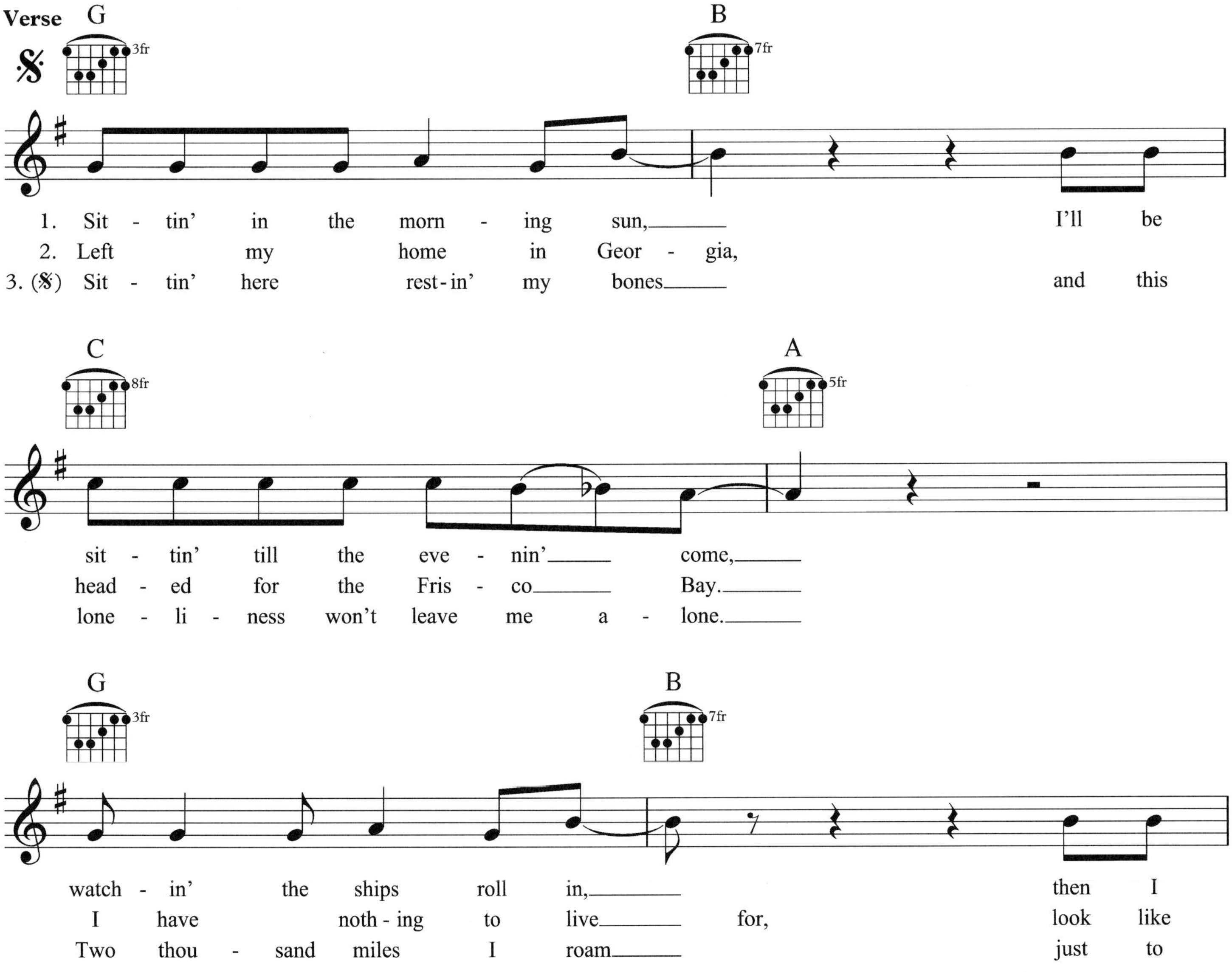

1 & 2 & 3 & 4 &

Intro
G
3fr

Verse
G 3fr
B 7fr
1. Sit - tin' in the morn - ing sun, I'll be
2. Left my home in Geor - gia,
3. (𝄋) Sit - tin' here rest - in' my bones and this
C 8fr
A 5fr
sit - tin' till the eve - nin' come,
head - ed for the Fris - co Bay.
lone - li - ness won't leave me a - lone.
G 3fr
B 7fr
watch - in' the ships roll in, then I
I have noth - ing to live for, look like
Two thou - sand miles I roam just to

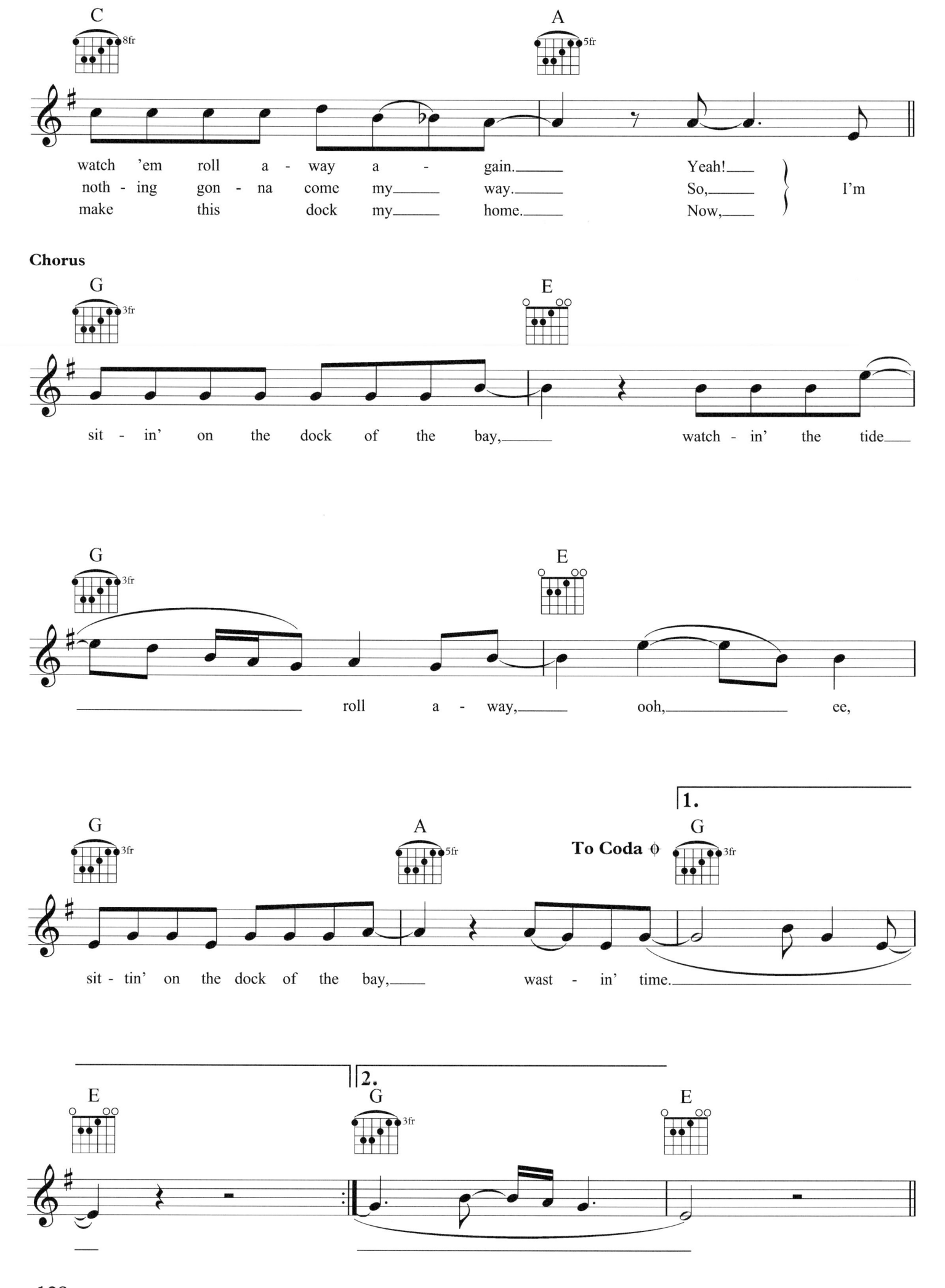

Bridge

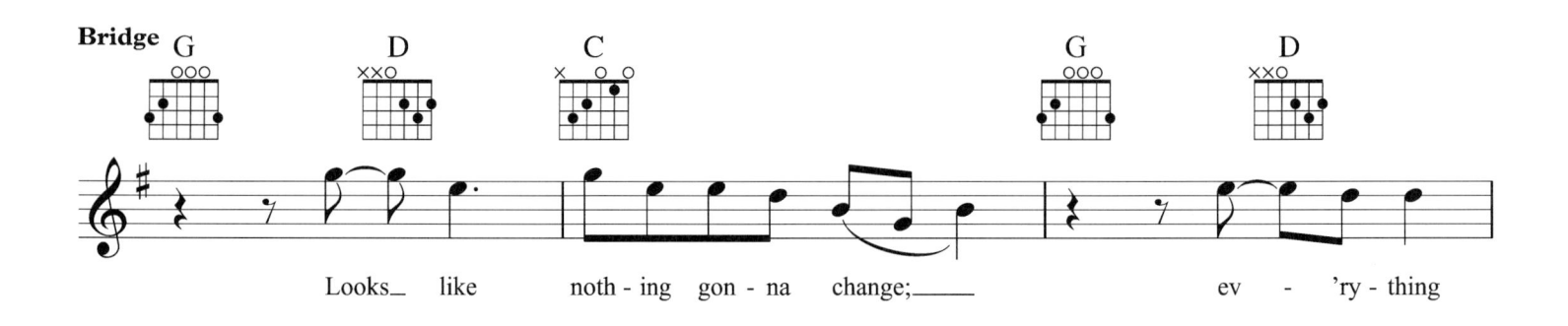

Looks_ like   noth - ing gon - na   change;_____   ev - 'ry - thing

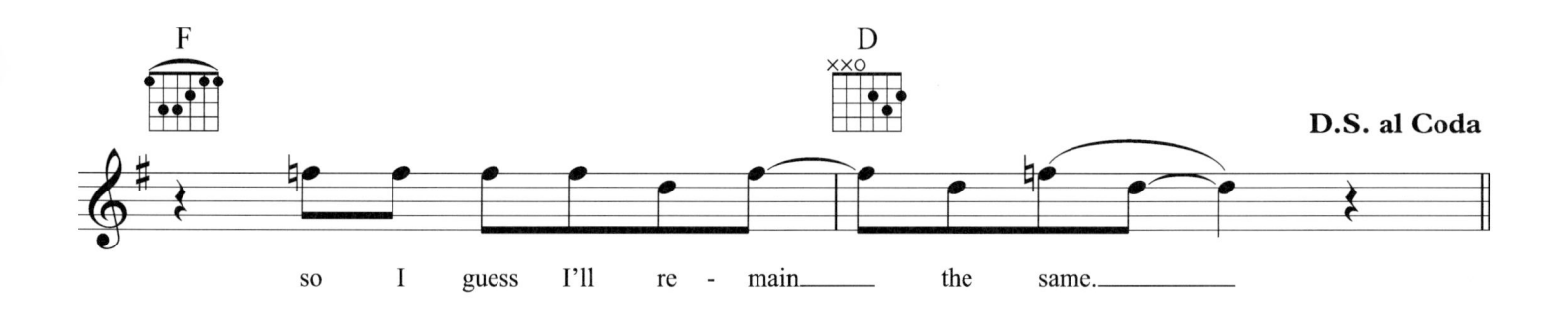

still re - mains the same._____   I_____ can't do what ten peo - ple tell me to do,_____

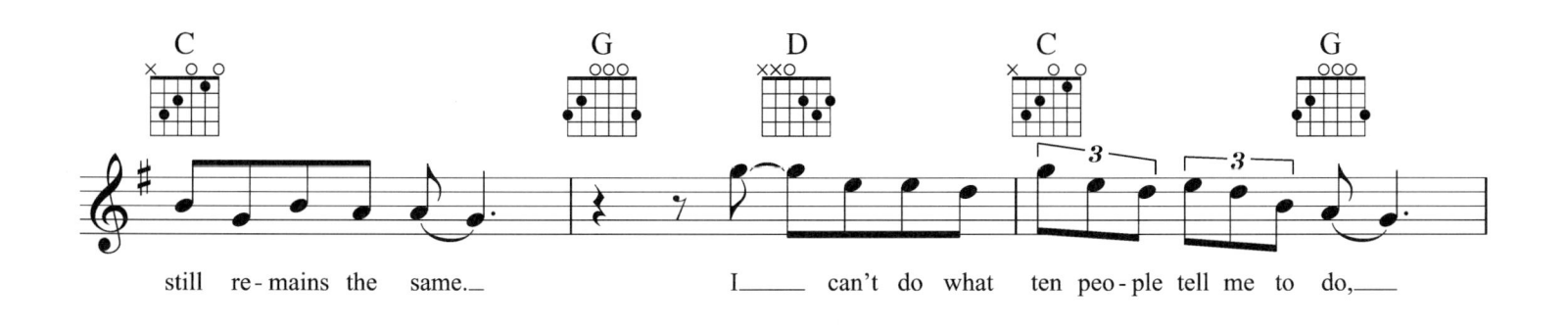

D.S. al Coda

so   I   guess I'll   re - main_____   the same._____

Coda

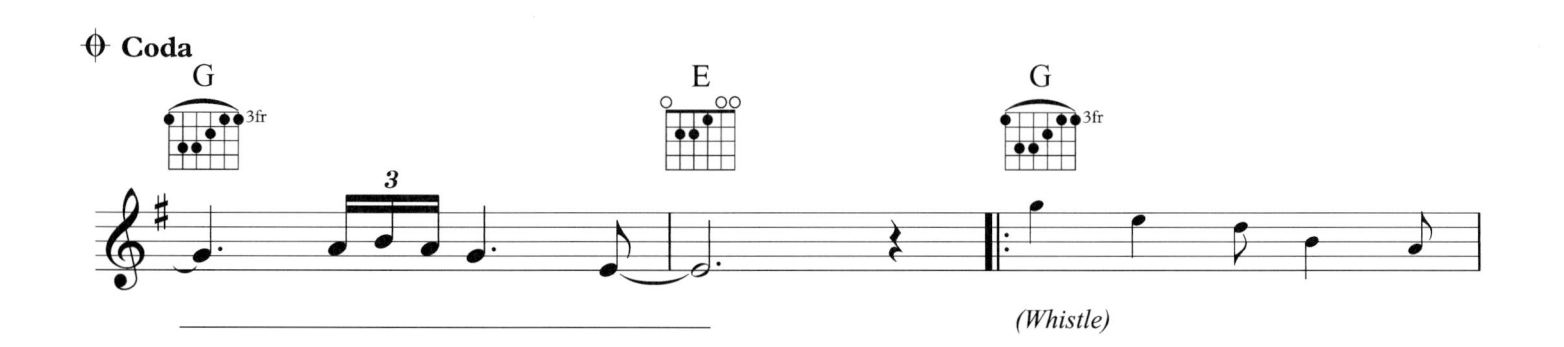

_____   *(Whistle)*

Repeat ad lib. to fade

Stay With Me

Words & Music by Tom Petty, Jeff Lynne
James Napier, Sam Smith & William Phillips

© Copyright 2014 Stellar Songs Limited/Naughty Words Limited/EMI April Music Inc/
Gone Gator Music/Salli Isaak Songs Limited/Method Paperwork Ltd.
Universal Music Publishing Limited/EMI Music Publishing Limited/
Sony/ATV Music Publishing/Wixen Music UK Ltd.
All Rights Reserved. International Copyright Secured.

Play very sparsely, with a single fi m down-strum for the Am7 and F chords.
The C chord is played with an up-strum just before the start of the following bar.

Strumming style:

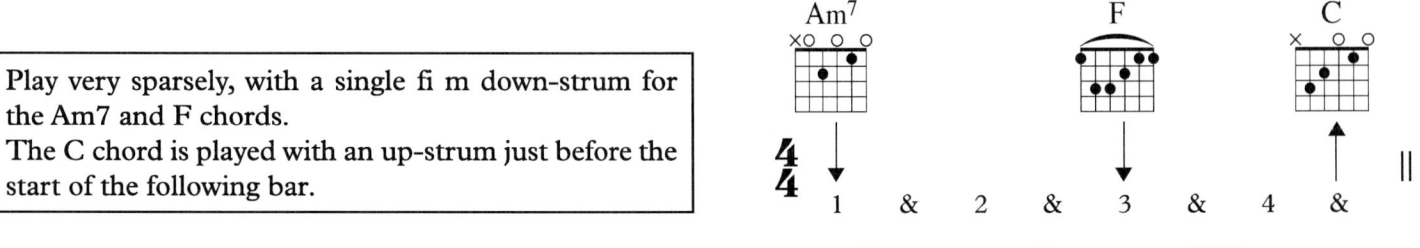

Intro

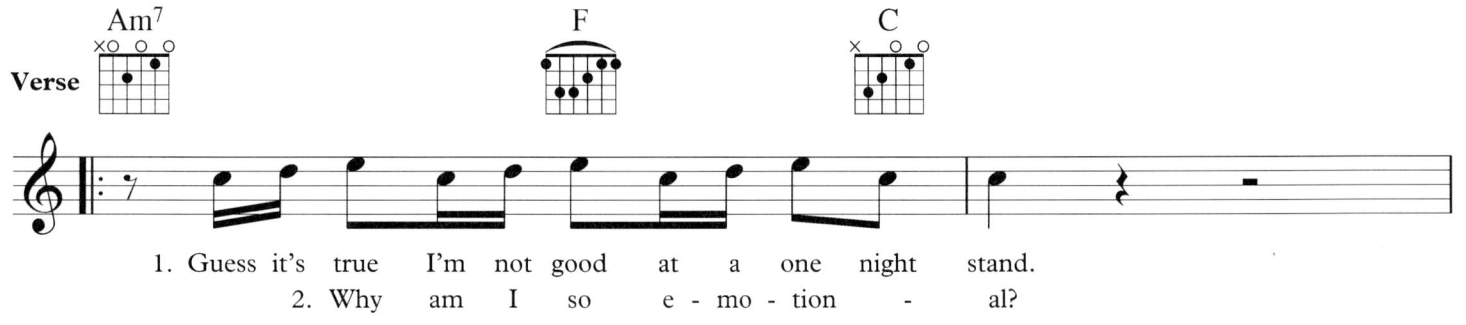

Verse

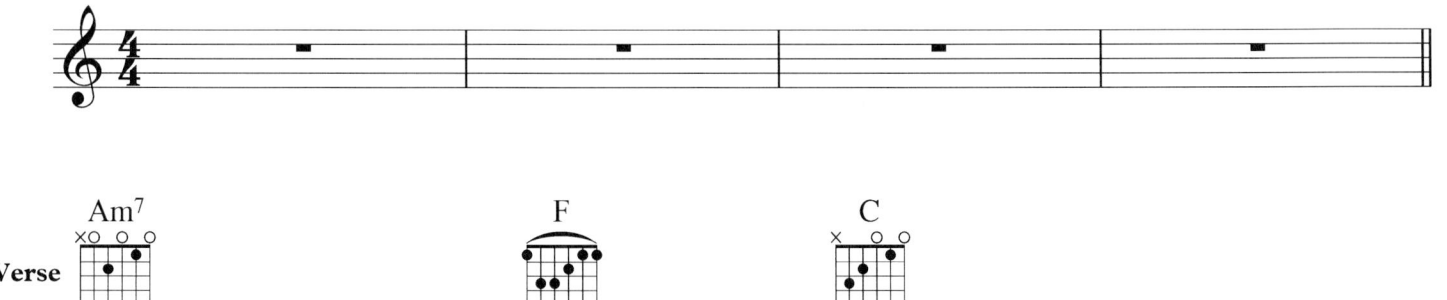

1. Guess it's true I'm not good at a one night stand.
2. Why am I so e - mo - tion - al?

But I still need love 'cause I'm just a man.___
No, it's not a good look, gain some self con - trol.___

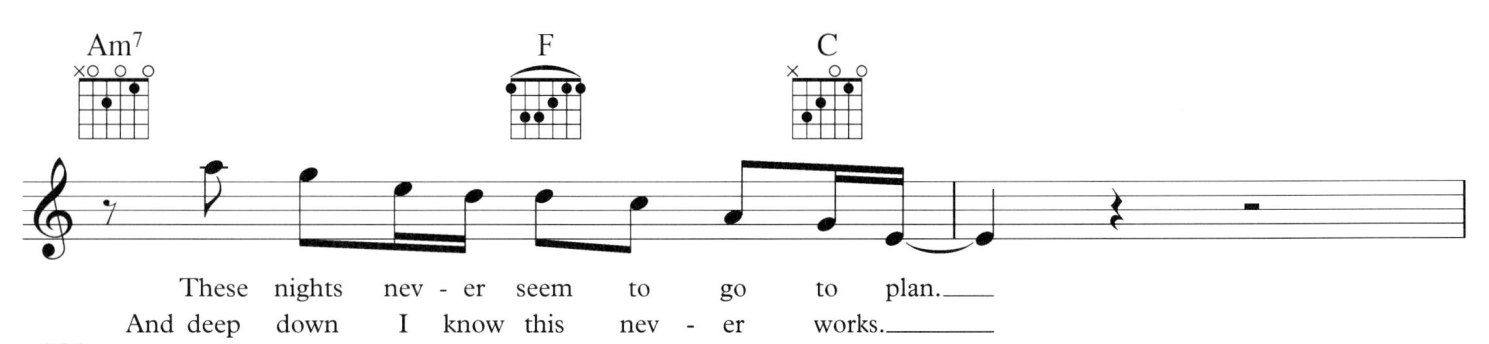

These nights nev - er seem to go to plan.___
And deep down I know this nev - er works.___

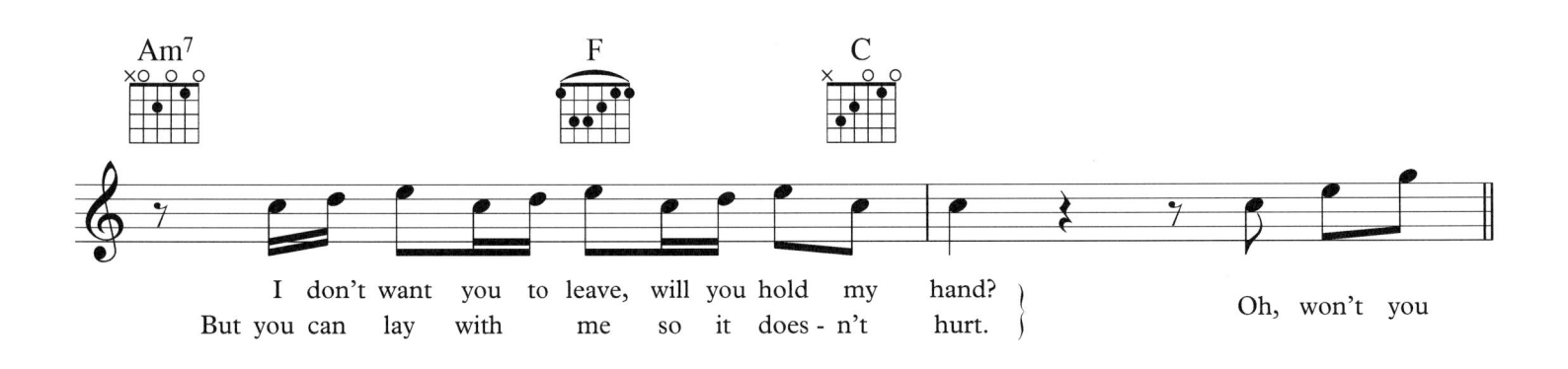

I don't want you to leave, will you hold my hand?
But you can lay with me so it does-n't hurt.

Oh, won't you

Chorus

stay_____ with me?_____ 'Cause you're____ all_____ I need..

To Coda ⊕

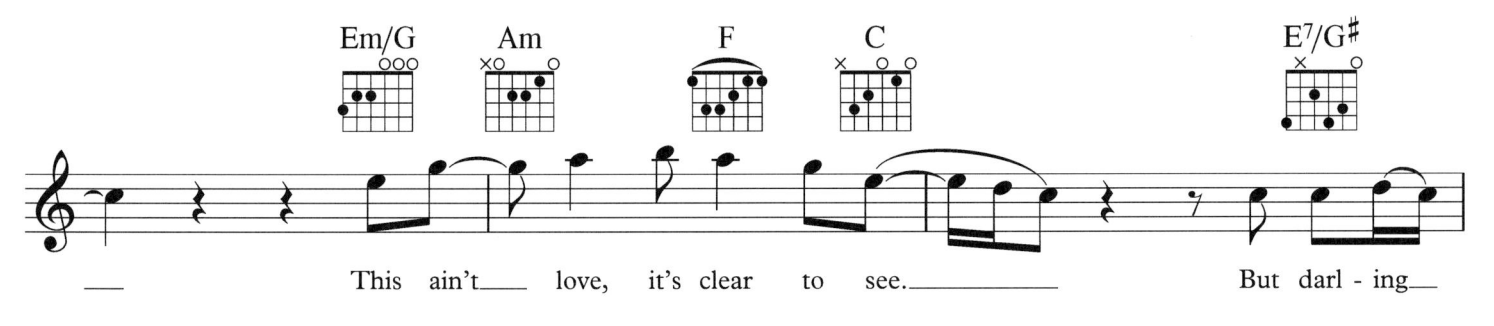

_____ This ain't____ love, it's clear to see._____ But darl - ing____

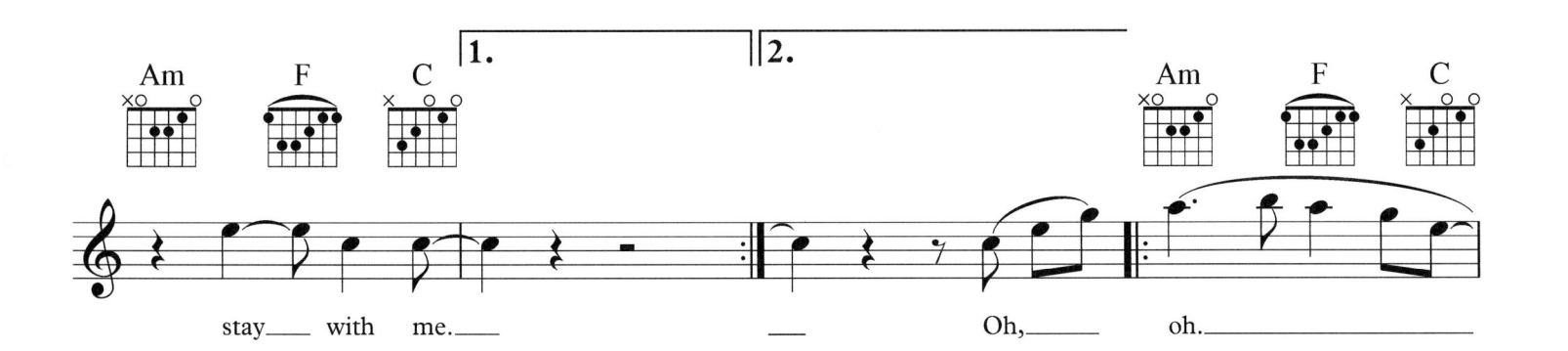

stay____ with me.____ ____ Oh,____ oh._____

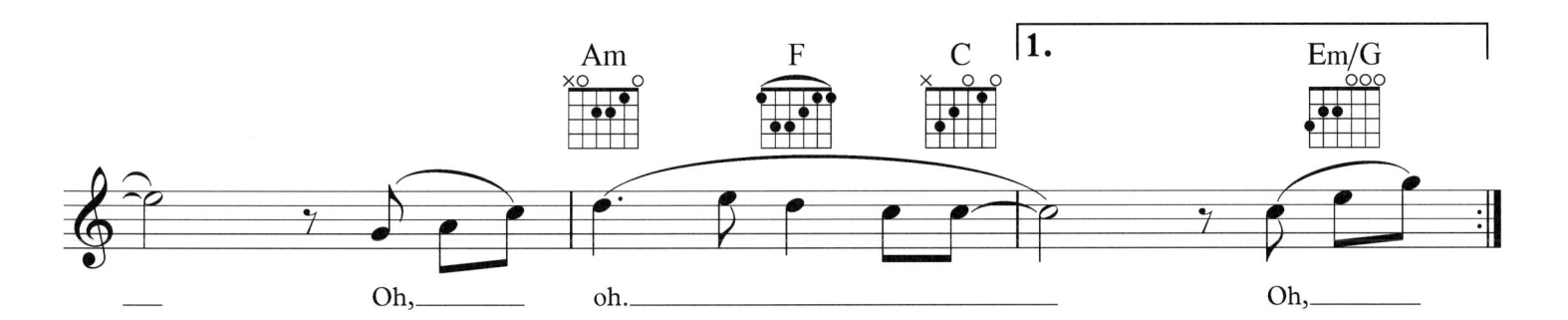

____ Oh,_____ oh.____ Oh,____

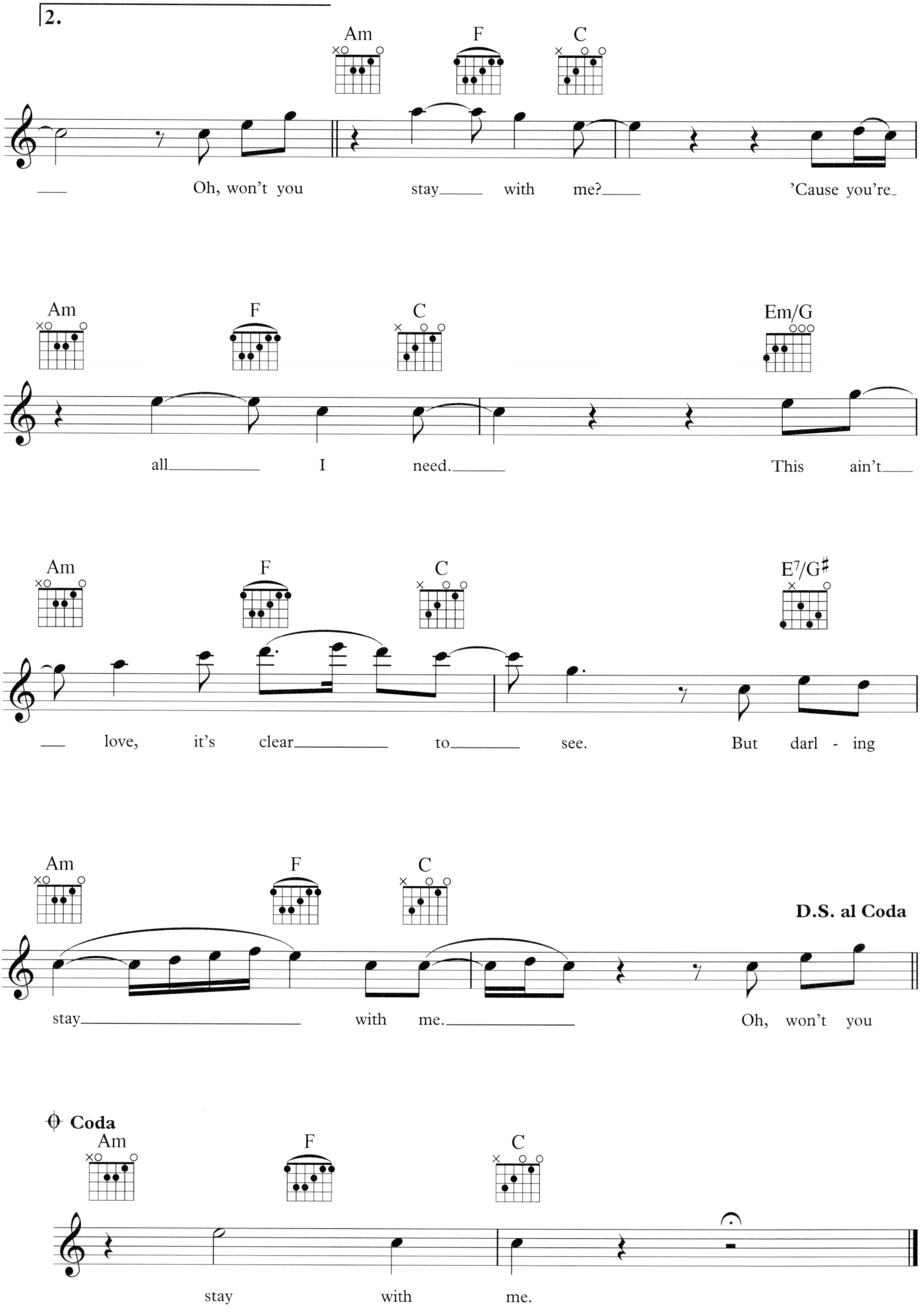

2.

Am   F   C

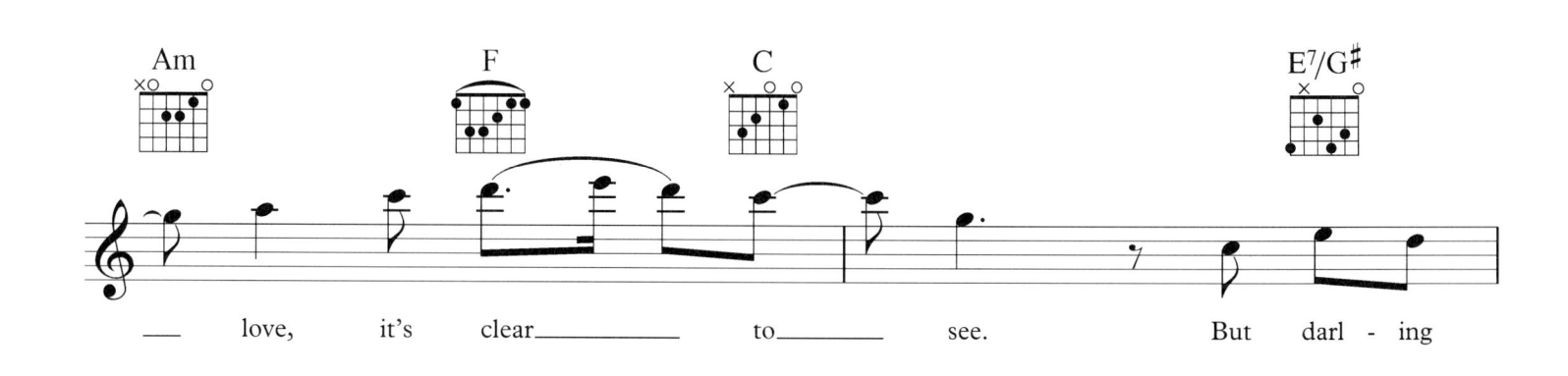

— Oh, won't you   stay___ with   me?___   'Cause you're_

Am   F   C   Em/G

all___   I   need.___   This   ain't___

Am   F   C   E⁷/G♯

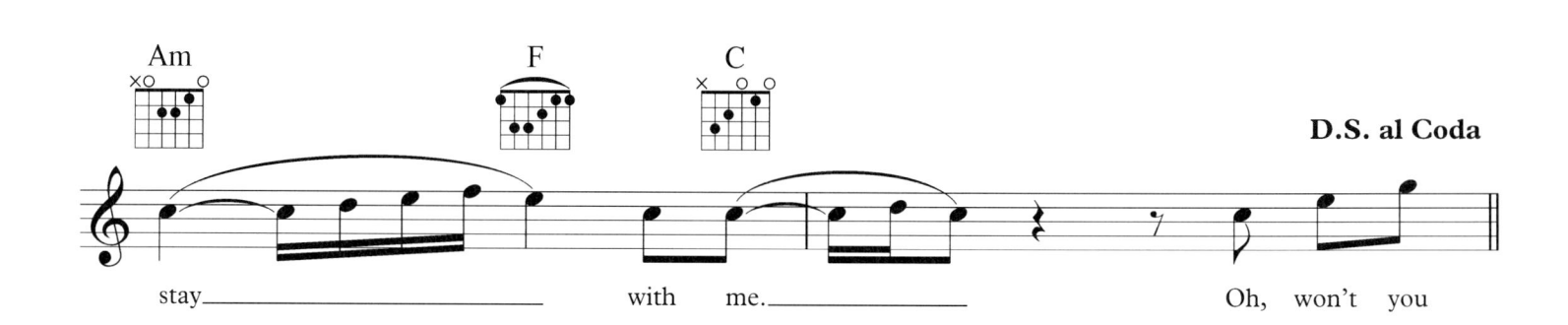

— love,   it's   clear___   to___   see.   But   darl - ing

Am   F   C

D.S. al Coda

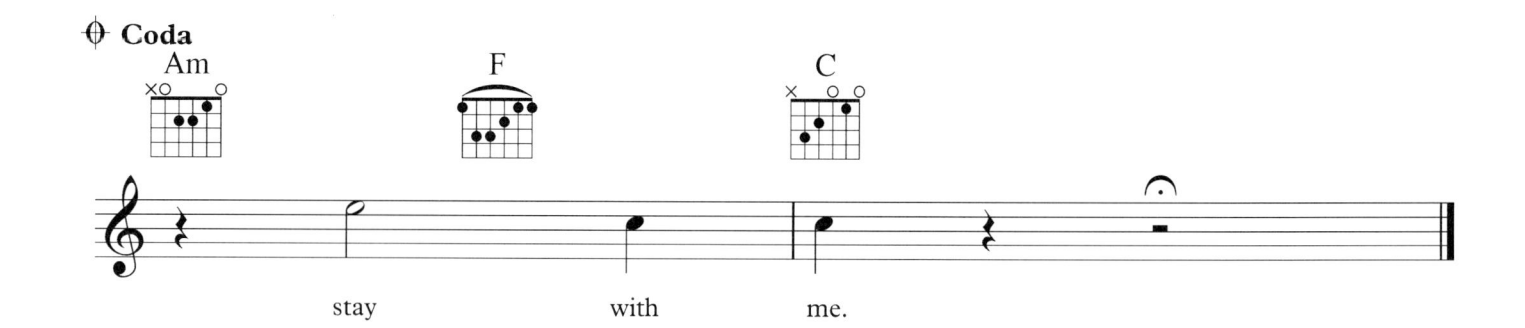

stay___   with   me.___   Oh, won't   you

⊕ **Coda**

Am   F   C

stay   with   me.

132

Streets Of London

Words & Music by Ralph McTell

© Copyright 1968 Westminster Music Limited.
All Rights Reserved. International Copyright Secured.

Capo: Fret 4

1. Have you seen the old man in the closed down mar-
2. Have you seen the old girl who walks the streets of
3. In the all night ca - fé at a quar - ter past el -
4. Have you seen the old man out - side the sea - man's

- ket, kick-ing up the pap - er with his worn out
Lon - don, dirt in her hair and her clothes in
- ev - en, same old man, sit-ting there on his
mis - sion, me-mo-ry fa - ding with the me - dal rib-bons that he

shoes? In his eyes___ you see no pride,___
rags? She's no time___ for talk - ing; she just___
own. Look - ing at the world___ o - ver the rim___
wears? In our win - ter ci - ty the rain

and held___ loose - ly at his side,___ yes - ter-day's
___ keeps right on walk - ing, Car - ry - ing___ her home___
___ of his tea - cup, each tea lasts an
cries a lit - tle pi - ty for one more for - got - ten he -

pa - per,___ tell - ing yes - ter - day's news.___
___ in two___ car - ri - er bags.___
hour, then he wan - ders home a - lone. So
- ro and a world that does - n't care.___

Chorus

how can you tell___ me___ you're lone - - ly,___

and say for you___ that the sun don't

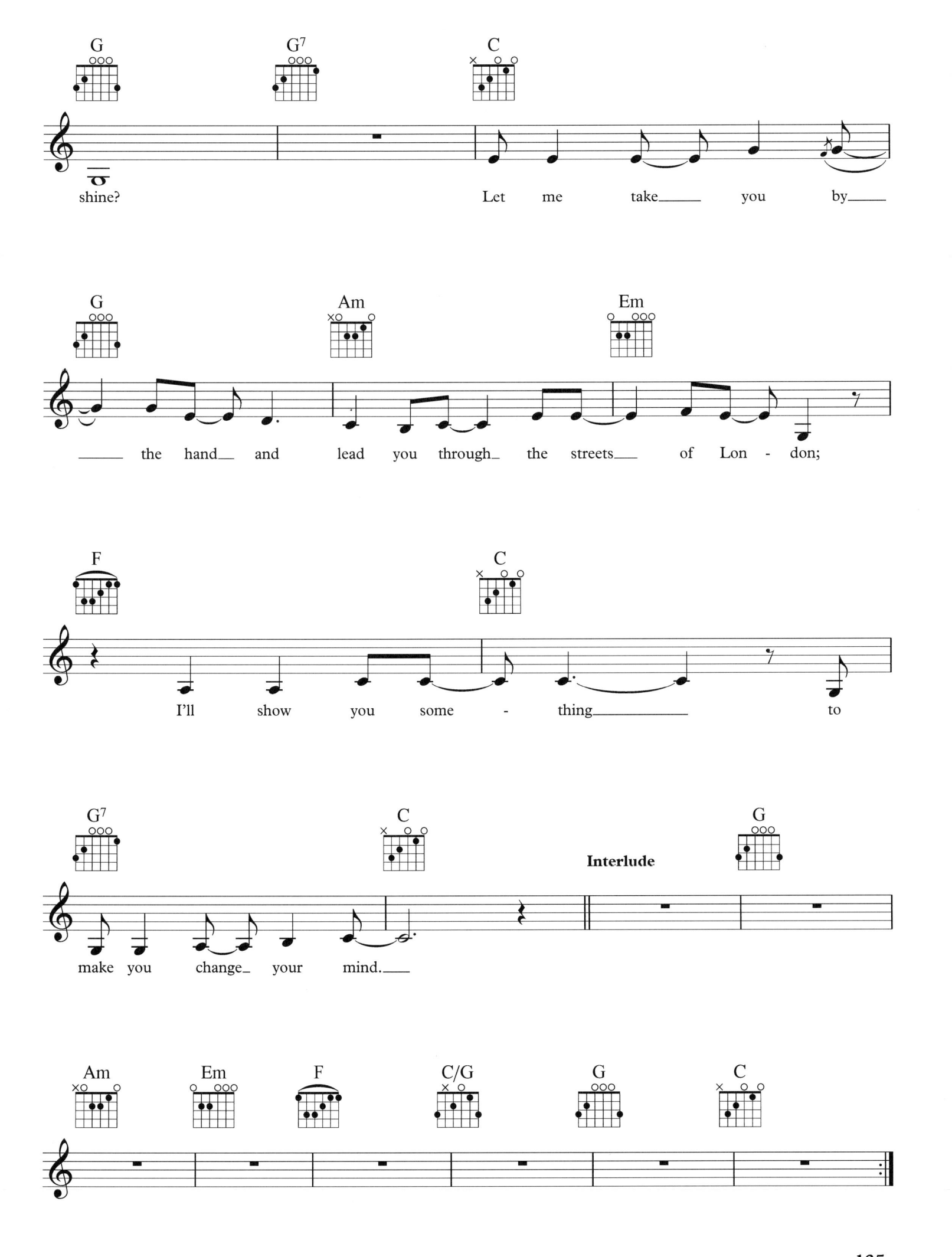

These Boots Are Made For Walking

Words & Music by Lee Hazlewood

© Copyright 1965 & 1966 Criterion Music Corporation.
Universal Music Publishing Limited.
All Rights Reserved. International Copyright Secured.

Strumming style:

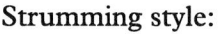

Pick heavy bass notes on beats 1 and 3, followed by pairs of eighth-note strums on beats 2 and 4.

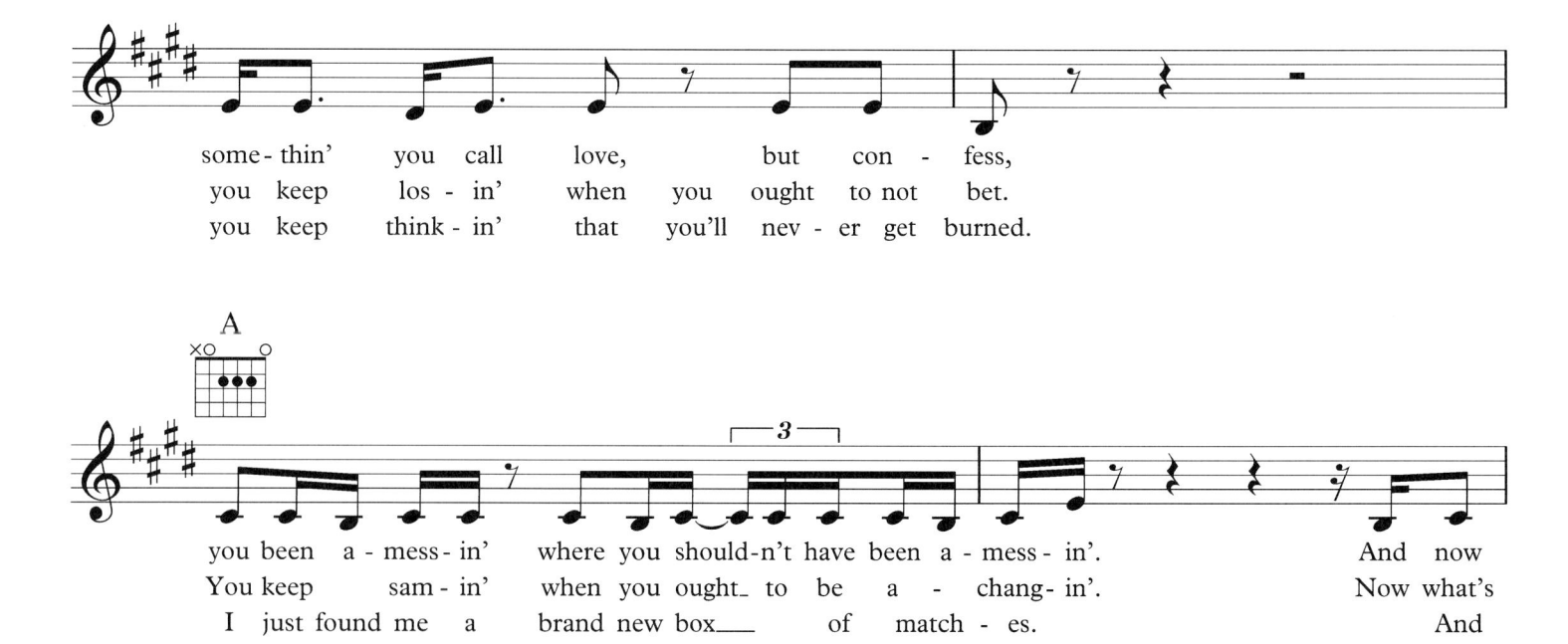

Intro

Verse

1. You keep say - in' you got some - thin' for me,
2. You keep ly - in' when you ought to be truth - in' and
3. You keep play - in' where you should - n't be play - in' and

some - thin' you call love, but con - fess,
you keep los - in' when you ought to not bet.
you keep think - in' that you'll nev - er get burned.

you been a - mess - in' where you should - n't have been a - mess - in'. And now
You keep sam - in' when you ought_ to be a - chang - in'. Now what's
I just found me a brand new box___ of match - es. And

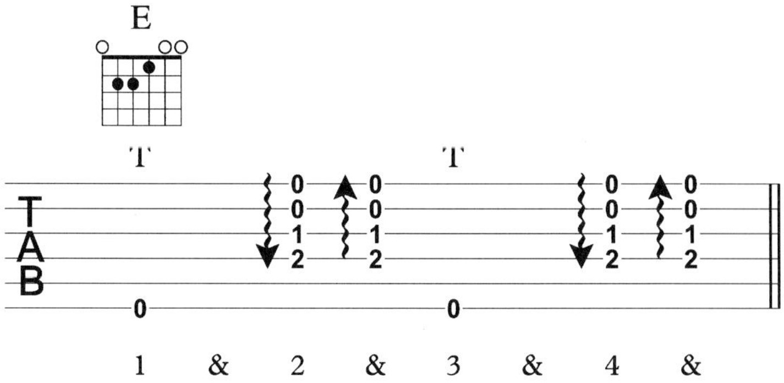

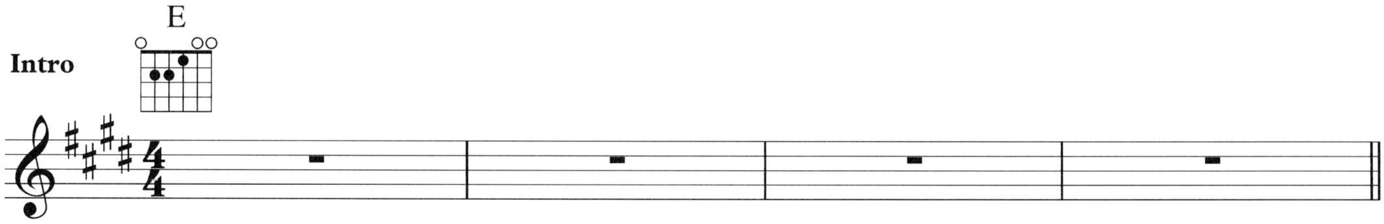

some-one else__ is get-tin' all__ your best.
right is right__ but you ain't been__ right yet.
what he knows you ain't had time__ to learn.

These

Chorus

boots are made__ for walk - ing and that's just what they'll do.

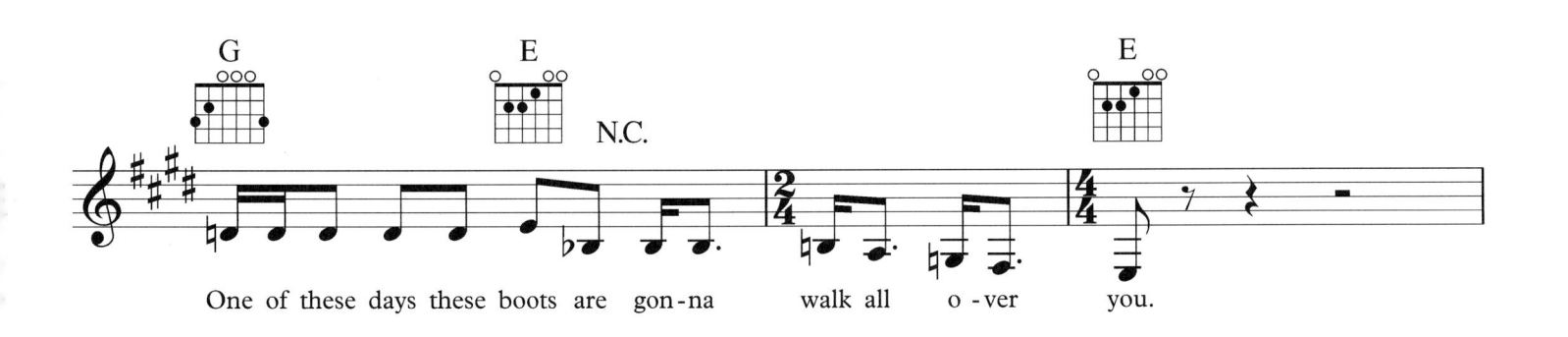

One of these days these boots are gon-na walk all o - ver you.

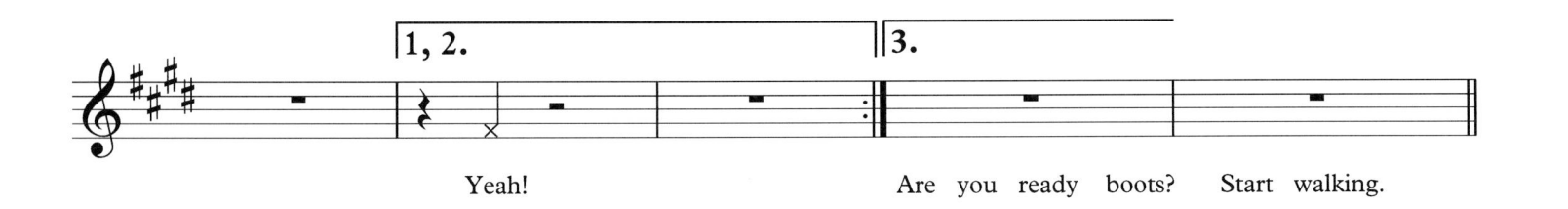

1, 2.

Yeah!

3.

Are you ready boots? Start walking.

Repeat ad lib. to fade

Trumpet

Thinking Out Loud

Words & Music by Ed Sheeran & Amy Wadge

© Copyright 2014 Sony/ATV Music Publishing/BDi Music Limited.
All Rights Reserved. International Copyright Secured.

Picking style:

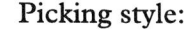

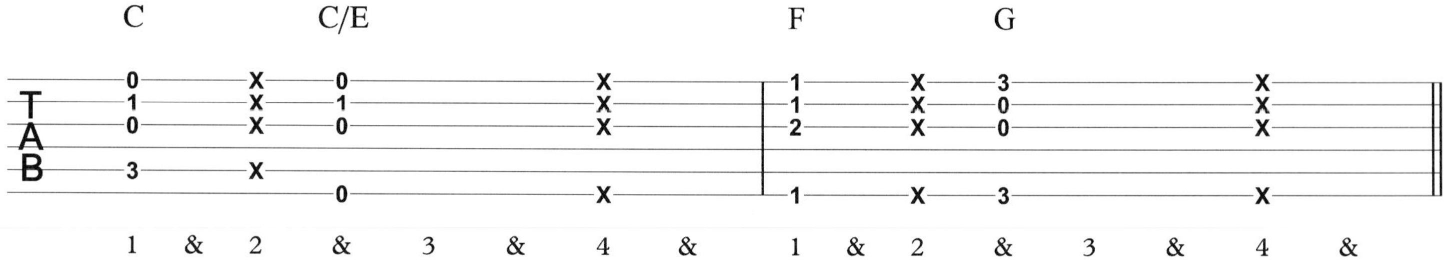

Capo: Fret 2

Verse

1. When your legs don't work like they used to be - fore
2. When my hair's all but gone and my mem - o - ry fades

and I can't sweep you off of your feet,
and the crowds don't re - mem - ber my name.

will your mouth still re - mem - ber the taste of my love?
When my hands don't__ play the__ strings the same way,

Will your eyes still smile from your cheeks? And darl - ing, I
I know you will still love me the same. 'Cause hon - ey your

will be lov-ing you till____ we're se-ven-ty.____
soul could nev-er grow old,____ it's ev-er-green.____

And ba-by, my heart could still fall as
And ba-by, your smile's for-ev-er in

hard____ at twen-ty-three._____ And I'm think-ing 'bout how____
my mind__ and mem-o-ry._____ And I'm think-ing 'bout how____

peo-ple fall in love in mys-ter - i-ous ways,____
peo-ple fall in love in mys-ter - i-ous ways,____ and

may-be just the touch of a hand.____ Well
may-be it's all part of a plan.____ Well

me I fall in love with you ev-'ry sin-gle day.____ And
I'll just keep on mak-ing the same____ mis-takes,____

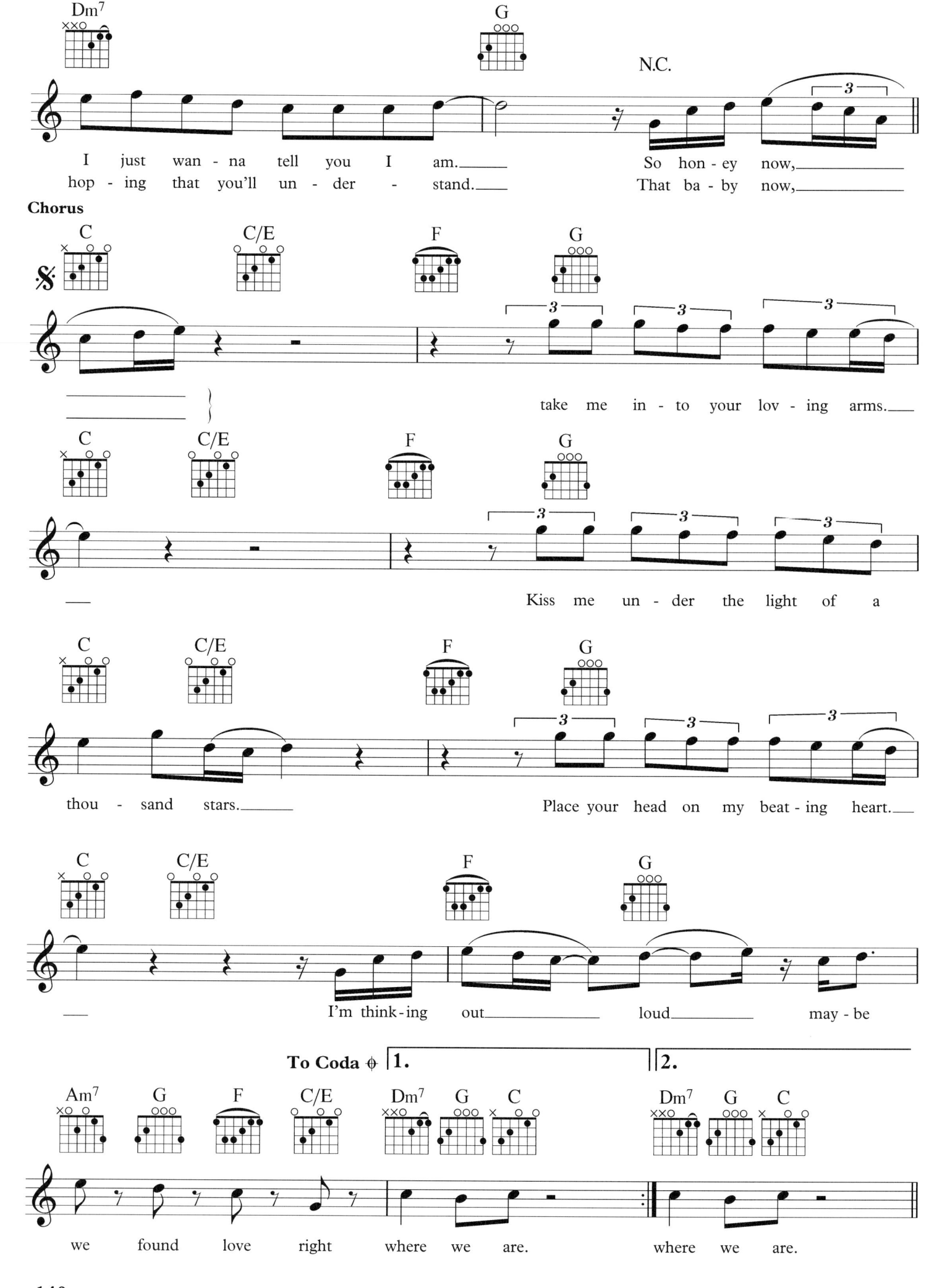

I just wan-na tell you I am._____ So hon-ey now,_____
hop - ing that you'll un - der - stand.____ That ba - by now,_____

Chorus

take me in - to your lov - ing arms.____

Kiss me un - der the light of a

thou - sand stars._____ Place your head on my beat - ing heart.____

I'm think - ing out____ loud____ may - be

we found love right where we are. where we are.

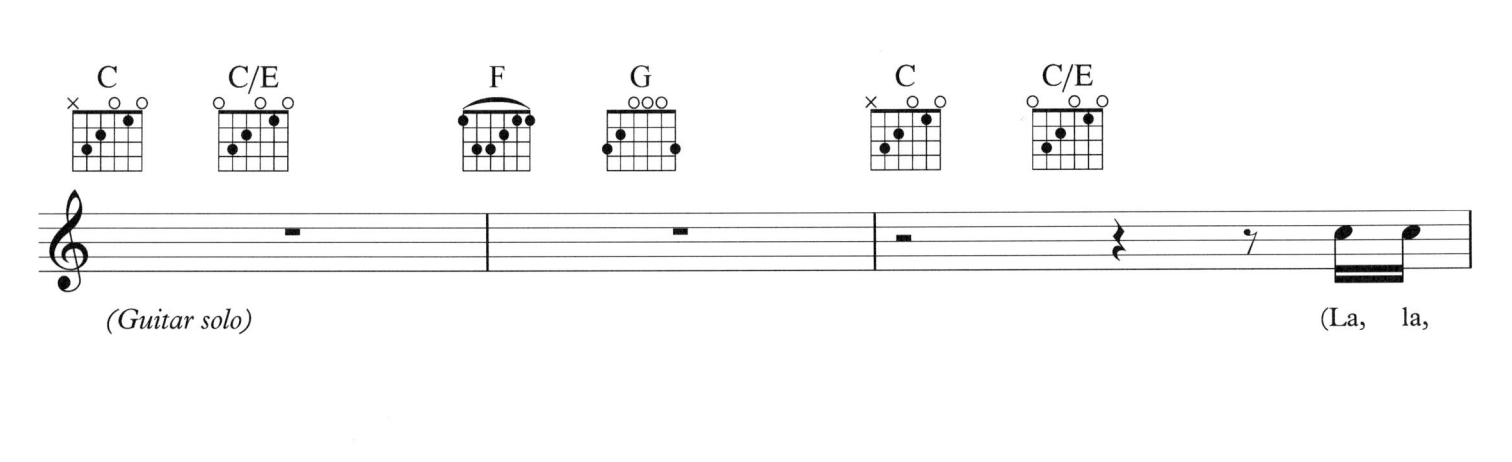

(Guitar solo)   (La,   la,

la,   la,   la,   la,   la,   la,   la,   la,   la,   la.)

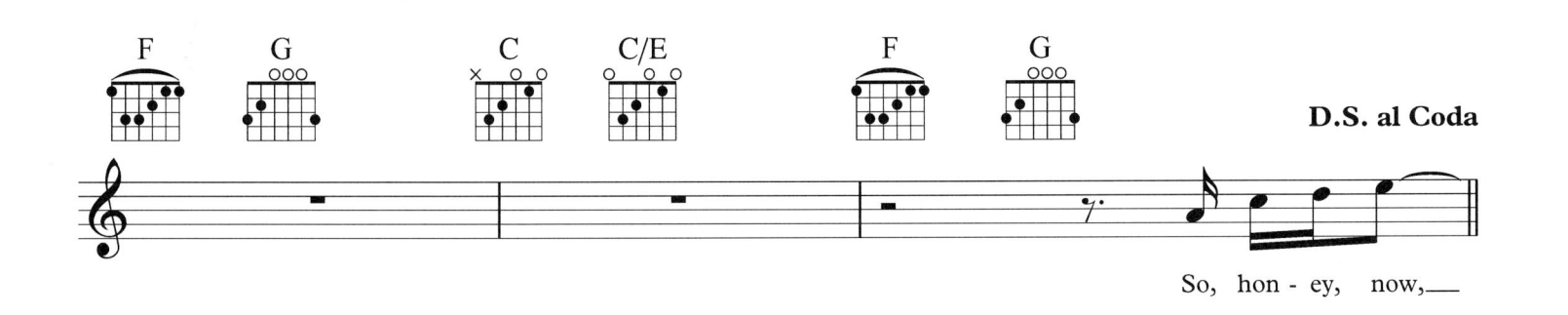

D.S. al Coda

So,   hon - ey,   now,___

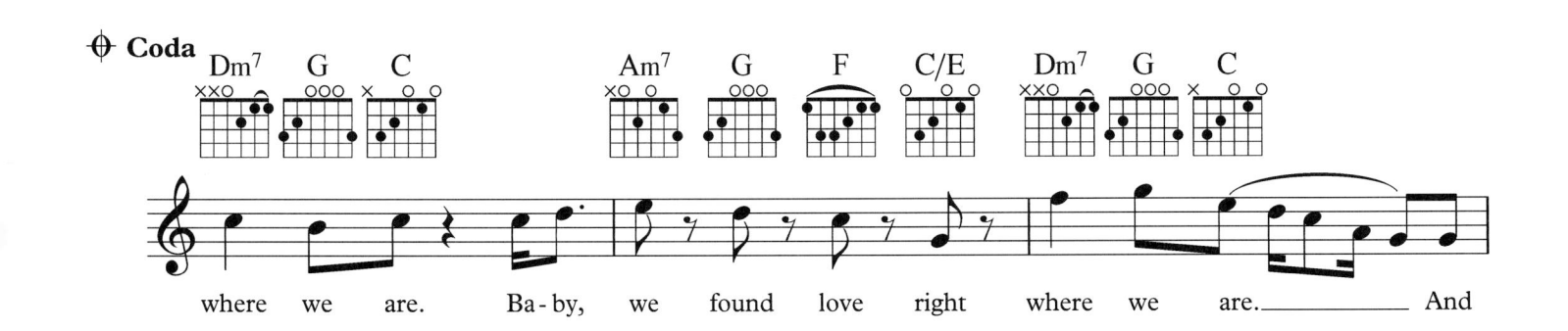

$\oplus$ **Coda**

where   we   are.   Ba - by,   we   found   love   right   where   we   are.___   And

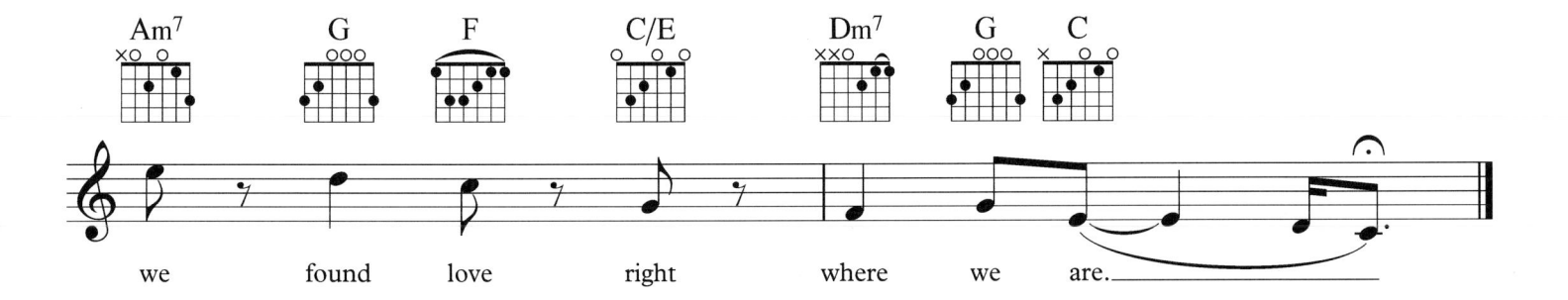

we   found   love   right   where   we   are.___

Take Me Home, Country Roads

Words & Music by John Denver, Bill Danoff & Taffy Ni ert

© Copyright 1971 (Renewed) BMG Ruby Songs.
Reservoir Media Management, Inc./BMG Rights Management (US) LLC.
All Rights Reserved. International Copyright Secured.

Picking style:

Pick the bass note of the chord on beat 1 and alternate the bass note to a different string on beat 3, to create the familiar country feel.

Intro

Verse

1. Al - most hea - ven,_ West Vir - gin - ia, Blue Ridge Moun - tains,
2. All my mem' - ries,_ ga - ther 'round_ her, min - er's la - dy,

Shen - an - do - ah Riv - er. Life is old there,_
stran - ger to blue wa - ter. Dark and dus - ty,_

old - er than the trees. Young-er than the moun - tains, grow-ing like a breeze. Coun-try
paint-ed on the sky, mis - ty taste of moon - shine, tear-drop in my eye.

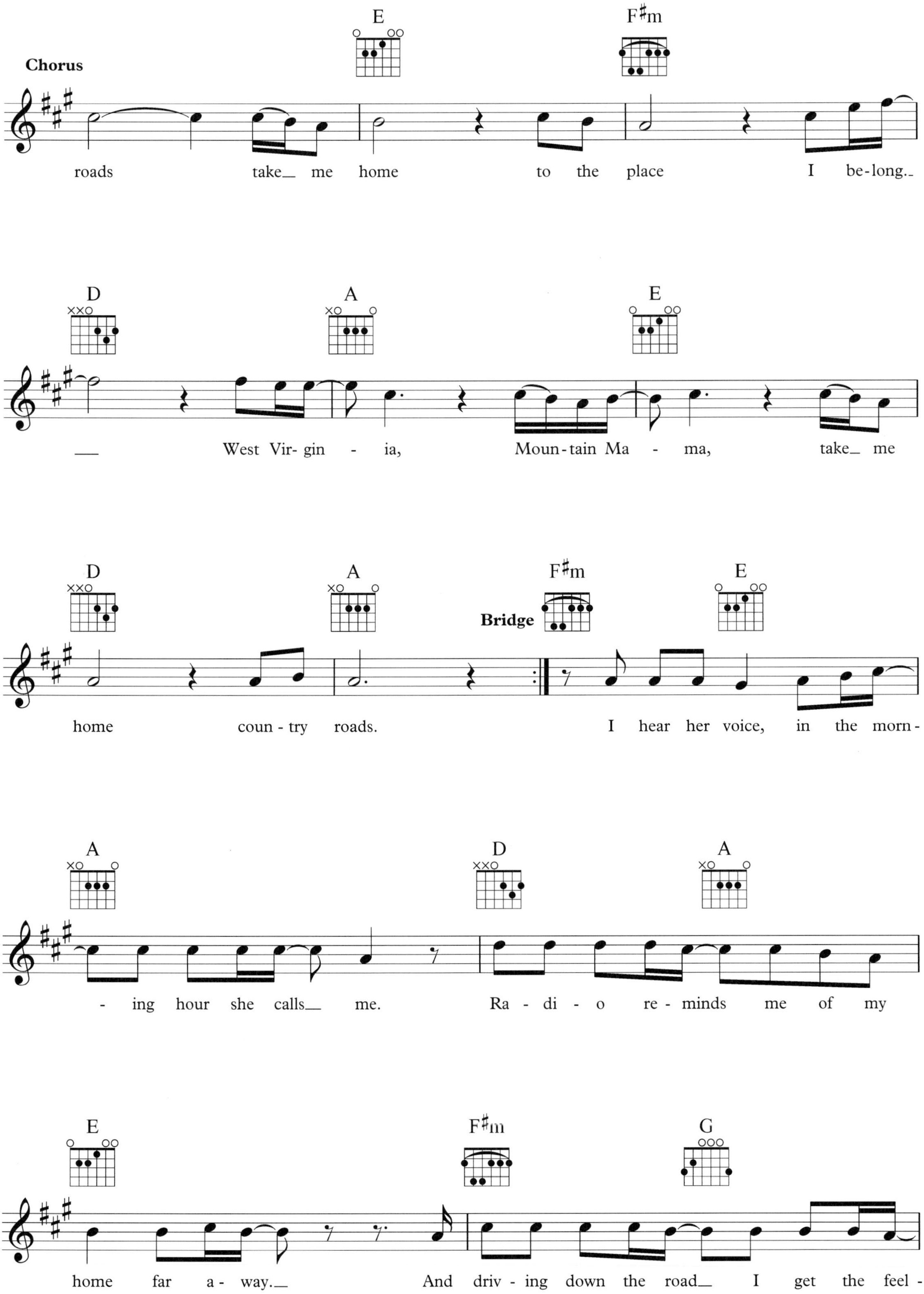

Chorus

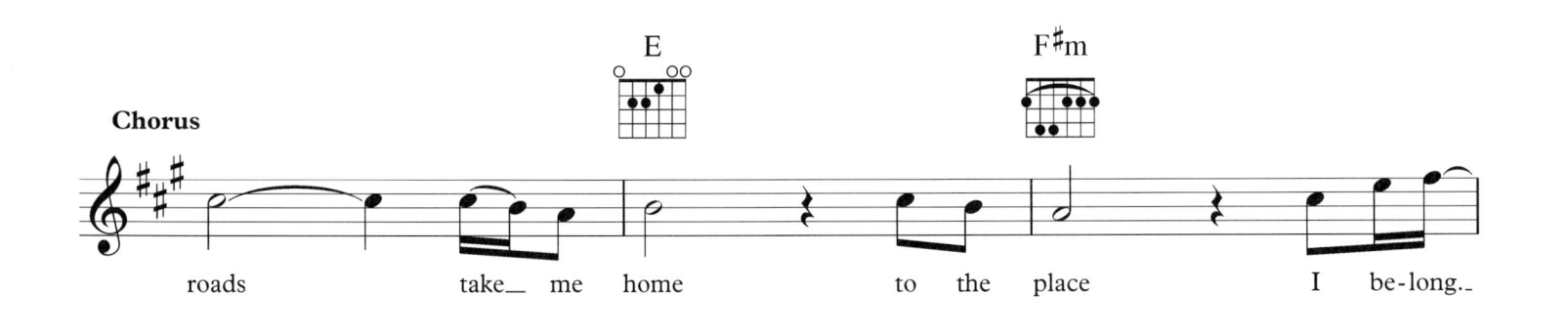

roads   take__ me home   to the place   I be-long.__

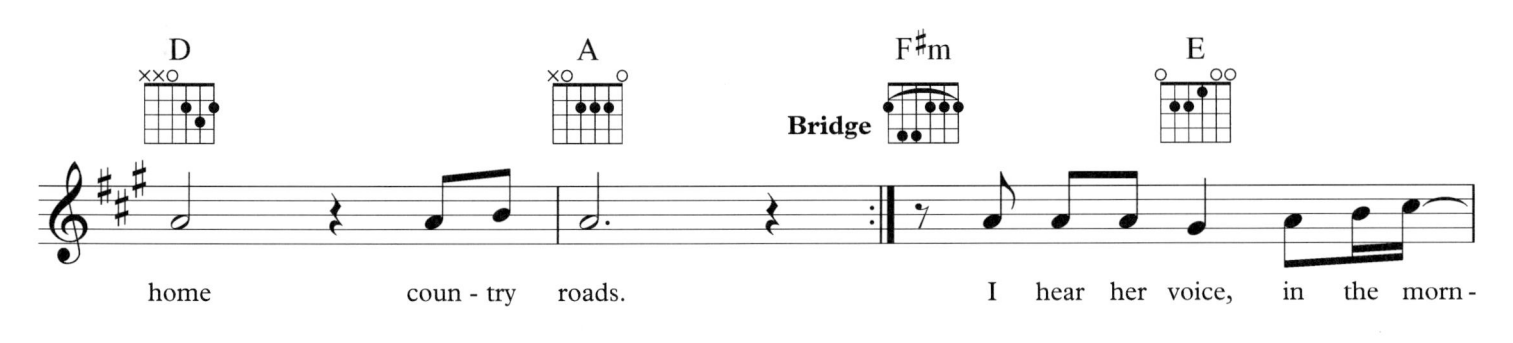

__   West Vir- gin - ia,   Moun-tain Ma - ma,   take__ me

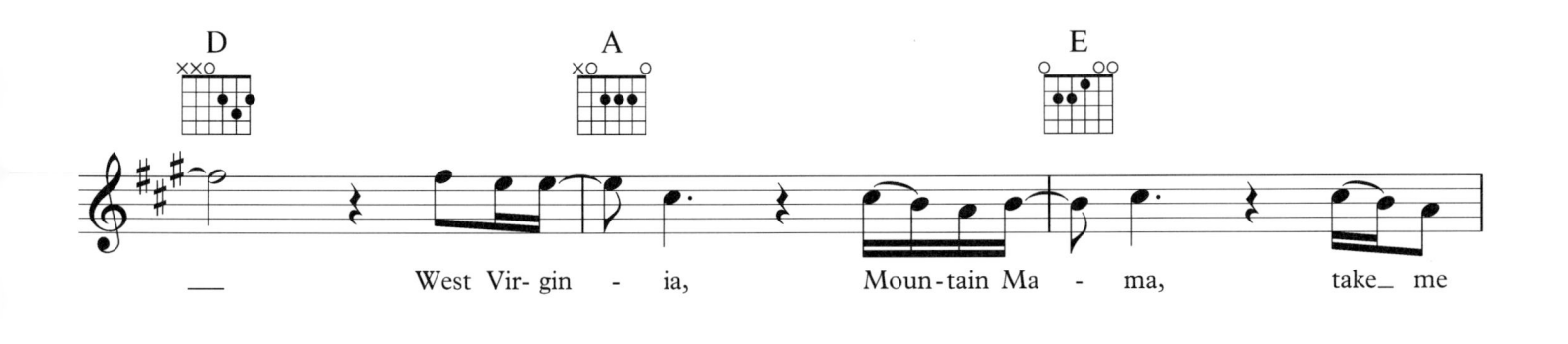

home   coun-try roads.   **Bridge**   I hear her voice, in the morn -

- ing hour she calls__ me.   Ra - di - o re - minds me of my

home far a - way.__   And driv-ing down the road__ I get the feel -

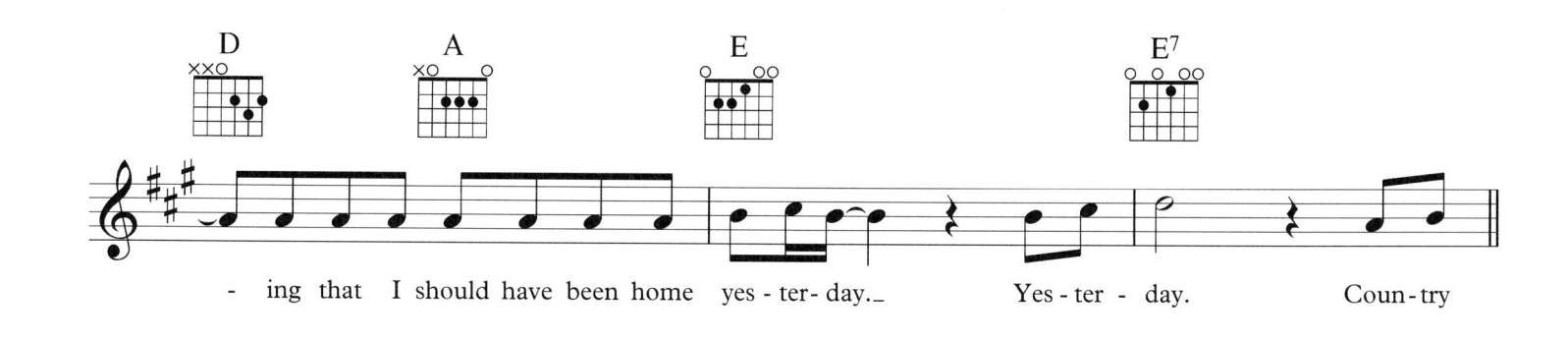

- ing that I should have been home yes - ter - day._ Yes - ter - day. Coun - try

Chorus

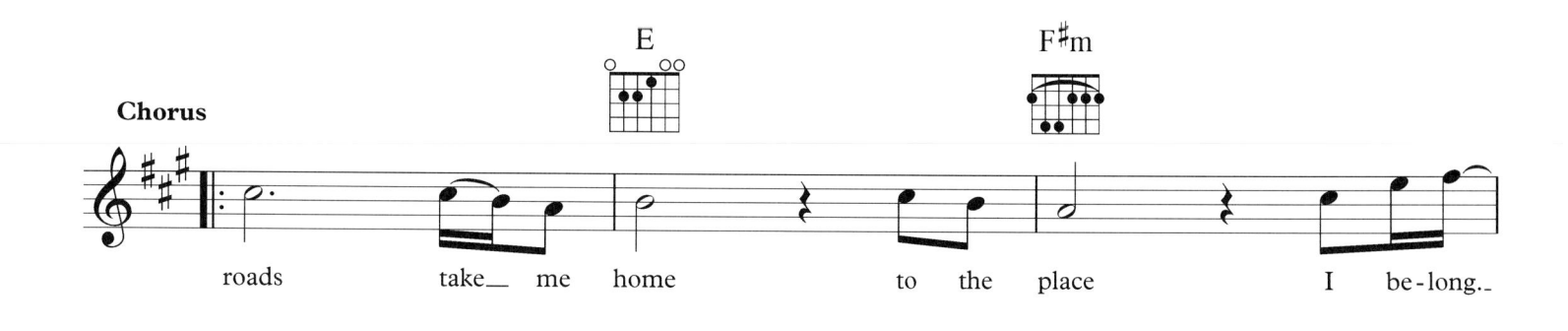

roads take__ me home to the place I be - long.__

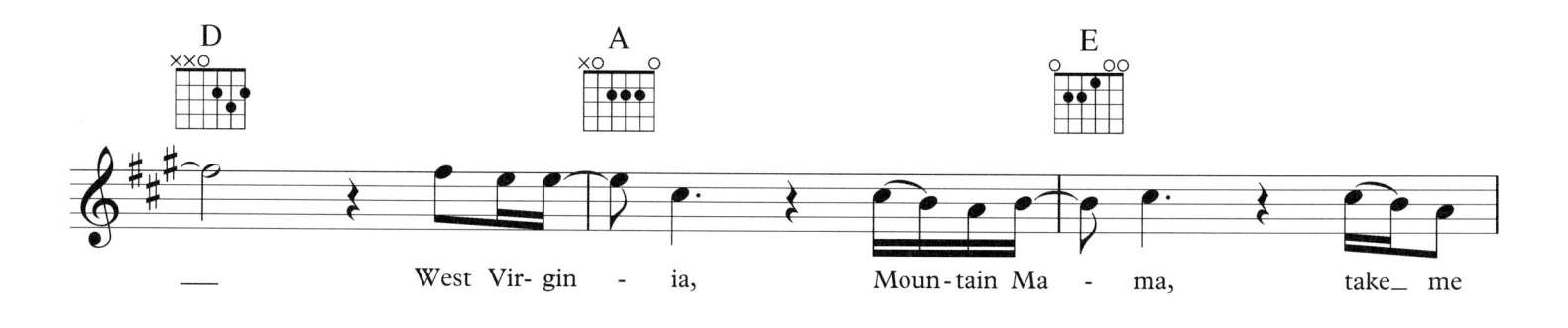

____ West Vir - gin - ia, Moun - tain Ma - ma, take__ me

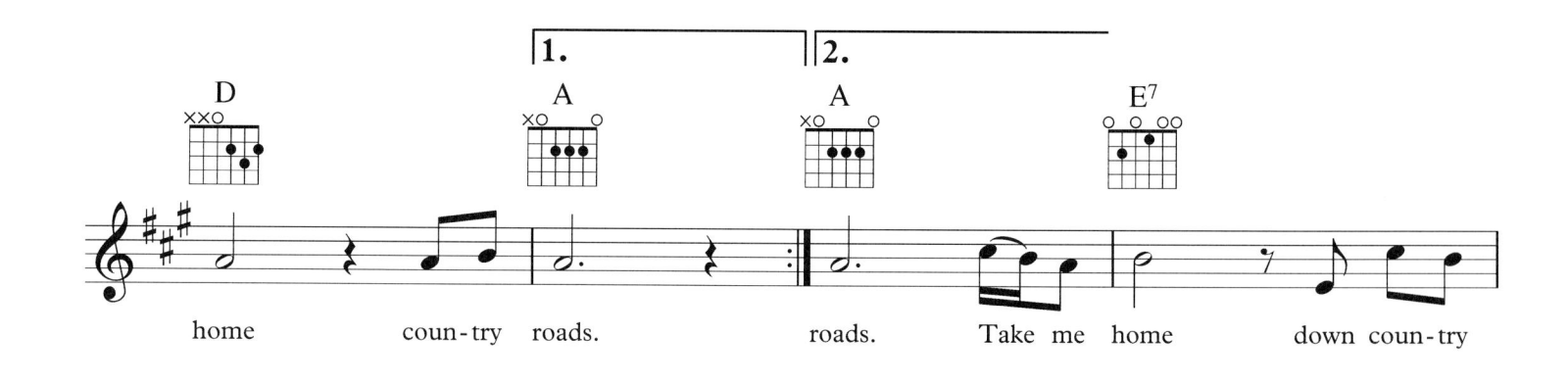

home coun - try roads. roads. Take me home down coun - try

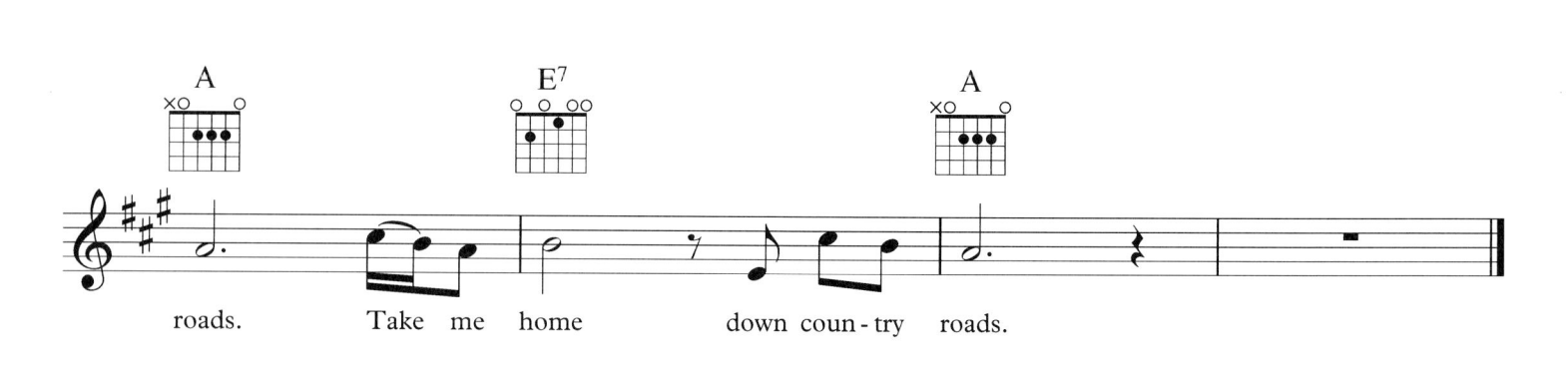

roads. Take me home down coun - try roads.

Tiny Dancer

Words & Music by Elton John & Bernie Taupin

© Copyright 1971 Dick James Music Limited.
Universal/Dick James Music Limited.
All Rights Reserved. International Copyright Secured.

Picking style:

C
F/A
T i m a m i m i T i m a m i m i
T
A
B
1 e & a 2 e & a 3 e & a 4 e & a

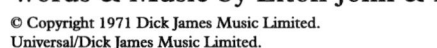

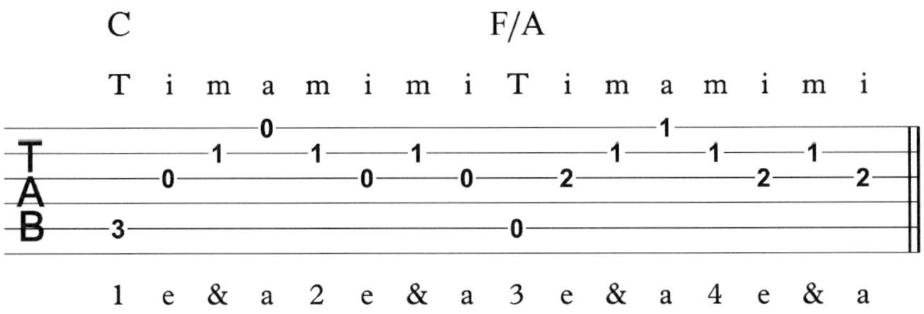

Intro

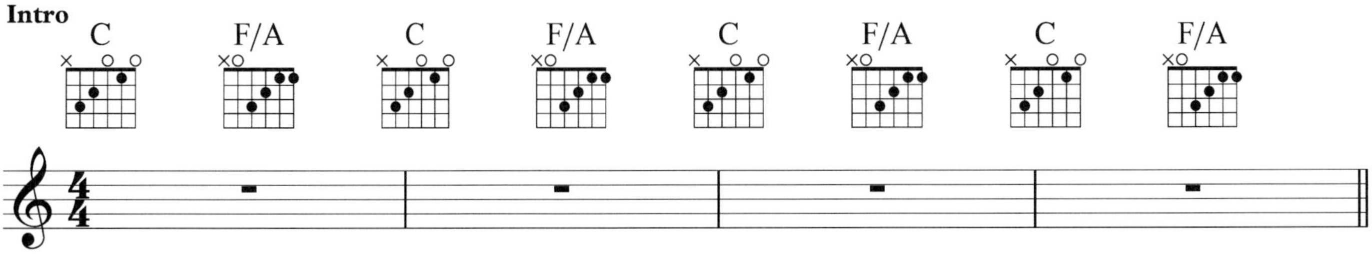

C
F/A
C
F/A
C
F/A
C
F/A

Verse

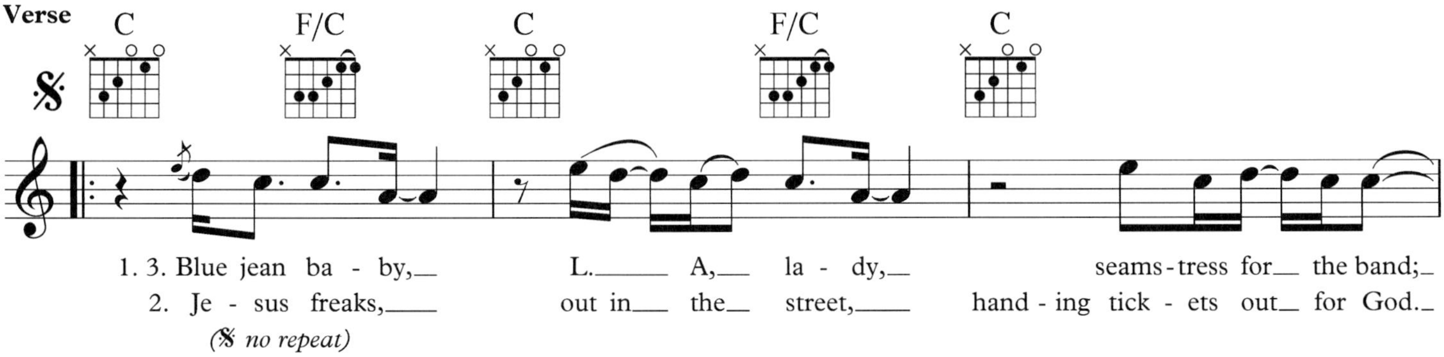

C
F/C
C
F/C
C
1. 3. Blue jean ba - by, L. A, la - dy, seams - tress for the band;
2. Je - sus freaks, out in the street, hand - ing tick - ets out for God.
(𝄋 no repeat)

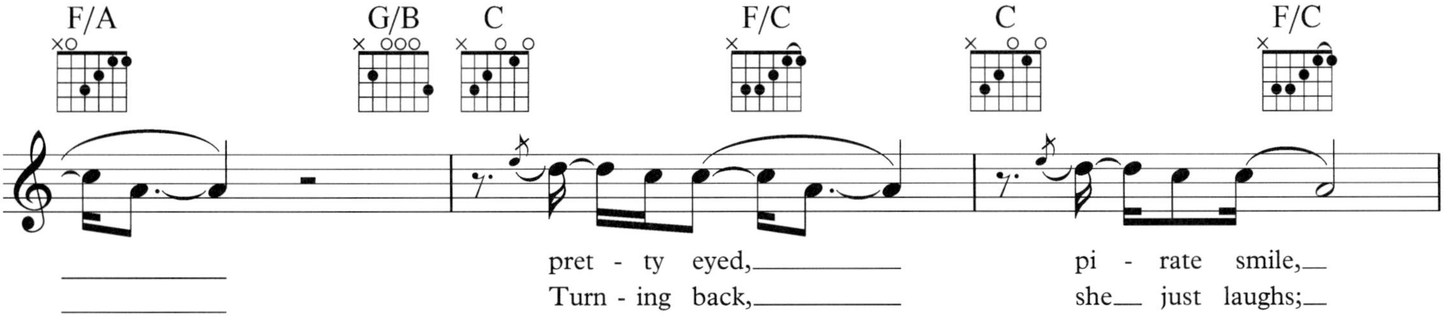

F/A
G/B
C
F/C
C
F/C
pret - ty eyed, pi - rate smile,
Turn - ing back, she just laughs;

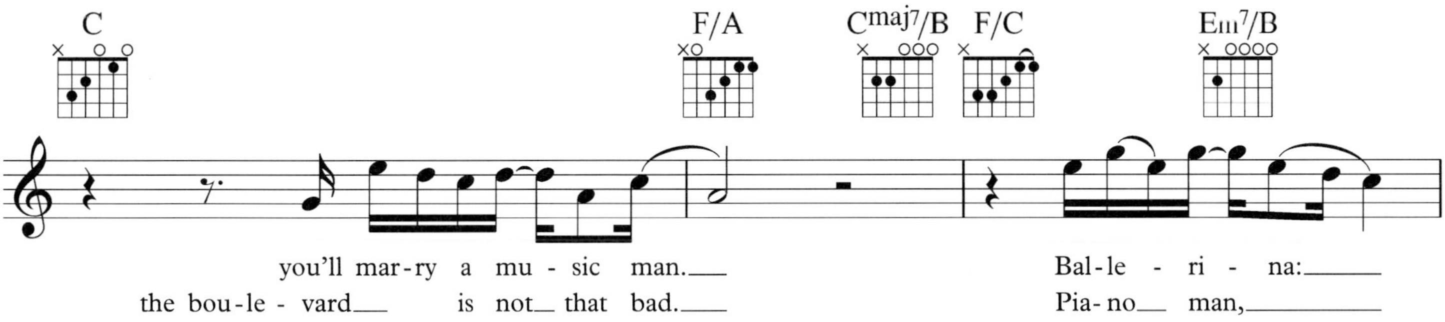

C
F/A
Cmaj7/B
F/C
Em7/B
you'll mar - ry a mu - sic man. Bal - le - ri - na:
the bou - le - vard is not that bad. Pia - no man,

Walk On The Wild Side

Words & Music by Lou Reed

© Copyright 1972 Oakfield Avenue Music Limited.
EMI Music Publishing Limited.
All Rights Reserved. International Copyright Secured.

Steady and continuous sixteenth-note strums can sound a bit too insistent if they're played heavily. A light touch and a little variation in accents creates just the right feel.

Strumming style:

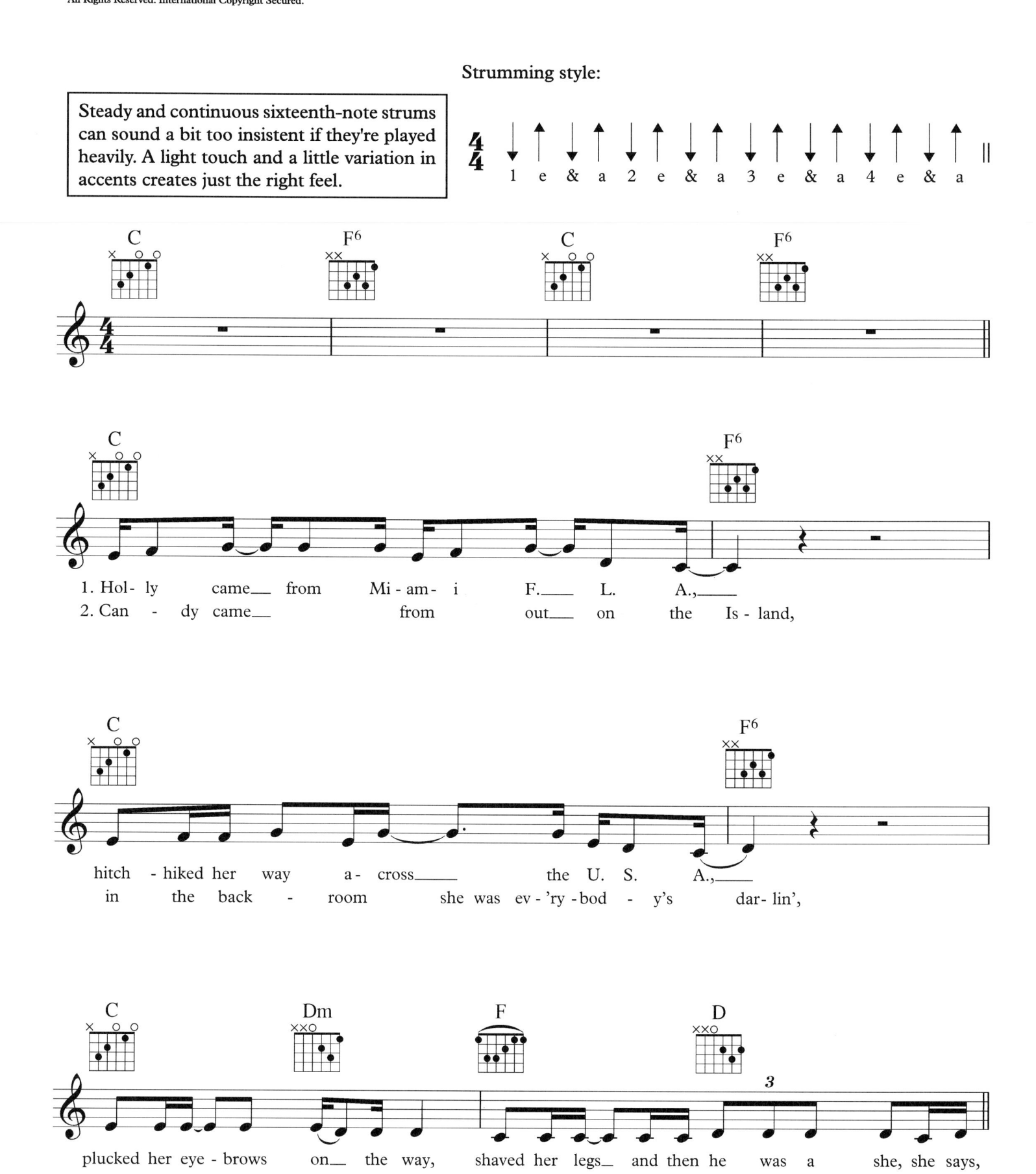

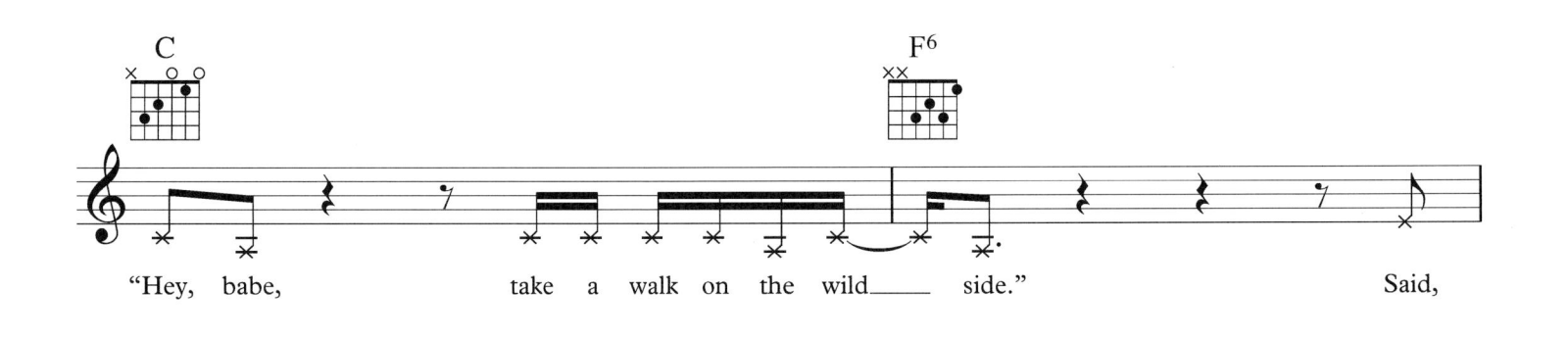

"Hey, babe, take a walk on the wild___ side." Said,

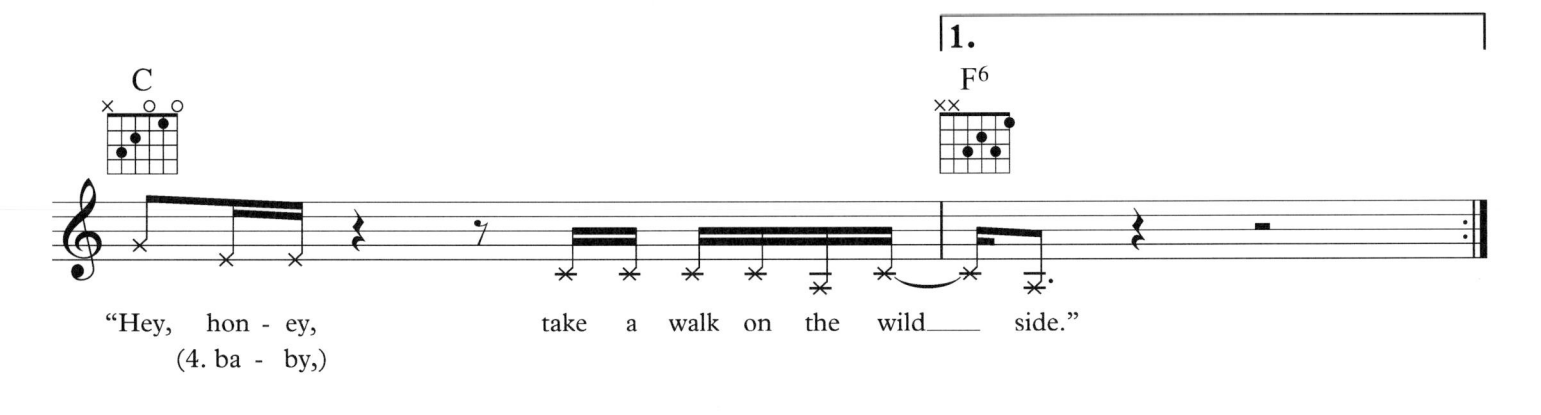

1.

"Hey, hon - ey, take a walk on the wild___ side."
(4. ba - by,)

2.

___ side." ___ And the col-oured girls go doo do doo do doo do___ do doo

doo do doo do doo do___ do doo doo do doo do doo do___ do doo doo do doo do doo do___ do doo

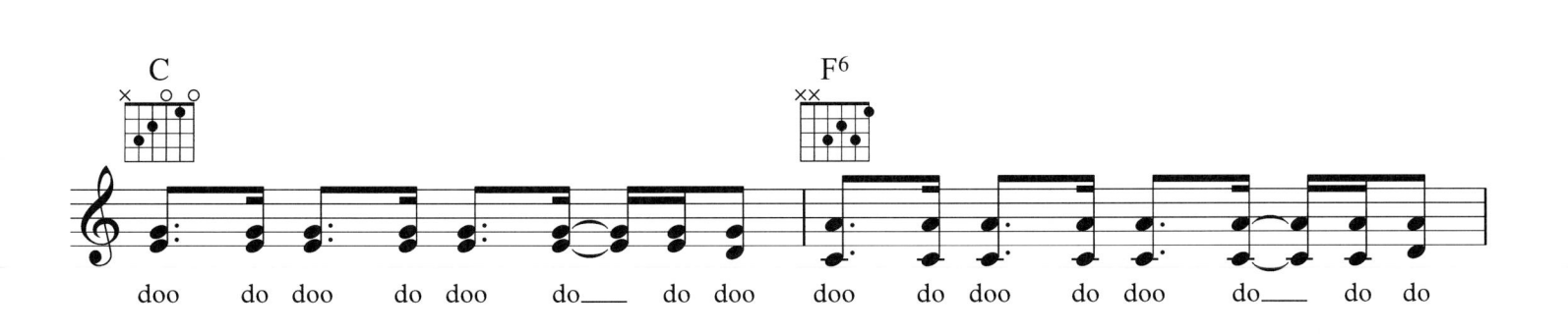

doo do doo do doo do___ do doo doo do doo do doo do___ do do

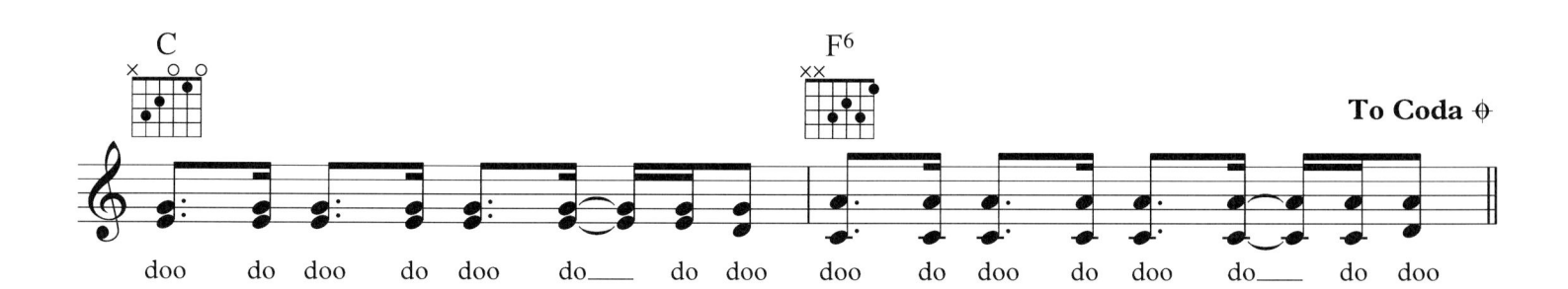

To Coda ⊕

doo   do doo   do doo   do____ do doo   doo   do doo   do doo   do____ do doo

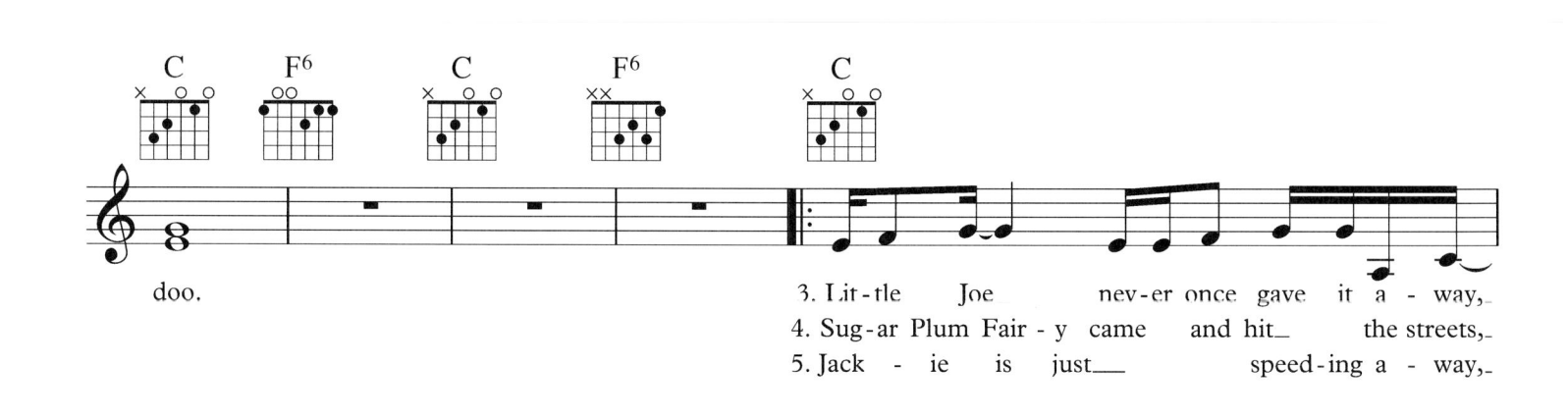

doo.

3. Lit-tle   Joe   nev-er once gave it a - way,__
4. Sug-ar Plum Fair - y came   and hit__ the streets,__
5. Jack - ie is just__   speed-ing a - way,__

ev - 'ry-bod - y   had   to pay__ and pay,___   a
look-in' for soul food and a place   to eat,__
thought she was_ James Dean   for a day.__

hus - tle here_ and a hus - tle there,   New York Cit-y's the   place where they say,__
went to the_ A-pol - lo,__ you should -'ve seen   them   go go go._ They said,
Then I guess she had to crash,   val - i-um_ would have helped that bash. I said,

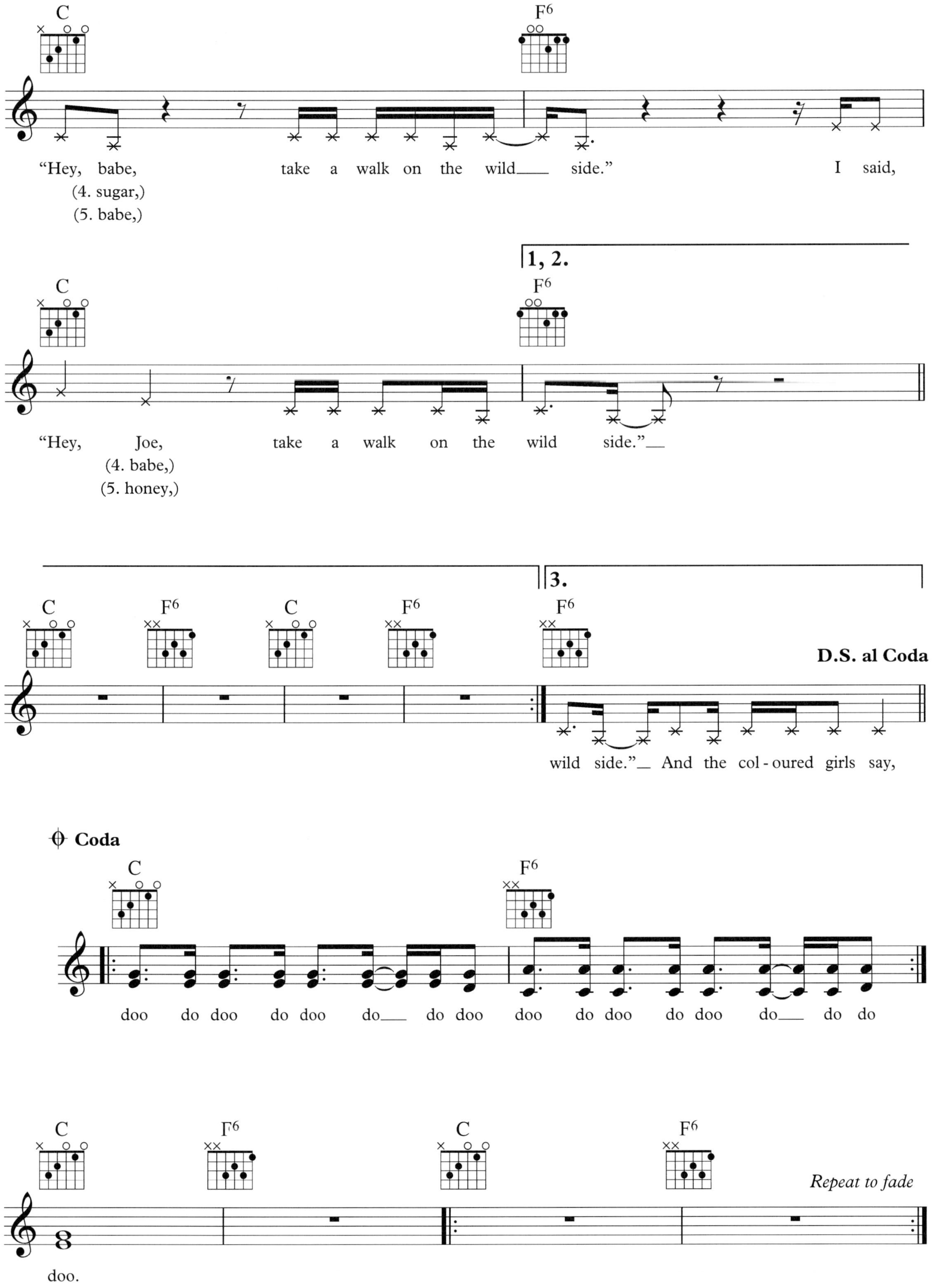

C   F^6

"Hey, babe,   take a walk on the wild___ side."   I said,
(4. sugar,)
(5. babe,)

1, 2.

C   F^6

"Hey, Joe,   take a walk on the wild side."___
(4. babe,)
(5. honey,)

3.

C   F^6 C   F^6 F^6

D.S. al Coda

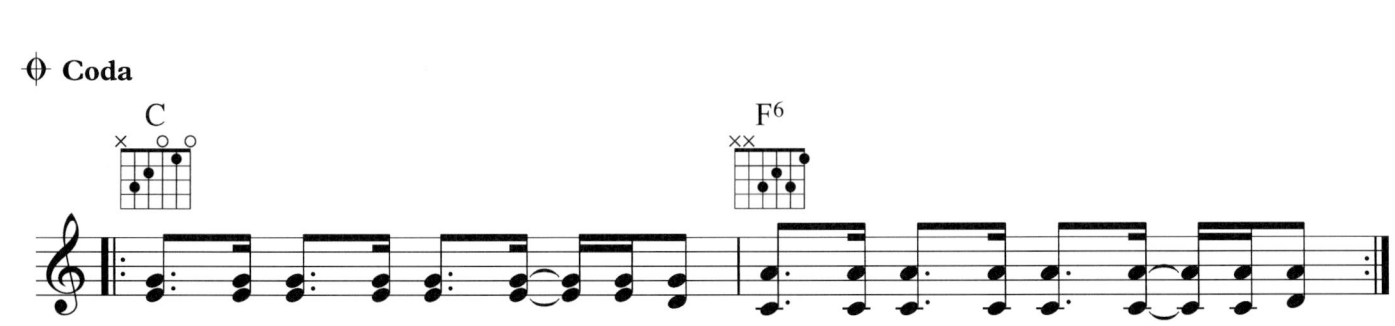

wild side."___ And the col-oured girls say,

$\oplus$ **Coda**

C   F^6

doo   do doo   do doo   do___ do doo   doo   do doo   do doo   do___ do do

C   F^6 C   F^6

Repeat to fade

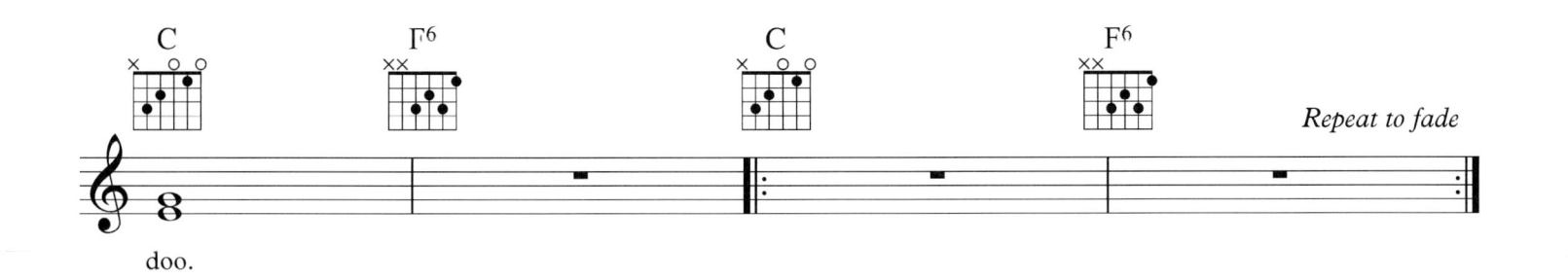

doo.

Waltz #2 (XO)

Words & Music by Elliott Smith

© Copyright 1998 Spent Bullets Music/Universal Music Careers.
Universal Music Publishing MGB Limited.
All Rights Reserved. International Copyright Secured.

Picking style:

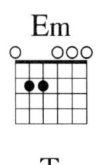

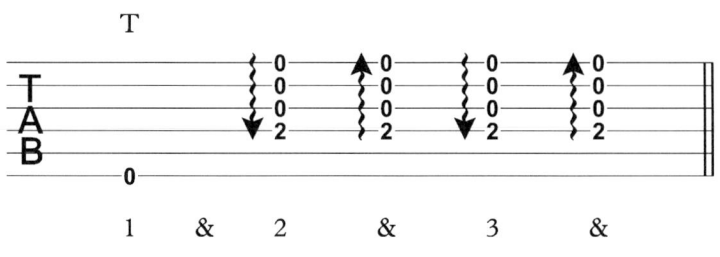

Capo: Fret 3

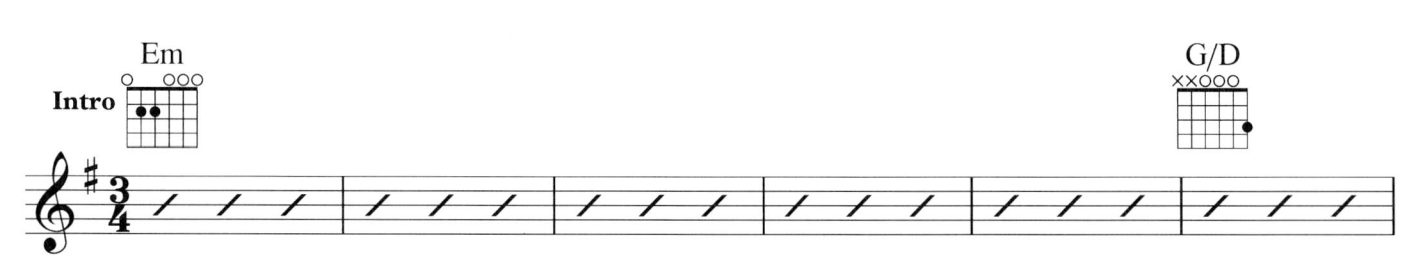

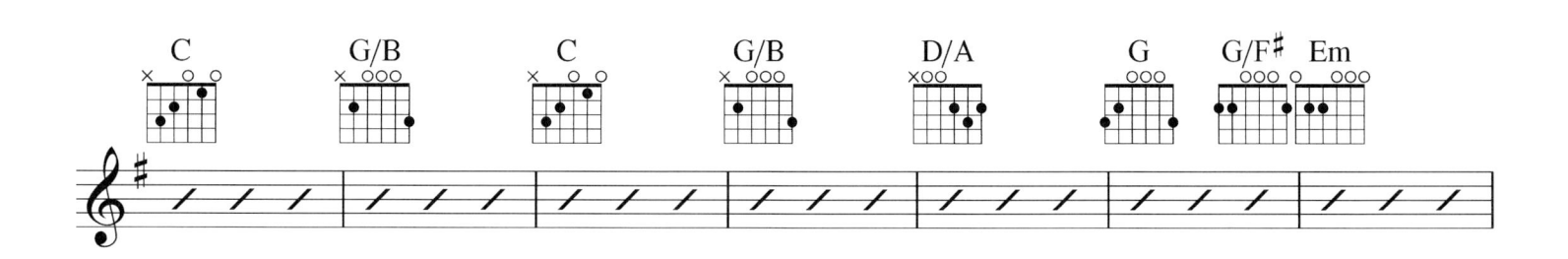

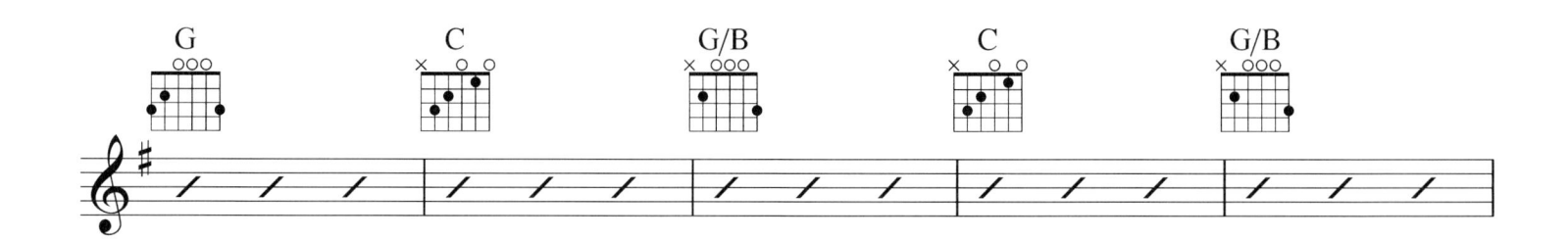

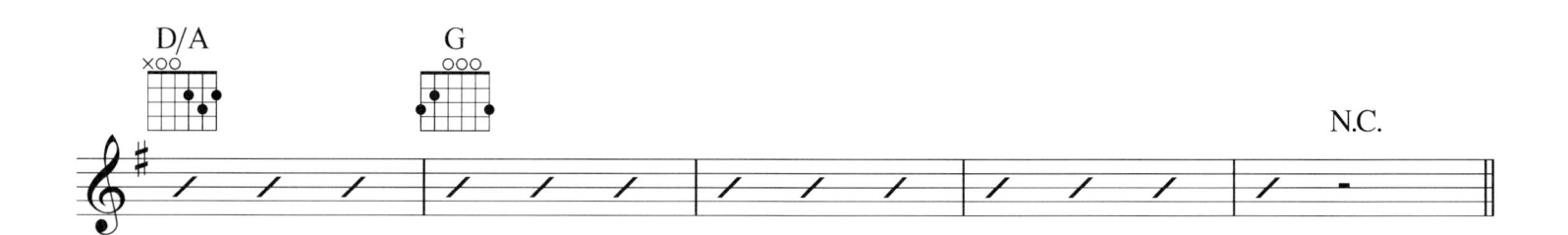

Chorus

To Coda ⊕

1.

I'm here to-day, expect-ed to stay on and on and on. I'm tired,

I'm tired.

I'm nev-er gon-na know you now, but I'm gon-na love you a-ny-how.

(Vocal tacet 3°)

We Have All The Time In The World

Words by Hal David
Music by John Barry

© Copyright 1969 EMI United Partnership Limited.
All Rights Reserved. International Copyright Secured.

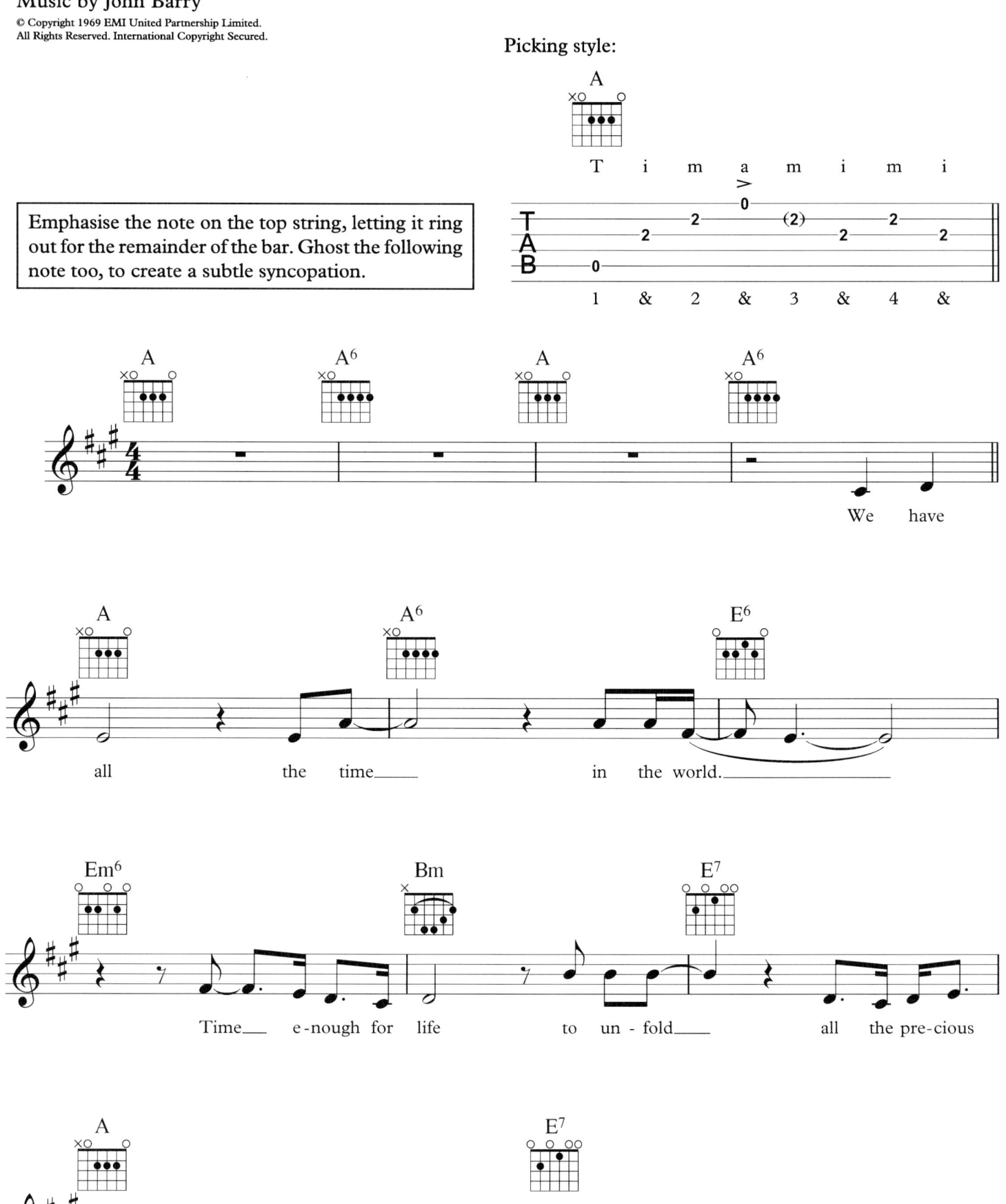

Who Knows Where The Time Goes?

Words & Music by Sandy Denny

© Copyright 1967 Fairwood Music (UK) Limited.
All Rights Reserved. International Copyright Secured.

> Strum loose sixteenth-notes, leaving a few rhythmic gaps as shown—and perhaps play a heavier, drawn-out down-strum at the beginning of the bar.

Wichita Lineman

Words & Music by Jimmy Webb

© Copyright 1968 Canopy Music Incorporated.
Universal Music Publishing Limited.
All Rights Reserved. International Copyright Secured.

Strumming style:

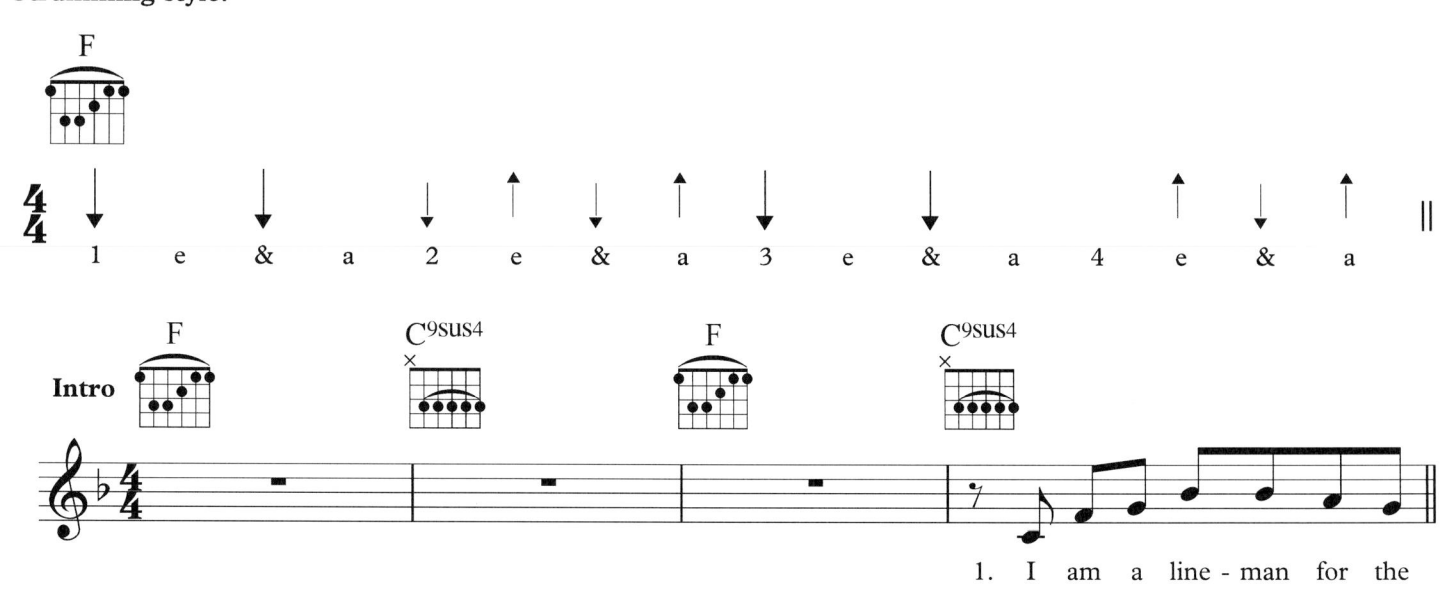

Intro

1. I am a line-man for the

Verse

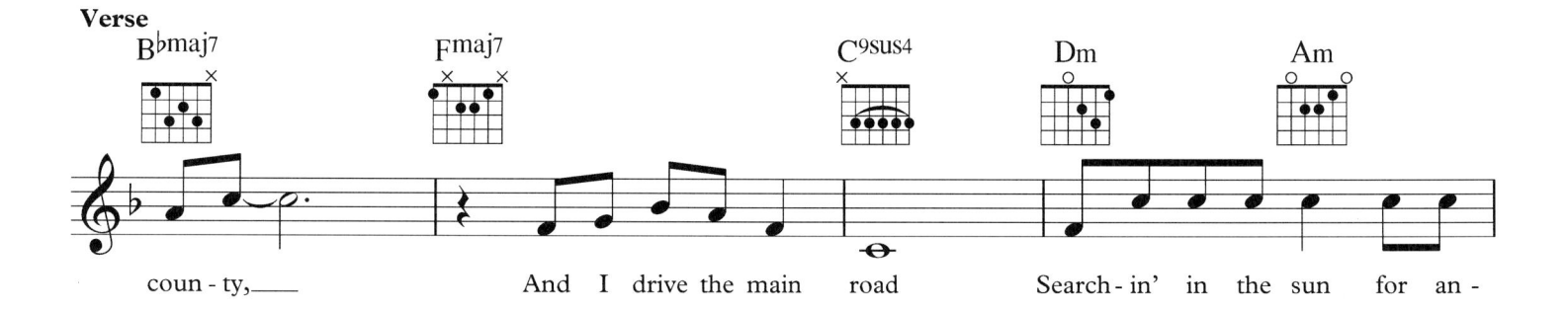

coun - ty,____ And I drive the main road Search-in' in the sun for an-

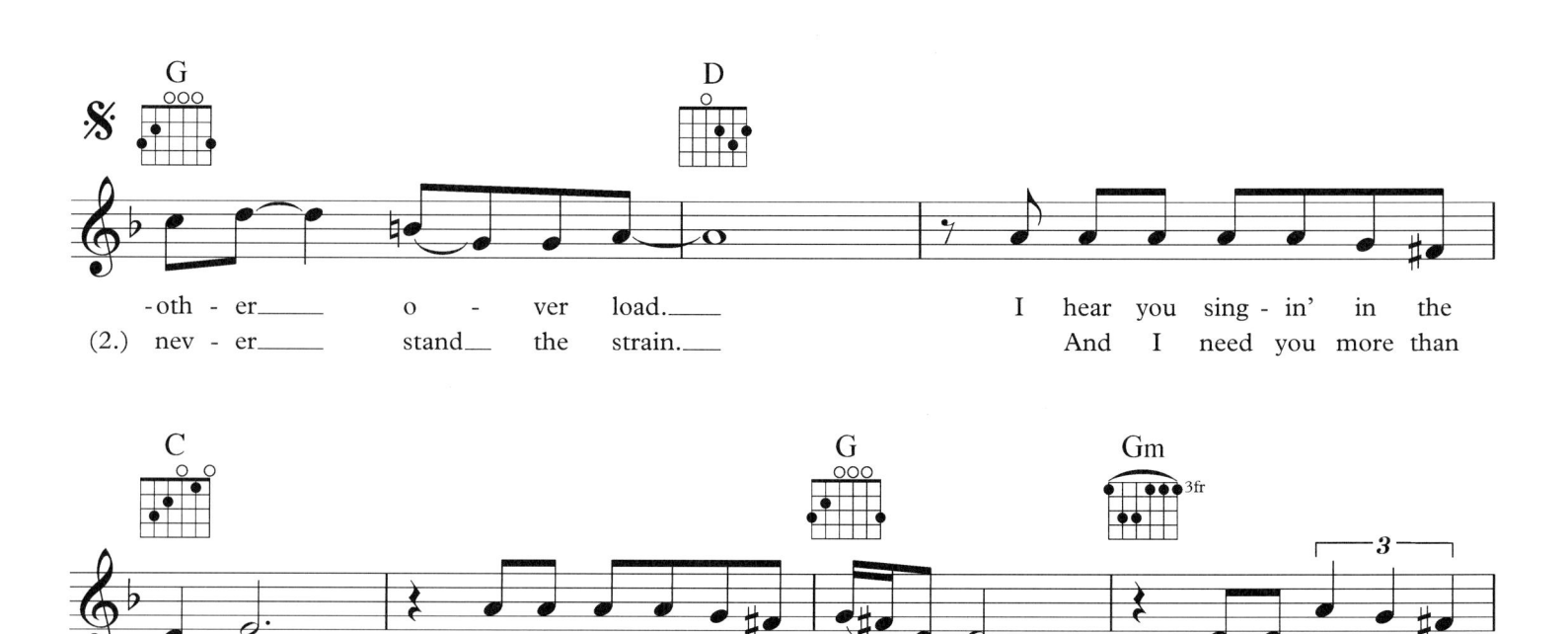

-oth-er____ o - ver load.____ I hear you sing-in' in the
(2.) nev - er____ stand__ the strain.____ And I need you more than

wi - res I can hear you thru the whine,____ And the Wi-chi-ta
want you, And I want you for all time,____ And the Wi-chi-ta

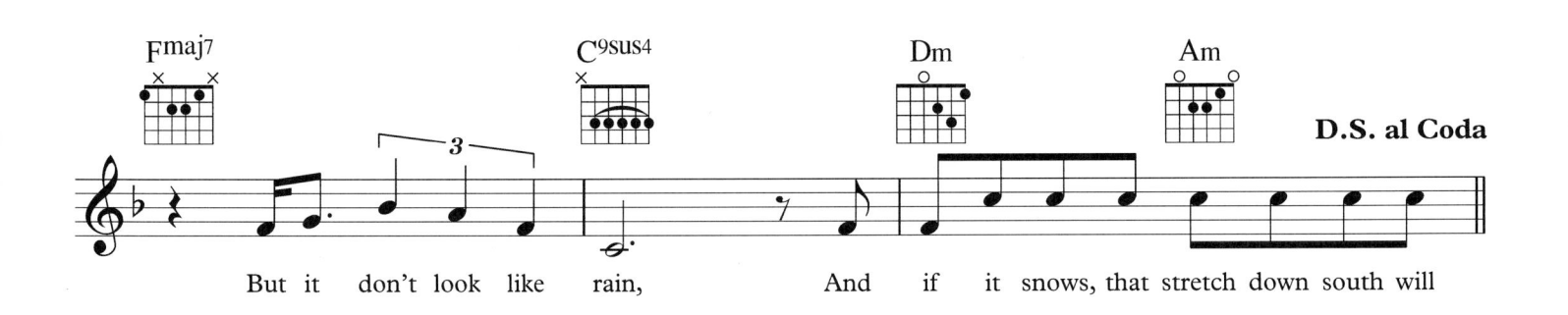

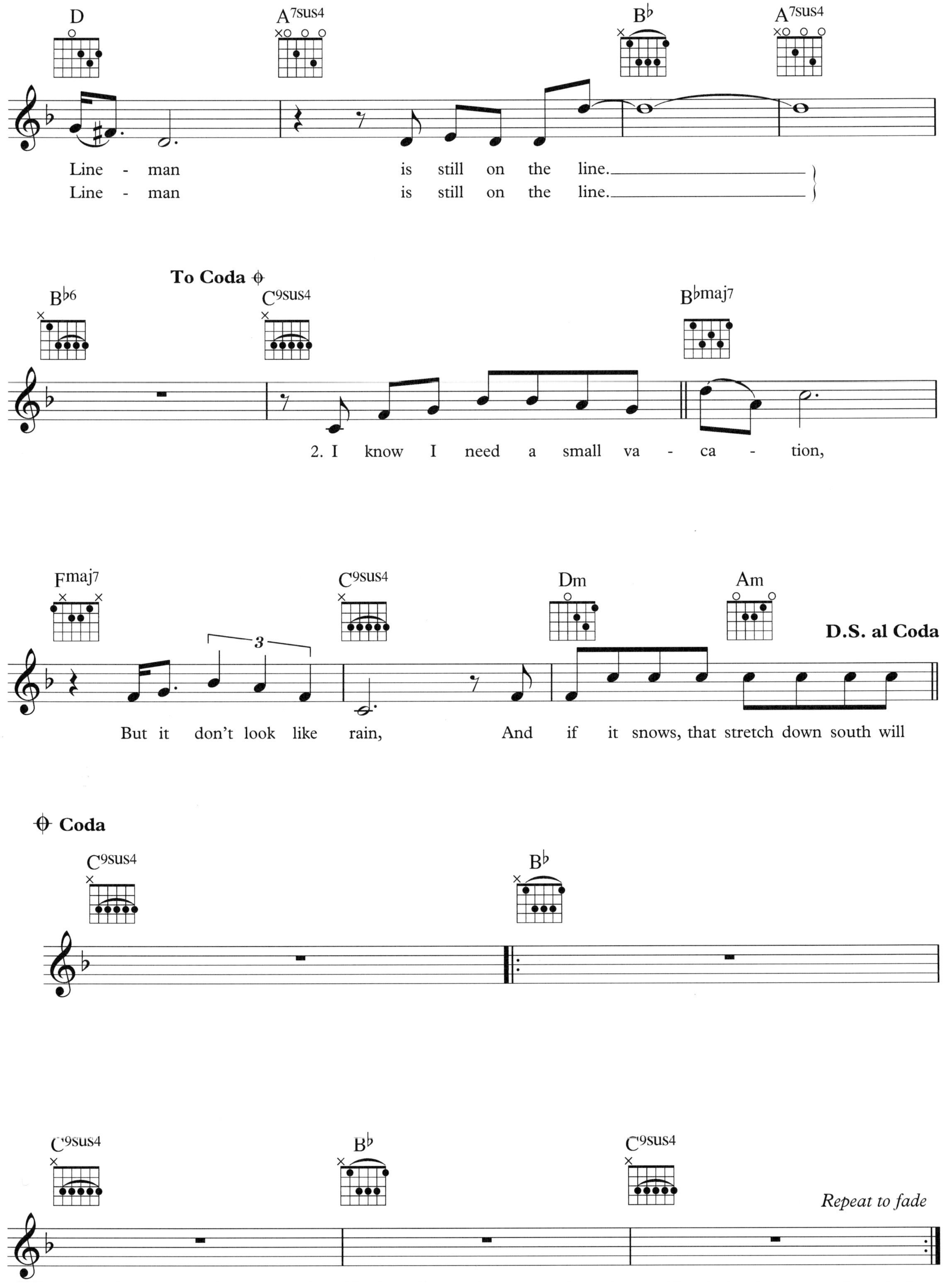

Line - man   is still on the line._____⎱
Line - man   is still on the line._____⎰

To Coda ⊕

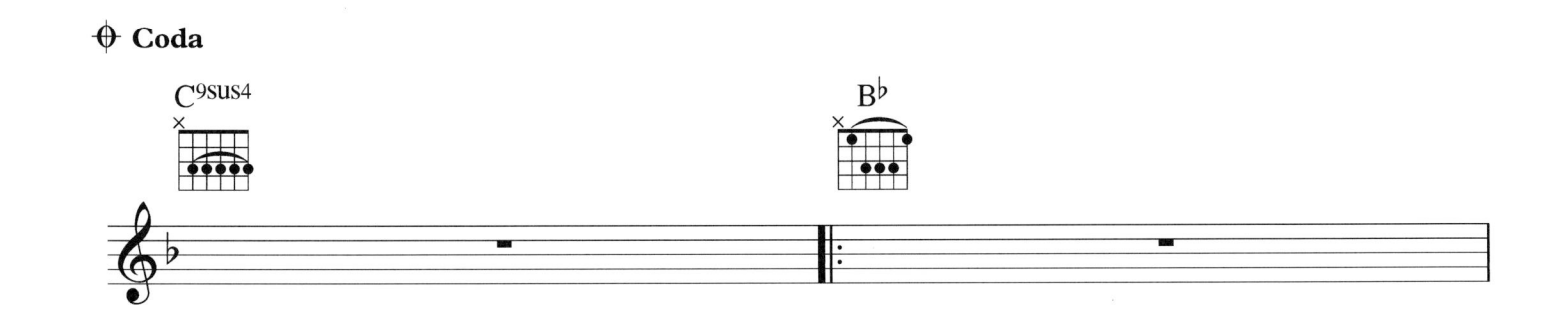

2. I know I need a small va - ca - tion,

But it don't look like rain,   And   if   it snows, that stretch down south will

D.S. al Coda

⊕ **Coda**

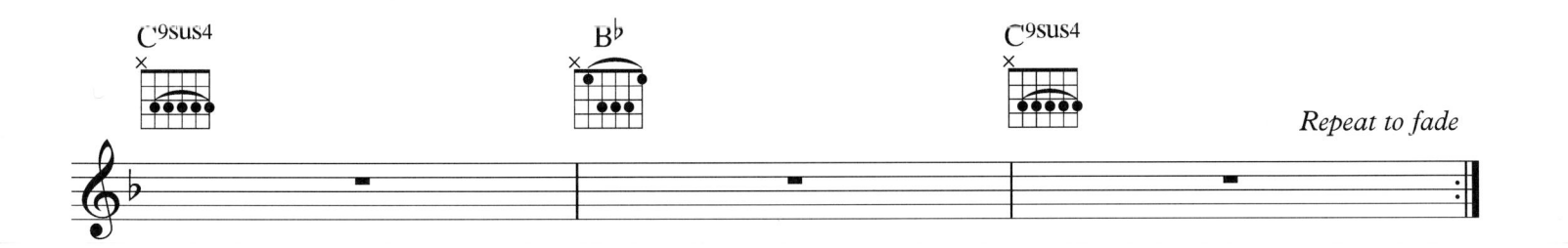

Repeat to fade

161

You're Beautiful

Words & Music by Sacha Skarbek, James Blunt & Amanda Ghost

© Copyright 2004 EMI Music Publishing Limited/Bucks Music Group Limited.
All Rights Reserved. International Copyright Secured.

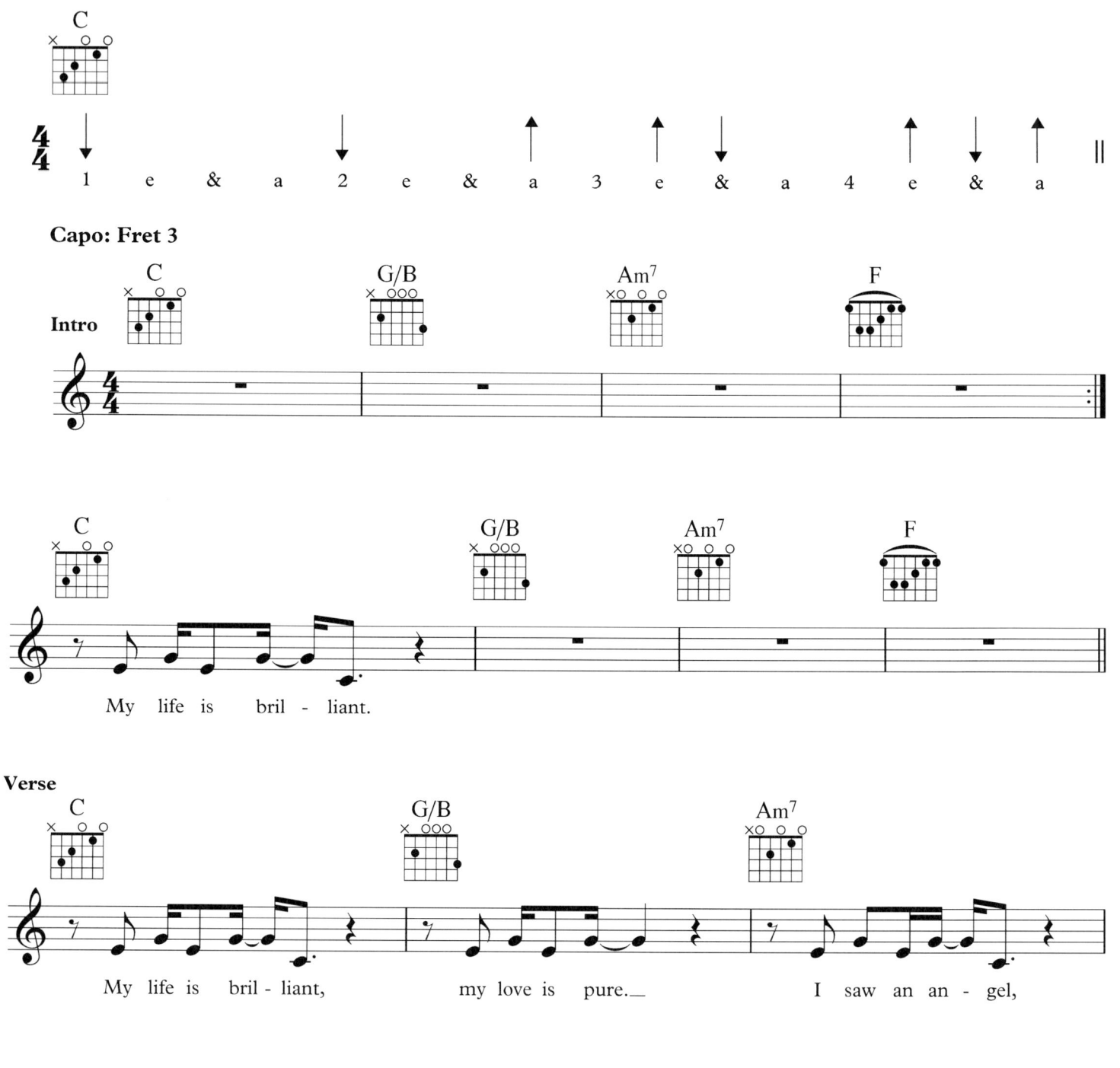

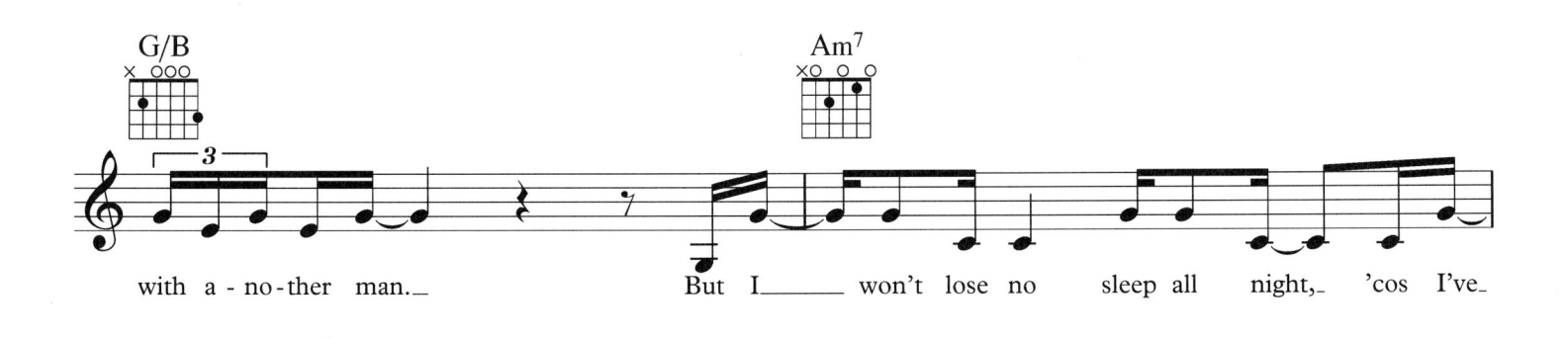

with a-no-ther man._ But I____ won't lose no sleep all night,_ 'cos I've_

Chorus

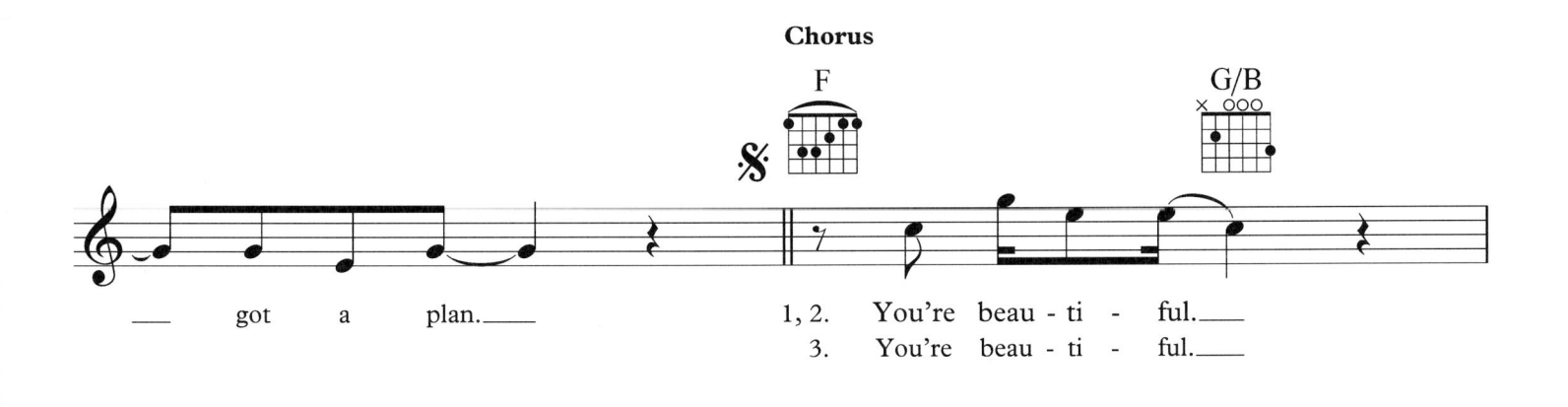

____ got a plan.____ 1, 2. You're beau-ti - ful.____
3. You're beau-ti - ful.____

You're beau-ti - ful._ You're beau-ti - ful,_ it's true.____ I saw_
You're beau-ti - ful._ You're beau-ti - ful,_ it's true.____ There must_

To Coda II ϕ

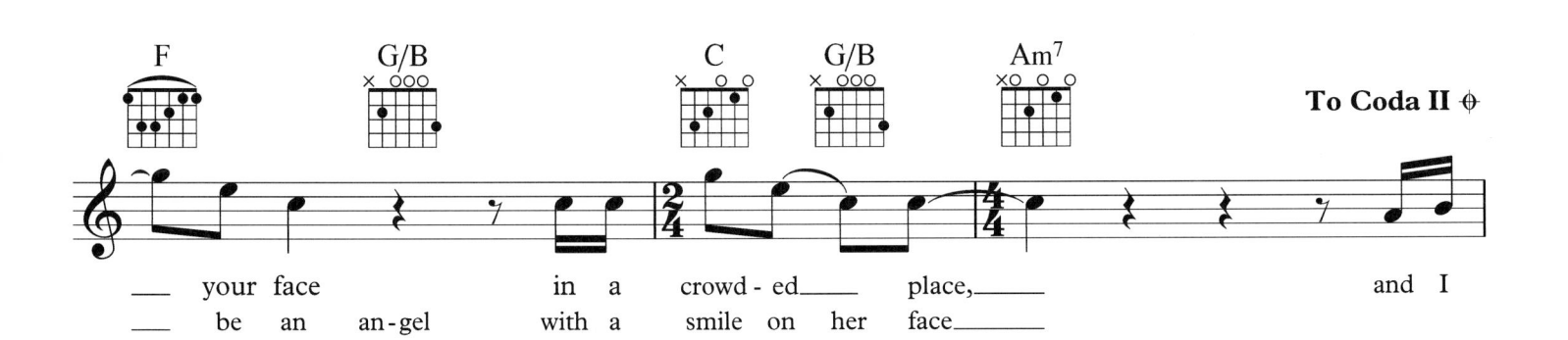

____ your face in a crowd-ed____ place,____ and I
____ be an an-gel with a smile on her face____

To Coda I ϕ

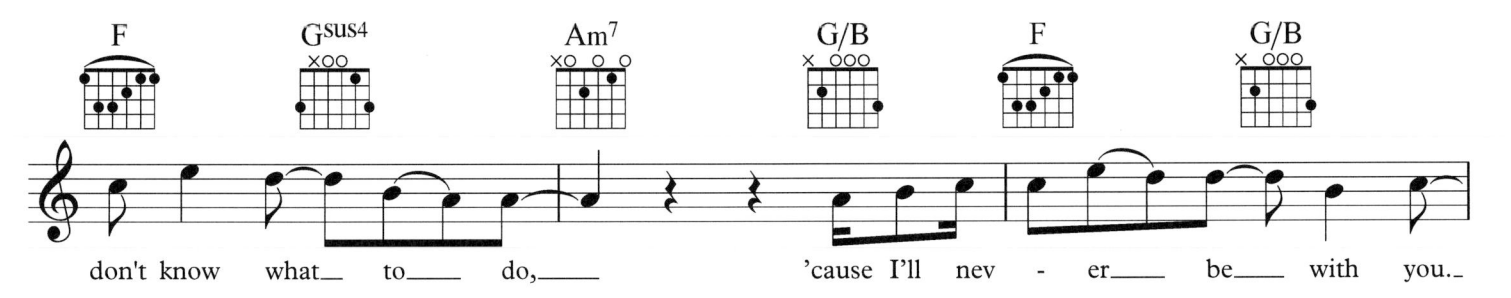

don't know what_ to___ do,____ 'cause I'll nev - er___ be___ with you._

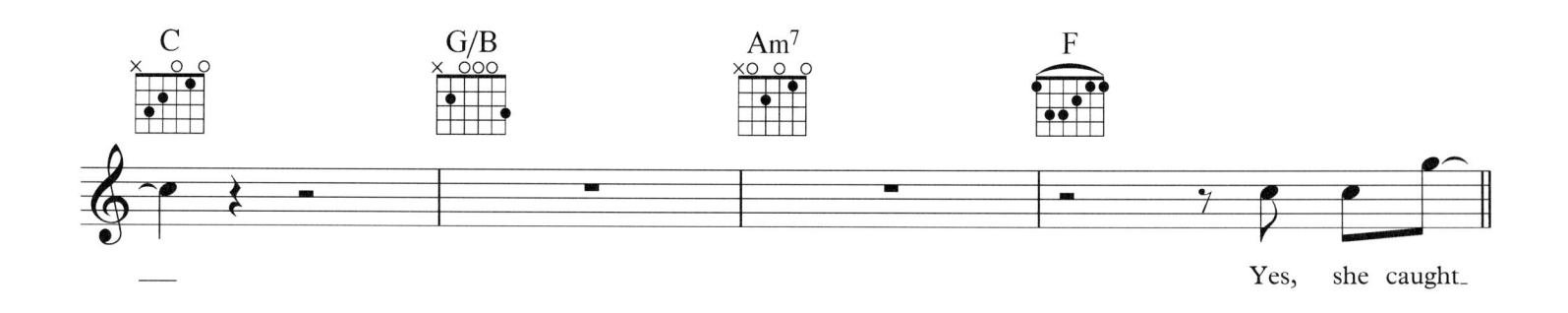

Yes, she caught

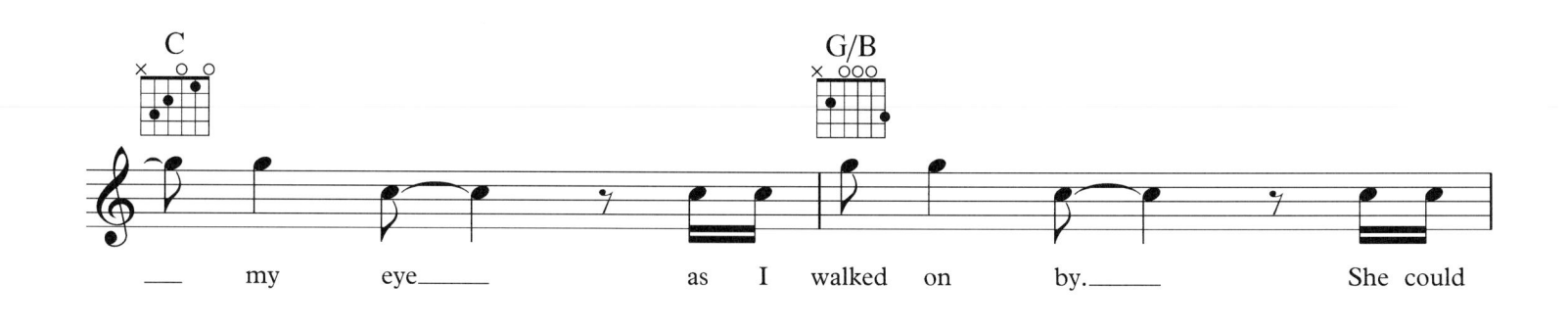

my eye___ as I walked on by.___ She could

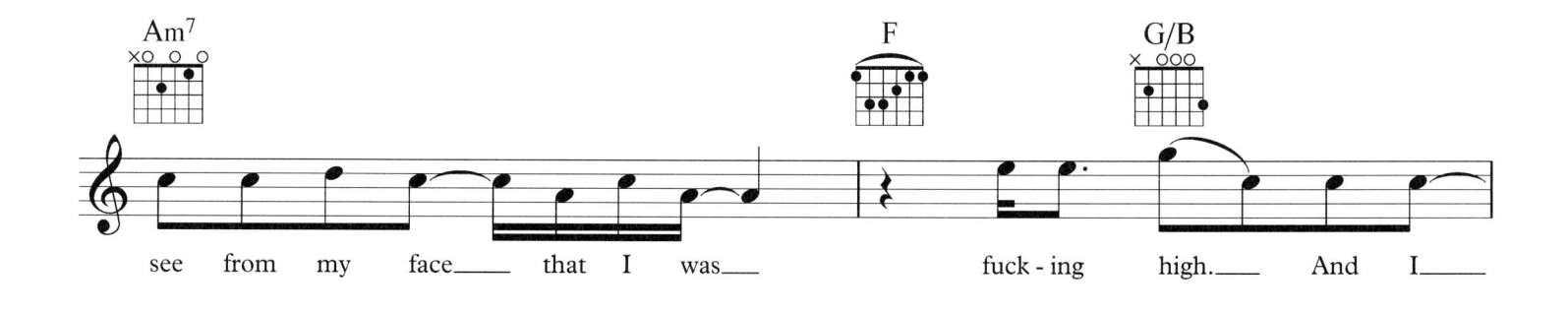

see from my face___ that I was___ fuck - ing high.___ And I___

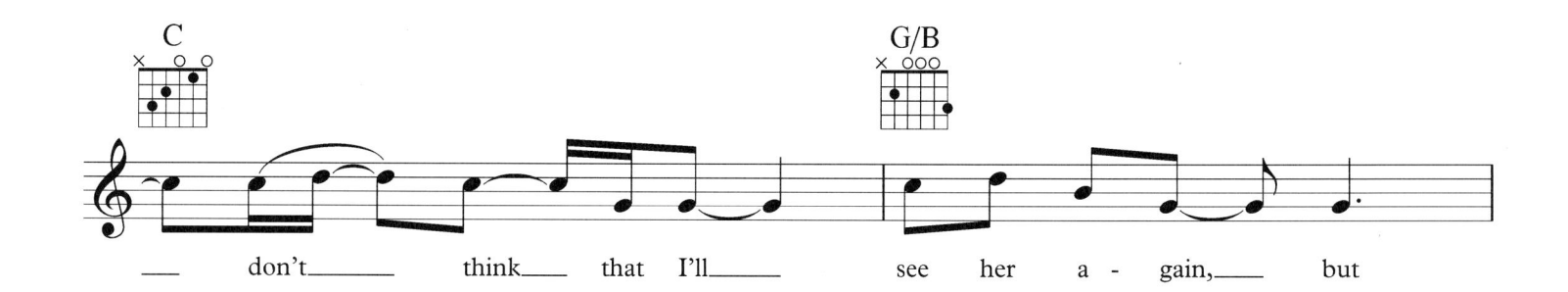

___ don't___ think___ that I'll___ see her a - gain,___ but

D.S. al Coda I

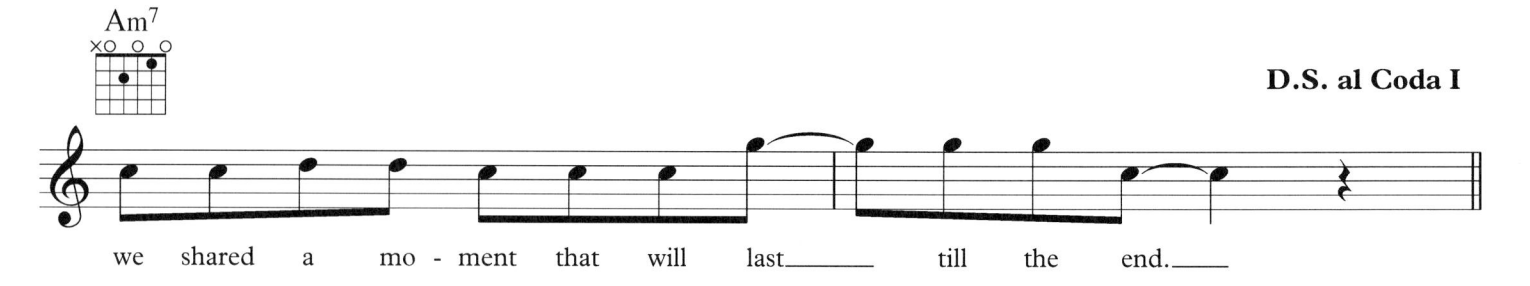

we shared a mo - ment that will last___ till the end.___

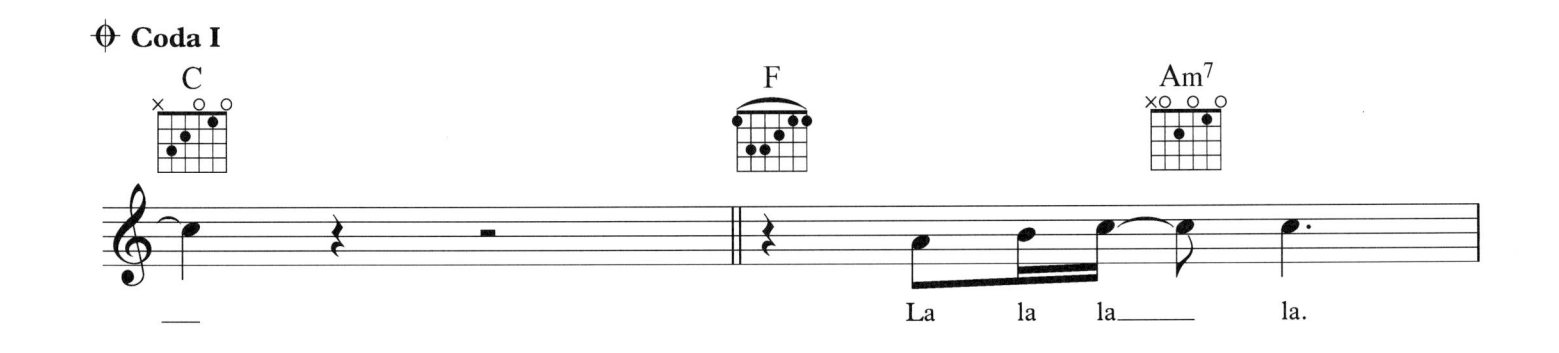

La la la____ la.

D.S. al Coda II

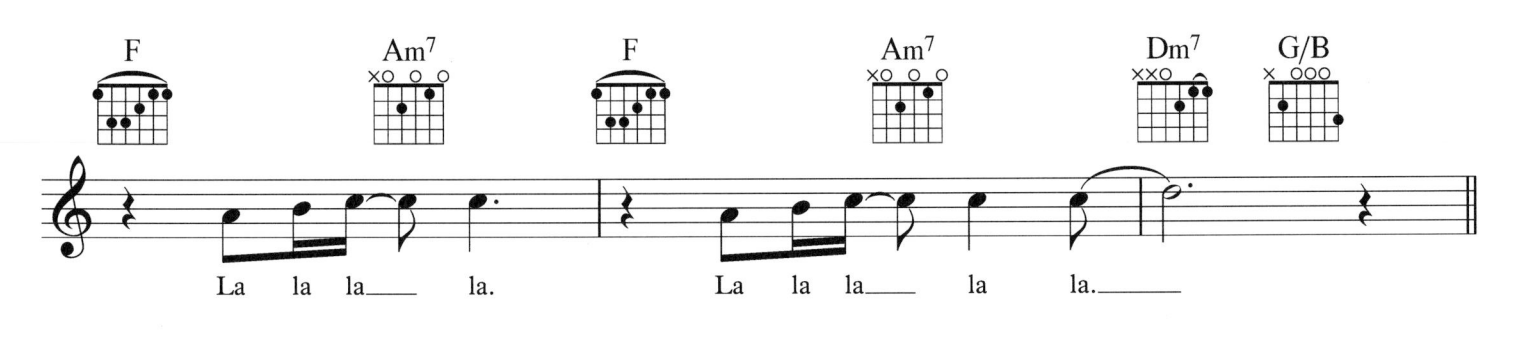

La la la____ la.   La la la____ la la.____

$\oplus$ **Coda II**

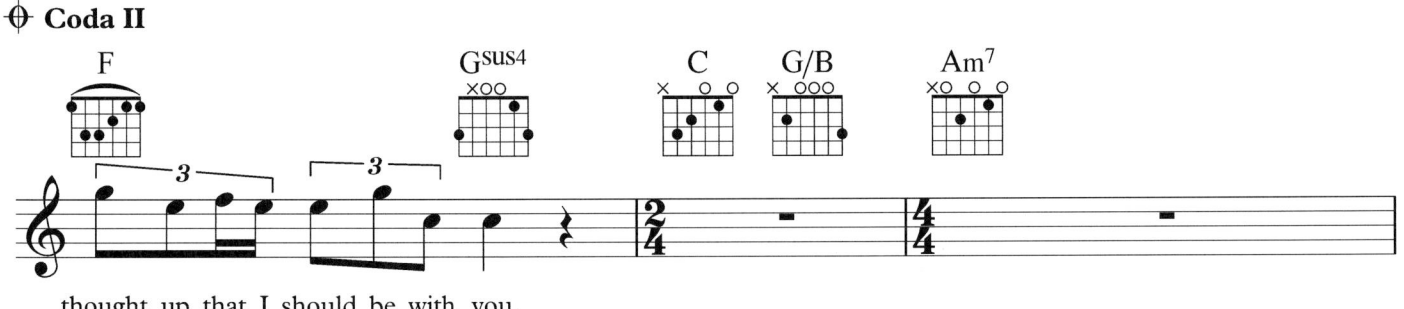

thought up that I should be with you.

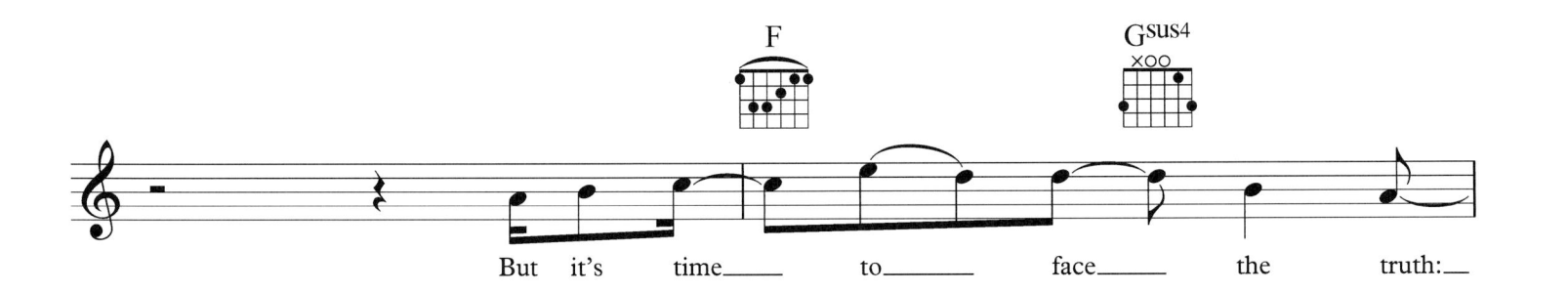

But it's time____ to____ face____ the truth:____

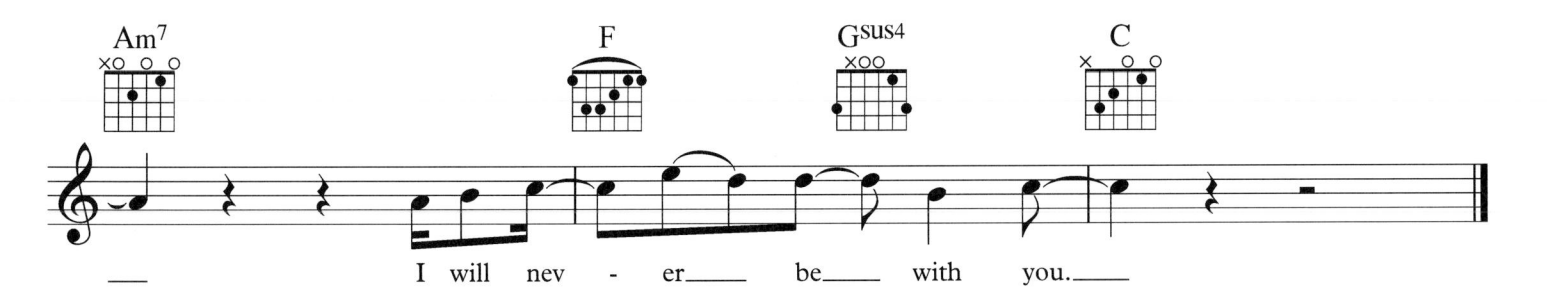

____ I will nev - er____ be____ with you.____

Wake Up Little Susie

Words & Music by Felice Bryant & Boudleaux Bryant

© Copyright 1957 Sony/ATV Acuff Rose Musi , USA.
Sony/ATV Music Publishing (UK) Limited.
All Rights Reserved. International Copyright Secured.

> Constant down-strums create a heavier, almost rock-like feel that's perfect for the intro.

Strumming style:

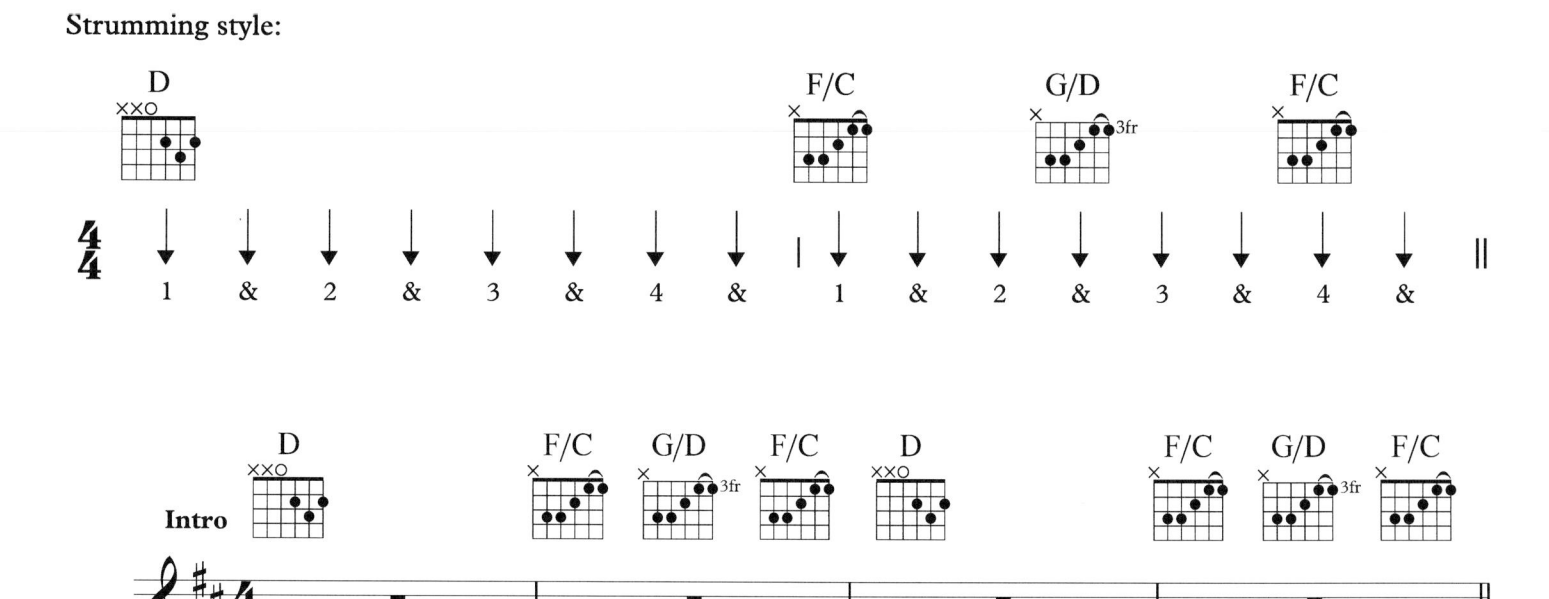

Intro

Chorus

Wake up,   Lit-tle Su - sie,___   wake up.

2.

Verse

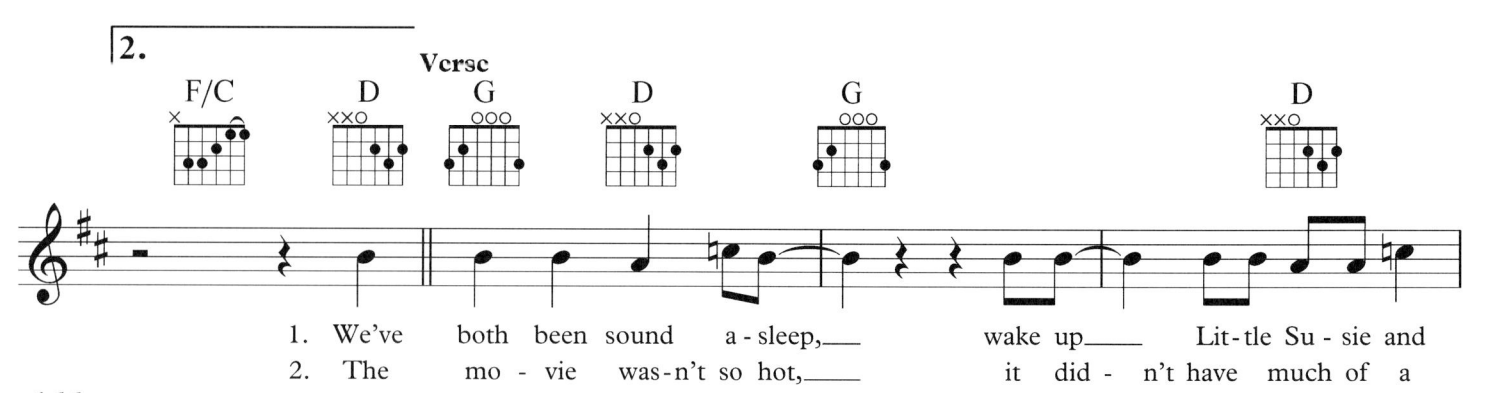

1. We've both been sound a - sleep,___   wake up___   Lit-tle Su - sie and
2. The mo - vie was-n't so hot,___   it did - n't have much of a

Well, Su - sie, ba - by, looks like we goofed a -

-gain._____ Wake up,__ Lit - tle Su - sie.__

Wake up,__ Lit - tle Su - sie.__ We've got - ta go

home.

Su - sie.__ Wake up,__ Lit - tle Su - sie._____

You're So Vain

Words & Music by Carly Simon

© Copyright 1972 C'est Music.
Quackenbush Music Limited, USA/Touch Tones Music Limited.
All Rights Reserved. International Copyright Secured.

Strumming style:

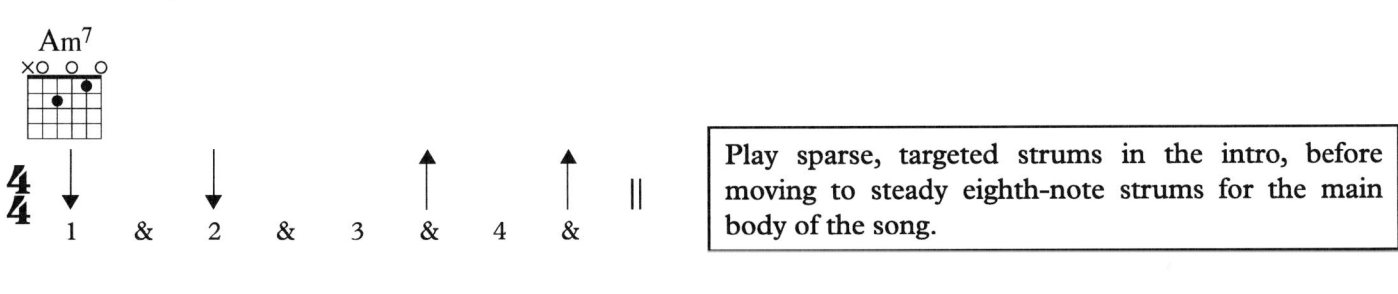

Play sparse, targeted strums in the intro, before moving to steady eighth-note strums for the main body of the song.

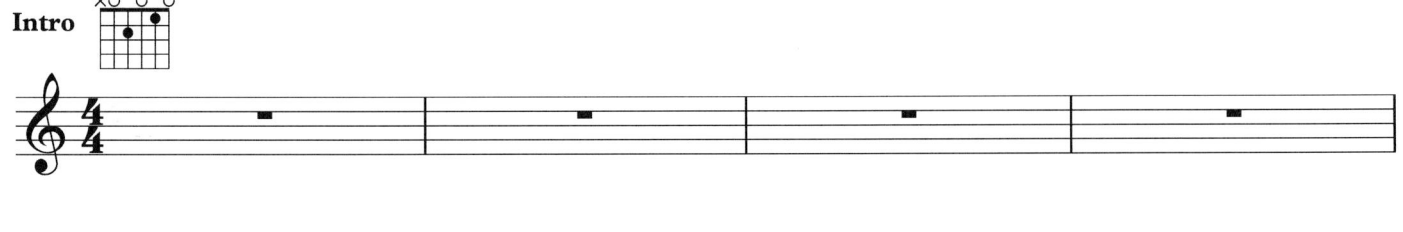

1. You

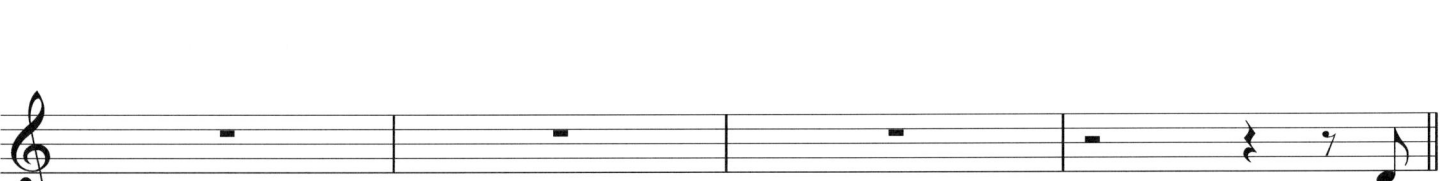

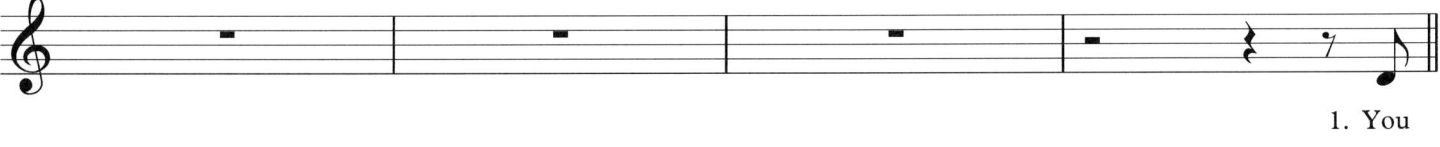

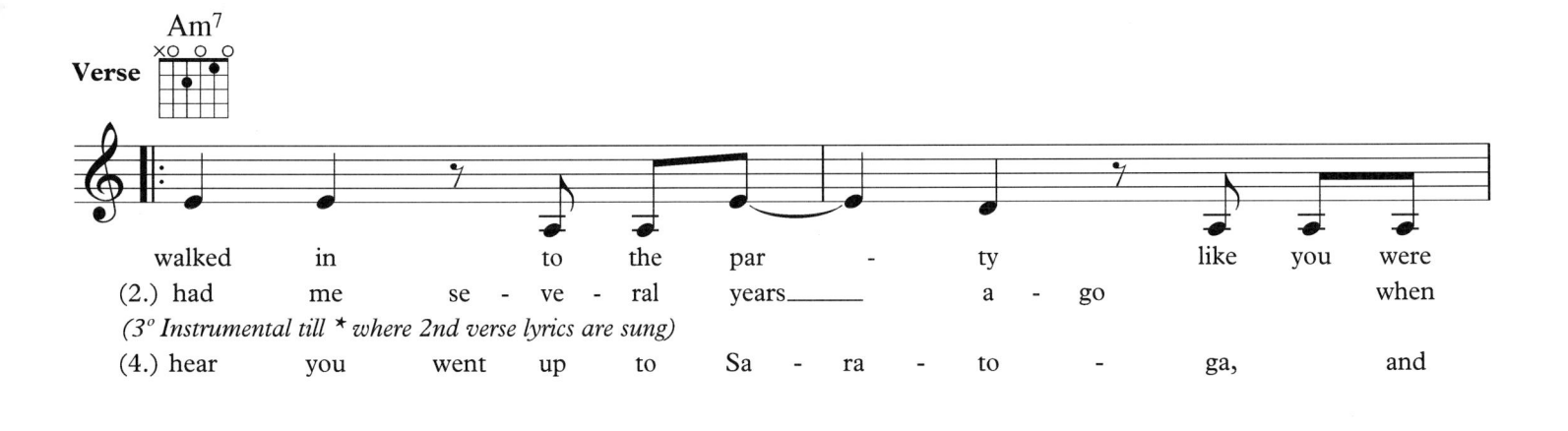

walked   in   to   the   par - ty   like   you   were
(2.) had   me   se - ve - ral   years_____   a - go   when
(3° Instrumental till ✱ where 2nd verse lyrics are sung)
(4.) hear   you   went   up   to   Sa - ra - to - ga,   and

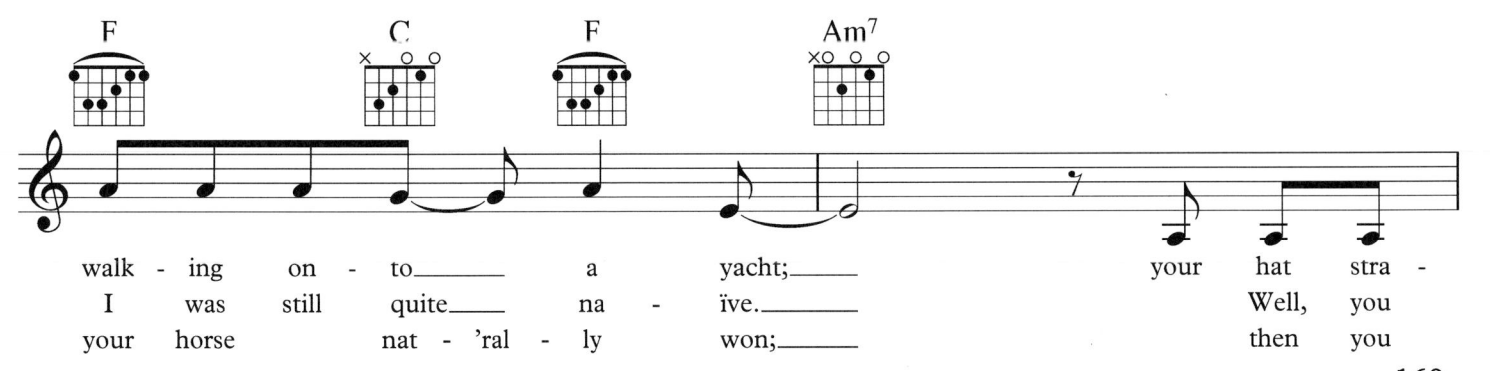

walk - ing   on - to_____   a   yacht;_____   your   hat   stra -
I   was   still   quite_____   na - ïve._____   Well,   you
your   horse   nat - 'ral - ly   won;_____   then   you

- te - gic - 'lly   dipped   be - low_____   one   eye,_____   your
said   that   we   made   such   a   pret - ty   pair,_____   and
flew   your   Lear - jet   up   to   No - va   Sco - tia,_____   to   see   the

F   C   F   Am⁷

scarf,   it   was   a - pri - cot._____   You   had
that   you   would   nev - er   leave._____   But   you
to - tal   e - clipse_____   of   the   sun._____   Well,   you're

F   G   Em   Am⁷

one   eye   in   the   mir - ror   as_____   you
gave   a - way   the   things   you   loved_____   and
where   you   should   be   all   the   time_____   and

F   C   G/B   F

watched   your - self_____   ga - votte,___   and___   all   the   girls_____   dreamed   that   they'd_
one   of   them   was___   me.___   * I___   had   some   dreams_____   there   were   clouds_
when   you're   not___   you're_   with___   some   un - der - world   spy_____   or   the   wife_

___   be   your   part - ner,   they'd_____   be   your   part - ner   and
___   in   my   cof - fee,   clouds_____   in   my   cof - fee   and
___   of   a   close   friend,   wife_____   of   a   close_____   friend   and

170

Chorus

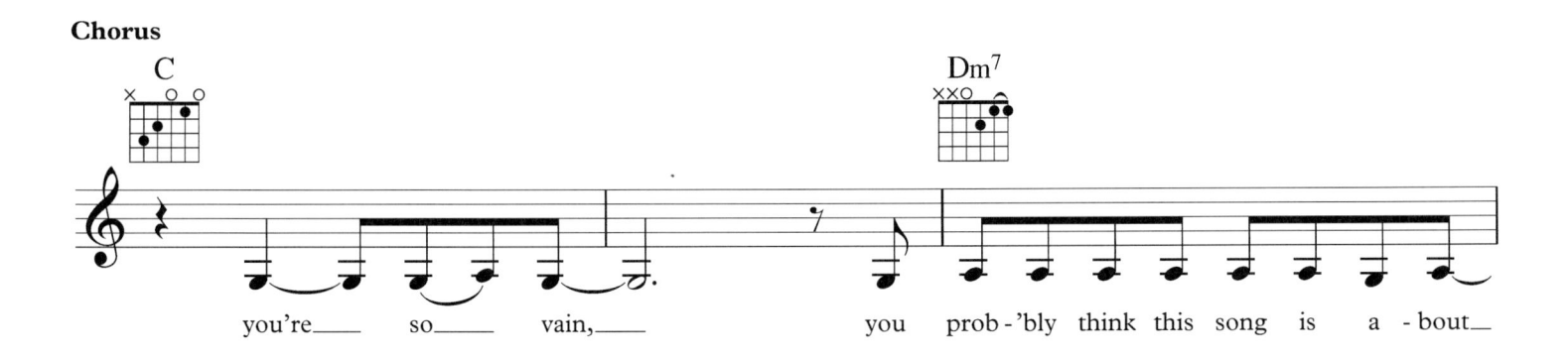

you're___ so___ vain,___ you prob-'bly think this song is a-bout___

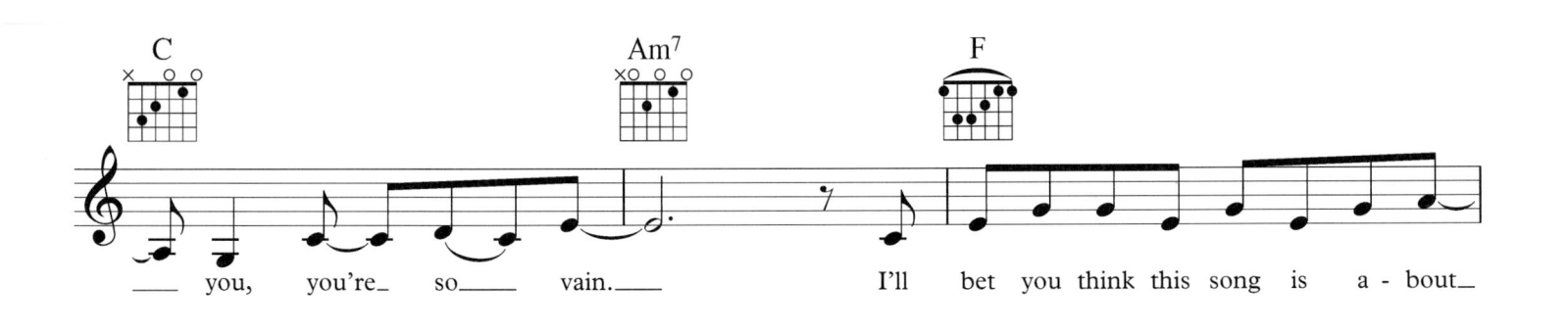

___ you, you're___ so___ vain.___ I'll bet you think this song is a-bout___

___ you. Don't__ you? Don't___ you?_____ 2. You ___ you? Don't__ you?

4. Well, I

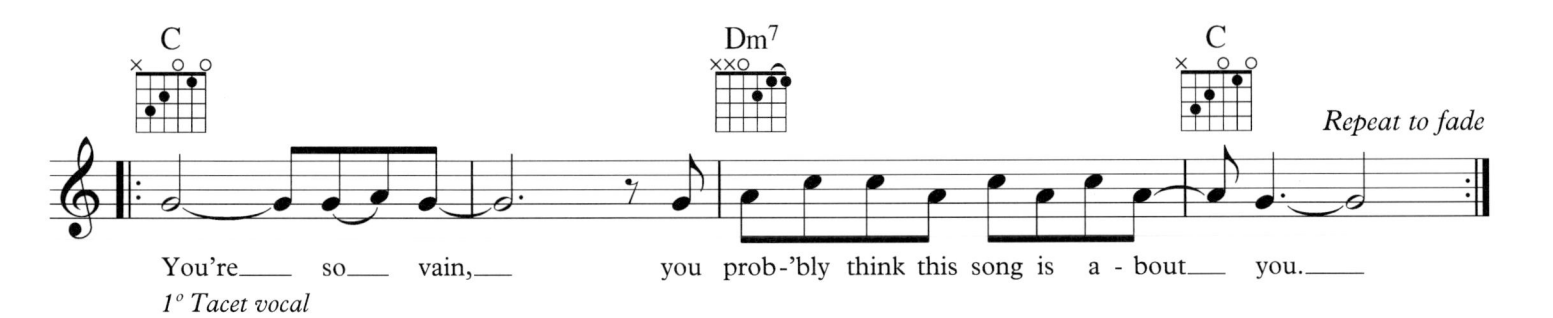

Repeat to fade

You're___ so___ vain,___ you prob-'bly think this song is a-bout___ you.___

1° Tacet vocal

Your Cheatin' Heart

Words & Music by Hank Williams

© Copyright 1952 Sony/ATV Acuff Rose Musi .
Sony/ATV Music Publishing.
All Rights Reserved. International Copyright Secured.

Strumming style:

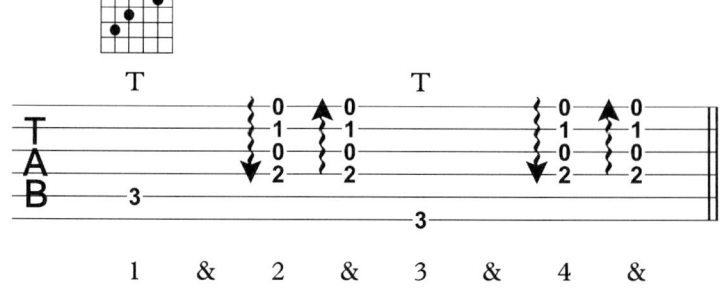

Play an alternating bass figure on beats 1 and 3 with a pair of heavy strums on beats 2 and 4.

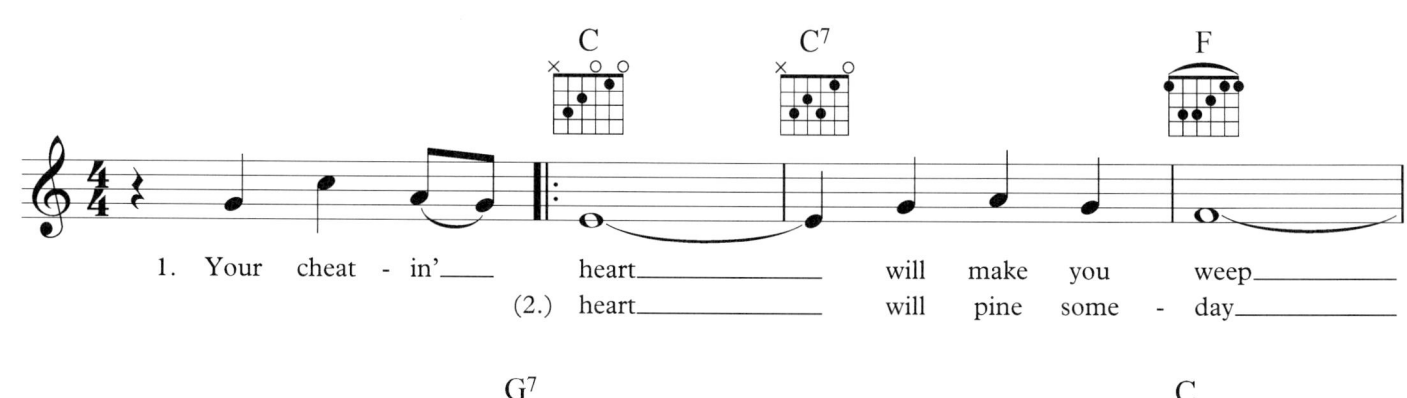

1. Your cheat - in'___ heart___ will make you weep___
(2.) heart___ will pine some - day___

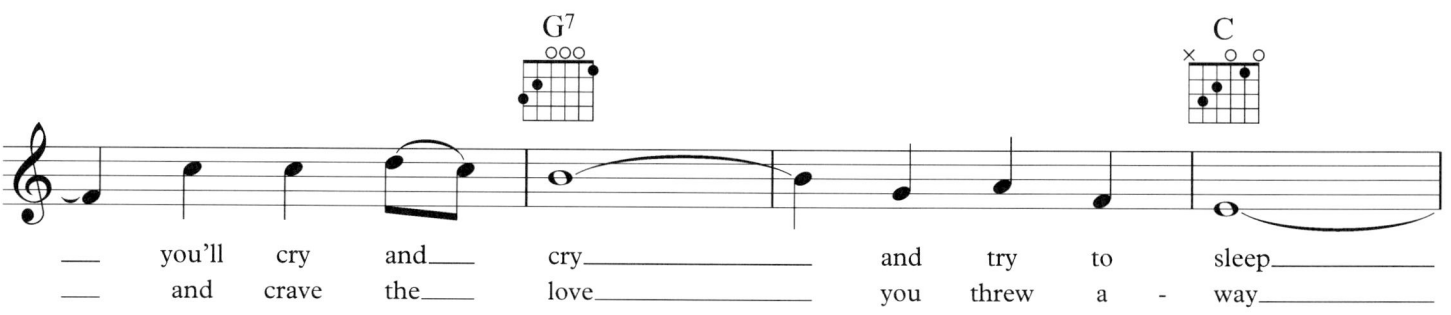

___ you'll cry and___ cry___ and try to sleep___
___ and crave the___ love___ you threw a - way___

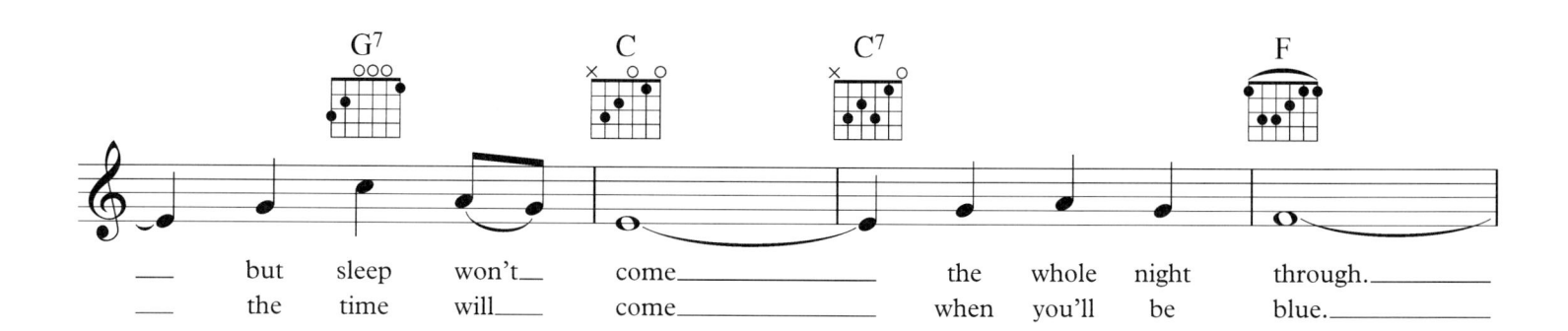

___ but sleep won't___ come___ the whole night through.___
___ the time will___ come___ when you'll be blue.___

___ } Your cheat - in'___ heart___ will tell on you.___ When tears come

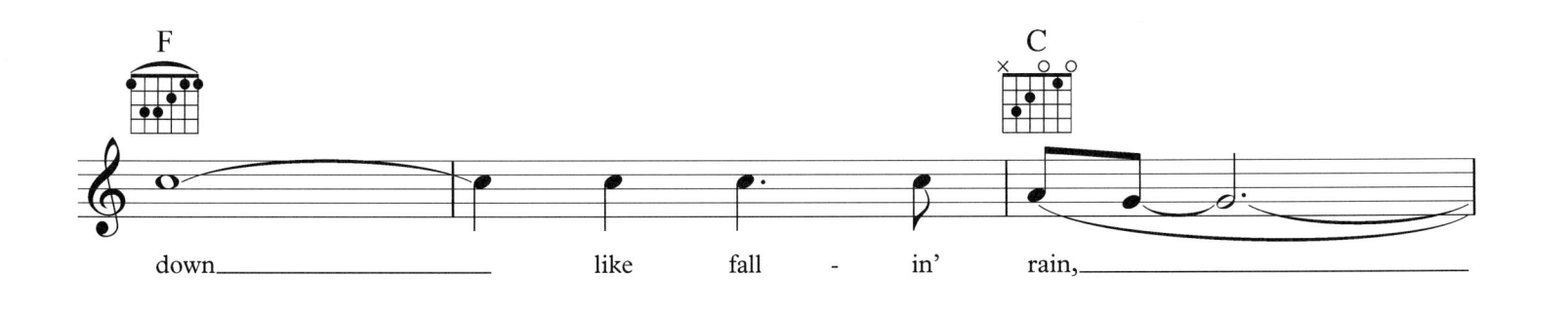

down_____ like fall - in' rain,_____

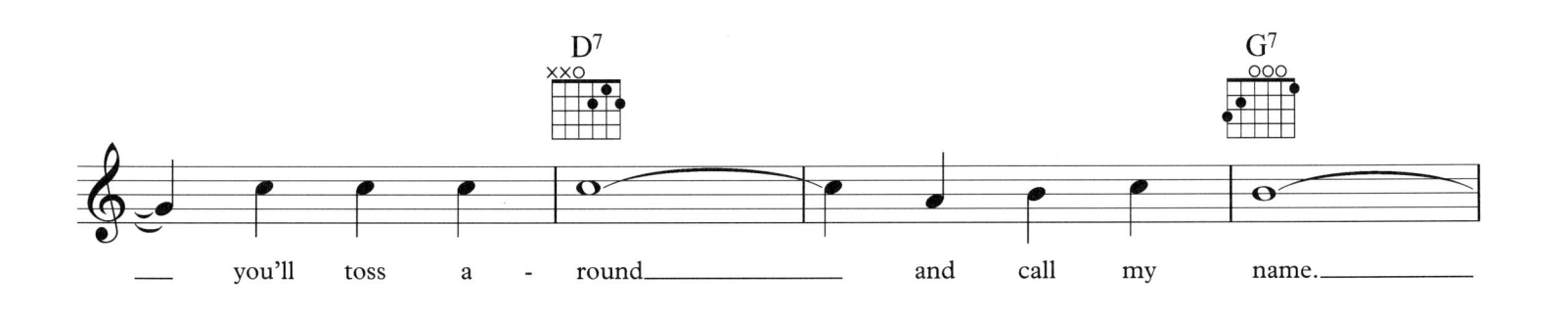

___ you'll toss a - round_____ and call my name._____

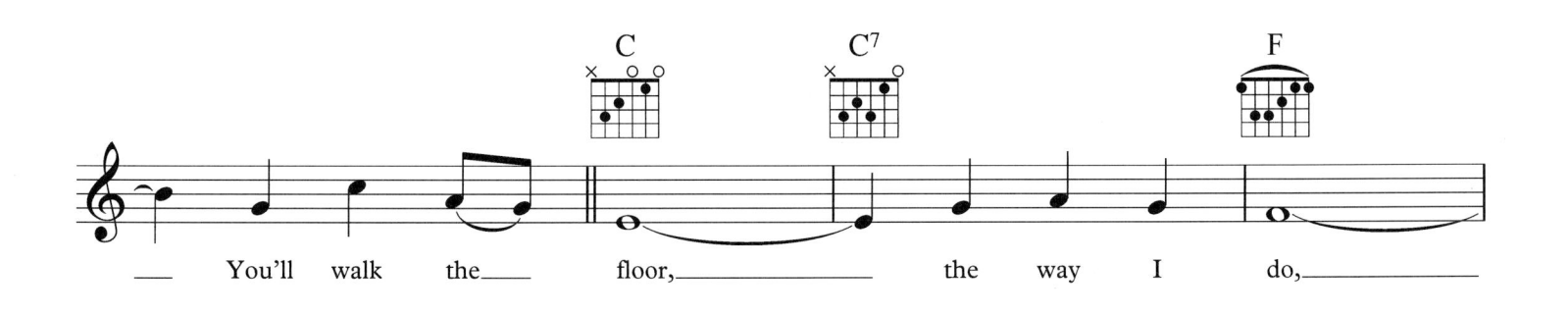

___ You'll walk the____ floor,_____ the way I do,_____

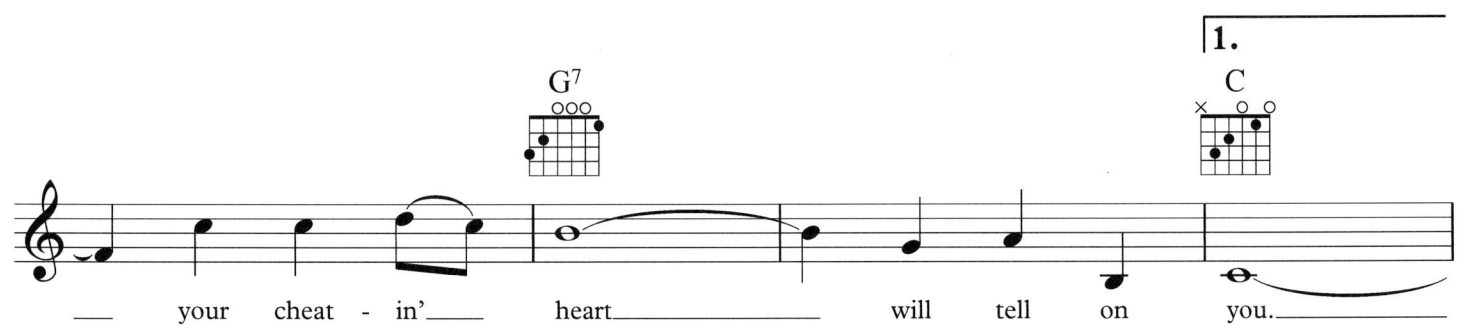

___ your cheat - in'____ heart_____ will tell on you._____

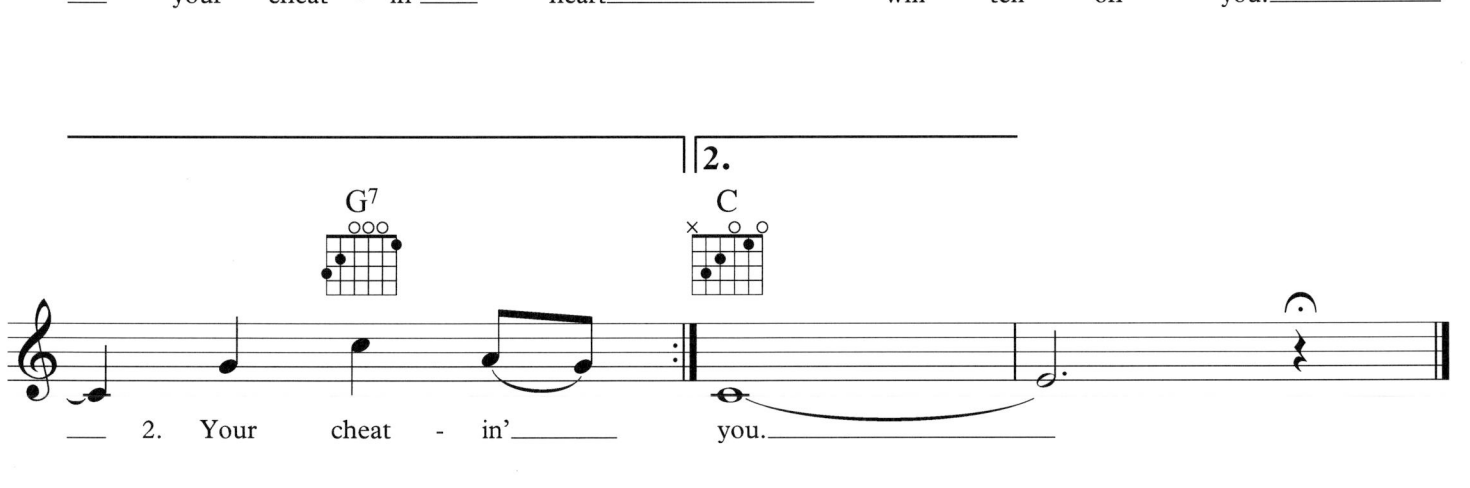

___ 2. Your cheat - in'_____ you._____